Techniques for Overcoming Objections.

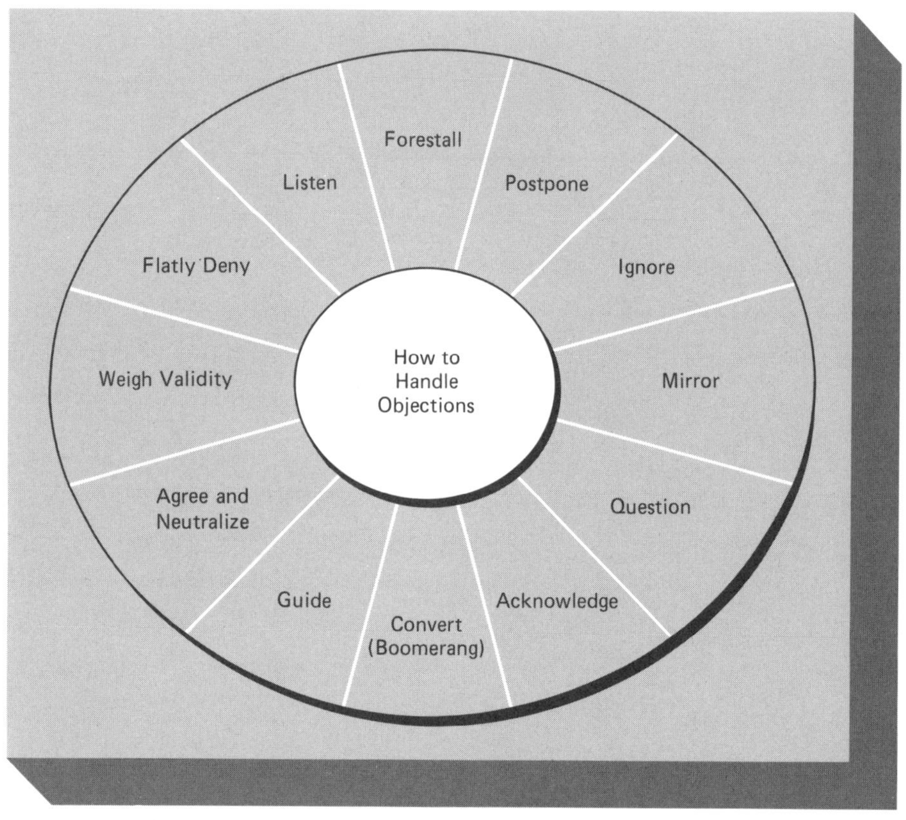

CREATIVE SELLING TODAY

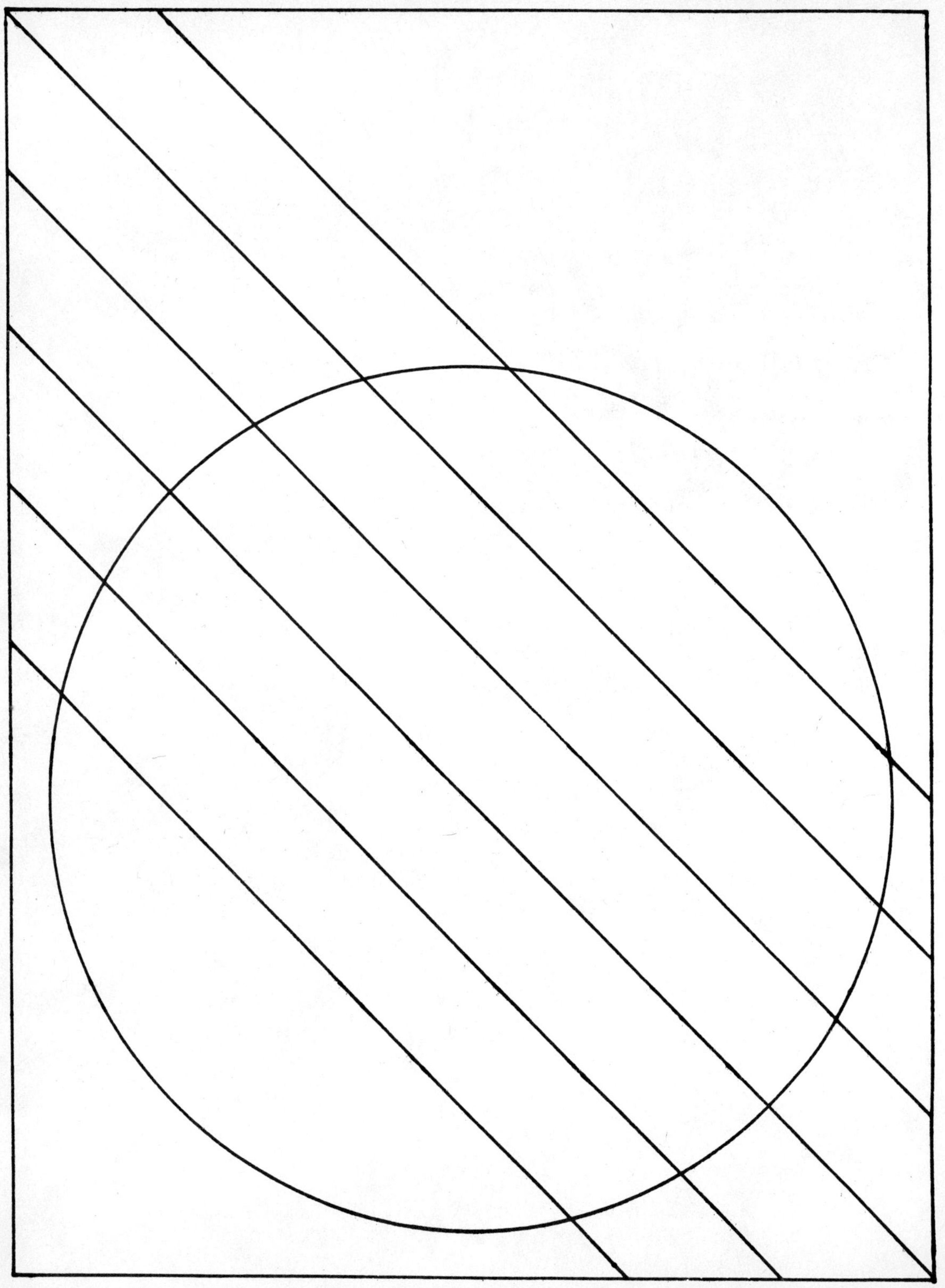

Third Edition

CREATIVE SELLING TODAY

STAN KOSSEN
MERRITT COLLEGE

HARPER & ROW, PUBLISHERS, New York
Cambridge, Philadelphia, San Francisco,
London, Mexico City, São Paulo, Singapore, Sydney

Sponsoring Editor: Jayne Maerker
Project Editor: Vivian Koenig
Text and Cover Design: Joseph Gillians
Text Art: Fine Line Illustrations Inc.
Production Manager: Jeanie Berke
Production Assistant: Paula Roppolo
Compositor: ComCom Division of Haddon Craftsmen, Inc.
Printer and Binder: R. R. Donnelley & Sons Co.
Cover Printer: NEBC

CREATIVE SELLING TODAY, Third Edition

Library of Congress Cataloging-in-Publication Data

Kossen, Stan, date.
Creative selling today / Stan Kossen.—3rd ed.
p. cm.
Includes index.
ISBN 0-06-043762-6
1. Selling. 2. Sales personnel. 3. Sales management. I. Title.
HF5438.25.K67 1989 88-21160
658.8′5—dc 19 CIP

88 89 90 91 9 8 7 6 5 4 3 2 1

To Cameron Marc and Jeremy Stuart:
two minors destined for the majors

Contents

Preface

The whole art of teaching is only the art of awakening the natural curiosity of young minds.

ANATOLE FRANCE

Once again, I would like to extend my gratitude to the many adopters of the previous editions of *Creative Selling Today.* The feedback received from numerous users is reflected in many of the modifications made in this, the third, edition.

Selling in today's environment continues to change substantially. Competition is keen. Many products are highly technical. Today's salespeople must have creative and imaginative minds to compete effectively with the many firms going after the same customers. Salespeople must focus on the needs of the buyer, all the while recognizing their equally important responsibilities to their firms, to society, and to their families. Accomplishing all of this creates a hefty burden, but also can provide exciting challenges and tremendous amounts of personal satisfaction. Those who develop effective selling skills frequently find opportunities opening up that are typicially lacking in other occupations.

THE AIMS OF *CREATIVE SELLING TODAY*

Students enrolled in selling courses often have diverse objectives. Many of them have no intention of pursuing a sales career (although many *will* take sales positions later). Recognizing this diversity, *Creative Selling Today* is designed to appeal to the needs of the following types of students:

1. Those who are *career-minded,* or intend to pursue a career in selling
2. Those who are *career-curious,* or have not yet decided on a specific career but are exploring
3. Those who are *management-oriented,* or hope one day to be managers and therefore desire to broaden their knowledge
4. Those who are *already in the sales field* and desire to improve their selling skills and knowledge

ORGANIZATION OF THE TEXT

Creative Selling Today, Third Edition, is divided into five parts plus a special section consisting of three appendixes. The organization is as follows:

1. The Nature of a Career in Selling
2. The Character of the Marketplace
3. The Need for Basic Selling Skills
4. The Selling Process
5. The Improvement of Sales Effectiveness

Appendixes: Specialized Areas of Selling

Appendix I: The Essentials of Retail Selling

Appendix II: Selling Real Estate

Appendix III: Selling in Foreign Markets

The text is a blend of essential background materials and practical information intended to aid in developing greater selling skills and effectiveness.

HOW STUDENTS CAN BENEFIT

Following are reasons why students can benefit from the use of *Creative Selling Today,* Third Edition:

1. They should find studying this text relatively easy because of the way each chapter is organized.
   a. Chapter-opening outline provides the reader with an organized overview of the chapter contents.
   b. Concise learning objectives appear at the beginning of each chapter.
   c. Opening statements in each chapter are designed to attract the attention of the reader.
   d. "Tickler questions" are placed in the margins to motivate the student to think about and to apply the presented concepts.
   e. Each page has been planned to aid in maintaining the reader's interest and desire to learn. Interspersed are related cartoons and main body quotations intended to create a more enjoyable reading atmosphere.
   f. Each chapter is followed by a summary of main concepts, questions for discussion, and an application section.
2. Although over two decades of experience in conducting selling classes and seminars as well as in actual selling preceded the writing of this text, I spent

many hours with sales managers and salespeople to make certain that the sales concepts in the text would relate to today's selling world.

3. A glossary at the back of the text lists key terms in alphabetical order.

HOW THE INSTRUCTOR CAN BENEFIT

It has been my experience that instructors appreciate all the help they can get to maximize their effectiveness in the use of time—that all-too-scarce commodity. With time pressures in mind, an instructor's guide for this volume has been prepared and is available upon request for adopters of the text.

The instructor's guide includes for each chapter the following aids:

1. A *lecture outline* (a real time-saver for the busy instructor who doesn't have time to reread the chapters each school term).
2. *Suggested answers to the discussion questions* located at the end of each chapter in the text.
3. *Suggested responses to chapter applications.*
4. *Supplementary materials and teaching aids,* a section intended to provide additional materials to aid in giving classes more variety.
5. *Thirty-four quizzes* (two for each chapter) consisting of 20 objective questions on each. These can be removed from the guide and reproduced.
6. *Three examinations* consisting of 30 multiple-choice questions and 40 true-false questions. (Multiple-choice questions can be assigned a value of 2 points each and true-false 1 point for a total of 100 points for each examination.)
7. A *final examination* covering all 17 chapters and consisting of 150 objective questions (50 multiple-choice and 100 true-false). Multiple-choice questions can be assigned a value of 2 points each and true-false 1 point each for a total of 200 points.
8. *Suggested course procedures.*
9. *Transparency masters,* available to adopters, containing material from the more significant tables and figures in the text.

NEW AND UPDATED MATERIALS

A variety of up-to-date and practical materials, fresh cartoons, and new end-of-chapter applications have been added throughout the third edition. Chapter 15, for example, was extensively revised with greater emphasis placed on the importance and practical use of telemarketing in the selling field. Chapter 16 includes new material on electronic sales promotion, with discussions of videotex, videodisc kiosks, and electronic mail. Chapter 17 was extensively reorganized and now includes an in-depth section on the use of computers by salespeople. These are only a few of the numerous changes made in the third edition of *Creative Selling Today.* Limited space prevents discussing all of the modifications in the preface.

ACKNOWLEDGMENTS

Far too many organizations and individuals in industry and education have contributed to and assisted with the three editions of *Creative Selling Today* to include all their names here. I do, however, want to express my indebtedness to them for their unselfish aid in the past.

Special appreciation is extended to the following professors of selling who provided me with helpful suggestions during the manuscript development phases of the third edition of *Creative Selling Today:* Robert E. Rose, Central Missouri State University; George W. Wynn, James Madison University; Peter J. Zayicek, Fulton-Montgomery Community College; Gus L. Kotoulas, Morton College; Douglass G. Norvell, Western Illinois University; Duane C. Brickner, South Mountain Community College; and Rusty Mitchell, Inver Hills Community College.

And finally, this edition would not be complete without providing a round of kudos for my ever-helpful, always patient editors, Jayne Maerker, Alice Lavin, and Vivian Koenig, three veritable powerhouses in the field of publishing. The four of us were kept mere milliseconds apart during the developmental and production stages of the manuscript due to the marvel of modern-day electronic and postal communications systems.

Stan Kossen

PART ONE

THE NATURE OF A CAREER IN SELLING

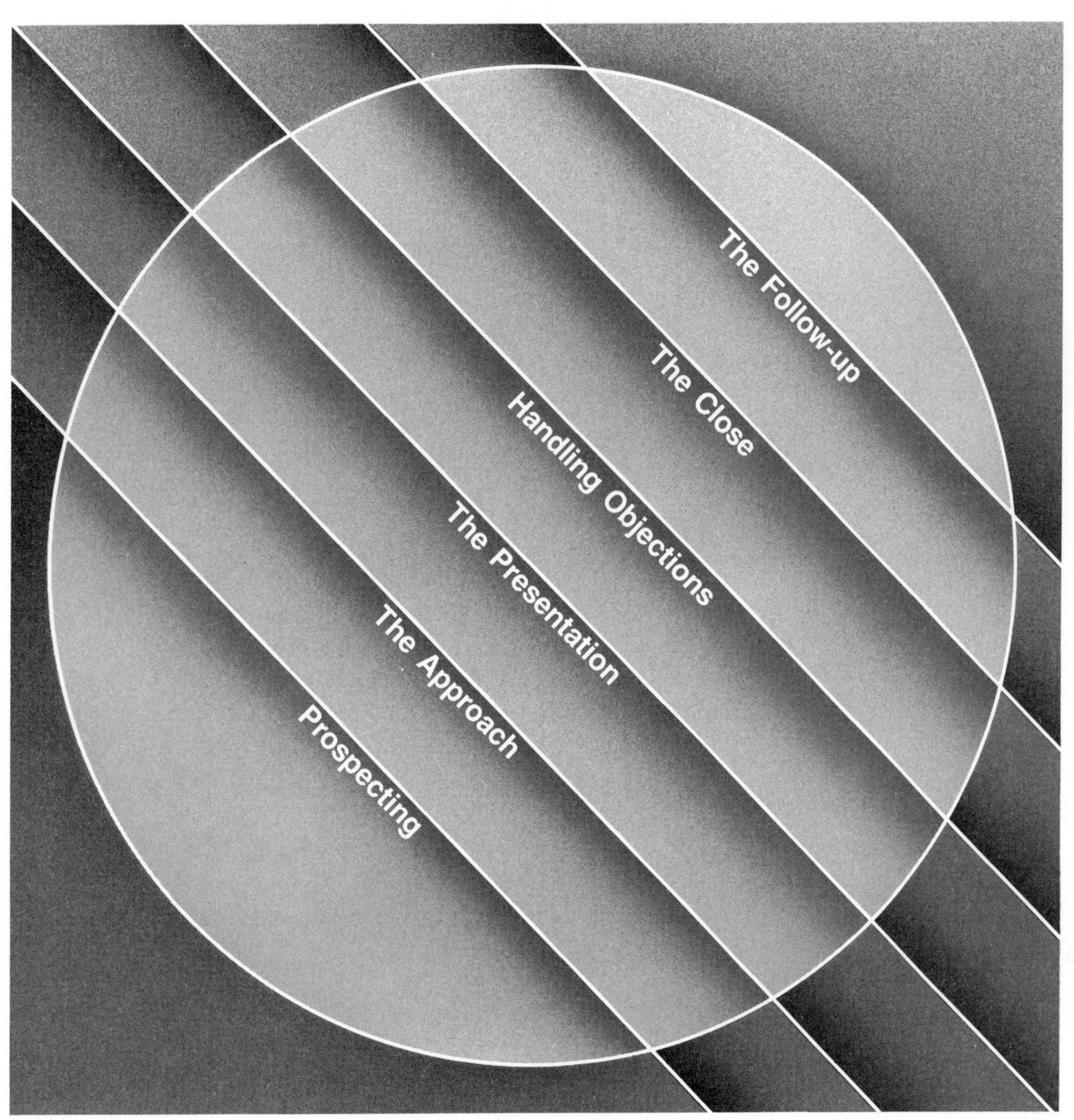

1 The Significance and Benefits of Sales Activities

What You Do *Is* Important!

THE UNIVERSALITY OF THE SALES PROCESS
What Do We Mean—Selling? ■ Are Salespeople Persuaders? ■ Who Doesn't Sell?

THE DIVERSITY OF THE SALES PROCESS

IS SELLING REALLY NECESSARY?
A Several-Trillion-Dollar Garbage Pile? ■ The Marketing of Mousetraps ■ Times Have Changed ■ The Self-Reliance of Consumers ■ Needs Versus Desires

COSTS AND THE PROCESS OF SELLING
Greater Output Can Reduce Unit Costs ■ Into the Publishing Business ■ Can Sales Activity Reduce Unit Costs?

THE BENEFITS OF SALES ACTIVITY
Benefits to Society ■ Benefits to Consumers ■ Benefits to Business Firms ■ Benefits to the Salesperson

NOW APPEARING—A BETTER IMAGE

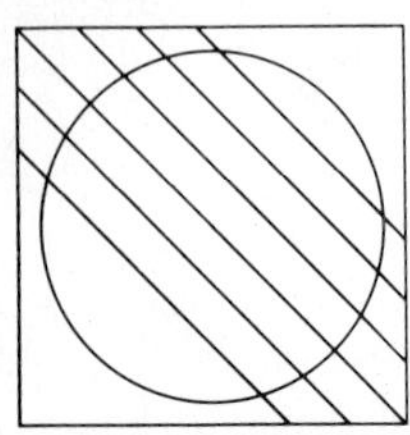

There is no one who is not in some degree a merchant; who has not something to buy or something to sell.
SAMUEL JOHNSON

Everyone lives by selling something.
ROBERT LOUIS STEVENSON

Here's what you should be able to do after studying this chapter:

1. Explain how everyone, regardless of occupation, engages in selling activities.
2. State why a highly developed and industrialized society requires a dynamic marketing process.
3. Describe how the selling process may actually *reduce* production costs and market prices of products.
4. Summarize how consumers, business firms, salespeople, and society in general can benefit from sales activities.
5. Discuss why the salesperson is one of the key individuals in determining the survival of a company.
6. Recognize the improved image that sales occupations have developed in recent years.

Are you considering a career in selling? A relatively small proportion of high school and college students actually intend to make selling their careers. Yet, if the future is anything like the recent past, between 12 and 18 percent of all college graduates will ultimately find themselves in selling occupations.

There are few occupations existing in our society today that are more challenging and demanding than selling. Salespeople have a gigantic responsibility, one of bringing together potential purchasers and producers. In a sense, every salesperson is a matchmaker attempting to develop a marriage of ideas—a meeting of the minds—on a variety of things such as purchase price, credit terms, and delivery dates.

As an activity, selling is nothing new. Some humorist-philosophers, tongue in cheek, have asserted that prostitution and the law are the world's two oldest professions. Perhaps they should also include selling—the attempt to influence and convince others—which is as old as humanity itself. As early as 4000 B.C., long before they sold oil to the energy-hungry West, Arabs journeyed by caravan bartering their wares in the region of the Tigris and Euphrates rivers. And even long before the sales activities of the Arab traders, cave dwellers, too, frequently practiced the art of persuasion. The cave dwellers' skills in selling may not have been as polished and sophisticated as those of today's high-tech sales representatives, but it has nonetheless been said that they could be forcefully persuasive upon discovering a startled enemy attempting to run off with their hard-won dinner!

Is selling an activity that only a small segment of society engages in, or is everyone involved in one way or another with selling efforts? Do selling activities really benefit anyone, or do they merely increase the market prices of goods and services? How are selling occupations perceived today—in a positive or negative light? We'll examine the answers to these specific questions in this chapter.

THE UNIVERSALITY OF THE SALES PROCESS

Our friends, the prehistoric cave dwellers, might have been outstandingly effective in their selling efforts. However, our concern will primarily focus on the types of sales activities that resolve customer problems and that creatively assist prospective customers in recognizing their needs for industrial, merchant, or consumer goods and services.

What Do We Mean—Selling?

The need to focus on needs.

Before proceeding any farther, we'd better establish a more precise meaning for the term **selling.** We shall define it as the process of analyzing the potential customers' *needs* and *wants* and assisting them in discovering how such needs and wants can be best satisfied by the purchase of a particular good, service, or idea. By this definition, you can see that a major focus of selling is on the *needs* and *wants* of customers rather than on the *features* of the item to be sold.

Are Salespeople Persuaders?

Is all *persuasion bad?*

Selling can be considered a process that involves the act of persuasion. Unfortunately, the word *persuasion* has negative connotations to some persons, often because of unpleasant experiences they may have had with "persuasive" individuals. However, persuasion is a skill. And like any skill, it can be either used or misused. In this text we consider persuasion as an art, as a creative act designed to *assist* prospective customers in satisfying their needs. For our purposes, the term does *not* mean the act of manipulating or duping prospects into purchasing unneeded goods or services.

Who Doesn't Sell?

When did you make your last sale?

If you give some serious thought to the subject, you probably will agree that virtually everyone engages in sales activity of a sort, even those who are not actively or directly concerned with the marketing of goods and services. To help us establish our point, let's examine the case of a young person named Cameron Carson who lives with his parents. Does Cameron sell? You bet he does! He might, for example, try to persuade (sell) his parents to lend him their sparkling new BMW this Friday evening so he can take his good friend Jennifer to a movie. He succeeds, but when he picks Jennifer up, he finds that she would rather go dancing. Cameron, however, was presold on seeing the film *Valentine's Day VI,* so he attempts to persuade (sell) Jennifer on the merits of attending the movie. He even offers to buy her a deep-dish, Chicago-style, thick-crusted, combination pizza afterward. Jennifer has never been able to pass up a juicy thick-crusted pizza, so she accepts Cameron's offer.

I'll buy that!

"Every individual, whether lawyer, union organizer, teacher, office manager, parent—in fact, whatever his or her occupation—regularly engages in the art of persuasion, that is, selling."

Some years later, after graduation from law school, Cameron needs a job and finds himself having to persuade (sell) prospective employers that he should be accepted as a junior partner. After extensive legwork, Cameron "makes a sale" to Mr. Phinger, of Phinger, Phinger, and Bhone Associates. Cameron then finds himself regularly having to persuade (sell) juries on the merits of his clients' cases.

Do you get the point? Every individual, whether lawyer, union organizer, teacher, office manager, parent—in fact, whatever his or her occupation—regularly engages in the art of persuasion, that is, selling.

THE DIVERSITY OF THE SALES PROCESS

Usually when we think of the selling process, we tend to think in terms of one human being directly involved with one or more other persons. Some selling, however, involves no direct face-to-face contact between a salesperson and a buyer. Think for a moment. What are some of the ways in which products and services are sold without the direct involvement of other individuals? How about vending machines? They sell a wide variety of products ranging from peanuts to insurance. Mail-order selling—which utilizes either catalogs, direct mail, or coupons in current publications—has been outstandingly successful for some companies. Other selling methods and aids to selling include advertising, telephone solicitation, direct mail, television home shopping, the use of samples, and trade fair displays.

Although most of the emphasis in this text will be on the personal selling process, advertising, which often paves the way for effective personal selling activities, is too significant a topic for us to omit. In a later section we'll examine advertising along with some of the specific aids—visual aids, the telephone, direct mail and computers—that sales personnel can use to assist them in their persuasive efforts.

Because of the variety of industries, products, and functions that exist in the marketplace, there is no generalized, simple description of the complex process of personal selling. It may involve highly experienced and knowledgeable individuals, sometimes called **senior account managers,** who call only on large or key accounts. Some firms employ representatives referred to as **sales engineers,** whose specialized backgrounds enable them to provide technical advice and assistance to their industrial accounts. Other representatives may be termed **missionary salespeople;** their activities include the promotion of products that are new on the market. To their regular wholesale and retail customers, missionary salespeople may also provide sales promotion assistance designed to help resell purchased products. Missionary sales representatives may even take orders from retailers to be turned over to their wholesaler customers.

IS SELLING REALLY NECESSARY?

Although other nations have made enormous economic progress over the years, America continues to be one of the most productive societies in the world. The total sales price of all goods and services **(gross national product)** produced annually in the United States is currently in excess of $4 trillion. It is estimated by the Conference Board to reach in excess of $6 trillion by the year 2000.[1]

A Several-Trillion-Dollar Garbage Pile?

Does all of this enormous output enhance everyone's standard of living and make everybody happy? Of course not. Much of it very quickly ends up in garbage containers along with the daily food scraps. Some production processes contaminate our environment and cost society money and effort in eliminating pollution and curing lung diseases. Some of our mammoth output, critics argue, uses up natural resources at too fast a rate, creating what they call a "several-trillion-dollar garbage pile." But a person doesn't have to be an adversary of free enterprise to take such a position. Even the most avid supporters of our present system would agree that there is a need for concern over the manner in which our resources and environment are utilized.

Assume, nevertheless, that most of us desire to improve the quality of our lives. How will this come about? Material possessions aren't the total answer, but a substantial proportion of such improvement unquestionably relates to the continued availability and distribution of large quantities of material goods and services. A better life, by most standards, doesn't seem to involve our squatting on the damp earth in a dark cave clad only in loincloths, pounding idly on rocks. (But who knows? Cave life might sound appealing to you after a strenuous day selling in your territory!)

How about a designer loincloth!

High levels of output require a large and skilled work force. At present, there are around 120 million persons in the American civilian labor force. Of these, almost 13 million are directly involved in sales work. If it were not for the dynamics of the marketing process, therefore, much of the work force would have difficulting in locating jobs. **Marketing** is a complex function, one defined by the American Management Associations as *the process of planning and executing the conception, pric-*

ing, promotion, and distribution of ideas, goods, and services to create exchanges that satisfy individual and organizational objectives.[2] Selling and sales promotion are essential parts of the marketing process.

The Marketing of Mousetraps

Have you ever heard that classic bit of advice, "Build a better mousetrap and the world will beat a path to your door." Such a belief is not only unfounded today but was probably never true. If you were to build a better mousetrap without attempting to market it, you would be more likely to observe untrampled grass growing knee-high on the narrow path in front of your doorstep. Stephen Leacock, a Canadian essayist and humorist writing in the Roaring Twenties, seemed to agree when he asserted:

> Without salesmanship we could not sell anything. If we could not sell anything we might as well not make anything, because if we made things and couldn't sell them it would be as bad as if we sold things and couldn't make them.[3]

Why do people buy better mousetraps?

Regardless of how superior or useful a product might be, potential customers must first learn of its existence and merits before they are likely to want it. Advertising has long assisted in providing information to consumers, but the process of selling is what has served to facilitate the distribution of goods and services from producers to consumers.

Times Have Changed

The selling function might be unnecessary if everyone were still a member of a family unit that produced all its own goods for consumption. But such is not the world in which we live. Instead, ours is a highly complex, specialized, and interdependent society where high levels of productivity and employment are unlikely to continue without the function of creative selling.

The Self-Reliance of Consumers

There are those who contend that the sales function is an unnecessary and costly frill, that consumers are bright enough to seek out on their own the products and services they want, and that much of what is sold isn't really needed anyway. Granted, many consumers *are* bright, and a sizable portion of our gross national production might be eliminated without their ever missing many of the products. But do these factors alone necessarily eliminate the need for creative selling?

"Often the only way in which consumers—either industrial or ultimate, intelligent or unintelligent—ever learn about many products is through sales and sales promotion activities."

Even bright consumers may lack certain kinds of knowledge. Do you, for example, fully understand the meaning of the terms *baud rates, acoustic coupler, RAM, ROM,* and *random access?* They are important terms for personal computer users. Regardless of how bright you are, the job of understanding your newly purchased personal computer can be made easier by a competent computer salesperson.

How bright are "bright" consumers?

Are most consumers necessarily as bright as we might hope? Some undoubtedly are—and others, well . . . let's take a look. Prior to the passage of truth-in-lending laws, "bright" consumers could have computed for themselves the precise rates of interest they were paying on revolving credit plans or credit cards, but in reality the typical consumer—bright or dull—had little awareness of how to compute true interest rates. Prior to **unit pricing** by grocery stores, did the average shopper necessarily buy products with the most value? (Some observers would argue that even *with* unit pricing, the typical consumer still doesn't purchase the items of greatest value!) Often the only way in which consumers—either industrial or ultimate, intelligent or unintelligent—ever learn about many products is through sales and sales promotion activities.

Needs Versus Desires

Do you **need** *an electric pickle peeler?*

Many items—such as first-class sections in airplanes, compact disc players and video tape recorders in living rooms, automatic ice makers in refrigerators, and desktop computers in homes and offices—may not be absolute necessities, but has humanity ever been so rational as to desire only the things it needed? Did prehistoric people *absolutely* need the wheel? True, this invention proved highly useful, but was it absolutely necessary for survival? Do San Franciscans *absolutely* need their picturesque cable cars?

How do **needs** *differ from* **desires***?*

The world in which we live has never been completely rational. There are many things people *desire* even though they are not needed for basic survival. Some products that people merely desire may significantly help to satisfy their psychological needs, such as the need for peer or social approval, for prestige, or for love and happiness. Might we not actually be imposing some of our own values and tastes onto others when we say that a person doesn't really need something?

COSTS AND THE PROCESS OF SELLING

Not every contact you make with a prospective customer will pay off immediately. Callbacks may be necessary. And each call that a salesperson makes is a costly item in a firm's budget, averaging $230 in a recent year, according to research by McGraw-Hill's Laboratory of Advertising Performance.[4] Simple logic dictates that the salaries plus the travel and entertainment expenses of salespeople must be paid by someone. Right? And the same brand of simple logic might imply that the somebody would probably be the purchaser of the product. Correct? Not necessarily. In fact, sales activities can actually result in lower prices to consumers. Let's try to discover how.

Greater Output Can Reduce Unit Costs

The selling function, as we know, involves **demand creation,** that is, *assisting others in recognizing their needs and desires for specific goods and services.* In a competitive society with numerous firms and industries competing for the limited amount of potential customer dollars, each firm finds it necessary to create a demand for its products or services. The creation of demand is given a boost by both advertising and personal sales efforts. But must the activity of demand creation, as some critics of the marketing process argue, necessarily increase costs and thus the sales price of each item produced?

Producing more costs less?

Economists and cost accountants play with a variety of figures and graphs that show how the cost of producing each unit of a product tends to decline as the size of a firm's productive operations (its plant) increases. They call this concept the **economies of scale.** This notion may sound confusing at first, so let's look at an example that should clarify it.

Into the Publishing Business

Certain expenses remain fixed.

And others vary.

Imagine that you have decided to venture into your own business and publish a magazine called *Horseplay,* designed to appeal to horse fanciers. As you might imagine, you will incur certain costs of operation that you can't avoid. These are called **fixed costs.** Whether you print ten or ten thousand copies, you will have certain expenses that are always with you, at least as long as you desire to stay in business. For example, you will have expenses related to heating your plant when it's cold. You'll have to pay for electricity to light your work areas and for power to run your presses. Then there will be minimum charges for your telephones, insurance premiums, depreciation expenses related to your equipment, and much, much more. This isn't the entire story, however. There are other costs, called **variable costs**—such as those for paper, ink, and postage—that will rise as your production or output increases, but usually at a declining rate. Why? One reason is that as your firm grows, you qualify for quantity discounts on your purchases of materials and supplies.

What happens to fixed costs as more equestrians buy your magazine? They remain roughly the same regardless of your level of output, but you are then able to "spread the overhead" (the fixed costs of heat, telephone, and so on) over your total production.

Can Sales Activity Reduce Unit Costs?

So bigger could be lower!

What, then, can expand the scale of your operations and reduce your **unit costs?** You've probably guessed it already: *demand creation.* What helps to create demand? You already know that answer: *persuasive sales activities.* Creative selling can enable a firm to expand its level of production and spread its overhead (fixed costs) over the larger number of units produced. This may still sound a bit confusing, but the major point, once again, is this: *some costs will continue regardless of how many magazines you print; but the more magazines you print, the less it will generally cost to print each copy.* Many magazines are competing for the consumer's dollar. With lower cost per magazine, you can offer the product at a lower price and maintain or expand your share of the market. In the absence of creative selling of your publication, however, you might find it necessary to cut back your output, which would increase your costs per magazine and create pressure on you to raise the cost of each copy. Another sales activity, the selling of advertising space in your publication, could also help to maintain a competitive price for your magazine.

"Creative selling can enable a firm to expand its level of production and spread its overhead (fixed costs) over the larger number of units produced."

Although there are many real-world examples that could help to illustrate our point, let's assume that you are not yet fully convinced that sales activity is beneficial, since you feel that producers will not necessarily pass savings in production costs on to the consumers. All right, then, let's move on to examine other more tangible benefits resulting from the process of selling.

THE BENEFITS OF SALES ACTIVITY

We seldom view selling as we might a field like medicine. We tend to place the medical doctor on a pedestal. The doctor, we rightfully feel, is a learned person who aids society by healing the sick and maintaining the healthy. In short, the doctor, we want to believe, serves humanity.

Do salespeople serve?

Could we place a similar halo above the head of the salesperson? Some individuals might chuckle if you asserted, "A salesperson serves humanity." But some of those same chucklers might agree that their own livelihoods—their jobs—and thus their standards of living, are highly dependent on the energetic and creative activities of the sales departments of their firms. In a sense seldom thought of, salespeople, too, serve humanity. They engage in a process that benefits not only *society* in general, as we shall soon see, but also assists *consumers, business firms,* and the *salespeople themselves.*

Benefits to Society

You may be wondering how society benefits from sales activities. If you've studied economics, you may have learned that most societies have specific economic goals. Two of the most important goals of any modern society are economic growth and maximum employment. The achievement of both goals means jobs and incomes for our labor force of approximately 120 million people. The number of people in our society who need jobs continues to expand, however, while some jobs have been eliminated because of automation, robotics, or technological obsolescence. Recognizing that there are problems associated with economic growth, we see that if jobs are to be available for all who want and expect them, our economy must continually

How does society benefit from sales activity?

expand its production of goods and services. This task requires sound government policies and the efficient use of people and technology. Equally important is the economy's need for individuals to sell what is produced. Through their persistent efforts to create and stimulate demand, salespeople become part of the lifeblood of a productive economic system. The large numbers of workers in the factories, offices, and service industries would be unneeded if someone weren't selling their goods and services.

To those not directly connected with the selling field, all of this might sound like so much sales puffery. However, a large proportion of today's salespeople are creative, professional individuals who sincerely believe in their products and firms and are truly interested in offering their customers a good product at a fair price accompanied by necessary service.

Benefits to Consumers

How can salespeople serve?

Professional salespeople seldom know every facet of a particular product, but they should know its major uses, limitations, and benefits so that they can serve their customers more effectively. For example, insurance agents can analyze the hazards and risks that confront a client's business or home situation, examine existing insurance coverage, and offer helpful advice designed to eliminate gaps or overlaps in coverage while also possibly saving the client money. Other salespeople are qualified to analyze office systems and offer creative recommendations for developing more efficient operations. Another type of salesperson, known as a **medical service representative,** can aid busy doctors by keeping them abreast of new drugs on the market. The list of sales workers who can offer assistance to customers is practically without end.

Benefits to Business Firms

What is your prime responsibility as a salesperson?

Both salespeople's own companies and their business customers stand to benefit from sales activities. You probably know the major reason why most businesses exist: to make a profit. Firms can make profits only if their total revenues exceed total costs of operation over prolonged periods of time. As a salesperson, your prime responsibility is to generate revenues, that is, to sell your firm's products at a profit. Almost anyone can give away or sell good products at a loss. The creative salesperson, however, helps to perpetuate the life of the firm by *profitably* selling goods or services. Can you see how both the firm's owners and their employees derive substantial economic benefit from sales activities?

"As a salesperson, your prime responsibility is to generate revenues, that is, to sell your firm's products at a profit."

Companies derive additional benefits from the various nonselling activities of their sales personnel. The sales worker in the field is in an ideal position to help the company keep abreast or ahead of competition. The resourceful salesperson engages in what could be termed **field intelligence** by providing important information about such things as the nature of competitors' activities and the changing needs of customers.

How does the business customer gain?

The sales force has the additional responsibility of serving the needs of businesses that buy its firm's products. Most firms cannot survive solely on the basis of one-shot sales activities; longer-term, repeat sales are necessary. Unless those in selling jobs truly serve their customers in a professional manner, they are likely to discover that their days are numbered. Our modern society has developed numerous built-in safeguards designed to protect buyers, and unethical or insincere approaches generally result in failure over time. On the other hand, buyers who transact business with inventive and professional sales personnel often reap substantial gains. A customer-oriented salesperson can perform a number of highly useful functions, such as:

1. Providing customers with product information and demonstrations
2. Training customers' employees in product use
3. Providing customers with sales advice on the merchandising and advertising of products purchased for resale
4. Assisting customers in the maintenance of inventories

Benefits to the Salesperson

How might you, the sales worker, benefit from sales activities? One of the more obvious benefits, of course, is *income*—the basic reason why most people work. Not all salespeople earn large sums of money, but for those who want to enjoy sizable earnings, the opportunities are probably greater in many types of sales positions than in most other occupations.

Money, money money!

Sales representatives whose incomes are derived principally from commission sales are usually limited only by their willingness to expend energy effectively. Their incomes are often directly proportional to the amount of creative effort they put forth in their territories. Ambitious salespeople can work more effectively or for longer hours and usually increase their incomes. Even sales workers on straight salaries, if productive, are in the position to command above-average incomes.

Free at last!

Potentially higher incomes are not the only benefits that salespeople receive, however. Sales representatives, especially those who work in what is generally referred to as "the field" (as opposed to a fixed location), usually enjoy greater degrees of *freedom of action and movement* than do office personnel. For the person who needs or prefers feelings of independence and freedom, for those who like to be "on the go," a career in sales can be a satisfying and challenging experience. Field representatives are frequently on their own. Their principal responsibility, as we have noted, is to produce new business profitably. How they accomplish their firm's goals is usually determined by the sales representatives themselves. The sales job provides the hard-working and persistent person with regular *feelings of accomplishment.*

I did it!

No one necessarily tells the salesperson what time to be on the job, on whom to make a sales call, or precisely what to say to customers. The relatively free and nonroutine atmosphere in which salespeople operate leads us to another advantage they have. They are, in effect, managers. They regularly engage in functions and activities not unlike those of managers, such as planning, organizing, staffing, directing, and controlling. A salesperson's activities are very useful for the *development of managerial skills.* People in the sales field work with and through other people. Effective managers also work with and through other people. The creative salesperson needs to be a self-motivated individual; so does the skilled manager. A recently reported survey of executives prepared by Korn/Ferry International indicates that sales and marketing jobs offer the "fastest route to the top."[5] Like salespeople, managers must be persuasive; they continually sell ideas. If you have aspirations to become a manager one day, you will find that experience in creative selling can help you gain the training and education necessary for such a leadership position.

Up the ladder!

NOW APPEARING—A BETTER IMAGE

What's your image of the salesperson?

Although nonprofessional hucksters have tainted the image of the salesperson, only a few careers in selling are of the "wheeler-dealer" variety, typified by authors like Arthur Miller in his *Death of a Salesman.* Most selling positions require self-disciplined, highly motivated, intelligent, and sincerely empathetic individuals who truly desire to aid customers with their needs and problems. It seems to be fashionable for "intellectuals," both in and out of business, to degrade the importance of the sales function and selling occupations. Yet if those who belittle selling as a career were to compare objectively their own job satisfaction with that of individuals in sales, they might experience a radical shift in their attitudes toward sales occupations. As is frequently the case, the lack of closeness to or awareness of a particular situation tends to develop prejudices or stereotypes toward it.

A higher proportion of today's salespeople are better educated than in the past. Most of them have completed college and also have had computer training. (It is estimated that by 1990, about 33 percent of all sales workers will utilize personal computers.[6])

We can see, therefore, that today's salesperson has every right to have a high regard for his or her occupation. To be effective over time in sales—or any occupation, for that matter—it's essential that you develop a favorable self-image. Fortunately, because of the increased complexity and challenges of the marketplace, maintaining pride as a salesperson will become much easier during the 1980s and 1990s.

Getting better all the time!

SUMMARY

Selling, the attempt to influence and convince others, is as old as humanity itself. Virtually all individuals engage in the art of persuasion throughout their entire lifetimes. Advanced societies, like those of the United States and the countries of western Europe and Asia, require dynamic marketing processes in order to create and maintain the demand for the myriad goods and services that result from high levels of productivity.

The sales function is a costly one. However, creative selling enables firms to operate at higher levels of output, and therefore—because of economies of scale—costs per unit of production may be lower than they would if the selling process were absent.

A variety of benefits result from sales activities. There are beneficial aspects not only for society in general but also for customers, business firms, and salespeople themselves. Since they are frequently the only contact that purchasers have with a supplying firm, salespeople are key individuals in determining the success or failure of their companies' operations.

Some persons, especially those who have had little contact with professional salespeople, have perceived selling in a somewhat unfavorable light in the past. However, attitudes toward sales jobs seem to have undergone a shift in recent years, with many better-educated individuals choosing careers in sales.

KEY TERMS

selling
senior account managers
sales engineers
missionary salespeople
gross national product (GNP)
marketing
unit pricing
demand creation
economies of scale
fixed costs
variable costs
unit costs
medical service representative
field intelligence

QUESTIONS

1. Evaluate the following statement: "Selling is an unnecessary activity. It deludes people into thinking they need something they could well do without, and it increases the price of products and services that people actually need."
2. List five examples of attempts at personal persuasion that you have made during the past month. How might your efforts have been more effective than they were?
3. In what way does a union official or a teacher attempt to sell?
4. How might the selling process result in lower, rather than higher, costs to the buying public?
5. Why is the old adage "Build a better mousetrap and they'll beat a path to your door" unlikely to be true in modern times?

6. Explain how society, consumers, business firms, and salespeople benefit from selling activity.
7. In what ways are the activities of field sales workers similar to those of managers? How do they differ?

APPLICATIONS

1.1 WHAT DO YOU THINK OF WHEN . . . ?

Select ten acquaintances and tell them the following: "I'm going to say a word in a moment. After I say it, write down the first three words that enter your mind. The word is 'salesperson.' "

Questions

1. What do you feel has influenced your acquaintances' word choices?
2. Did those who had positive responses have a closer relationship to the selling field in the past?

1.2 SELLING SELLING

Assume that you are a guest speaker at a nearby high school. Your topic is "Selling—One of the Best Professions." How would you respond if you were confronted with some of the following comments during the question-and-answer period?

Selling is a job—not a profession or a career.

Salespeople must lie and be deceitful in order to succeed.

Selling brings out the worst in people.

To be a good salesperson, you have to be psychologically maladjusted.

One must be arrogant and overbearing to succeed in selling.

Salespeople lead a degrading and disgusting life because they must pretend all the time.

The personal relations involved in selling are repulsive.

Selling benefits only the seller.

Salespeople are prostitutes because they sell all their values for money.

Selling is no job for a person with talent and brains.

1.3 FAST—BUT IS IT EFFECTIVE?

Sales experience has been said to provide a person with a "fast track to the top" of American corporations. What are some typical characteristics of many sales job that might act as detriments to a salesperson's becoming an effective manager?

NOTES

1. "Looking Back—and Ahead," *Newsweek International,* April 20, 1987, p. 9.

2. "AMA Board Approves New Marketing Definition," *Marketing News,* March 1, 1985, p. 1.

3. Stephen Leacock, "The Perfect Salesman—A Complete Guide to Business," in *The Garden of Folly* (New York: Dodd, Mead, 1924), pp. 101–112.

4. "Significant Trends," *Sales & Marketing Management,* August 1986, p. 94.

5. According to a Korn/Ferry International executive survey that asked the question, "What jobs offer the fastest route to the top," those surveyed said: marketing/sales, 34 percent; finance/accounting, 25 percent; general management, 24 percent; professional/technical, 7 percent; as reported in "The Fast Track," *The Wall Street Journal,* January 6, 1987, p. 31.

6. "Computers in the Work Force," *The World Almanac* (New York: Pharos Books, 1986), p. 96.

2 Characteristics of Selling Careers

You Are the Company

THE MYTH OF THE BORN SALESPERSON
Skills Can Be Developed ■ Sincerity Is Necessary

PERSONAL CHARACTERISTICS AND ATTITUDES
Is Your Behavior Ethical? ■ Is Your Appearance Favorable? ■ Do You Avoid Distracting Mannerisms? ■ Are You Motivated to Succeed? ■ Are You People-Oriented? ■ Are You Emotionally Stable? ■ Are Your Manners Acceptable? ■ Do You Attempt to Maintain a Good Sense of Humor? ■ Do You Maintain a Positive Attitude? ■ Are You Enthusiastic? ■ Are You Developing Good Work Habits?

SKILLS AND EDUCATION
Social Sensitivity ■ Perception—The Ability to See What Is Actually There ■ The Ability to Communicate Effectively ■ Educational Requirements for Selling ■ The Maintenance of Education and Skills

NO JOB IS PERFECT
Long Working Days ■ Need for Self-Discipline ■ High Degree of Pressure ■ Regular Travel Away from Home ■ Handling Disgruntled Customers

CAREERS IN PERSONAL SELLING
An Improved Image ■ Types of Sales Positions Available

THE FINANCIAL AND NONFINANCIAL REWARDS OF SELLING
Straight, or Guaranteed, Salary ■ Straight Commission ■ Salary Plus Commission ■ Salary Plus Individual Bonus ■ Salary Plus Group Bonus ■ Salary Plus Commission Plus Bonus ■ Noncash Sales Compensation

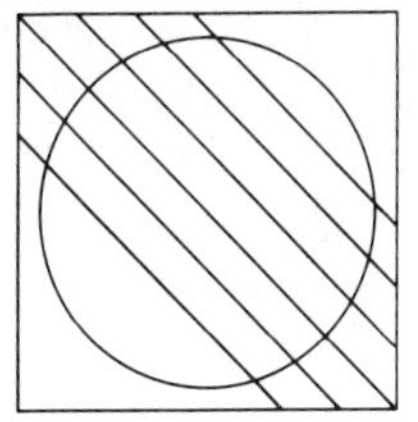

A good salesperson must have a need to achieve, which is a particular kind of ego drive that makes a person want and need to make the sale in a personal, or "ego," way, not merely for the money to be gained.
DAVID MAYER

Here's what you should be able to do after studying this chapter:

1. Summarize the personal characteristics that contribute toward greater sales effectiveness.
2. Describe the importance of *social sensitivity* as a developed sales skill.
3. Explain why individuals in selling should develop skills in communication and perception.
4. List the college courses that can enhance your selling effectiveness.
5. Describe some of the ways in which your level of education and skills can be maintained.
6. Explain how work habits influence sales results.
7. Recognize at least five potentially undesirable features of a career in sales.
8. Summarize the principal types of sales positions by kinds of responsibilities.
9. Explain the financial and nonfinancial rewards of selling.

How would you describe an ideal salesperson? If you were to ask ten people to list what they believe to be the personal characteristics necessary for a successful career in selling, chances are they would come up with ten different lists.

One of the main difficulties in developing a precise list of characteristics to fit all situations is that there are so many different types of jobs in the selling field. Driver sales jobs consisting principally of providing service—delivering products such as milk, fuel, or clean diapers to the home—probably do not require a highly developed ability to persuade, handle objections, or close sales. Individuals in such fields, however, should have friendly and cordial manners so as not to alienate their customers. Those people selling intangibles like insurance or advertising usually need more highly developed skills of persuasion and communication. And industrial salespeople who sell items like electronic spectrum analyzers and other highly sophisticated types of capital equipment and systems generally require higher levels of education and technical skill than salespeople in the other groups.

Even within specific industries, sales characteristics and qualifications will vary, depending on company policies and the nature of territories. Purchasing managers know that good salespeople come in all shapes, sizes, sexes, and colors. Purchasers have to deal with salespeople whose personalities differ greatly—some extroverts, some introverts, and some combinations of both.

Although there appears to be agreement that no single type of personality ensures success in the field of selling, there seem to be certain characteristics that, when present, contribute toward greater sales effectiveness. In this chapter, we'll take a closer look at some of the significant *characteristics* and *qualifications* that can assist you—the salesperson—to function more effectively in your organization.

Also in this chapter we'll examine some of the types of *skills* and *education* that can enhance your selling effectiveness. Although a sales career offers many advantages, we shouldn't ignore those factors that are perceived as potentially undesirable aspects of selling positions—another topic to be covered. We'll also look at the principal types of sales positions and conclude by exploring some of the major forms of financial and nonfinancial rewards provided to salespeople.

THE MYTH OF THE BORN SALESPERSON

"She's a born salesperson." Have you ever heard that comment? It's a fairly common one. But does it really make sense? Would you ever say that a person is a born doctor or a born plumber or a born secretary? Not very likely. These are occupations that require the development of skills through practice and training. The same should be said of selling.

Skills Can Be Developed

A more realistic cliché might be that "people are born babies." Of course, babies are not all born with the same physical capabilities or innate capacity for learning. And no infants are predestined to become members of selling teams. Instead, environmental and educational experiences, along with the development of specific skills, exert a strong influence on their future occupational aptitudes.

Is there one "best" sales personality?

The person who wants to play well at tennis, racquetball, or golf must develop the requisite skills. The same holds true for sales: skill to sell must be developed. Contrary to popular belief, you needn't be an extreme extrovert—that is, an outgoing, backslapping, jovial type person—to succeed at selling. In fact, there isn't any one personality type that makes the best kind of salesperson. Out of any group of productive salespeople, you can find soft-spoken, quiet individuals who sometimes seem introverted and mild-mannered. You can also find the opposite: highly energetic, outgoing, enthusiastic individuals who seem to raise the energy level of any room they enter. Furthermore, a complete range of personality types can exist between these two groups.

Far more significant for you than acquiring a particular type of personality is learning the skills of your profession, understanding how to prospect for new accounts, developing persuasive sales presentations, learning how to close a sale, and servicing accounts adequately after they have been sold.

"Insincerity tends to become transparent; customers are likely to see through it quickly and easily."

Sincerity Is Necessary

It is also important that you feel and convey a sincere interest in your customers and their problems. Insincerity tends to become transparent; customers are likely to see through it quickly and easily. The development of useful sales skills, along with a sincere interest in assisting your customers, can make you appear to be a "born salesperson" to others.

PERSONAL CHARACTERISTICS AND ATTITUDES

"Know thyself," advised Socrates.

Many years ago a persuasive Grecian from Athens called Socrates regularly suggested to his friends and acquaintances that perhaps they should attempt to know their own selves a bit better. His advice was a succinct "Know thyself." To his friends with more time to spare, he would sometimes add, "Know your strengths and your weaknesses, your potentialities, your aims and purposes; take stock of yourself." Socrates, one of the best and most creative salespersons of his time, believed that before individuals could really understand how to deal effectively with the problems of others, they first had to look within and become better acquainted with themselves.

Salespeople should seriously consider the advice of Socrates and attempt to recognize how their own personal characteristics and attitudes can significantly influence their effectiveness in selling. One way for you to gain an improved understanding of yourself is periodically to answer the following questions:

How many yesses can you offer?

1. Am I honest and ethical in my dealings with others?
2. Is my appearance favorable?
3. Do I avoid distracting mannerisms?
4. Am I motivated to succeed?

5. Am I people-oriented?
6. Am I emotionally stable?
7. Are my manners acceptable?
8. Do I attempt to maintain a good sense of humor?
9. Do I maintain a positive attitude?
10. Am I enthusiastic about what I do?
11. Am I developing good work habits?

If your answer to any of these questions is no, you might also ask yourself what you might do to change it. Let's now briefly discuss each of the questions separately.

Is Your Behavior Ethical?

The subject of ethics is so important that an entire chapter will be devoted to it. At this juncture, however, it is important to point out that honest and ethical behavior is essential for those who intend to pursue a career in sales.

Is negative gain worth the risk?

Success and achievement became important to young people in the 1980s. There were highly publicized examples involving well-educated Wall Street workers who unfortunately seemed to think more about their own monetary achievements than about the rightness or wrongness of their actions. The lack of ethical practices on their part cost many individuals their careers.[1] You will discover that your own self-image will be much more favorable when you know that your goals have been accomplished in an ethical and legitimate manner.

Is Your Appearance Favorable?

It has been quite soundly suggested that a book should never be judged by its cover. True as that statement might be, don't you sometimes find yourself gravitating toward books with appealing covers? Our personal judgments, especially our first impressions, are frequently based on outward appearances.*

How might the obsessive quest for freedom actually imprison?

The "liberated" male and female may feel that their personal appearance ought to be nobody's business but their own. In an ideal sense, perhaps they are right. Unfortunately, however, what *ought to be* and what *is* are often two different things in the real world. Some people, in their intense desire to be free, actually tend to imprison themselves. The desire for freedom can become so much of a fetish that it actually prevents them from entering doors of opportunity that might otherwise be open to them. People who resist the standards of appearance of their firm should try to understand the words adapted from a prayer by Reinhold Niebuhr: "God grant me the serenity to accept the things I cannot change; the courage to change the things I can; and the wisdom to know the difference."

---

*Experienced salespeople recognize, however, that judging a prospect solely on his or her appearance can sometimes be misleading and lose potential sales.

"What might be an acceptable standard of dress in downtown Chicago could seem bizarre in the desert town of El Centro."

There are no hard and fast rules for dress that can apply to every situation. What might be an acceptable standard of dress in downtown Chicago could seem bizarre in the desert town of El Centro. Some organizations prefer to convey a conservative image to their customers; others prefer a more modern one.

The key point is this: you should familiarize yourself with the acceptable standards of personal appearance of both your company and your territory and try to maintain a standard that does not cause prospective customers to be distracted during your sales presentations. We'll explore some specific suggestions related to personal appearance in a later chapter.

Do You Avoid Distracting Mannerisms?

Have you ever heard that smoking **helped** *make a sale?*

Not all of your prospective customers will be from the same ethnic or cultural backgrounds. Some people react negatively to such things as being touched during conversations, while others feel such contact is normal. Do you try to understand your customers' feelings and avoid mannerisms that might be considered offensive, such as smoking in the presence of a nonsmoking customer, nervously fingering your moustache or hair, or anxiously tapping your pen on a desk?

Are You Motivated to Succeed?

Do you want to get ahead?

Success is a concept with different meanings to different people. To many salespeople it means being a winner. Sales managers tend to agree that the most effective salespeople generally have a strong urge to achieve; that is, they are highly motivated to accomplish their goals. They derive intense personal satisfaction from the act of consummating sales. And they enjoy the process of selling because it offers them continual challenges they can strive to meet and overcome.

Are You People-Oriented?

Do you sincerely like people?

You needn't be an extrovert to be an effective salesperson, but you should genuinely enjoy the company of other people. There is nothing particularly wrong with enjoying occasional periods of solitude—in fact, such experiences can be psychologically beneficial. But the salespeople who have achieved the best results are those who not only enjoy the company of others but also have a strong desire to be of service to them. The successful salesperson spends a considerable amount of time in assisting, not just selling, his or her customers.

Are You Emotionally Stable?

Is your head on straight?

As a salesperson you are frequently on the move and under substantial pressure. Consequently, it's sometimes difficult to be patient with your associates and customers. Effective salespeople, however, have learned to maintain their composure even

Reprinted with permission from *Sales & Marketing Management* magazine; © 1986.

under stress and strain. In dealing with a customer with a strong complaint against your company, a natural reaction is to strike back—perhaps arguing with him or her. But try to remember this sage bit of advice offered by a philosopher long ago:

Win the argument
and
lose the sale.

Are Your Manners Acceptable?

Manners relate to generally acceptable modes of social conduct. There are certain types of social conduct that most reasonable people would avoid, such as belching in the presence of others. Yet, there are more subtle types of behavior that can be equally offensive to some of the people whom you, as a salesperson, may be attempting to influence positively. An awareness of generally accepted standards of social behavior, such as "proper" eating habits, is another characteristic that can enhance your self-confidence and self-image. You will create obstacles for yourself at such

Which spoon do I use?

functions as business luncheons if you are continually anxious about your eating habits. Acceptable manners should be practiced in low-risk situations so that they become virtually automatic behavior in business settings.

Do You Attempt to Maintain a Good Sense of Humor?

With violence, terrorism, destruction, and scandal all about us and the old AIDS-plagued home planet apparently crumbling a bit more each day beneath our feet, maintaining a sense of humor and a positive attitude is no easy matter. Negative and critical responses may seem, at times, like an easy way out, serving to release pent-up tensions. Most of us, however, prefer the company of cheerful rather than complaining people. A sense of humor is an essential characteristic for a salesperson. Not only can it assist you through difficult and trying situations but it can also help to ease the tensions of your workday.

What good is a sense of humor?

"Your customers probably enjoy your laughing with them, but few appreciate your laughing at them."

Your sense of humor, however, *should make sense.* And it should be *situational.* A humorous quip would be out of place, for example, when your account appears visibly tense or preoccupied with a serious problem. Some comedians, such as Joan Rivers and Don Rickles, became famous for their ability to "put down" others. But they were paid to be masters of insult; you are not. Remember, your customers probably enjoy your laughing *with* them, but few appreciate your laughing *at* them.

Do You Maintain a Positive Attitude?

Once upon a time there was a small community, and residing in this community was a family with identical twin daughters. One daughter was a pessimist, the other an optimist. One year when their birthdays rolled around, a friend of the family—the town psychiatrist—and the girls' parents decided to conduct an experiment. For her birthday, the mother and father gave the pessimistic daughter a shiny new bicycle, a water gun, and a colorful hat. The optimistic child was given a roomful of fresh horse manure and a small green shovel.

About 15 impatient minutes later, the nimble psychiatrist and the anxious parents went into the pessimist's room and enthusiastically asked her how she liked her presents. The sulking young girl snapped, "The bicycle is no good, the water gun doesn't shoot far enough, and the hat is too small." Then they went into the optimist's room and asked her how she liked her gifts. Within the room busily shoveling horse manure about in an excited fashion was the optimistic child, who looked up and cheerfully replied, "It's a lot of work, but I know there's a pony in here somewhere!"

If you look for the positive, you'll find it!

This amusing story helps to point out the way in which attitudes strongly influence how you cope with the pressure inherent in many sales jobs. Some salespeople, not unlike the pessimistic youngster in the story, continually focus on the negative—and they can usually find it, for there always seem to be certain undesirable aspects to any situation or sales job.

Are You Enthusiastic?

One, two, three-*enthusiasm!!*

One, two, three-*chaaaarge!!*

One, two, three-*enthusiasm!!*

One, two, three-*chaaaarge!!*

One, two, three-*enthusiasm!!*

One, two, three-*chaaaarge!!*

Was high school all bad?

These are the words that a sales manager for one of the largest insurance companies in the United States had his field representatives shout vociferously during periodic sales meetings. Some of the salespeople at the meeting felt that the manager's approach was somewhat "high schoolish," but since they were a captive audience, they went along with his program. After three or four experiences with the approach, however, even the biggest skeptics had to admit that it did release some of their pent-up tensions and help liven up their spirits. Some people might feel strange shouting at the top of their lungs in public, but try it yourself sometime in private: you might be surprised at its effects. The important point is that you *can* influence your own moods.

Frank Bettger, a salesman-author, believed that enthusiasm is by far the biggest single factor in successful selling. Naturally, no single factor will ensure success, but an enthusiastic attitude tends to influence customers in a positive manner. Prospects who see salespeople exuding genuine enthusiasm in their presentations tend to develop more positive feelings about the products. Would you be likely to develop much interest if a salesperson presented a product in a dull, unenthusiastic manner, acting as though it were just another one of many such products on the market?

"Some people influence their moods by altering their environment."

What's good for a case of the "blues"?

There are many ways to maintain or develop enthusiasm. You should try to discover what specific methods work most effectively for you. Some people influence their moods by altering their environment. Lively music, for example, can make you feel more energetic. Associating with optimistic and enthusiastic people can likewise help you maintain an enthusiastic attitude.

Knowing your company and its products, knowing your job and customers, and being well organized can also help you maintain self-confidence and enthusiasm in your activities.

Poor physical and mental health make enthusiasm difficult to maintain. Your mind and body are inseparable. A poorly maintained body can adversely affect your

How can you rid yourself of tensions?

mind, and vice versa. Do you follow a program of regular exercise? Physical activity can be of value to practically every part of your body and can make a big difference to whether you feel energetic or sluggish. One of its greatest benefits, however, is to the mind, for exercise, such as a daily routine of running, brisk walking, or swimming, can help relieve you mentally of the anger, pressures, worries, or frustrations that can build up on a job. Enthusiasm is far easier to maintain if you exercise regularly and stick to a proper diet.

Are You Developing Good Work Habits?

A farsighted philosopher once said, "What I am to be I am now becoming." Can you see how this belief could apply to you or anyone in the field of selling? The habits you are now developing are likely to exert significant influence on how you will function in the future. Examine the following checklist. Ask yourself how each question applies to your current situation. Can you answer yes to each? Are you currently developing good habits that will help you in both your selling and nonselling activities?

1. Are you usually dependable?
2. Do you follow through with your commitments?
3. Do you turn in reports on time?
4. Are you sincere and honest in all of your human relationships?
5. Do you assume responsibility for your own mistakes instead of being a buck passer?
6. Do you usually plan and organize your activities?
7. Do you usually try to arrive somewhat early for appointments in order to allow for possible delays while traveling?

This is only a representative list of the positive types of habits salespeople should try to develop. It could be expanded to include any regularly recurring activities that have an influence on your selling effectiveness.

SKILLS AND EDUCATION

Developing a skill is significantly different from acquiring an education. Although a skill, such as the ability to communicate clearly, may result from education, it is more often developed through practice. One of the major purposes of education is to enable people to reason more logically. Education shouldn't be designed to stuff your head with quickly outdated facts; instead, it should help you know where to find facts that are useful in analyzing and resolving problems.

The level of skill necessary for a salesperson depends not only on *the nature of the particular job* but also on *the type of territory, company, and industry involved.*

In the following section, we'll examine some of the skills and educational characteristics that seem to increase in importance as the nature of the selling job becomes more complex.

Social Sensitivity

Can you be both tough and sensitive?

As a salesperson, you will sometimes find yourself in a difficult position. On the one hand, you must maintain a fairly thick skin so that undue criticism and streaks of poor selling luck don't get you down. On the other hand, you must maintain a high degree of **social sensitivity** toward your prospects and customers.

Behavioral scientists have categorized social sensitivity in a variety of ways. You certainly should be sympathetic toward the problems of your customers. **Sympathy** can be defined as *the state of feeling sorry for someone.* Assume, for example, that one of your customers purchased a large quantity of a product from you and then had difficulty reselling the product because your firm recently introduced a new and improved model. A sympathetic approach on your part would be to tell your account how sorry you were that this problem situation had arisen. The capacity to feel sympathy is certainly not an undesirable characteristic for you to have.

There is, however, a characteristic that can be more helpful to your account than the ability to be sympathetic—the ability to be empathetic. **Empathy** is a feeling that goes beyond sympathy; it is the *ability to feel as the other person does*—in effect, to put yourself into the other person's shoes. Sympathy won't help your customer out of a financial bind. With empathy, however, you feel the situation as would your customer. By so doing you might be more inclined to use some of your expertise and skills to help your customer develop an effective sales promotion campaign and thus to dispose of the product without serious financial losses.

"Empathy is a feeling that goes beyond sympathy; it is the ability to feel as the other person does—in effect, to put yourself into the other person's shoes."

Some salespeople have developed a type of social sensitivity that behavioral scientists call first-person and second-person sensitivity; both are related to the concept of empathy.

You are said to have **first-person sensitivity** if you have developed the ability to perceive what the other person *thinks about you.* In other words, you can feel and understand, with a fair degree of accuracy, the impressions that you are making on another person. Although it is quite possible to misinterpret the sense of what you think you're receiving from another person, first-person sensitivity is a skill that can be developed with experience. Some salespeople, for example, have learned that certain facial expressions and bodily motions indicate how they are coming across to their customers.

First-person sensitivity, as we have indicated, refers to your ability to perceive how the other person feels *about you.* A related concept is called **second-person sensitivity,** a skill that refers to the ability to perceive what others are feeling, thinking, or experiencing *about a particular situation or problem.* Both first- and second-person sensitivity are forms of empathy. However, regardless of the labels attached to these specific skills, you should attempt to develop the ability to feel as your customers do in order to be of more help to them.

Perception—The Ability to See What Is Actually There

A skill closely related to social sensitivity is the ability to see what is actually there—**perception.** Read the short sentence in Figure 2.1. Have you read it? Okay, will you now reread it and count—that's right, *count*—the number of times the letter *F* appears. How many do you see?

Seeing the truth may take some effort.

Did you count three *F*s? Most readers will; others will count four or five; still others will find six. There are six. Did you see them all immediately? If not, why not? Did you overlook half of the letters—the *F* in the word *of?* Unimportant detail, you may say, but you were specifically requested to count *F*s, weren't you? Can you figure out how this simple quiz might relate to the topic of consumer buying motives?

We've already concluded that a need or want must be recognized before a person is likely to act on it. How a person perceives a particular situation will significantly influence his or her actions. As in the case of the *F* quiz above, prospective customers may not perceive all of the relevant details in their situations. Equally important, salespeople who are aware of the major factors that influence perception are in a better position to help potential customers recognize their needs and wants. The determinants of perception will be covered in a later chapter when we examine the motives of buyers.

The Ability to Communicate Effectively

Salespeople are communicators. They must develop **presentation skills,** that is, the ability to deliver well-organized, persuasive presentations to individuals and groups. Their effectiveness is significantly influenced by how skillfully they transmit their messages and listen to customers. Certain words, for example, seem to make a product almost come to life, while others make the product seem dull and insipid. The late Elmer Wheeler once suggested that a creative salesperson should "sell the sizzle, not the steak." Calling a product "nice" says little about it, especially to a prospective buyer.

Elmer said, "Sell the sizzle."

"Salespeople are communicators. Their effectiveness is significantly influenced by how skillfully they transmit their messages to customers."

Figure 2.1

FINISHED FILES ARE THE RE-
SULT OF YEARS OF SCIENTIFIC
STUDY COMBINED WITH THE EX-
PERIENCE OF MANY YEARS.

Imagine that you are seated in a fine restaurant. Your waiter arrives at your side. Which of the following two statements (assuming you're not a vegetarian!) would tickle your palate the most? "Well, Mac, you oughta try our house special—it's a nice hunk of bloody, dead cow meat served with a side order of dried mushrooms." or, "Monsieur, I should like to recommend the *spécialité de la maison*—a tender and juicy morsel of exquisite filet mignon, delicately laced with fresh baby mushrooms, the taste of which will cause your taste buds to tingle with excitement!"

The topic of effective communication is so important that Chapter 7 is devoted entirely to it.

Educational Requirements for Selling

What determines the amount of education necessary for selling?

The amount of education necessary for a selling position varies with the industry, the philosophy of each company, and the nature of the job itself. Hewlett-Packard, for example, requires degrees in engineering and from four to five years of technical experience for representatives selling its instrumentation line. For its calculator line, degrees are also required, but usually in the area of general business or finance. As another example, the Clorox Company prefers individuals with college degrees, but the degree need not be in any particular field. To be considered for sales employment with the Clorox Company, applicants must have had from four to six years prior experience, preferably in the retail grocery industry.

"A college degree will not ensure that you will be a creative salesperson, but it is evidence to a prospective employer that you were capable of meeting the standards established by an educational institution."

Some firms won't even consider applicants for positions in sales if they lack college degrees, while others feel that factors such as personal characteristics and experience are more essential. In general, however, educational requirements for selling occupations have increased over the years. A college degree will not ensure that you will be a creative salesperson, but it is evidence to a prospective employer that you were capable of meeting the standards established by an educational institution. College training can help open doors leading to careers in selling.

What college courses might help you become a more effective salesperson? Virtually any course can assist you, not only by broadening your interests and frame of reference but also by providing you with experience in applying self-discipline to your daily activities. Students, as you know, must meet deadlines; so must salespeople. Students have to turn in reports; so do salespeople. Students have to use their imaginations and ingenuity (we hope!); so do salespeople. Almost any useful habit established in college is likely to carry over into your sales job. In some respects, your educational experiences and activities may be more important than your major while in college.

How do college experiences aid the prospective salesperson?

Although numerous skills can be developed through experience and through trial and error, certain courses do tend to reduce the time necessary to acquire such skills and, consequently, the frequency of errors caused when they are lacking. See Table 2.1 for a list of courses that can help you develop selling skills more quickly.

The Maintenance of Education and Skills

In recent decades, demands placed on most sales personnel have increased as products have become more sophisticated and complex. Consumer and price legislation have placed additional burdens on those involved in the distribution of goods and services. Recurring periods of high-cost borrowing for housing has required real estate salespeople to develop creative and novel methods for financing the purchase of dwellings. Buying committees and trends toward centralized purchasing have created the need for a more professional type of salesperson in the marketplace.

Skills not honed get dull.

Present-day salespeople, therefore, must maintain levels of skill and education seldom required in the past. Previously acquired education quickly becomes outdated and, like a subscription to your favorite magazine, must be renewed periodically. The following checklist may assist you in maintaining and revitalizing your sales skills:

1. Do you maintain your education by reading and studying regularly?
2. Do you keep up to date on your company, its products, its customers, and its competition?
3. Do you strive to improve the effectiveness of your selling techniques?

TABLE 2.1 College Courses of Particular Benefit to Persons Contemplating Careers in Selling.

Marketing
Selling
Sales Management
Principles of Management
Language Arts
Speech
Economics
Organizational Behavior
Psychology
Sociology
Time Management
Managing Stress
Business Mathematics
Accounting
Business Law
Computer Science
Drama

4. Do you apply the concepts of effective communication and listening?
5. Do you engage in **situational selling**—that is, do you logically analyze each situation and draw on past knowledge and experience while also recognizing that each prospect or customer may have unique problems and requirements?
6. Have you developed a set of attainable personal goals?

Can you think of any additional factors that could improve your selling abilities?

NO JOB IS PERFECT

Although attitudes probably influence job satisfaction and morale as much as the job itself, we know from Chapter 1 that many selling jobs offer advantages seldom found in other occupations. Among the major benefits are advancement opportunities, relatively high incomes, feelings of accomplishment, and considerable freedom. If you are looking for the perfect job, however, you had better obtain some extra footwear, for you will probably wear out many pairs of shoes during your lengthy search. Few jobs are ever likely to be all things to all people. Any job tends to have both advantages and disadvantages. An important consideration if you are contemplating a career in selling is whether the advantages of a sales occupation outweigh the disadvantages TO YOU—not to your brother, mother, or uncle on your father's side but to *you.* We have already covered some of the principal advantages of a career in sales. It is essential, however, that you be aware of some of the less pleasant characteristics of certain sales jobs. Among these are:

1. Long working days
2. The need for self-discipline
3. Considerable job-related pressure
4. Travel away from home
5. The handling of disgruntled customers

If you are considering a career in sales, ask yourself whether you are mentally prepared to accept such conditions.

Long Working Days

Ever worked a 26-hour day?

Many sales jobs are a far cry from typical nine-to-five jobs. Appointments with some customers may have to be scheduled for early mornings, before normal working hours begin, while with other accounts appointments may be possible only during evenings. Nonselling activities—such as planning, writing up orders, and other types of required paperwork—may absorb some of your nights. Occasionally even your weekends may be occupied if you are expected to attend training workshops, conferences, or trade fairs. For many real estate salespeople, Saturdays and Sundays are the most productive days of the week.

Need for Self-Discipline

Are you a self-starter, or do you have to be cranked?

One of the main advantages of selling occupations—a greater degree of freedom—is considered by some to be a disadvantage. Sales representatives are typically on their own more than are nonsales personnel. Often, sales managers don't have the slightest idea where field personnel are at any given moment. Managers can positively influence the motivation of their sales force, but skillful techniques of motivation alone are not enough. Sales representatives have to be "self-starters." They must have initiative and **self-discipline.** They should be the type of person who actually seeks to influence events rather than passively accept situations. A career in sales is probably not the place for the person who needs a substantial amount of direction and close supervision.

Excuses for all reasons and seasons!

It is fairly easy for a salesperson to make excuses for not calling on customers. "Monday mornings are no good; my accounts want to open their mail." "Friday afternoons are no good; my accounts want to get ready for their weekends." "Just before holidays is no good; my accounts have their minds on other things." "Just after holidays is no good; most people are broke from the holidays." And so on ad infinitum. Some sales representatives waste substantial time making up alibis for doing things other than making sales calls. Salespeople who search long and hard enough can even find an excuse for each month in the year (see Figure 2.2). A creative and conscientious salesperson knows the characteristics of regular accounts and generally has a fair idea when calls can or cannot be made. Times that are bad for some customers may be very good for others.

Figure 2.2 Monthly Alibis for Not Making Sales Calls.[2]

January—Too soon after Christmas

February—Too cold

March—Unpredictable weather

April—Customers too busy with spring planting, cleaning, and repairing the ravages of winter

May—Too many customers afflicted with spring fever

June—Time for swimming, boating, fishing, and gala summer weddings

July—Too hot

August—Vacation time

September—Back to school time; customers also too busy preparing for winter

October—Football games, hunting, and time to enjoy the fall season

November—Lots of sickness and colds because of colder weather

December—Customers too busy preparing for Christmas

"A creative and conscientious salesperson knows the characteristics of regular accounts and generally has a fair idea when calls can or cannot be made."

High Degree of Pressure

Most jobs with responsibility involve a certain amount of pressure. Sales positions, however, seem to carry greater pressures than most. Salespeople, especially those whose incomes are derived principally from commissions, soon discover that their standards of living and sometimes their very survival depend on their ability to make successful sales contacts consistently. Even those paid on a straight-salaried basis are usually under pressure to develop new accounts and to improve their sales records if they want to keep their jobs.

In general, salespeople tend to be in the limelight regularly. In a sense, their position is similar to that of front-line troops in combat. Supportive military forces working in the background are essential, but the responsibility for the success of a military operation is primarily on front-line troops. Salespeople also need efficient backup support personnel, but the success of a company's operation is highly dependent on the effectiveness of sales activities. As a result, salespeople are continually in the limelight, a situation that can not only create pressures for the sales representatives but may also cause problems of jealousy and animosity between sales and other personnel, such as service representatives.

How could being in the limelight turn into a lemon?

Regular Travel Away from Home

The size of sales territories varies substantially among companies, even among firms operating within the same industry. For example, book publishers employ sales representatives who call on college and university professors in order to familiarize them with the latest textbooks. A representative with one book company might cover the colleges and universities within a 50-mile radius or less, while a representative with another firm, or one who works in a more sparsely settled territory, might cover the colleges in eight or more states.

The point is that some representatives must be prepared to spend occasional nights away from home. It's a situation that might seem exciting at first, but generally the social life of traveling sales representatives tends to be limited since they may spend only a day or two in each community. This lack of a regular home life can sometimes cause feelings of loneliness.

My suitcase is my clothes closet!

Handling Disgruntled Customers

For the moment, put yourself in the shoes of an experienced purchasing manager. As a purchasing manager, you probably discovered long ago how important are the salespeople from whom you regularly purchase thousands (or possible even millions) of dollars worth of items. You probably also discovered that sales representatives are virtually your sole contact with the companies that supply your firm with needed products. But you, the purchasing manager, are only human; you have your good

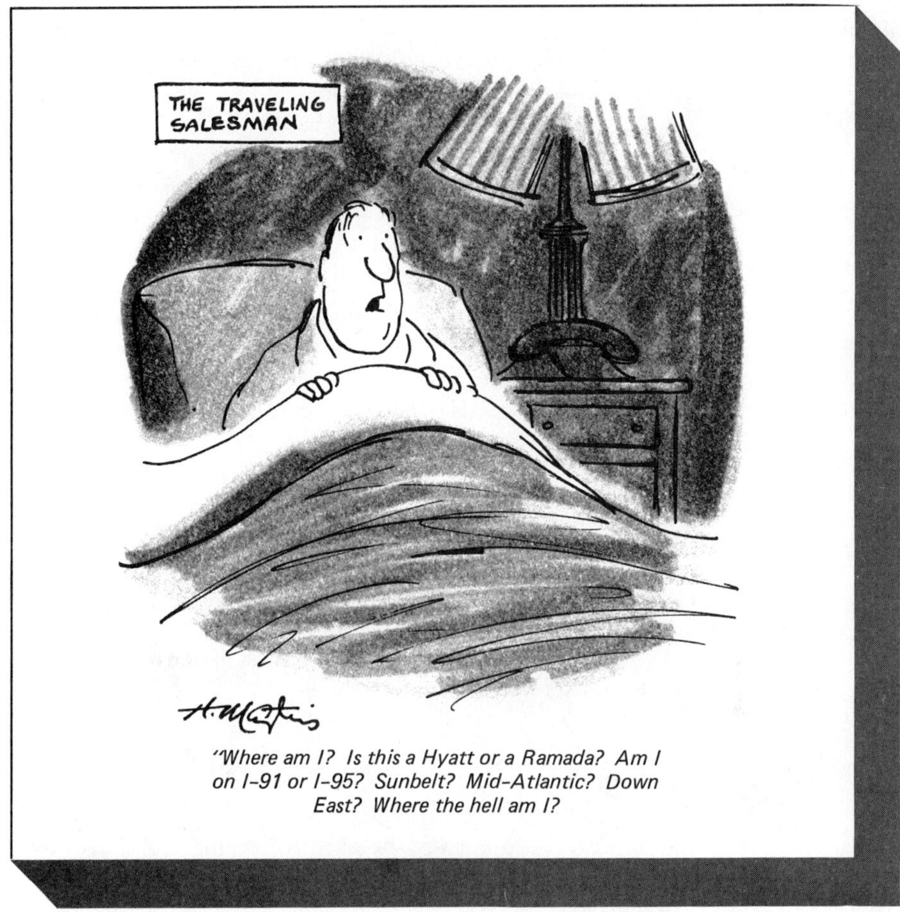

Reprinted with permission from *Sales & Marketing Management* magazine; © 1985.

days and your bad ones, like anyone else. Unfortunately, sales representatives sometimes receive the full impact of your bad days, whatever the reason for them—an unpleasant morning at home, difficulties at the office, or problems with a purchased product or its supplier.

"Sales representatives must be tough enough to fend off unpleasant verbal attacks but sensitive enough to recognize valid customer problems, complaints, and criticisms when they arise in order to deal with them effectively and objectively."

Why don't you jump out of that purchasing manager's shoes before your feet start aching and bounce back into the oxfords of a salesperson? As you might imagine, any complaints relating to your company or to the products that you sell

To a purchaser, who is the company?

will generally be thrown into your lap, since, to the purchasing manager, *you* are the company. Let's assume that you have always been conscientious and have attempted to serve all your customers in an outstanding fashion. Yet occasionally they jump all over you. You could easily become discouraged. Sales representatives, however, must be tough enough to fend off unpleasant verbal attacks but sensitive enough to recognize valid customer problems, complaints, and criticisms when they arise in order to deal with them effectively and objectively.

No job is perfect; most have advantages and disadvantages. Individuals contemplating careers in sales should become aware of the potentially unpleasant as well as the desirable aspects of selling. They should attempt to be both flexible in their thinking and willing to adjust to the pressures and occasional inconveniences. For the adaptable person who looks upon such conditions as a challenge rather than as drudgery, the rewards of a selling career generally outweigh the disadvantages.

CAREERS IN PERSONAL SELLING

As already mentioned in Chapter 1, ours is a highly productive society. With a total national output valued in excess of $4 trillion, there is likely to be a continuing need for creative, high-level salespeople to assist in one of the most crucial parts of getting goods and services distributed.

An Improved Image

Creative selling is not mere order taking; it involves direct and persuasive communication skills accompanied by effective selling techniques and a sincere desire to understand the motives and needs of buyers. The individual who understands human relationships and has developed the ability and willingness to persuade others to purchase products or services is likely to find that a job in the selling field is easy to obtain. The professional salesperson of today is much less likely to have the unfavorable image of the huckster of yesteryear. Sales representatives are expected to have achieved reasonably high educational levels. Professional degrees are now more commonplace in some fields, such as insurance and real estate. Educational backgrounds in chemistry, engineering, and metallurgy as well as in business have become increasingly important in a world that has rapidly become more complex and competitive.

"The professional salesperson of the future is much less likely to have the unfavorable image of the huckster of yesteryear."

Types of Sales Positions Available

Sales positions vary widely in their scope and activities, ranging from the salesclerk who takes your order for a hamburger and fries at a fast-food outlet to the highly professional field representative of an electronics firm, a person who may be required to hold degrees in both electrical engineering and business administration. If you look at Table 2.2, you will see a summary of the various categories of selling positions described by their major responsibilities. Virtually any sales position can fit into one of these categories.

THE FINANCIAL AND NONFINANCIAL REWARDS OF SELLING

Income, of course, is a topic of concern to the person in the field of selling. Salespeople typically receive any of the following types of financial compensation:

1. Straight, or guaranteed, salary
2. Straight commission
3. Salary plus commission

TABLE 2.2 Types of Sales Positions and Primary Responsibilities.

Types of sales position	Primary responsibilities
Driver salesperson	Principal responsibility is to deliver product to retail outlets. Efficient, courteous service may lead to increased sales.
Inside order taker	Primarily responsible for taking orders rather than selling but may engage in suggestive selling, as in fast-food outlets or self-service discount stores.
Outside order taker	Primarily responsible for writing predetermined orders, as in the case of field salespeople who call on retail food chains. May be responsible to sell retailers on "positioning" products to highlight certain product lines.
Missionary salesperson	Generally does not take purchase orders. Principally responsible for promoting the future purchase of a product, such as book publisher's representative who calls on college professors and medical service representative who calls on medical doctors.
Sales engineer	A sales position, such as a field engineer for an electronics firm, requiring a high degree of technical knowledge.
Tangible product salesperson	Responsible for locating customers for such products as heavy machinery, airplanes, houses, automobiles, or any product for which a customer can be made to realize a need or want. Some are inside and others outside salespeople.
Intangible service salesperson	Responsible for locating customers for products that are difficult to demonstrate, such as insurance, advertising, and consulting, banking, and accounting services.

4. Salary plus individual bonus
5. Salary plus group bonus
6. Salary plus commission plus bonus

Not every sales manager agrees as to which method of compensation is best. Instead, the choice is often determined by the standards of the particular industry, the nature of the product to be sold, and the specific managerial philosophies of the firm. As you can see from Table 2.3, more than three-fourths of surveyed companies tend to favor offering their sales representatives some sort of incentive pay as a means of motivating them.

Straight, or Guaranteed, Salary

Give it to me straight!

Some salespeople, especially those new to a sales position, are paid on a **straight, or guaranteed, salary** basis. A straight salary provides a salesperson with a fixed sum of money each pay period regardless of his or her volume of sales. This method helps to take some of the negative pressure off of the salesperson who lacks sufficient experience to make an adequate income based on the number of units sold. As the new salesperson gains expertise, he or she may be switched to one of the other forms of remuneration.

However, some salespeople remain on a straight salary basis, which may be considered more practicable in fields that require a substantial amount of a salesperson's time in nonselling activities, such as servicing accounts, market research, and sales promotion. This method of compensation tends to avoid a problem that can exist when salespeople are paid on the basis of how many units they sell: the tendency to neglect prime accounts that require a high degree of attention and service. About 17 percent of surveyed companies offer their salespeople a straight salary with no additional incentives.

TABLE 2.3 Typical Methods of Compensation for Salespeople (Ranked by Utilization).

Method	Percent
Salary + individual bonus	34
Salary + commission	31
Straight salary	17
Salary + commission + bonus	9
Straight commission	6
Salary + group bonus	3

Source: Adapted from "Sales Incentives," as developed by Wyatt Company's Executive Compensation Service Inc. and reported in *The Wall Street Journal,* December 18, 1985, p. 29.

Straight Commission

I get what I deserve!

Some salespeople—about 6 percent—are paid on a basis that is directly and solely related to their sales performance. This system, the **straight commission** method, typically pays a specific percentage of an item's selling price as income to the salesperson. For example, a salesperson will receive a $105 commission if the commission rate on an automobile insurance policy is 15 percent of the first year's total premium of $700. Some salespeople on a pure commission basis feel considerable pressure and insecurity, since they receive income only when they have completed sales. Other salespeople, however, are motivated by the opportunity to earn what they believe to be virtually unlimited amounts of compensation.

An increasing number of firms have begun to relate commission rates to the profitability of the items sold. Termed **varied commission** plans, commissions under such arrangements are higher on items that bring in greater gross profits to the firm and are lower on items of lesser profitability.

Salary Plus Commission

Mix it up!

An income approach preferred by many salespeople, and second most common, is the **salary plus commission** method. With this compensation system, salespeople are given a predetermined and guaranteed floor below which their income will not fall regardless of their sales volume. In addition they are provided with an incentive to increase sales volume by having the opportunity to receive a commission on sales amounts above the floor. In many cases, the income floor is considered to be a **drawing account,** which provides salespeople with advances charged (drawn) against future commissions. These amounts ultimately must be earned through actual sales.

Salary Plus Individual Bonus

More for more!

Another form of sales compensation—the most common—is **salary plus individual bonus.** Under this plan, salespeople receive a fixed salary plus rewards for particular achievements, such as the attainment of previously established goals. **Sales quotas** are common types of goals assigned to salespeople as a means of motivating them. A sales quota is a sales target expressed in dollar volume or number of units of a product or products that a salesperson is expected to attain within a specified period, usually one year. Typically the salesperson's bonus income is directly related to the attainment of the established goals. Sales quotas are generally more effective as motivators when the salesperson has worked mutually with the sales manager in determining goals and objectives.

Salary Plus Group Bonus

More for the group!

Salespeople in a small percentage of companies—about 3 percent—receive a **salary plus group bonus,** rather than individual bonuses. The added rewards, therefore, are based on an entire sales department, or sometimes the company as a whole, achieving or exceeding predetermined goals.

Salary Plus Commission Plus Bonus

More plus more plus more!

As can be seen by Table 2.3, about 9 percent of surveyed companies offer their salespeople a **salary plus commission plus bonus.** The salary serves as a floor, or minimum, level of compensation. Commissions and bonuses are provided in addition to the salary and are related to actual performance.

Noncash Sales Compensation

After the training session, let's bob for beer cans at Pismo Beach!

Some firms provide salespeople with benefits other than cash, such as company cars that can be used for business and personal purposes. A variety of types of **noncash sales compensation** exists. For example, salespeople who must travel overnight are typically on **expense accounts** and need not pay for their own meals, lodging, travel, and other business-related expenses. Another common perquisite is the opportunity to attend training sessions at "glamour resorts" where salespeople can relax or enjoy the facilities during their off hours. Many firms also hold **sales contests,** which frequently pit one salesperson against others in a region or one division against other divisions. Prizes for the victorious salespeople typically include vacation travel or consumer goods.

Many firms also include salespeople under their **employee benefit programs,** which are indirect financial rewards that include paid leave, insurance, retirement plans, stock options, and educational assistance.

SUMMARY

The skills necessary for creative selling are not inborn; they must be learned. At the same time, no one type of personality makes the best salesperson. More important than a particular type of sales personality is an understanding of the techniques of creative persuasion along with a sincere interest in the welfare and needs of customers.

Although it is generally agreed that there is no such thing as the ideal personality for all sales jobs, there are certain personal characteristics and qualifications that tend to help individuals function more effectively as salespeople. Among the more significant characteristics are honesty, ethical behavior, a favorable appearance, a lack of distracting mannerisms, a high degree of motivation, a sincere liking for people, emotional stability, acceptable manners, a good sense of humor, positive attitudes, and enthusiasm.

In addition to the requisite basic personal characteristics, successful salespeople customarily develop certain skills that enable them to fulfill their responsibilities with greater effectiveness. Among these skills are a sensitivity toward the feelings of others, the ability to perceive what is really there, and the ability to communicate effectively.

Although college training is not a prerequisite for all sales jobs, many sales managers have discovered that individuals with prior college experience tend to learn selling more rapidly.

As any tennis player or golfer recognizes, skills can become rusty without practice; the same holds true for the salesperson and his or her selling skills. Since work habits developed at school tend to be long-lasting, it is essential for those interested in developing effective selling skills to exert a conscious effort to maintain positive work habits.

Few—if any—jobs are perfect. We learned that selling positions offer many rewards and satisfactions, but they also have certain aspects that may be perceived as less desirable.

In this chapter, we also examined the principal types of selling positions from the standpoint of their major types of responsibilities.

We concluded the chapter by examining the major forms of financial and nonfinancial rewards associated with a career in selling.

KEY TERMS

social sensitivity
sympathy
empathy
first-person sensitivity
second-person sensitivity
perception
presentation skills
situational selling
self-discipline
straight/guaranteed salary
straight commission
varied commission
salary plus commission
drawing account
salary plus individual bonus
sales quotas
salary plus group bonus
salary plus commission plus bonus
noncash sales compensation
expense accounts
sales contests
employee benefit programs

QUESTIONS

1. What, if anything, should you do if you don't agree with the standards of personal appearance expected by your company?
2. List some typical mannerisms that might alienate prospective customers.
3. Why should a person in sales, probably more so than in most other occupations, be a highly motivated and self-starting individual?
4. Why, in effect, does a salesperson seldom *win* an argument?
5. How might "having a sense of humor" differ from "being a joker"?
6. Assume that you have been emotionally depressed for about three days and this condition has begun to affect the quality of your work. What might you do to help yourself out of your blue mood?
7. What are some typical excuses often given for not exercising? Are they valid?

8. If you were interviewing applicants for sales positions in your chosen field, what personal characteristics, ranked in order of importance, would you look for?

9. Why does education, not unlike an automobile insurance policy, have to be renewed periodically?

10. Assume that a friend of yours has attempted to talk you out of pursuing a career in sales. He cites such disadvantages as long working days, extreme job pressures, travel away from home, and the necessity of facing disgruntled and seemingly unappreciative customers. Try to convince your friend that each of the disadvantages cited could also be considered an advantage.

APPLICATIONS

2.1 THE UNKEMPT BANK WORKER

One Friday afternoon, Mr. Seamore Strait, president of Bear International Data Processing Machines Company, entered the downtown branch of the West Valley First National Bank to make a deposit in his personal account. While waiting for a teller, he observed a young man near the rear of the office explaining the use of an office machine to one of the bank clerks.

Mr. Strait was somewhat taken aback at the young man's sloppy appearance. He was wearing a crumpled and slightly soiled corduroy suit, no necktie, and shoes that appeared to have been used on a mountain-climbing expedition in the Himalayas during the rainy season.

As Mr. Strait was about to leave the bank, he happened to meet Ms. Sara Schock, a manager in the bank, and the following conversation ensued:

Strait Good afternoon, Ms. Schock. Say, I wanted to tell you I'm somewhat surprised at the standards of dress you now permit among the employees of your bank.

Schock What do you mean, Mr. Strait?

Strait What do I mean? Take a look at the unkempt young fellow with the wrinkled yellow corduroy suit and the unshined shoes.

Schock (Laughing) Mr. Strait, he doesn't work for West Valley; he's a salesperson with your company!

Questions

1. If you were Mr. Strait, what would you do about this situation?
2. What would you say to a salesperson who told you, "My appearance is my own business. As long as I'm doing my job, nobody has the right to hassle me about how I look"?

2.2 WHAT I AM TO BE I AM NOW BECOMING

Larry Lassit is a young community college student from a fairly wealthy family. Larry, somewhat accustomed to "the good life," is certain that one day he will operate his own business and become rich. He believes that he has the natural ability to sell successfully any product his future company will market.

Larry loves to talk; in fact, he is considered an incessant chatterbox. He is also a bit brusque with his friends and is continually insulting them. Most of Larry's friends are willing to tolerate these traits, especially since Larry has a beautiful automobile and is quite generous with his money.

Larry also considers himself to be quite deft with the ladies. His custom is to "trade one in" on the average of every three weeks. Larry feels that his persuasive skills with young women will be excellent experience for his future business activities.

A slightly below-average student, Larry does little studying or homework and receives C's and D's. So far during his college career he has been on and off probation three times. Larry doesn't particularly worry about keeping up with reading and homework assignments, since he usually can cram the evening before an examination and squeeze by with at least a C minus. Most of Larry's professors accept his late homework.

Questions

1. What do you see as likely problems for Larry in the future?
2. If Larry truly has aspirations to become a successful businessperson, what habits should he attempt to develop in the present?
3. Is it likely that Larry can "coast" through college developing undesirable habits and then suddenly change after he enters the world of work? Explain your answer.
4. Larry considers himself to be a smooth talker with women. Why will this alone not guarantee him success in the sales field?
5. If you were a college counselor, what would you recommend to Larry?

2.3 TWO O'CLOCK FRIDAY—THIS MUST BE SANTA CLARA!

Stirring somewhere in the back of my thoughts as I, Betty Diamond, was driving toward Santa Clara was the chapter in a book I recently read on selling that described the benefits of being a salesperson: "Be your own boss, earn an unlimited income, and name your hours."

Back at the office, as if quoting from the same book, my boss had drilled, "Learn your presentation, know your product, organize your leads, and make your phone calls early in the day."

"Will two o'clock Friday or seven o'clock be a better time for you?" was my standard line when setting up appointments. The book had said to go for the appointment and never sell your product on the phone, a practiced skill that was easy enough.

Soon I found myself standing in a fogged-up telephone booth in downtown Santa Clara. The rain was beating down on the steel roof, puddles were forming everywhere, and the temperature had dropped to a chilly 45 degrees. Undaunted by the rain or the temperature, with a roll of coins broken open on the tray beneath the phone and my yellow "lead" cards propped up against the cold glass wall, I made my appointments to sell cancer insurance for the American Cancer and Life Insurance Company. It was my first day in the field and I already had six appointments for the afternoon and early evening.

The rain stopped and I leaped over a few puddles on my way back to the car. Once in the driver's seat, I spread the map of Santa Clara over the steering wheel and started looking up the streets. With a red pencil I circled the spot on the map indicated by J-9. Card number 2 was F-6, card number 3, L-2; card 4, J-3; and so on. Quite spread out but no problem, as I had allowed travel time between appointments.

The "lead" cards had been sent to the company by the prospective clients. They were under no obligation to purchase this supplemental insurance protection, but as the program was sanctioned by their local union, they had been encouraged to listen to the sales representative, who was going to be in the area only once. Enrollment was on a one-time basis only. Also, it was part of my presentation to name the seven danger signals of cancer, so even if they refused the policy, I would have the good feeling that they had been properly educated.

I reached for my sunglasses and carefully nudged the car out onto the Bayshore Highway. St. Frances Acres and my two o'clock appointment were a few minutes away. Mulberry Drive was lined with attractive homes. I pulled up in front of Mr. and Mrs. Aiken's home, grabbed my briefcase, and headed for the double front doors. A tan cocker spaniel greeted me with a wag of its tail and we both stood outside waiting to be let in.

Mrs. Aiken opened the door, formalities were exchanged, and she ushered me into the living room. When Mr. Aiken entered, I presented my credentials and asked if we could sit at the dining room table. "How are you today, Mr. Aiken?" I asked, as I spread out the blank forms. While he answered me, I opened my hardcover book that contained the visual aids for my presentation.

"Well," he said, "it would be better for me if I was working more. I'm only getting twenty hours a week on the job. Local 48 plumbers are just not getting any new contracts, and the work available is divided among the workers. It's been this way since November."

I said I was sorry to hear that, and believe me, I was more than sorry because this could affect the amount of the sale or the entire sale itself. I did agree with him, however, that economic conditions were rough for some people these days. "Let me show you our program. It's designed just for you and Mrs. Aiken." I went ahead with my sales presentation.

My flawless presentation left no stone unturned. The Aikens asked many intelligent questions. To close the sale, I asked that they put their names at the bottom of the application and said they could make me out a check for the first year's premium. (If I could get the full premium, there was a $50 bonus waiting for me.)

Mr. and Mrs. Aiken decided on a three-month premium, due to their squeezed income, and I had made a sale. The phone rang and Mr. Aiken showed me to the front door. The cocker spaniel sat waving goodbye with its tail.

My next appointment was across town in one hour. I had time to reflect. So this is what it is all about. Equal pay for equal time, be your own boss, pick your hours, and serve your customers. I had just made $85 in commission, had had a pleasant chat with Mr. and Mrs. Aiken, and had really sold my first policy.

I returned to my map to locate Acorn Lane, turned on the ignition, and eased the car away from the curb. "Look out, people! Here I come, and I am full of enthusiasm!" I shouted at Santa Clara.

Questions

1. The current chapter relates some of the undesirable features of sales work. Betty Diamond, however, appears to focus on the more positive. What are some of the positive aspects of a sales career that Betty touches on in her account of her first day of selling?
2. What would you suggest to Betty to help her maintain sales enthusiasm over extended periods of time?

NOTES

1. David Clark Scott, "As Inside Trades Boil, Business Deans Ponder Ethics Role," *The Christian Science Monitor,* June 27, 1986, p. 16.
2. Richard H. Howland and Roger H. Hermanson, *Principles of Salesmanship* (Homewood, IL: Irwin, 1972), p. 74.

3 Ethical Practices and Responsibilities of the Sales Force

But . . . I Was Only Following Orders

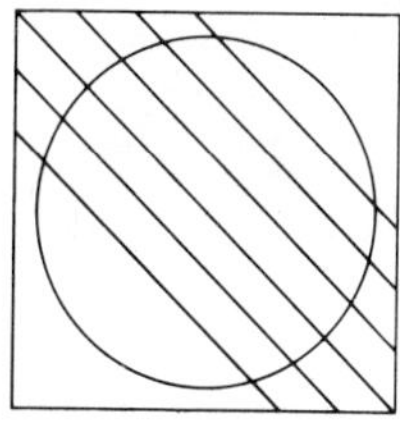

Nothing is more efficient than honesty; those who break the law or abuse the basic moral code in the name of profit are doing more to make "profit" a dirty word than all of the critics of the free-enterprise system put together.

WILLIAM SIMON

People may doubt what you say, but they will believe what you do.

ANON.

Here's what you should be able to do after studying this chapter:

1. Restate the difficulties surrounding the question of business ethics.
2. Recognize the specific groups toward whom salespeople have important responsibilities and obligations.
3. Summarize the principal types of consumer protection legislation.
4. Understand the importance of maintaining or developing personal faith and trust in yourself and others.
5. State specific ways in which work addicts can derive greater satisfaction from life.

"Irangate," political chicanery, lurid tales of adultery and hush-money payments related to TV evangelists, coupled with insider-trading abuses on Wall Street. Do you remember seeing some of the headlines associated with such scandals during the late 1980s? They caused immeasurable damage to society's faith in public, private, and even religious institutions.

Ethics in the world of business has been a perennially popular subject, one that has received renewed attention whenever new corporate abuses reach the public eye. Highly publicized activities in recent years seem to have renewed the public's concern about ethics. Some observers, however, contend that young people's growing concern about their own personal success and achievement during the 1980s caused them to discount the significance of ethical practices in their business dealings.[1]

Is it true that young people don't care about the issues of right and wrong? Have those in the business world actually become less ethical than they were in the past? Not necessarily, but with the speed and efficiency of today's communications media, undesirable business practices and behavior can be revealed around the world almost as soon as they occur. One of the great dangers of such instant communication, however, is that their frequency has convinced some people that "right is wrong,

wrong is right, everybody does it, so—what the heck—I might as well get my share, too!"

As we progress in this textbook, we shall see that both an extensive knowledge of sales factors and well-developed selling skills are essential for success in selling. But there is an additional factor—far less tangible than the others, perhaps—that has long-lasting effects on a salesperson's self-image, personal satisfaction, and feeling of success. We're referring to the salesperson's need to establish *ethical values* and to develop an objective understanding of *responsibilities to others and to self.* These nonselling responsibilities of salespeople—a topic as significant as any dealing with selling skills—will be the major focus of this chapter.

We start with a brief examination of the concept of ethics itself, followed by a general overview of the responsibilities that salespeople have toward specific groups. Of course, one of the major responsibilities of individuals in the sales field is to serve their customers. But they should recognize that their obligations vary, extending also to their own companies as well as their customers, competitors, fellow employees, society, themselves, and, of course, their families. Let's briefly examine each of these topics.

ETHICS AND THE SALESPERSON

Does everyone agree on what is ethical?

Ethics is a term that is probably easier to define than to illustrate. Basically, ethics deals with *standards of conduct or morals established by the current and past attitudes, moods, and practices of a particular society.* Business ethics, in simple terms, relates to standards of "right" and "wrong" conduct in business relationships. A factor complicating the concept of ethics is that what is considered "wrong" by one person, firm, industry, or country may be considered "right" or even desirable, by another.

Changing Standards of Ethics

It's difficult, then, to determine in absolute terms what constitutes ethical behavior. The problem is further complicated by changing standards. Practices once considered unethical have later been accepted and, therefore, have become ethical. Here's an example of changing standards. Prior to the 1980s, debates raged as to whether advertising by doctors, dentists, pharmacists, and lawyers should have been considered a breach of professional ethics. Today, however, advertisements by "legal advisers" and other professionals are relatively commonplace.

The charging of interest on loans was once considered unethical. According to ancient Hebraic and Christian dogma, the practice of charging interest for the use of money is usurious and immoral. This doctrine ultimately gave way when it was recognized that a lender is entitled to some compensation for making a loan. Usury laws still exist, however; they place limits on the amount of gain that a lender can enjoy. Nevertheless, yesterday's usurious moneychangers in the temples are today's respectable bankers in the towers.

"A factor complicating the concept of ethics is that what is considered 'wrong' by one person, firm, industry, or country may be considered 'right,' or even desirable, by another."

Legal Versus Moral Standards

There is a significant difference between *legal* standards and *ethical* standards. The former can be enforced by statute, while the latter are determined by custom and attitudes. Many *unethical* practices are also *illegal,* but can you think of an activity that's *legal* but considered *unethical?* Here's one example: selling a product that meets legal standards but is borderline with regard to consumer safety. Another example could be selling a product or service that a customer can't use. Falling into the first category were the three wheel all-terrain vehicles (ATVs), which killed an estimated 900 people over a five year period and injured people at a rate of nearly 7,000 per month. ATVs were legal until 1988 when the Justice Department, backed by the Consumer Product Safety Commission, outlawed their future sales.[2] A later section of this chapter discusses some of the legal types of protection provided to consumers.

Can moral law differ from legal law?

In general, a good measure of whether or not a business practice is unethical is found in the answers to two questions:

1. Is the activity contrary to current acceptable legal and moral practices?
2. Is the activity likely to be injurious to others?

Affirmative responses to these questions could mean disaster for some firms.

We could, of course, discuss the philosophical meaning of ethics at great length. For our purposes, however, it's more fruitful to examine ethics in the light of specific sales practices and responsibilities. Our approach, then, will be to look at the activities of salespeople from the perspective of their responsibilities toward specific groups and toward themselves.

RESPONSIBILITY TOWARD YOUR CUSTOMERS

As a salesperson, one of your major responsibilities is to serve your customers. The types of salespeople we have been concerned with in this text are professionals, honest and sincere individuals who are genuinely concerned with serving and assisting customers with their problems and needs and who follow through promptly on complaints. The kind of salespeople in demand among today's marketing organizations are not the con artists but rather individuals who can readily adapt their style and approach to fit the characteristics and needs of their customers. Getting the order is only the beginning for the creative, professional salesperson. Repeat orders, which significantly influence the survival of most companies, are directly dependent on the goodwill established by the salesperson.

How can you show your customers that you really care?

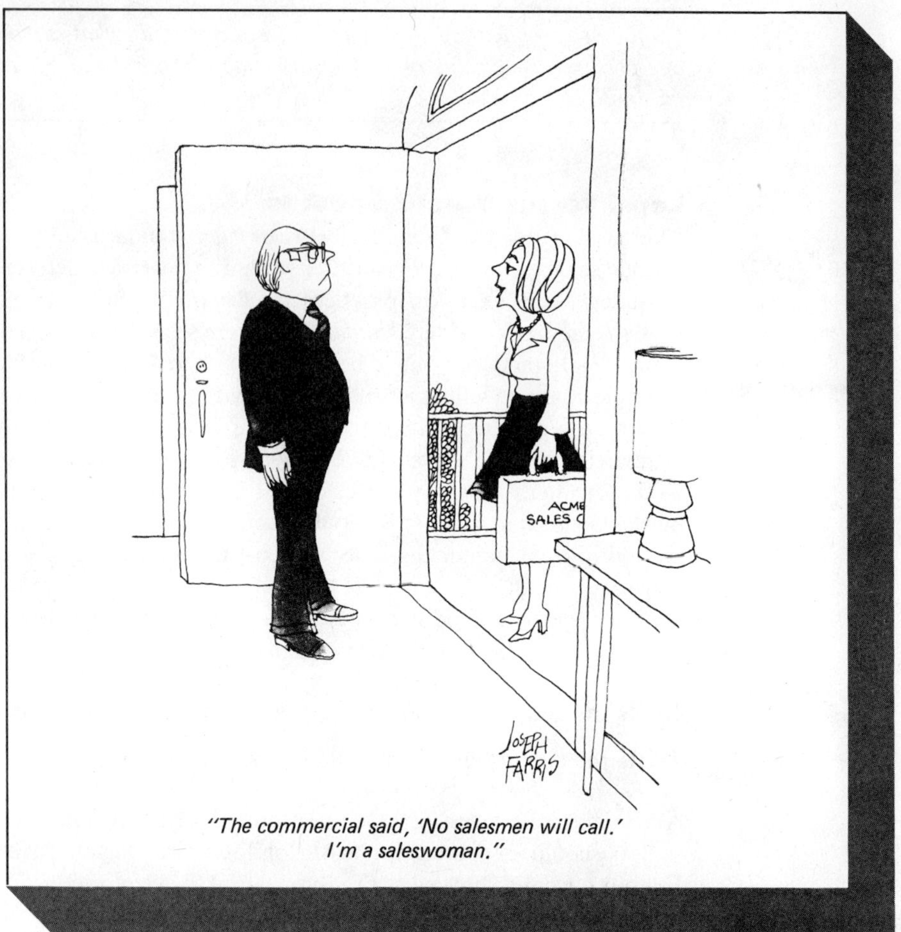

"The commercial said, 'No salesmen will call.' I'm a saleswoman."

Reprinted with permission from *Sales & Marketing Management* magazine; © 1979.

"Getting the order is only the beginning for the creative, professional salesperson."

As a salesperson who is aware of all this, you are likely to find yourself facing innumerable pressures and temptations in relation to your customers. Areas of conflict sometimes arise involving bribes, gifts, confidential information, entertainment, and reciprocity. Let's discuss each of these briefly.

Bribes

Much publicity has surrounded the use of **bribes** in the business world. A bribe is an effort to buy business from customers through kickbacks or by giving elaborate gifts. Unfortunately, there seem to be no clear-cut guidelines in this matter for business in general, but some specific firms have developed their own policies regarding bribes and gift giving.

American businesspeople doing business abroad sometimes find themselves in a dilemma. They contend that the bribing of foreign officials and businesspeople to acquire sales contracts is standard practice in some countries, that such activities are considered by locals as "financial favors," something similar to how Americans perceive tips. Some American businesspeople argue that they must engage in **situational ethics,** which is the application of moral standards that relate to the attitudes and laws in a particular social and cultural environment. In general, however, American government officials have considered the offering of financial favors—that is, bribes to foreign officials and businesspeople—to be illegal.

Is bribing really a form of creative selling?

Aside from their dubious legality, however, a key question is whether or not bribes are actually necessary for obtaining business. In a sense, if you have to *buy* business from your customers, aren't you admitting that you haven't adequately *sold* your company, its products, and its service? If you get orders because of bribes and gift giving, aren't you likely to lose orders when someone with a bribe more tantalizing than yours comes along? Do bribes really make for more stable and long-lasting business relationships? And even beyond the ethical question, bribes are often blatantly illegal and thus jeopardize the careers of those involved.

Gratuities

Gratuities are not far removed from bribes but are considered more acceptable and are offered more openly as a business practice. Many salespeople are expected to give their customers specialty items like pens and appointment books, which are advertising as well as goodwill-building devices.

Do you know your customers' policies regarding gratuities?

It's important that you try to become familiar with the policies of both your firm and your customers' firms regarding gift giving and gift receiving. Some firms openly offer gifts, including the use of recreational facilities, to their customers, while others consider such activities to be a form of unethical bribery. Many firms have developed policies against gratuities of any sort. (See Figure 3.1 for an example of a letter concerning gratuities that was sent out by a large corporation to all of its suppliers.) Finally, the Internal Revenue Service carefully scrutinizes gift giving by businesses. It places a dollar limit on the value of a gift that can be deducted for tax purposes.

Confidential Information

As a salesperson, you may have several customers who are each others' competitors. Typically, you get to know quite a bit about such firms' future operations and plans. You may also find yourself in the awkward position where one of your customers will try to get you to provide confidential information about its competitors.

When you lose their trust . . .

You should attempt to perceive yourself as having a **fiduciary relationship** with all of your customers; that is, a position of trust, confidence, and responsibility in your obligations to your customers. When asked by a customer for information that might injure one of your other customers, you might merely state with firmness

ACEITE PETROLEUM COMPANY
422 South Daisy Street. Los Angeles, California, 90054-4411

December 5, 1988

Dear Supplier:

I believe you will be interested in knowing that once again we are reaffirming to our employees the Aceite Petroleum Company's long-standing policy concerning gratuities. Our view is that gifts between business associates are unnecessary and sometimes raise questions that may injure the development of mutually beneficial and cordial business relationships.

Employees who represented our Company in dealings with other firms and individuals are instructed to do business solely on the basis of quality equipment, materials and services at reasonable cost and to show no preference because of personal considerations. It is contrary to our policy for any of our employees at any time to solicit or accept gifts or other personal benefits from anyone with whom the Company is or is likely to be doing business. This prohibition applies to gifts of merchandise, payments, loans, services, excessive entertainment, pleasure trips, travel or other tangible or intangible things of value, either directly or indirectly through relatives or friends. Items of token or little intrinsic value such as advertising give-aways or a small sample of a company's product are excepted.

We wish to express our appreciation for your past services and hope you will understand and appreciate the business intent of this letter. It is our sincere conviction that strict adherence to this policy will avoid embarrassments and is in the best interest of all concerned.

Respectfully yours,

Victor Packer

Victor Packer
Regional Procurement Manager
West Coast Divison

VP:bs

Figure 3.1 Adapted from an Actual Letter Sent by a Large Petroleum Company Manager to Suppliers.

something like, "I'm really sorry, Jason, but I'm really not in the position to provide you with that kind of information." If pressed further, you might say, "Jason, isn't it likely that if I blabbed about your competitors *to you* that I probably would be doing the same with your competitors *about you.* You would lose my respect if I did. Quite frankly, I refuse to do anything that might damage either you or them." Such an approach is likely to gain you even greater respect of your customers.

Entertainment

Entertaining customers is closely akin to gift giving and is common practice in many industries. A few firms, however, have policies discouraging salespeople from entertaining customers except in certain situations.

Creative selling, as we have learned, is the attempt to persuade another person to recognize and act upon a need to obtain your goods or services. Many salespeople feel that an occasional lunch or nightclub outing helps to make potential customers more receptive to sales messages. In general, however, if your customers don't feel you have a product they need, it is unlikely that lunches in plush restaurants will lead them to make affirmative buying decisions.

Will a lunch substitute for a good product?

Some salespeople use entertaining as a substitute for creative selling, hoping that the customer will feel an indebtedness or obligation to buy their products. If you were the customer, however, would you necessarily feel obligated to purchase something you weren't sold on because of a free lunch? Or wouldn't you be more concerned with obtaining a quality product and dependable service?

"In general . . . if your customers don't feel you have a product they need, it is unlikely that lunches in plush restaurants will lead them to make affirmative buying decisions."

Since you are likely to entertain customers occasionally, however, you should be somewhat careful about your behavior, especially in relation to the consumption of alcohol. You needn't be a teetotaler, but you should be aware of your capacity for holding drinks. Otherwise, you could find yourself behaving in a fashion that could lose—rather than gain—orders and goodwill. That's not all you might lose. You could also lose an important sales tool—your right to drive an automobile—if caught driving in an intoxicated state.

Reciprocity

Purchasers sometimes make buying decision based on nonrational motives. An example is **reciprocity,** a mutual exchange of benefits that occurs when a firm buys products from its own customers.

What are the potential dangers of a "back-scratching" relationship?

Some salespeople use reciprocity in a manner that borders on the unethical. These salespeople approach firms that supply their own company and attempt to persuade them to buy out of obligation, implying that orders will not be forthcoming in the future without reciprocal purchases.

Reciprocity may be acceptable in situations where both parties benefit, but there is always a danger that it will be interpreted as a form of blackmail by customers who are pressured into buying because they have sold products to your firm. In general, the "you scratch my back and I'll scratch yours" approach to business transactions is of questionable merit in instances where a purchase is made regardless of price, quality, or dependability of the product and service.

SELLERS BEWARE—THE CUSTOMER HAS A PROTECTIVE SHIELD

Years ago there was little legal protection for consumers. If a salesperson, for example, sold a product that later proved to be unsafe, the seller would often say something like, "Tough darts, Charlie! You bought it, so it's yours, problems and all."

Because of such abuses in the past, salespeople are now forced by legal statutes to engage in ethical practices. Customers have numerous laws available to them that are intended to protect them against unfair sales practices.

"But I didn't know, judge." "That's too bad!"

As a salesperson, you're expected to be familiar with the laws affecting your sales activities. A plea of ignorance will count for little in a court of law. A major challenge you must face, however, is that of keeping up with the extensive amounts of legislation, since new laws are continually added and old ones modified. Of course, we can't cover all aspects of commercial law in the limited space available here. We will look at some of the more significant laws that could affect you as a salesperson in your dealings with customers.

"I Changed My Mind"—The Right to Cancel

House-to-house salespeople are affected by a number of rules enforced by the **Federal Trade Commission (FTC).** One such rule relates to a **cooling-off period** that must be provided to people purchasing merchandise from a house-to-house salesperson. In short, the rule states that a buyer can cancel the order within 72 hours of the transaction and receive full refund if the value of the items exceeds $25. Further, the salesperson is required to provide a written notice of the right to cancel, such as the one illustrated in Figure 3.2.

Most states have similar right-to-cancel laws. Such legislation was passed as a result of complaints from consumers indicating that they were pressured into buying unwanted merchandise.

Don't Say It If You Don't Mean It

Consumers are also protected from false and misleading claims made in advertising or promotion or by the salesperson. False and misleading advertising or promotion of any good or service is considered illegal.

Although you personally may have little to do with the creation of advertising or promotional campaigns, you are in the position of making statements about what you sell. You could be considered guilty of **fraud** or **breach of warranty** if you make either false or misleading statements or conceal relevant information about your product or service.

The legal aspects of warranties are important to sellers of goods and services. Basically there are two types of warranties: expressed and implied. An **expressed warranty** exists when a seller makes a statement, either in writing or orally, about the product or service that induces a person to make a purchase. An **implied warranty**, however, doesn't have to be stated; it's assumed to exist. For example,

NOTICE OF CANCELLATION

Date of Transaction:

You may cancel this transaction, without any penalty or obligation, within three business days from the above date.

If you cancel, any property traded in, any payments made by you under the contract or sale, and any negotiable instrument executed by you will be returned within 10 business days following receipt by the seller of your cancellation notice, and any security interest arising out of the transaction will be canceled.

If you cancel, you must make available to the seller at your residence, in substantially as good condition as when received, any goods delivered to you under this contract or sale; or you may, if you wish, comply with the instructions of the seller regarding the return shipment of the goods at the seller's expense and risk.

If you do make the goods available to the seller and the seller does not pick them up within 20 days of the date of your notice of cancellation, you may retain or dispose of the goods without any further obligation. If you fail to make the goods available to the seller, or if you agree to return the goods to the seller and fail to do so, then you remain liable for performance of all obligations under the contract.

To cancel this transaction, mail or deliver a signed and dated copy of this cancellation notice, or send a telegram, to (name of seller) ____,

at (address of seller's place of business) ____ ____,

not later than midnight of (date) ____________________.

I hereby cancel this transaction.

Date: ____________________

(Your Signature) ____________________

Figure 3.2 Sample Cancellation Notice Provided to Purchasers of Merchandise from House-to-House Vendors. **Source:** Federal Trade Commission.

there's an implied warranty that any product a person buys is free from defects and can be put to the specific uses suggested by the seller's presentation.

Consumer protection laws currently require manufacturers to include with the product an expressed warranty that relates to its performance and that indicates what the purchaser must do if the product is defective.

You Really Wouldn't Want That One—Ye Olde Bait-and-Switch Ploy

Fishing for trouble!

Another selling practice frowned upon by the FTC is what is termed the **bait-and-switch tactic.** In using this ploy, a retailer advertises a lower-priced item to attract (bait) customers, then attempts to switch them to higher-priced items. The following is an example of this practice.

Ned Neater has wanted to purchase a portable cassette recorder for some time but has felt that most sets were out of his price range. In this morning's paper, however, he saw what he'd been looking for: a portable AM/FM stereo cassette recorder on sale for only $48.00. "This is the price I've been waiting for," Ned said to himself.

Ned hopped into his car, headed out to the the Happy Valley Shopping Center, and went into the SaveMuch Value Outlet, where the salesperson told him: "I really wouldn't want to sell you that cheaper set. I would feel guilty if I did. For example, it lacks the high-speed dubbing feature that is so popular these days. It also doesn't have the five-band graphic equalizer for custom-shaped sound available in our better model. Nor does it have that all-essential feature—a Dolby noise reducer. You can't even record your own voice along with the music. What I really want you to take home is our quality model here, which is only about $100 more but has all those necessary features lacking in the cheaper model. How would you like to pay, cash or charge?"

Retailers who have been investigated by the FTC for playing the bait-and-switch game have received substantial unfavorable publicity that has tended to tarnish their public images.

Don't Blame Me . . . I Only *Deliver* the Mail

I didn't ask for it, but I'll keep it!

The FTC also investigates the unfair practice of sending people merchandise they never ordered. According to the FTC, householders, for example, who receive such items as books, records, and cosmetics have certain options available to them. They can either refuse to accept the merchandise or they can keep the unsolicited item and refuse to pay for it. However, these rules don't apply to merchandise sent to the wrong address; it must be returned.

To Tell the Truth

¡Compra sin dinero!

Many consumers make their purchases with credit. A law designed to provide consumers with more information regarding their credit charges is the **Truth in Lending Act.** The purpose of this law is to let consumers know exactly what it will cost them to make use of credit and to help them compare the charges made by different credit sources. The law requires that customers be made aware of two things regarding the cost of credit: (1) the **finance charge**—the amount of money the customer pays to obtain credit—and (2) the **annual percentage rate,** which enables the customer to compare credit costs regardless of the dollar amount of those costs or the period of time over which the payments must be made. Both the finance charge and the annual percentage rate must be displayed prominently on the forms and statements used by the lender.

Don't Dun Me!

The flip side of credit is debt. Naturally, you expect customers who have made purchases from you on credit to pay their debts. Some customers, however, don't pay their bills. You might find occasion, therefore, to turn over an unpaid bill to a collection agency. Because of some of the past practices of debt collection agencies, Congress passed the **Fair Debt Collection Practices Act.** This law prohibits debt collection agencies from using unfair or abusive collection practices. However, the law doesn't apply to creditors who collect their own bills or lawyers who are collecting on behalf of a client. Table 3.1 summarizes the principal types of debt collection practices prohibited by the act.

You dun me in!

The Feminine Side of Credit

Another area of FTC concern relates to women and credit. Women have had problems developing credit ratings, since credit accounts in the past were often listed only under their husbands' names. Many women assumed the responsibility for

TABLE 3.1 Prohibited Practices Under the Fair Debt Collection Practices Act.

Harassment and Abuse. A debt collector can no longer use threats of violence or harm to a consumer's person, family, property, or reputation. Obscene or profane language is also out. The improper use of the telephone—repeated calls to annoy or harass, calling without giving full identification, calling at all hours of the day and night—is also against the law.

Falsehoods. Debt collectors may not imply that they are lawyers or agents of the federal, state, or local government or that they work for a credit bureau when they do not. A collector must not misrepresent the amount of your debt or falsely imply that you committed a crime by not paying your debt. Nor can a collector threaten court action if no such action is planned or may not legally be taken. In fact, the law prohibits a debt collector from using *any* false or deceptive means to collect a debt.

Privacy. A debt is a private matter—and the law keeps it that way. Therefore, a debt collector cannot send you a collection notice by postcard. The word *collection* cannot appear on an envelope sent to you; nor is anything else allowed on the envelope that might indicate a message inside concerning a debt you owe. Also, the debt collector may not publish your name as a debtor or in any other way advertise your debt or you as a debtor. The debt collector may call your friends or your boss to verify where you live or work but may not discuss your debts with them. In fact, the debt collector may not discuss your debts with anyone but you (without permission from you or a court).

Unfairness. A debt collector may not charge you additional interest or fees unless the law of your state (or the state where you signed the original contract) authorizes them. If a debt collector calls you or sends you telegrams *collect,* you don't have to accept the charges. In addition, a debt collector can't deposit your postdated check before the date you agreed upon.

Source: Federal Trade Commission.

"Sorry, lady—you don't exist."

paying monthly bills on time, but credit bureaus kept all account records in their husbands' files. As a result, problems often arise when a woman is widowed or divorced or simply wants credit in her own name. Creditors requesting a credit report about her may get a "no file" response from the credit bureau. She might have an excellent credit history—but it's all in her husband's name.

A woman who gets married and changes her name can have similar problems, The old accounts held in her maiden name may not be transferred to the file listed under her married name, and—for all practical purposes—her credit history may get lost.

A federal law now attempts to overcome this problem. Entitled the **Equal Credit Opportunity Act,** it prohibits creditors from discriminating on the basis of sex or marital status in any aspect of a credit transaction. The act also forbids discrimination on the basis of race, color, age, national origin, religion, receipt of public assistance payments, or the fact that an applicant has exercised rights under federal consumer credit protection laws.

Avoiding Costly Lawsuits

Misrepresentation and breach of warranty lawsuits can prove to be expensive to your company, even if charges are eventually dropped, because of the large expenditures of time and legal expense. In addition, your company may experience bad publicity in the process. Table 3.2 suggests some ways in which salespeople can minimize exposure to costly misrepresentation and breach of warranty lawsuits.

TABLE 3.2 Suggestions for Avoiding Costly Misrepresentation and Breach of Warranty Lawsuits.

1. Understand the distinction between general statements of praise and statements of fact made during the sales presentation (and the legal consequences).
2. Thoroughly inform the customer about the specific qualities of the product before making the sale.
3. Be accurate when describing a product's capabilities.
4. Know the technical specifications of the product.
5. Avoid making exaggerated claims about product safety.
6. Be familiar with federal and state laws regarding warranties and guarantees.
7. Be well versed in the capabilities and characteristics of your products and services.
8. Keep current with all design changes and revisions in your product's operating manual.
9. Avoid offering opinions when the customer asks about what a product or service will accomplish unless your company has tested the product and has statistical evidence.
10. Never overstep authority, especially when discussing prices or company policy. Your statements can bind your company.

Sources: Adapted from Steven Mitchell Sack, "Legal Puffery: Truth or Consequences," *Sales & Marketing Management,* October 1986, pp. 59, 60; and Steven Mitchell Sack, "The High Risk of Dirty Tricks," *Sales & Marketing Management,* November 11, 1985, pp. 56–59.

RESPONSIBILITY TOWARD YOUR COMPANY

Your organization needs you and other salespeople. But so do you need your organization. And you have certain important responsibilities toward it, such as generating profitable revenues, being familiar with its products, engaging in field intelligence activities (collecting marketing information), submitting reports on time, and helping to maintain a positive company image by adequately servicing your accounts. You significantly influence the success or failure of your company. According to Dun and Bradstreet, each month there are approximately 5000 business failures in the United States.[3] There is no single cause for these failures, but poor management of sales territories, along with inadequate understanding of responsibilities by employees contributes extensively.

Passing the Buck

Why does the "passed buck" fly back to your face?

When one of your customers presents you with a complaint, don't pass the buck by criticizing other individuals in your company. If you blame them—or anything else about your company, including your computer—you are, in effect, blaming yourself, since to your customers, *you*—the salesperson—*are the company.* Your customers don't really separate you from your firm.

Misuse of Company Time and Resources

Moonlight becomes you not.

There are some salespeople who would never stoop to stealing company equipment or supplies yet feel no guilt when stealing another valuable resource—time. An ethical question can be raised as to whether or not a salesperson should be **moonlighting**—that is, holding a second job. Most sales managers are opposed to their salespeople moonlighting since the added work tends to reduce efficiency in their primary job of selling. Sometimes the second job involves promoting another firm's products or pursuing self-interest, activities that a sales manager would certainly not consider loyalty to the firm.

Other unethical activities that tend to misuse company resources are *padding expense accounts, juggling sales orders during sales campaigns and contests,* and *putting company assets to personal use.* You will continually be faced with ethical questions and temptations. When in doubt as to the "proper" course of action, ask yourself the following questions:

1. If I owned this company, would I approve of my employees doing the same thing?
2. How might my career be affected if my actions became known by my boss?

RESPONSIBILITY TOWARD COMPETITORS

At first glance you might find it strange that, as a salesperson, you even have certain ethical responsibilities to firms actively competing with yours. But although the responsibility is somewhat indirect, it does exist. Some behavior in relation to competition is blatantly unethical, such as making false claims about or unfair comparisons with competing products and firms. Some sales representatives have been known to sabotage the competition's products so that the performance of these products couldn't match that of their own.

Such behavior is obviously unethical and highly dangerous. Overaggressive sales behavior of this nature is also likely to be discovered, resulting in untold damage to the reputation of the offending company and its sales staff. Let's now examine two less obvious aspects of a salesperson's responsibility toward competitors.

Criticizing the Competition

Inexperienced salespeople sometimes feel that an effective way to meet and beat competition is to attack it. Nothing could be further from reality. An important rule you should remember is:

> Do not knock thy competitors.

How might knocking your competition hurt you?

Put yourself in the shoes of a person who has been purchasing a particular product for about two years and is quite satisfied with it. If a salesperson tells you that the product you have been purchasing is no good, he or she is, in a sense, criticizing you and your judgment. The criticism may even place you in the position of having to defend a product you previously acquired. Instead of criticizing your competition, you as a salesperson should stress the positive and beneficial features of your own products and relate them to your prospect's needs.

For example, assume that you, a respresentative of a securities brokerage firm, approach a prospective client whose account has been handled in the past by a discount broker. Don't attack or criticize your prospect's brokerage firm. The prospect may have had highly favorable experience with the firm or may even be a personal friend of one of the principals. You are likely to be more effective if you stress how the prospect will benefit from the service facilities of your own firm and say as little as possible about your competition. Besides, why give your competition a free plug?

You have to be prudent when comparing the qualities and characteristics of your product or service with a competitor's during the sales presentation. False statements are illegal and could result in costly lawsuits against you and your company. Lawyer Steven Mitchell Sack suggests avoiding four types of comments when talking to customers:

1. Untrue remarks that a competitor engages in illegal or unfair business practices.
2. Untrue remarks that a competitor fails to live up to his or her contractual obligations and responsibilities. For example, saying that the competitor ships defective goods or is always being sued.

3. Untrue statements regarding a competitor's financial condition. Example: stating that the competitor has discontinued its operations, is financially unstable, or is going bankrupt.
4. Untrue statements that a principal in the competitor's business is incompetent, of poor moral character, unreliable, or dishonest.[4]

Learning from the Competition

How might your competition assist you?

Maintaining a good relationship with salespeople from competing firms can help you more often than you realize. They can not only provide you with helpful information about a potential prospect but might also refer sales to you that, for various reasons, they can't handle. You can meet salespeople from competing firms in many places, such as customer's offices, trade fairs, and conventions. When you do, why not invite them out occasionally for a cup of coffee? You can ask a few open-ended questions and often learn things that can be useful in your own sales activities. Most persons enjoy talking about their work, so some carefully framed open questions might provide you with valuable information about your competitors' activities. However, watch out for the competitor who's as clever as you. You could lose far more than a cup of coffee!

RESPONSIBILITY TOWARD FELLOW EMPLOYEES

How might inside and service personnel affect an unsympathetic sales rep?

Salespeople, as we have learned, are frequently placed on pedestals because of their revenue-generating activities. But this elevated position can be a bit precarious at times. Even though you may regularly find yourself in the limelight, you should guard against appearing to be a prima donna. Your direct contact with service or inside personnel may be infrequent, but it can be highly significant. Remember that service and inside personnel *support* your field activities. By recognizing their feelings and problems, you are likely to find them far more receptive to the needs and problems you face with your customers. If you don't, well . . . you should be able to figure out what obstacles you could encounter.

RESPONSIBILITY TOWARD SOCIETY

As a salesperson, your responsibility toward society is difficult to define in absolute terms since we all perceive our fellow humans and our environment in different ways. You shouldn't forget, however, that in addition to being a salesperson you are also a member of the human race. Consequently, you have certain responsibilities to others that cannot—indeed, should not—be ignored, especially as a result of an expanded public consciousness regarding the environment and consumers' rights. Firms whose members operate with a blatant disregard for the well-being of society or ignore laws relating to product safety or price and employee discrimination may find difficulty in attracting qualified employees and maintaining markets. In recent

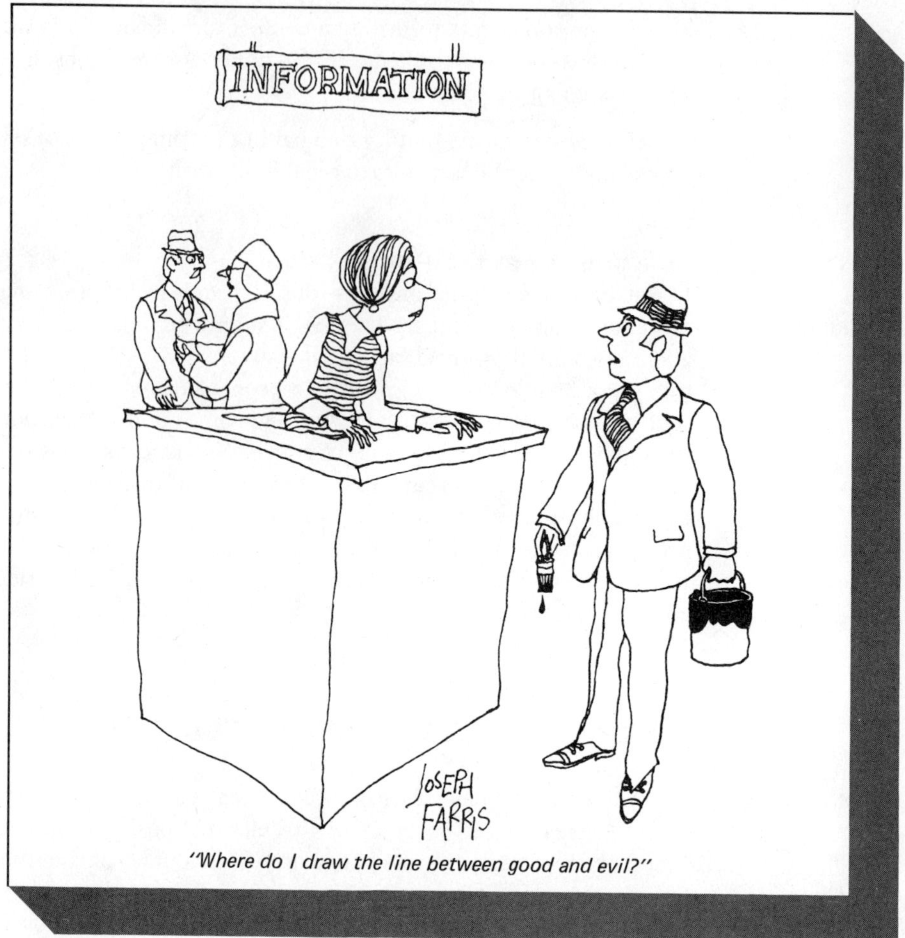

"Where do I draw the line between good and evil?"

Reprinted with permission from *Sales & Marketing Management* magazine; © 1979.

years, **caveat emptor** (let the buyer beware) attitudes by some businesses have been highly publicized and have damaged the reputations of reputable organizations while tarnishing the image of free enterprise.

"Firms whose members operate with a blatant disregard for the well-being of society or ignore laws relating to product safety or price and employee discrimination may find difficulty in attracting qualified employees and maintaining markets."

Salespeople who consistently engage in socially unacceptable activities, those bordering on the unethical or illegal, are likely to experience fewer personal job satisfactions than those who are proud of their activities. Socially concerned salespeople are often involved with civic affairs that not only help the community but can also help maintain and create goodwill for their firms.

Like many progressive companies today, the Xerox Corporation has developed a statement of corporate policy regarding the ethical practices of its sales representatives (see Figure 3.3).

RESPONSIBILITY TOWARD YOURSELF

Do you realize how many hours are spent on the job during a typical lifetime? Assuming that you have an eight-hour workday (probably a low estimate, considering travel and preparation time or jobs with differing responsibilities), you will spend roughly 1,900 hours a year at your job. In a lifetime of 40 years of employment, you will have spent at least 76,000 hours (9,500 workdays) on your job. If during your entire career you literally dread your work and are not proud of your activities, a substantial part of your lifetime will seem dull and full of drudgery. Don't you owe yourself more than that?

The Need to Establish Ethical Values

To make your work and personal life more satisfying, you need a certain degree of faith and trust both in yourself and in others. One way to maintain greater trust is to be trustworthy yourself. Salespeople, like individuals in all kinds of occupations, are constantly faced with difficult choices. Unfortunately, any discussion of this nature runs the risk of sounding "goodie-goodie" or possibly even prudish, but think seriously about the following: If you continually engage in unethical practices with others, say your customers or your own company, two principal types of problems might confront you. The first relates to *living with your own conscience* and the second to the tendency of *assuming that others are as unethical* in their dealings as you are.

An example of a situation that could strain your ethical values might be one in which your boss directs you to do something you believe is either unethical or illegal. Assume that you are a sales representative and your boss, Mr. Nomore Straight, asks you to keep a separate set of records—one with padded expense figures—for income tax purposes.

What do you do when you're between the devil and the deep blue sea?

In a figurative sense, your boss has placed you between the Scylla of willful disobedience and the Charybdis of facing the ethical or legal consequences of your act.* If you do as directed, you may be as legally responsible (or as criminally negligent) as your boss. If you don't do as directed, you also run risks since your boss determines your pay raises, territories, and promotions. What do you do then? How might your personal financial responsibilities influence or change your decision? What about the long-run effects on your own conscience? If you are caught, and the chances are fairly good that you will be, how might your future career be affected?

*Scylla, in ancient mythology, was a female monster who lured sailors onto the rocks along the Sicilian coast opposite a whirlpool called Charybdis. Mariners thus had to sail between two equally hazardous alternatives.

The Ethics of Selling for Xerox.

A customer buys from Xerox for two reasons. He wants the product. He trusts the Sales Representative.

These two factors mesh like two gear wheels. Neither is going very far without the other. Together, they move.

Our technology may be superb, the reputation of our products may be unmatched. A man buys from the salesman he trusts.

Don't sell ethics short. Xerox doesn't. We lay claim to idealism in our company and make no apologies for that. But we also recognize the simple economic fact that our success rests heavily on your relationship with each of your customers—the service you provide, and the confidence each customer has in it and in you.

Because your performance in this respect is so important, because it can be critical in our competitive business environment, Xerox has developed a specific code of ethical selling practice for Sales Representatives. We ask you to understand it! We insist you adhere to it; your work will be measured against it.

The first five points involve the fundamental integrity of the entire corporation in the eyes of the public. You are responsible for meeting established revenue, net-addition and expense objectives—but in doing that you are also the custodian of the company's reputation. You are indeed Xerox to your customers, to your own immediate competitors. And you are Xerox in a legal sense. Your obligations are precise and not negotiable.

The last three points are essentially internal. They are no less compelling, no less significant than the first five.

Xerox management has its own clear responsibilities—obligations to you—under this code. It must keep informed—it must encourage a free flow of communication from Sales Representatives and Sales Managers. It must determine quickly and fairly the validity of any seeming infractions. It must act promptly and decisively when deviations from the code occur. It is obligated to you to make the code work and help you make it work.

The Xerox Selling Code.

1. The only sales proposal you present to a customer is the proposal that best meets that customer's real needs: what it takes to do his job effectively without wasted capacity, equipment, or products. Anything else hurts Xerox in the long run—in the short run, too, for that matter.

2. You make sure that customers understand exactly what they are contracting for, what their contractual obligations are to Xerox. You make equally sure that they understand just as clearly what Xerox contracts to do.

3. You never knowingly misrepresent any Xerox product or service or price. You exercise initiative and responsibility to avoid doing so unknowingly.

4. You never knowingly misrepresent any competitive product or service or price. You exercise initiative and responsibility to avoid doing so unknowingly.

5. You make no disparaging statements, directly or by any kind of inference or innuendo, about competitors and their products and services—even if you believe them to be true.

6. You conduct your activities so that they do not impinge in any way on the personal or business interests and integrity of your Xerox associates.

   - You do not knowingly engage in any practice that provides personal gain at the expense of others.
   - Territory and accounts are so managed as to permit territory transition and account changes without affecting other sales people adversely.

7. You recognize your responsibility to understand this code and to operate within it without exception.

8. You recognize the importance of bringing any problems you experience in implementing the code, internally or externally, to the attention of your management.

Courtesy: The Xerox Corporation.

Figure 3.3 Xerox Corporation's Statement of Corporate Policy Regarding the Ethical Practices of Its Sales Representatives.

You should continually remind yourself when confronted with certain temptations that ethical values are not necessarily obsolete. You will discover that you can live a far more confident existence if, in your mind, your sales activities do not border on the unethical or illegal. Think about the words of Professor Gus L. Kotoulas, who has warned, "Underhanded dealings act like a cancer that slowly eat away at a salesperson and often cause him to leave selling because of the anxiety they create."[5]

Work and Personal Satisfaction

Since you probably are destined to spend considerable time on your job, you should try to find a sales position that will give you personal satisfaction and a feeling of accomplishment. Don't however, spend a lot of time looking for a perfect situation; such jobs are rare if not totally nonexistent.

Does **work** *have to be a nasty four-letter word?*

To some salespeople, the word *work* is equated with drudgery—dull, unpleasant, irksome activities that mainly serve as the means (the commission check?) to far more satisfying ends (a videocassette recorder or some new skis?). To other sales personnel, though, *work* has no such unfavorable connotation. They look forward not only to paydays but also to nearly every day and to every account on whom they must call. Open your eyes wide, look carefully, and you *will* see people who truly enjoy their work.

You have a responsibility to yourself. Of course, the nature of your job has some influence over how you react to work, but even more important is your *attitude.* If you look for negative factors in any situation, you'll find them; but if you maintain a positive and enthusiastic attitude, you'll see a lot more that's positive.

The Need for Life Enrichment

Salespeople need time for leisure activities. Unfortunately, though, a surprisingly large number of salespeople suffer from an affliction believed to be worse in some

"Excuse me, sir, but I'm on a
working vacation. Would you like to buy a tie?"

Drawing by C. Barsotti; © 1974. The New Yorker Magazine, Inc.

respects than excessive drinking. The malady is called **workaholism (work addiction).** Some people apparently overwork for the same reason that alcoholics overdrink: to try to escape frustration. There is nothing particularly wrong with being a hard worker, but a hard worker is not a work addict. Addicts feel guilty when they are not working; hard workers do not.

"A surprisingly large number of salespeople suffer from an affliction believed to be worse in some respects than excessive drinking. The malady is called work addiction."

Can you develop a balance between work and play?

Enriching your life off the job can help enrich your on-the-job activities. Time spent on hobbies, on evening courses in art or music, in exercise, or in any other activity that interests you can not only relieve some of your job-created tensions but also help you recharge your run-down, tired batteries. Salesworkers should establish a balance between work and leisure activities. As Bertrand Russell once advised, "To be able to fill leisure intelligently is the last product of civilization." Individuals who have not learned how to unwind, whose tensions strain their tolerance, sometimes discover that mother nature helps them slow down through heart attacks and increased accidents. A bit morbid, but too often true, is this bit of philosophy found written on a washroom wall in San Francisco: "Death is nature's way of telling you to slow down." Think about those words.

RESPONSIBILITY TOWARD YOUR FAMILY

Many salespeople have families, and many salespeople are very ambitious. These two characteristics are not necessarily incompatible, but sometimes salespeople make them so. Although there is nothing wrong with your having a burning yearning to achieve, it shouldn't be at the expense of your family. Of course, the same should hold true for a "significant other."

"Although there is nothing wrong with your having a burning yearning to achieve, it shouldn't be at the expense of your family."

The disadvantages inherent in some sales jobs, such as extensive travel and long working hours, can also be disadvantages to the home lives of salespeople. As usual, of course, if you are aware of the potential hazards, you're often more likely to be able to avoid them, or at least lessen their effects. You're likely to work far more effectively and accomplish your goals more readily and with greater job satisfaction if the members of your family are reasonably satisfied with their situation. Look at the following guidelines for fulfilling your responsibility toward your family. Can you add to the list any that relate to your specific family situation?

1. Do you plan and organize your activities effectively? Disorganized salespeople are so busy "putting out fires" that they tend to have little time available for their families.
2. Do you share some of your more interesting experiences with your family?
3. Do your family members have an opportunity to share their daily experiences with you?
4. Do you devote at least one entire day a week to activities with your family, excluding all thoughts of work?
5. Do you take regular vacations or trips with your family?
6. Do you plan your next vacation soon after finishing one? This activity can give both you and your family something to look forward to.

SUMMARY

The question of ethics is a difficult one since each person perceives what is right or wrong in his or her own way. There are, however, certain generally accepted standards of business behavior that are essential if continuity and predictability are to exist in business.

The duties and responsibilities of those in selling are far more varied than is usually recognized. The primary function of salespeople, of course, is to sell goods and services at a profit for their companies. But the job of selling carries with it as well other duties and responsibilities, such as planning, traveling, collecting, forecasting, and report preparation. Of equal importance are the responsibilities salespeople have toward specific groups, including customers, their own companies, competitors, fellow employees, society, themselves, and their own families.

KEY TERMS

ethics
bribes
situational ethics
gratuities
fiduciary relationship
entertaining customers
reciprocity
Federal Trade Commission (FTC)
cooling-off period
fraud
breach of warranty
expressed warranty
implied warranty
bait-and-switch tactic
Truth in Lending Act
finance charge
annual percentage rate
Fair Debt Collection Practices Act
Equal Credit Opportunity Act
moonlighting
caveat emptor
workaholism (work addiction)

QUESTIONS

1. Why is it sometimes difficult to determine what is or isn't ethical behavior?
2. What is your opinion of the *cooling-off period* as applied to house-to-house purchases?
3. In what way might criticizing specific inside personnel or departments in your company for inadvertent errors tend to hurt your own chances for future sales? Would passing the buck to a computer foul-up be acceptable? Explain.
4. What kinds of useful information might you be able to learn from a salesperson with a competing firm? How might you obtain such information?
5. In addition to being somewhat rude, why is it bad practice for a salesperson to snub or alienate his or her fellow employees?
6. Assume that you have been asked by your manager to deliver a 5- to 10-minute address to a group of 20 new sales trainees. The topic is to be "The responsibility of the salesperson to the community at large." What would you say to the new employees?
7. Explain how being a hard worker is different from being a work addict. What significance is there in the distinction?
8. Assume that a friend of yours bares her troubles to you. You discover that she has not learned how to establish a balance between work and leisure activities. What would you advise her?

9. In what ways not cited in the text can a salesperson enhance his or her family relationships?

10. If you are an unmarried salesperson, how might the section in this chapter entitled "Responsibility Toward Your Family" relate to you?

APPLICATIONS

3.1 THE IMMINENT PRICE CHANGE

Assume that you work as a sales representative for a steel supply company and that you have called on one of your customers, Gib Gilbert, who wants to place an unusually large order with your firm. However, earlier this morning you learned that in five days your company intends to make a 5 percent price reduction on the types of materials Mr. Gilbert wants to buy. You have at least two options: you can take the order for the materials at today's prices or you can inform Mr. Gilbert that the price is about to drop and save him a considerable sum of money. If you enable your customer to purchase the materials at next week's lower price, the revenues to your firm and your commission (paycheck) will also be substantially lower.

Questions

1. Based on the facts cited in the case, what would you do?

2. What are the long-run implications of your decision?

3.2 THE SLOW DELIVERIES

As a cost-cutting measure, the XYZ firm has closed its warehouse storage operations located in Fort Worth and consolidated them with its operations in Dallas. As a result, deliveries of orders to the customers of Willie Weeper, an XYZ sales representative, have been one to two weeks late. Some of Willie's customers have begun to complain about the delays. Willie's approach has been to say: "Mr. Customer, don't blame me. You know I always do my best for you. The problem is with XYZ. They're trying to cut down on costs and so they moved their storage facilities to Dallas. But don't worry, I'll tell them you're upset."

Questions

1. What is your reaction to Willie's approach?

2. What would have been a more desirable approach?

3.3 CAUGHT BETWEEN SCYLLA AND CHARYBDIS

Wilma Wohri is a sales representative for a medium-sized consumer products firm, Kitem and Voler, Inc., and has the responsibility of calling on buyers for supermarket chains to promote K&V's products. Wilma is a voracious reader. Recently she learned from a foreign publication that a Swiss government agency in Zurich has banned the sale in Switzerland of an antiperspirant spray that K&V currently manufactures and distributes under a different brand name in the United States and Canada. The Zurich government agency uncovered what it believes to be positive evidence that the antiperspirant's active ingredient, zirconium, has the potential to cause inflammation in the human lung that, over the long run, can interfere with the organ's function. The substance was shown by Zurich researchers to create an inflammatory response, known as granuloma, in tissue. According to the article that Wilma read, a panel of Swiss experts stated that the risks in using zirconium-containing aerosol antiperspirants "are insupportable in view of the benefits likely to be derived from their use. Safer antiperspirant drug products, which achieve comparable perspiration control without risk of pulmonary disease, are available."

Not long after reading the Zurich report, Wilma was asked by her boss, Mr. Filbert Finchpenny, to come to his office. During the session, Mr. Finchpenny informed Wilma that the sale of Sprayitough, the American trade name of the antiperspirant, had not been particularly good in her territory. He suggested that she begin to promote Sprayitough to her accounts with greater vigor.

Wilma explained to Finchpenny that Sprayitough is K&V's name for the same spray that was removed from the Swiss market. Finchpenny glossed over the Swiss experience and mumbled something about "those moneychangers in Switzerland know nothing about antiperspirants." He informed Wilma of the tremendous capital investment that K&V had sunk into the research, development, and advertising of Sprayitough. "We're already getting hit on all sides by the public with their narrow-minded attitudes toward aerosol applicators. All we need now is another phoney scare like you've brought up. If we don't recover our investment," warned Finchpenny, "all of us here at K&V are going to end up on welfare."

Wilma was disturbed by Finchpenny's attitude, so she told him that the company should not be "pushing" a product that might cause bodily harm to consumers. Finchpenny stressed that the firm had hardly begun to recover the tremendous investment already made on Sprayitough. He also made an allusion to her being a widow with a substantial mortgage and two children at an out-of-state university who are dependent on her support. Finchpenny closed the discussion with the comment, "I expect to see some positive results on your next monthly production statement!"

Questions

1. What sort of a problem does Wilma face?
2. Assume that you are a close friend of Wilma's and that she has come to you for advice. What would you say to her?

3.4 WAS ORVILLE RIGHT?

Orville Niswonger is a sales representative for the Needling Supply House of Walla Walla, Washington. Orville has a territory consisting of 45 accounts. One of his newer accounts, Harry Hartford, has been a customer for the past six months. Harry's purchase volume has been quite satisfactory, but payments on his account have been at least 40 days late during each of the last three billing periods.

Doris Debit is the manager of the credit department of the Needling Supply House, Orville's employer. She has requested that Orville call on Harry to ask him to improve his habits of payment.

At Harry's office, Orville and he had the following conversation:

Orville Good morning, Harry. How are you today?

Harry Hello, Orville, I'm sure glad you're here because I've got one big complaint to hand you. That credit department of yours, and especially that pushy female manager you've got, has been offensive as all get out in her letters to me, and that's what I'm about ready to do—*get out!* I've bought a lot of goods from you during this past six months, but I don't have to take that kind of crap from your credit department or anybody else. There are plenty of suppliers with products as good as yours that I can deal with.

Orville I don't blame you, Harry. You know how credit people are, and when they're women it's even worse. They should have kept Doris in the steno pool. But I'm on your side, Harry. I don't want to lose your business. Do the best you can and don't pay any attention to our credit department.

Questions

1. Was Orville right in the way he handled this situation? Explain.
2. What might have been a more desirable approach for Orville to have taken?

3.5 UNDER-THE-TABLE INFLUENCE

Assume that you are a salesperson representing the Flying Zebras Cargo Lines. Your principal responsibility is to sell air cargo space to manufacturers of components and finished products. You are paid on the basis of a guaranteed salary of $2150 per month, which is a draw on (that is, it's deducted from) future commission sales.

Competition for customers has been keen in your industry, with the activities of some of your major competitors bordering on the unethical. The industry has been plagued recently with newspaper reports of illegal under-the-table bribes and kickbacks for the purpose of influencing buying decisions.

The philosophy of your firm, however, has been to sell cargo space on the basis of service, speed, and dependability. Furthermore, Flying Zebras has stressed a formal policy stating that gratuities should be avoided wherever possible, and under no circumstances should gifts or entertainment expenses exceed $150 for any one account during a calendar year.

During one of your recent sales calls on a prospective customer, Mr. Wheeler D. Lehr, you were faced with a somewhat difficult situation. Lehr is a traffic manager for SIL-CON, Inc., one of the world's largest manufacturers of silicon chips for electronic devices. The annual shipping volume of SIL-CON is tremendous. Lehr recently contacted your office and expressed an interest in using the shipping facilities of Flying Zebras. During a subsequent meeting with you Lehr said:

> We haven't been fully satisfied with Divisor Air Freight, the carrier we've been using for the shipment of our chips. It seems as though the attitudes of their representatives have deteriorated a lot since we first started using Divisor. As you probably know, we do a lot of shipping each year so it's worthwhile for any shipper to play our kind of ball. We're now in the stage of deciding which air carrier to switch to.
>
> We've contacted the representatives of the Texonata Lines. We're not too sure about them yet. And we've also decided to see what you have to offer. Frankly, I think that Flying Zebras has a fairly good chance of getting the business.
>
> A factor that could help me make up my mind could be . . . of course, what I'm about to say is hush-hush, understand? You see, my wife and I have been wanting for some time to spend a weekend in Palm Springs, but we've just never gotten around to it. I think that expenses for the entire weekend wouldn't exceed $1400. Now, I'm certainly not asking you to arrange this for us, but I will say that a weekend in Palm Springs could certainly give me the opportunity and time to do some serious thinking about which carrier to choose to ship our chips in the future. Any comments?

Problem

How would you handle this situation?

NOTES

1. David Clark Scott, "As Inside Trades Boil, Business Deans Ponder Ethics Role," *The Christian Science Monitor,* June 27, 1986, pp. 16–17.
2. "Outlawing a Three-Wheeler," *Time International Edition,* January 11, 1988, p. 39.

3. "Bankruptcies Increase in 1985," *The World Almanac & Book of Facts 1987* (New York: Pharos Books), p. 123.

4. Steven Mitchell Sack, "Watch the Words," *Sales & Marketing Management,* July 1, 1985, pp. 56, 58.

5. Extracted from a review of Stan Kossen's *Creative Selling Today,* 2nd ed. (New York: Harper & Row, 1982).

PART TWO

THE CHARACTER OF THE MARKETPLACE

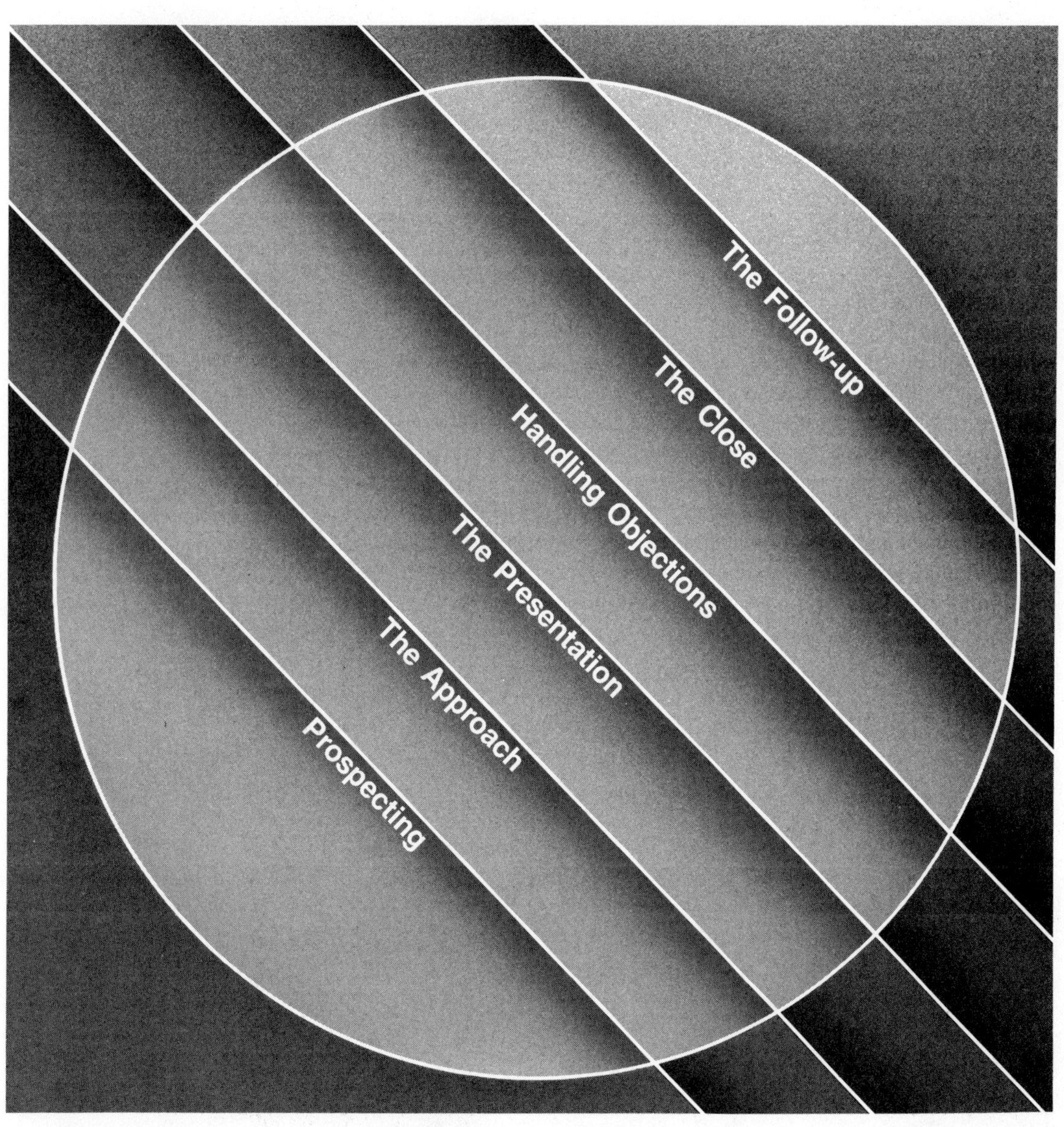

4 Understanding Markets

Who *Really* Are Your Customers?

THE NATURE OF MARKETS
Marketing and Markets Defined

MAKING IT MANAGEABLE—MARKET SEGMENTATION AND THE CHANNELS OF DISTRIBUTION
Selling Industrial Goods ■ Selling Consumer Goods ■ Doing Business Across Borders ■ Degree of Segmentation Relates to Product

REQUIREMENTS FOR EFFECTIVE MARKET SEGMENTATION
Market Potential ■ Needs Potential ■ Effective Demand Potential ■ Accessibility ■ Profit Potential

FOCUSING ON CUSTOMER NEEDS AND WANTS
And in the Beginning . . . ■ When Selling Was All-Important ■ Concern Out of Necessity—The Marketing Concept

THE PRODUCT LIFE CYCLE
Stage 1—Introduction ■ Stage 2—Growth ■ Stage 3—Maturity ■ Stage 4—Decline ■ Management of the Product Life Cycle

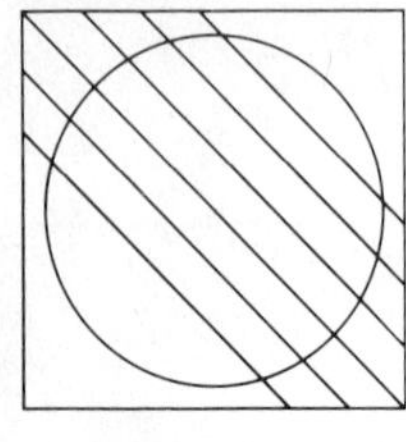

The market is not a single cohesive unit; it is a seething, disparate, pullulating, antagonistic, infinitely varied sea of differing human beings—every one of them as distinct from every other one as fingerprints.
WALTER WEIR

The day after you have introduced a new product, you are one day closer to the obsolescence of that product.
GABRIEL S. CARLIN

Here's what you should be able to do after studying this chapter:

1. Describe the nature of marketing and markets.
2. Cite the general ways in which markets can be segmented.
3. Explain how industrial markets differ from consumer markets.
4. Review the major channels of distribution.
5. Identify the ingredients essential for effective market segmentation.
6. Contrast the production and sales concepts with the marketing concept.
7. Illustrate the concept of the product life cycle.

You probably have some ideas already about what marketing is. But have you ever thought about how essential the marketing process is today? All of the motions that marketing managers go through to get goods into people's hands might be unnecessary if everyone were still a member of a family unit that produced all of its own goods for consumption. But such is not the highly productive world we live in today. Instead, we are members of a highly complex, specialized, and interdependent society where high levels of productivity and employment are unlikely to continue without the highly significant activity that we call *marketing.*

Since selling is an essential part of the marketing process, salespeople especially should be aware of *the nature of markets*—the principal thrust of the current chapter. This chapter will also briefly introduce you to the important concepts of *marketing segmentation,* the various *channels of distribution,* the factors that influence the extent of *market segmentation,* the shift from the *production* and *sales concepts* to the *marketing concept,* and the *product life cycle,* all topics that should help to clarify your interpretation of the environment in which you as a salesperson operate.

THE NATURE OF MARKETS

The United States has long been known as the world's "melting pot." Yet has the pot really melted? Not entirely. The American population of over 245 million people continues to be diverse—a factor that especially needs to be recognized by those involved in any sort of marketing activities.

Marketing and Markets Defined

Marketing, as defined in Chapter 1, is the process of planning and executing the conception, pricing, promotion, and distribution of ideas, goods, and services to create exchanges that satisfy individual and organizational objectives. In broader terms, marketing is a complex set of functions concerned with all of the activities involved in enabling an exchange intended to satisfy needs and wants.[1]

In Chapter 1 we learned that everyone sells something. The same holds true for marketing—everyone markets something, since selling is one aspect of the marketing process.

You now have a general idea of what marketing is, but what about the term *market?* Can we develop a simple and precise definition of this concept? Not really. Let's illustrate why not. Do you remember the rhyme that begins "This little piggy went to market," that childhood favorite that tickled you so—especially your feet? What does the word *market* really mean? In the nursery rhyme it presumably means that the piggy went *shopping.* But in another context, couldn't it mean that the piggy went to the market to *be sold?* Or couldn't it even mean the "this little piggy" went to *sell something* at the market?

Where did "this little piggy"* really *go?

"Anyone involved with the marketing of goods, services, or even ideas . . . should recognize that tastes change quite fast."

So you see the meaning of the term *market* depends considerably on how it's used. In a large and highly diversified country with a mobile population, there is no such thing as a *single* national market for all goods and services. Instead, markets are generally identified by groups, or segments, so that marketers of a particular product or service can appeal to the wants of specific groups of consumers. A fairly useful definition of a **market** for our purposes, then, is this: *a group of people who share some common needs or wants and have the financial authority and ability to buy certain products.*

Anyone involved with the marketing of goods, services, or even ideas (such as a promoter of political ideologies) should recognize that tastes change quite fast. As we'll learn shortly most products enjoy anything but an endless life. The future of any product is subject to the whims and trends of the marketplace. Today's hot seller may become tomorrow's bummer.

MAKING IT MANAGEABLE—MARKET SEGMENTATION AND THE CHANNELS OF DISTRIBUTION

The term **market segmentation** symbolizes another significant concept to individuals concerned with the marketing of goods and services. Basically, *market segmentation is the grouping or categorizing of customers into two general areas:*

1. Selling industrial goods
2. Selling consumer goods

Let's now examine each of these.

Selling Industrial Goods

The **industrial market** is highly significant and diverse, involving the purchase of billions of dollars worth of goods and services each year. The industrial market consists of businesses and institutions that purchase products for use either within their own organizations or in manufacturing other goods. Such products, called **industrial goods,** aid—either directly or indirectly—in the production of consumer goods or other types of industrial goods for resale. Examples of industrial goods include raw materials, building materials, office equipment, component parts, processed materials, and supplies. If you were a marketer of industrial goods, your customers might include manufacturers, retailers, wholesalers, institutions, and government units.

Examples of **institutional buyers** are schools, hotels, hospitals, and restaurants. Institutions purchase large quantities of relatively standard items—towels, soap, and furniture, for example—and tend to have strong bargaining strength regarding price.

Industrial goods differ from consumer goods, but the distinction isn't always clear. A particular good, such as a personal computer, can be considered an industrial good when purchased by a business firm and a consumer good when purchased by a college student.

"A particular good, such as a personal computer, can be considered an industrial good when purchased by a business firm and a consumer good when purchased by a college student."

The key factor determining whether a good is an industrial or a consumer good, therefore, is the nature of the buyer and the intended use of the good or service.

Government markets are generally included in any discussion of industrial markets. The sheer size of government markets—which include those at local, state, and federal levels—makes this area a target that many marketers desire to shoot for. Governments perform a variety of functions and services, including police and fire protection, national defense, road building and maintenance, employment counseling, welfare assistance, and schooling. All of these activities require goods of an industrial nature.

Selling industrial goods is a complex and varied activity. Although there are, of course, numerous exceptions, industrial buyers are often highly sophisticated, knowledgeable, and rational in their buying motives. Industrial sales representatives generally have fewer but larger accounts. They also are expected to have a sound technical knowledge of products in order to assist customers more creatively with their needs.

If you were the producer of an industrial good, through what channels would you market it? Judging from the wide variety of marketing channels that are used, there doesn't seem to be any "best" channel that fits all situations. The choice of a particular distribution path seems to depend more on the nature of the industry, the types of products produced, and the personal attitudes of the marketing managers.

What's the best? It all depends.

A marketing channel or **channel of distribution** is the route that a product takes as it moves to its segmented market. The channel includes the producer of the product, the users of the product (industrial or consumer), and any wholesaler or agents involved in the product movement. Some channel intermediaries take title to but not possession of the goods. Others take neither possession of nor title to the goods; they serve to facilitate the distribution of goods through marketing channels.

Some channels of distribution are quite short, with the salesperson dealing directly with industrial buyers. Other producers of industrial goods may sell exclusively to **merchant wholesalers**, who in turn sell the products to industrial buyers.

In other cases, a producer may utilize its own sales force for large accounts *and* work through a type of wholesalers called **industrial distributors** for selling to smaller accounts. Producers find that industrial distributors perform a variety of useful and efficient services by maintaining inventories, thus resulting in the faster delivery of relatively small orders.

Figure 4.1 shows four typical routes that industrial goods may take from producer to industrial, institutional, or government buyers. A brief discussion of each route follows:

1. *Producer* to *industrial buyer.* No merchant wholesaler is involved in this channel. Manufacturers of expensive items often use this route. Boeing, in the sale of aircraft, and General Dynamics, in the sale of tactical missiles and submarines, are examples of producers that sell directly to industry or government without the aid of intermediaries.

Wanna buy a missile?

2. *Producer* to *industrial distributor* to *industrial buyer.* This route utilizes a full-service wholesaler—industrial distributors—to sell to industrial markets. Producers of building supplies and various types of major custom-made equipment are likely to use this channel. Industrial distributors typically take title to the goods they sell.

Wanna buy a brick?

3. *Producer* to *agent* to *industrial buyer.* Producers who are new to a particular market or who lack their own marketing departments might employ a channel that utilizes *agents* or *brokers,* which are wholesaling intermediaries that do not take title to the goods.

Wanna buy something new and different?

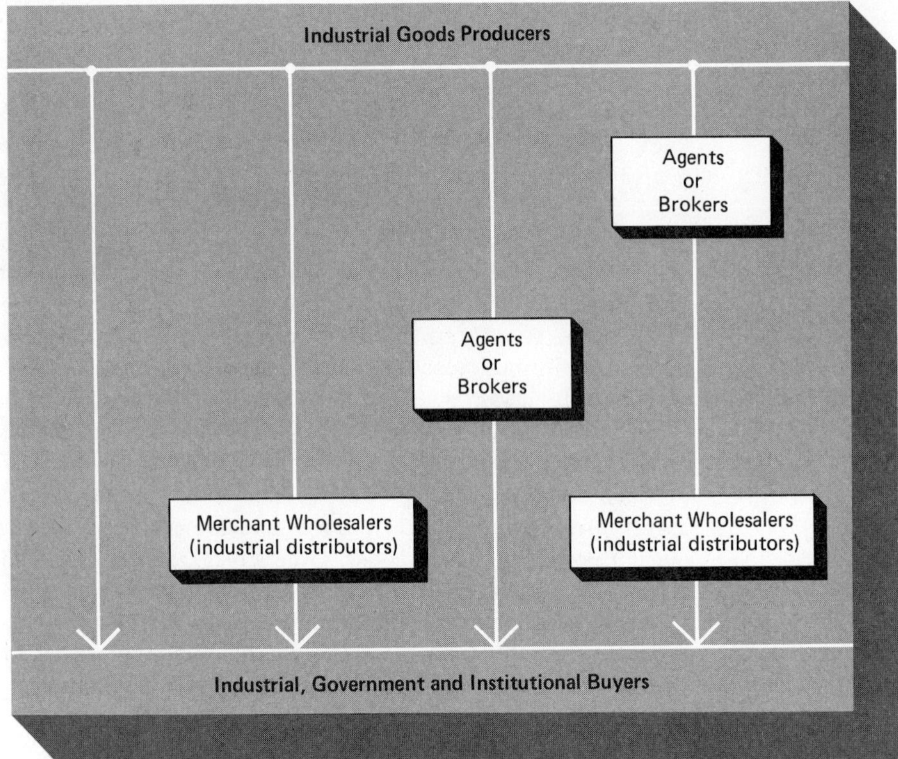

Figure 4.1 Channels of Distribution from Industrial Producers to Industrial, Government, and Institutional Buyers.

Wanna buy some lettuce for your cafeteria?

4. *Producer* to *agent* to *industrial distributor* to *industrial buyer.* This channel may be used when a producer needs broader services than an agent alone can provide yet believes that an agent can provide additional service and customer exposure than would be provided by an industrial distributor alone.

Selling Consumer Goods

Consumer goods are products that are purchased by individuals and householders for their own personal consumption rather than for business use. These people make up the **consumer market** and are referred to as **ultimate consumers**. Virtually everyone is a consumer of some sort, since everyone consumes goods and services. The ways in which the consumer market can be segmented are numerous and include the following:

1. *Demographic data* (that is, family income, geographic location, and race)
2. *Behavior patterns* (such as amount of a specific product consumed, social status, and language spoken)
3. *Physical characteristics* (such as sex, age, and health)

4. *Psychological traits* (such as interests, hobbies, and psychological needs)
5. *Marketing conditions* (such as channels of distribution and degree of competition

For a more comprehensive breakdown of ways in which consumer markets can be segmented, see Table 4.1.

To aid in segmenting the market, consumer goods can be further broken down into specific categories, which include *convenience, shopping, specialty,* and *unsought goods.* As we'll see shortly, the behavior and attitudes of shoppers influence which of these four categories a particular consumer good falls into.

Convenience Goods There are some products that consumers are willing to purchase with little expenditure of time, effort, and money. These are known as **convenience goods,** and consumers typically have little **brand loyalty** for such products.

TABLE 4.1 Ways in Which Markets Can Be Segmented.

Demographic data	a. Geographic area b. Family composition c. Family size d. Education of household head e. Occupation of household head	f. Family income g. Ethnic origin h. Race i. Home ownership j. Marital status k. Number of wage earners in family
Behavior patterns	a. Amount of given product consumed b. Previous experience with product c. Brand loyalty d. Language spoken	e. Social-class status f. Life-cycle status g. Social or fraternal affiliation h. Religion
Physical characteristics	a. Sex b. Age c. Health status	d. Physical differences (such as dry skin, tough beard)
Psychological traits	a. Intelligence level b. Personality characteristics	c. Avocational interests d. Psychological needs and preferences
Marketing conditions	a. Channels of distribution	b. Degree of competition

Source: Adapted from Dik Warren Twedt, "The Concept of Market Segmentation," *Handbook of Modern Marketing,* edited by Victor P. Buell and Carl Heye (New York: McGraw-Hill, 1970), pp. 2-4, 2-5.

Examples of convenience goods include readily available items such as notebook paper, pencils, and candy. Convenience goods are typically sold by retail stores.

Shopping Goods Convenience goods, as the name implies, are obtained conveniently and with little shopping effort. **Shopping goods,** on the other hand, are usually obtained only after considerable effort has been expended. Brand loyalty typically isn't an important factor in the case of shopping goods, since consumers generally *shop around* to compare prices, quality, and the "best buy." Examples of shopping goods include furniture, household appliances, jewelry, and used cars.

Specialty Goods A third category of consumer goods that purchasers are willing to spend time and effort to purchase are **specialty goods.** Consumers typically have a strong brand preference for such products because of their unique characteristics. Some customers may search specifically for a particular brand of clothes because of the reputation of the designer. Or they may look only for Klipsch stereo speakers, a JVC videocassette recorder, or a Head tennis racket. Customers of specialty goods usually won't settle for substitutes. Specialty goods are typically considered expensive items.

Something special!

Unsought Goods Our fourth classification of consumer goods is termed **unsought goods.** As the name implies, these are goods or services that consumers don't necessarily want to buy; typically they feel that they have little choice in the matter because the purchase is necessary. For example, most consumers don't have a burning yearning to purchase a burial plot, life insurance, or a prescription drug. As with convenience goods, consumers have little brand loyalty for unsought goods and are unwilling to spend much effort in obtaining them.

You need—but really don't want—it.

A word of warning is in order. For purposes of classification, it may appear that all consumer goods fit neatly into one of the four categories discussed. Such is not the case, however, in the real world of markets. To one consumer—Pam—chewing gum is a convenience good. Pam couldn't care less which brand she obtains. To another consumer—Fran—chewing gum may be a specialty item. The only brand Fran is willing to buy, for example, is Figley's Swordmint Sugarless Chewing Gum. No substitutes will ever enter Fran's gum-chomping mouth. The process of classifying consumer goods, therefore, can assist the marketer in determining overall marketing strategy. Of course, individual judgment and careful analysis have to be applied in the process if marketing strategy is to be successful. See Table 4.2 for a summary of the principal categories of consumer goods.

Sales to ultimate consumers have traditionally been made either by clerks employed with retail establishments or by outside sales workers, who follow referred leads or prospect for new customers. Newer channels of distribution include catalog sales, home shopping by cable TV, and vending machines. Channels of distribution, once again, vary with the firm. A small proportion of consumer sales, about 5 percent, moves directly from producers to consumers. Some insurance companies, such as State Farm Mutual, deal directly with the public through company representatives; others, such as Fireman's Fund, sell through independent agent or broker

TABLE 4.2 Principal Categories of Consumer Goods.

Types of consumer goods	Typical examples
Convenience goods	Notebook paper Pencils Candy
Shopping goods	Furniture Household appliances Jewelry
Specialty goods	Designer clothes Health foods Certain brands of stereo equipment
Unsought goods	Burial plots Life insurance Prescription drugs

intermediaries. Distribution in the cosmetic industry varies also; some cosmetics are sold only house to house, a direct channel from manufacturer to consumer, and others are sold through wholesalers to retailers to consumers, the latter being one of the most common channels of distribution for consumer goods. Figure 4.2 shows some examples of the typical channels of distribution to ultimate consumers.

How might inside salespeople be creative?

Some observers of the marketing scene contend that modern retail merchandising has virtually eliminated the need for creative inside sales personnel. They point to large self-service outlets, catalog purchasing, buyers' clubs, and home shopping by cable TV, which seem to lend some degree of support to their arguments. However, in spite of numerous changes in retailing over the years, retail sales personnel can still do a lot to aid their customers in purchasing consumer products. Techniques employed by inside salespeople can often make or break sales transactions. Inept approaches can result in disgruntled customers and a costly deterioration in a firm's established goodwill.

". . . in spite of numerous changes in retailing over the years, retail sales personnel can still do a lot to aid their customers in purchasing consumer products."

Some salespeople are involved with outside consumer selling, which generally takes place in potential customers' homes and offices; sometimes, when the seller is a street vendor, it even takes place on city sidewalks or at flea markets. Groups engaged in outside selling include the Fuller Brush and Avon Cosmetics companies,

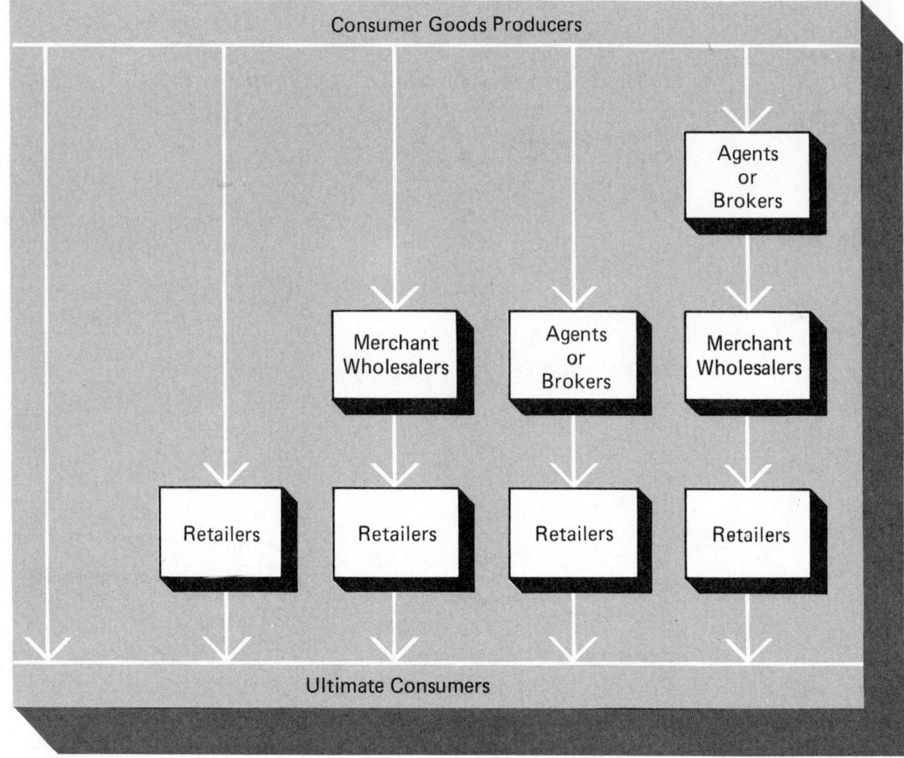

Figure 4.2 Channels of Distribution from Consumer Goods Producers to Ultimate Consumers.

who have long used house-to-house selling; insurance and securities sales representatives; magazine solicitors; and sidewalk merchants hawking such items as belts and jewelry.

Doing Business Across Borders

Hi! . . . I mean, Bonjour, monsieur.

The chances aren't too unlikely that one day you could find yourself working for a company that does business across borders—that is, sells its products or services in a **foreign market.** Segmentation in foreign markets occurs along the same lines as in domestic markets: industrial, government, merchant intermediaries, and consumer. However, cultural and business customs often vary considerably from those practiced in your own home country. Take a look at Appendix III in this book if you have a deeper interest in conducting business in foreign markets.

Degree of Segmentation Relates to Product

Some products need little segmentation. Toothpaste, for example, is a product that appeals to a mass market. Drilling equipment, on the other hand, would appeal to

What would influence the degree of segmentation?

a more limited, industrial segment of the market, such as firms involved in the exploration of oil reserves. The possible ways in which markets can be segmented, or grouped, are practically endless. Within the limited space of a single chapter, we can barely scratch the surface.

REQUIREMENTS FOR EFFECTIVE MARKET SEGMENTATION

Since each person in any country is a unique being, the ultimate in market segmentation would be to develop a different marketing strategy for each individual. Obviously, such a breakdown would be neither feasible nor practical. What, then, would influence the extent of market segmentation? As can be seen in Figure 4.3, five factors are essential for effective segmentation:

1. Market potential
2. Needs potential
3. Effective demand potential

Figure 4.3 The Essential Ingredients for Effective Market Segmentation.

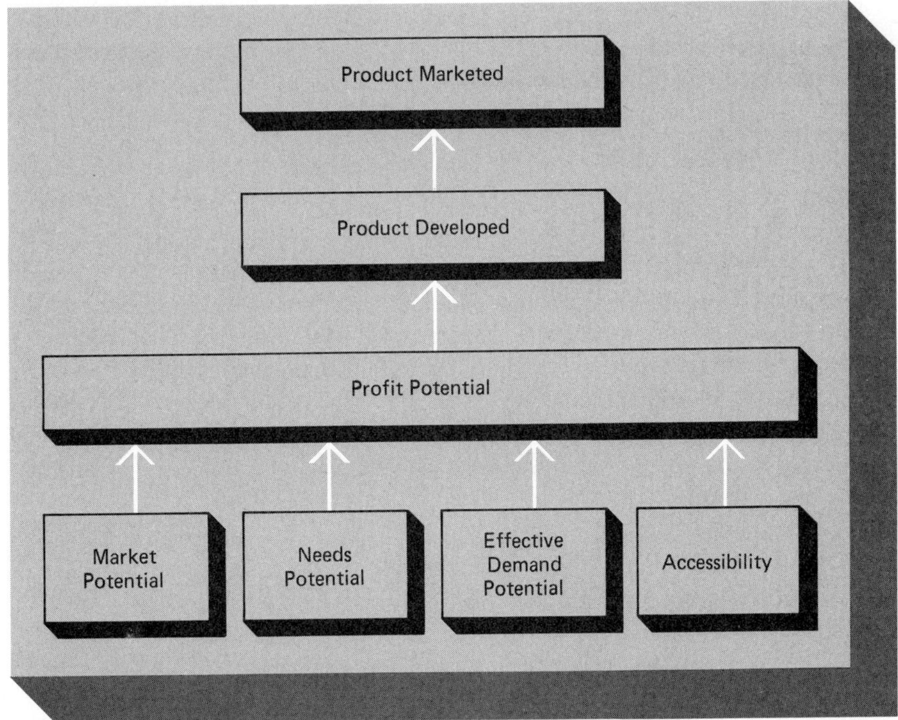

4. Accessibility
5. Profit potential

Market Potential

Is there a market?

Would you be likely to try selling air conditioning at the North Pole or snowmobiles in the desert regions of Death Valley? Not quite! The reason relates to our first requirement for effective market segmentation and should be fairly apparent: there is virtually no market for air conditioning in the North Pole or snowmobiles in Death Valley. For market segmentation to be effective, there must be sufficient numbers of potential purchasers in a specific market to justify investments in capital and human resources. The North Pole, or even better, the Mountain States, would have far greater potential as a market for snowmobiles, and the inland regions of California greater potential as a market for air conditioners.

"For market segmentation to be effective, there must be sufficient numbers of potential purchasers in a specific market to justify investments in capital and human resources."

Needs Potential

Is the public convinced of the need?

Another criterion for successful market segmentation relates to the needs of potential consumers. Consumers in a specific market must either already have a need for a particular product or, through effective sales promotion and demand creation activities, be convinced of its desirability.

Effective Demand Potential

What makes demand effective?

Consumer desire for a particular product is seldom enough to satisfy our third requirement for effective market segmentation. That desire, or demand, must be **effective demand.** Demand, in order to be effective, requires purchasing power, which relates to income and credit ratings. Let's assume that you want a sleek new Porsche automobile. You might confidently stroll into an automobile dealer's showroom and demand the most expensive vehicle in the house, but without effective buying power, you would probably return home by the same means that you arrived—and without a new car.

Accessibility

Is the market reachable?

The fourth requirement for effective market segmentation is accessibility through available marketing means. In other words, can a chosen market be reached with reasonable effort and cost? Marketers often attempt to reach segmented markets through selective types of media, including regional editions of such publications as *The Wall Street Journal, Time,* and *Sports Illustrated.* Certain types of television programs may also be used for reaching segments of the buying public that are known to watch these programs.

Profit Potential

What really measures marketing success?

The fifth requirement for market segmentation, and one to which all others relate, is *profit potential,* the true measurement of marketing success. No firm can survive for long without the existence of profits. Mistakes can be and often are made by marketers, but their frequency and severity can be minimized through careful and intelligent research and profit analysis *prior* to the expenditure of large sums of risk capital. Many firms, for example, will test-market their products in selected regions in order to predict the likely success of broader-scale efforts.

FOCUSING ON CUSTOMER NEEDS AND WANTS

It takes more than **producing** *a good product!*

The road to the marketplace is hazardous, a route filled with ups and downs, twists and turns, and even a soft shoulder here and there. Only a small proportion of those "great new and different" ideas for a product ever make it to the display shelves of stores. And a shockingly large proportion of those that do make it to market fail within one year of their introduction. The Bank of America reports that as much as 75 percent of total new-product expenditures are wasted on unsuccessful products.

There are numerous causes for product failures, such as faulty design, poor timing when introducing a new product, and pricing mistakes. A key cause, however, involves the failure of firms to consider a highly significant business philosophy known as the *marketing concept,* one that contrasts greatly with two other approaches that are referred to as the *production* and *sales concepts.* Let's examine how these approaches differ in focus.

And in the Beginning . . .

F. W. Taylor entered the organizational scene in the early 1900s. His principal concern was with efficiency and productivity in organizations, often referred to as the **production concept.**

Produce it and it will sell itself!

The attempt to produce as much as possible at the least cost made fair sense in those days, since incomes were relatively low, mass production techniques were virtually unheard of, and the public's demand was high for the basics, such as food, shelter, and clothing.

When Selling Was All-Important

During the production concept period (1900–1930), firms didn't have to worry too much about selling their products. Reduced production costs and higher personal incomes made it fairly easy to dispose of products. Producers enjoyed what has been referred to as a **sellers' market.** They didn't really worry much about the needs of consumers.

Sell it regardless!

Then came the Great Depression of the 1930s. With almost 25 percent of the work force unemployed in 1933, firms developed substantial excess production capacity. Aggressive selling tactics were increasingly believed to be necessary to dispose of the increasing stocks of product inventories. The emphasis developed on selling, known as the **sales concept.**

Concern Out of Necessity—The Marketing Concept

It's what **the customer** *wants that's important!*

Most consumer purchases were substantially restricted during the World War II. Goods remained scarce during the years immediately following the war. However, the pendulum swung to the buyer's side during the 1950s, when products once again became plentiful. Even the Korean War couldn't utilize all of the productive capacity that had developed. A buyers' market had developed. Competition for the consumer's dollar heightened and, out of necessity, a new marketing philosophy—the **marketing concept**—was born. The marketing concept, as with the approach of today's professional salespeople, focuses on *customer needs and wants.* Market researchers first identify the needs and wants of the market and then produce, promote, and distribute the products that will profitably satisfy those needs and wants. In summary, then, the *production concept* is concerned primarily with producing the most goods at the least cost. The *sales concept* rests on the belief that a marketer's main responsibility is to convince consumers to buy the products that have been manufactured regardless of their needs or desires. The contrary holds true for the *marketing concept,* in which needs and wants are first determined through market research; then decisions are made on how to satisfy such desires profitably.

THE PRODUCT LIFE CYCLE

Most products, just like people, pass through a series of stages during their lives. Every person, if lucky, passes through infancy, adolescence, adulthood, retirement, old age, and death. Products aren't much different from people; they pass through what is termed a **product life cycle.** Although the duration of each stage (as with the aging process in humans) varies with the product, most products go through four distinct phases. These are:

1. Introduction
2. Growth
3. Maturity
4. Decline

Let's now examine each stage separately.

Stage 1—Introduction

It's important for those involved with marketing activities to recognize which stage a particular product is in at any given time since this factor has a significant influence over marketing approaches. As you can see in Figure 4.4, a company's sales and profits are typically low at the **introduction stage** of a product. During this period, sizable amounts of resources are usually allocated for promoting the product. Many larger companies proceed cautiously at this stage by first **test marketing** in specific cities or regions before launching into full-scale production and marketing of a new product.

"Most products, just like people, pass through a series of stages during their lives."

Are consumers in Azusa, Calif. typical of the nation?

Services, too, may be test-marketed. Insurance companies, for example, sometimes introduce a new type of insurance coverage or policy in only one or two states in order to determine consumer acceptance and probable claims experience. If a new product or service proves unacceptable or too expensive to market, it will be far less costly—and far less damaging to a company's image—to discontinue it in a small region than to withdraw it from national or international markets.

Figure 4.4 The Typical Stages of Life for Products.

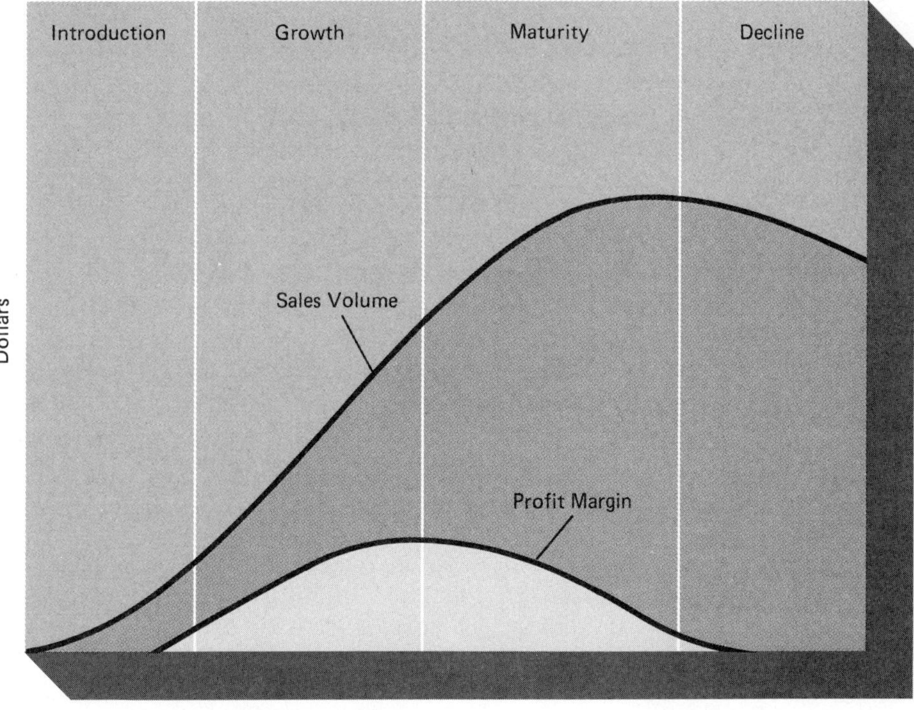

Stage 2—Growth

After initial sales resistance has been met and overcome, a product may enter the **growth stage.** At this stage, marketing efforts are likely to be expanded, perhaps on a national or international basis. These increased marketing efforts tend to result in increasing sales and profit margins. However, profits typically begin their descent toward the end of the growth stage.

During the second half of the 1980s, for example, compact disc players and cellular telephones entered the growth stage of their product life cycle.

Stage 3—Maturity

The next phase in the product life cycle—the **maturity stage**—is a crucial one. If, for example, a product has been successful in achieving favorable sales and profits, its marketing managers are likely to find competitors flocking to the marketplace with similar competing products. Cutthroat competition sometimes results, with drastic price cutting and squeezed profit margins, as was the case with digital watches and personal computers during the 1980s. Firms without adequate resources to withstand such intense competition may fall by the wayside during this stage of the cycle.

Stage 4—Decline

Some products—the yo-yo, flying discs, particular brands of chewing gum, and French perfumes—may retain consumer loyalty for many years and never reach the final phase, the **decline stage.** For products that reach the decline stage, however, demand virtually disappears because the product ceases to satisfy consumers' tastes and desires. The rise of the electronic hand-held calculator has hastened the demise of the slide rule, for example. The desire for a more traditional, conservative look in the late 1980s resulted in a decline in the sale of digital watches.

Management of the Product Life Cycle

Not all companies experience the same life cycles with their products. Certain products, such as fad items, travel rapidly through the cycle, peaking out in one to three years. Most toys, for example, have a relatively short life cycle. Approximately 60 percent of all toys on store shelves at a given time are unlikely to have been there the previous year. As Gabriel S. Carlin, executive vice president of the Savin Corporation, has said, "The day after you have introduced a new product you are one day closer to the obsolescence of that product."

Marketing managers especially find themselves in challenging situations during both the maturity and decline stages of the product life cycle. Astute managers attempt to anticipate the need for change before sales and profits decline significantly. Related to such changes are some difficult questions that arise for which practical answers are essential:

1. Should product managers be involved with **restaging;** that is, utilize a new ingredient, package design, or marketing technique to extract additional profits

from the marketplace? (The *Sgt. Pepper's Lonely Hearts Club Band* album by The Beatles is an example of a product that has twice experienced the life cycle as a result of its being reintroduced on compact disc in 1987.)

2. Can unprofitable models or sizes of the product be pruned out? (This tactic could result in decreased sales but higher profits.)
3. Should the product be gradually phased out or discontinued immediately? (Managers frequently dislike phasing out products since doing so appears to be an admission of failure.)

SUMMARY

In this chapter we learned that the concept of a market is difficult to pinpoint with precision since there is no such thing as a single national or world market for all goods and services. As a result, markets are usually broken down into segments, or groups, so that appeals can be made to the buying needs and motives of specific groups of buyers. We focused on the general categories of customer segments known as industrial markets, consumer markets, institutional markets, and foreign markets. Goods produced for these segments are marketed through so-called channels of distribution. Such channels vary with the product, firm, industry, and country.

Although there are exceptions, many observers of today's business world feel that emphasis has shifted from the production and sales concepts to the marketing concept, thus focusing to a greater extent than in the past on the needs and desires of the buyers in the marketplace.

Those who are concerned with the marketing of goods should recognize that most products tend to go through product life-cycle periods ranging from introduction to growth to maturity to decline. Astute marketers attempt to make certain that improved and new products are made available before existing products have outlived their usefulness.

The factors that influence the extent of market segmentation are market potential, needs potential, effective demand potential, accessibility, and profit potential.

KEY TERMS

market
market segmentation
industrial market
industrial goods
institutional buyers
government markets
channels of distribution
merchant wholesalers
industrial distributors
consumer goods
consumer market
ultimate consumers
convenience goods
brand loyalty
shopping goods
specialty goods
unsought goods
foreign market

effective demand
production concept
sellers' market
sales concept
marketing concept
product life cycle
introduction stage
test marketing
growth stage
maturity stage
decline stage
restaging

QUESTIONS

1. Why is it difficult to apply a simple and precise definition to the concept of a "market"?
2. What advantages do you feel result from the segmentation of markets?
3. What are the broad categories of markets? What are their major differences?
4. Hispanics are one of the fastest growing ethnic groups in the United States. In your opinion, should marketers consider them a segment different from so-called mainstream Americans? If so, in what manner should they be segmented differently?
5. Evaluate the following statement: "Markets are markets. It doesn't really matter if your customers are in the United States, France, or Spain. All buyers engage in about the same types of behavior."
6. What is the purpose of breaking down consumer goods into the specific categories of convenience, shopping, specialty, and unsought goods?
7. Which of the five factors essential for effective market segmentation do you feel is the most important? Why?
8. Which do you feel is more realistic as a marketing philosophy—the production, sales, or marketing concepts? Why?
9. Can the concept of the product life cycle be realistically applied to all products? Explain.

APPLICATIONS

4.1 BOATOWNERS' INSURANCE PROVES DOOR OPENER

A combination of effective advertising and use of FIRSTCO boatowners' insurance policies as lead items has enabled the agency of Fellaton and Co. to achieve the distinction of being one of the fastest-growing agencies in the area around Hayward, California. By using boatowners' insurance as a door opener to other lines, Ami Fellaton, the agency owner, has developed his enterprise from a "scratch" start five years ago to a business doing more than $5 million of annual premium volume.

Like many agents, Ami has consistently advertised under the FIRSTCO logo in the yellow pages and has developed a substantial number of new auto and homeowner accounts as a result. However, he has gone one step further in yellow pages advertising. He uses a display advertisement that emphasizes boat and yacht insurance.

Ami got this idea from a young woman selling space in the yellow pages. She suggested that he insert a boat advertisement along with his regular listings. Her reason was that she and her husband had purchased a boat two months earlier and had wanted boat insurance. They had looked in the yellow pages and were amazed to find not one agency featuring boat insurance. Consequently, the couple had to call a number of agents before finding one with a good boat insurance policy.

Ami pondered this idea. He wondered—if this family looked in the yellow pages specifically for boat insurance, how many other people must do the same thing? For about three years thereafter, Fellaton and Co. had had the only boat advertisement in the yellow pages. Ami enthusiastically exclaims that a substantial volume of new boat insurance business resulted from this advertising.

The yellow pages were not the only source of boat insurance leads. Ami knew that FIRSTCO's yacht and outboard yacht policies were among the broadest and most competitive products then on the market. Consequently, he knew that members of yacht clubs would be interested in listening to what he had to say about boat insurance.

He acquired the names of every yacht club member in the San Francisco–Oakland Bay area from yacht club yearbooks. He then systematically mailed to each member a letter that described the FIRSTCO yacht policy. This was accompanied by an example of rates for a typical boat, a return envelope, and an inquiry card.

The response was excellent—more than 20 percent replied. And Ami was able to close about 90 percent of those who did respond. He followed up with a telephone call to those who did not immediately reply.

Ami sailed into additional profits through the use of account selling. While delivering a boat policy, he would frequently sell the prospect a homeowners policy. He never failed to depart with at least two expirations (renewal dates of existing insurance policies carried with other agents) and often had the opportunity to survey the commercial accounts of his new prospects.

He is well aware of the need for knowledge of his products. He has made an effort to learn everything about the coverage of the FIRSTCO boatowners' policies, so that when questions arise, the answers are at his fingertips. In addition, he realizes that if an agent is to use boat insurance as a lead item, he must be able to speak easily about boats. As a result, Ami has studied nautical terms, is familiar with the waterways in the Bay Area, and is active every weekend as a water skier. Enthusiastically, he points out, "I feel that my clients have far more confidence in me as their insurance agent when they can discuss boats and know that I understand their jargon."

Ami Fellaton has not been content merely to insure boatowners. He has also insured a number of marine supply companies in the Bay Area and has discovered that they are excellent sources of leads. He now receives a substantial number of referrals directly from the marine supply companies.

Questions

1. How does this case relate to the concept of market segmentation?
2. List two products other than insurance that could lend themselves to the market segment selected by Ami Fellaton.
3. How can salespeople use the concepts of market segmentation to locate customers more readily?

4.2 HOW QUICKLY YOUTH FADES

The makeup of the U.S. population is changing significantly. For one thing, it is getting older. The birthrate has dropped sharply since 1970, and the median age of the nation's residents has slowly risen from 27.9 years to 32 years. It is expected to continue to rise. (The median age is that which has the same number of people above and below it.)

What's happening is that all those kids born during the "baby boom" period—1947 to 1961—have gotten older. Almost 60 million Americans were born during that period, and these now account for about 40 percent of the adult population. At the beginning of the 1980s, people in this group were 19 to 33 years old. By the end of the 1980s, they were 29 to 43. Consequently, the group comprising middle-aged Americans—those between 35 and 54—has grown faster than any other age group. And by 1990, the number of "middle-aged crazys" will have grown by 13.5 million, or 28 percent.

That's not all. The number of teenagers is shrinking. By 1990, their numbers will fall by about 4.6 million, or 17 percent. In fact, it won't be long before there will be more people over 65 than there will be teenagers. By 1990, the over-65 set will be made up of almost 30 million people—a gain of about 20 percent.

Questions

1. As a marketer of consumer goods, how might you interpret and utilize these data about the changing population makeup of the United States?
2. Do the population figures suggest that jeans makers like Blue Bell, Inc., and Levi Strauss and Co. are doomed to a future of declining sales? Explain.

4.3 A NEW AND IMPROVED FLYING DISC? SOME FUN!

If you had been a member of the "Yuppie" generation of the '80s, liked money but also enjoyed fun, what would you have done to satisfy those wants? One high achiever, Michael Sandeen, while in his late twenties, decided to try to accomplish both of these desires.

An inventive type, Sandeen had attempted several times previously to both make a lot money and still have what he calls "fun" with his creations. For example, he developed a fitting for a washing machine hose. It sold satisfactorily, but he didn't consider it a *fun* product. He tried other inventions, most of which were somewhat complex and required moving parts. None were fun. He believed that there must be some sort of a device waiting to be created that would be simple to produce, profitable to market, and, above all, *fun!*

One day during the winter of 1985, Sandeen was throwing a Frisbee with a friend. His friend could throw the disc satisfactorily, as can many people, but he couldn't do what is the envy of all flying disc throwers—the basis for most disc tricks—spin or stall the disc on his finger. According to Sandeen, only about 2000 people in North America can spin or stall a conventional flying disc on their fingers.

Sandeen spent three sleepless days and nights trying to develop a dishlike object that could be spun on a finger with ease and still fly as well as the others. He got the idea to form a concave cone that he inserted into a cut out portion of the center of a flying disc. His principal challenge became that of how to prevent the cone from falling out. He tried tape, glue, chewing gum, and anything else adhesive. But the continual bumping and jarring of the disc always knocked the center cone off of the body of the disc. Sandeen worked out that problem by designing the disc and cone as a one-piece injection-molded plastic item.

Back to money and fun! Sandeen wondered if he could acquire both of them with his new creation. The principal competition, Wham-O's Frisbee, had been around since the mid-1950s, more than 30 years. Sales of flying discs had become somewhat constant at about 5 million units per year. He wondered what the legal ramifications were in producing and marketing a flying disc, since his product was similar to the Frisbee. Would there be any likelihood of a lawsuit? Sandeen also wondered how he could obtain the capital necessary to produce and promote the product. Further, how should the product be promoted once it was produced? Should he try to do the marketing himself or should he hire a professional staff? What should he name his flying disc? How important was the packaging of the product?

Although first selecting the name "Trixster" for his disc, Sandeen was later convinced that the name "SpinJAMMER" would have greater appeal. He didn't want it to be considered "just another pretty disc," so he called the concave cone a "whatchamastallit," the "stall" portion of this term symbolizing the ability to spin—that is, *stall*—the object on one finger. Sandeen made the decision to go ahead with his pursuit of financial rewards and fun.

Questions

1. What is your opinion of Sandeen's entering a market that had been dominated for over 30 years by the Frisbee product? Would you have been willing to attempt it? Why or why not?

2. At what stage of the product life cycle was the flying disc at the time Sandeen entered the market? Would the SpinJAMMER be considered at

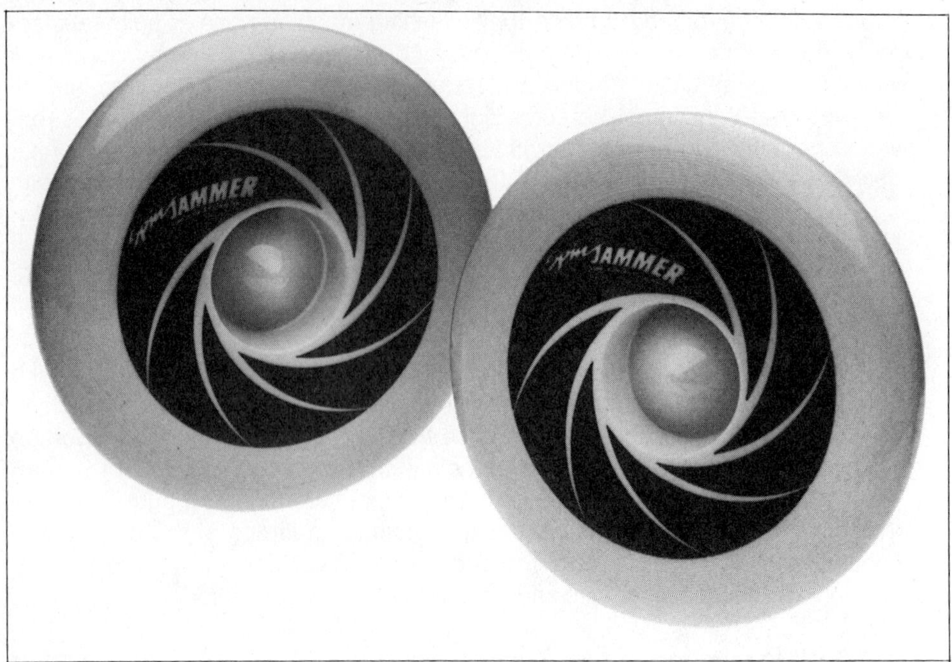

SpinJAMMER © Sandeen, Inc.

the same stage of the product life cycle as were flying discs in general? Explain.

3. If the SpinJAMMER were your invention, what would be your specific plans for financing, promoting and selling the product?

4. What would be your future plans, if any, for restaging the existing product—SpinJAMMER—and possibly adding any other product lines?

NOTE

1. General definition adapted from William J. Stanton and Charles Futrell, *Fundamentals of Marketing* (New York: McGraw-Hill, 1987), p. 4.

5

The Motives of Buyers

Why Do They Do It?

THE CAUSES OF CONSUMER BEHAVIOR
Wanted—Part-Time Selling Psychologists

THE NATURE OF NEEDS AND MOTIVES
Felt Needs Motivate ■ Satisfied Needs No Longer Motivate ■ The Priority of Needs ■ Needs Are Not Mutually Exclusive

CULTURE AND CONSUMER BEHAVIOR
Changing Cultural Influences

ATTITUDES AND CONSUMER BEHAVIOR
Reference Groups ■ What Causes Attitudes to Change? ■ Putting Customer Attitudes to Use

SOCIAL CLASS AND CONSUMER BEHAVIOR

PERCEPTION AND CONSUMER BEHAVIOR
Determinants of Perception ■ Snap Judgments ■ Selective Perception ■ Peer Pressures

THE PURCHASE DECISION PROCESS AND CONSUMER BEHAVIOR
Stage 1—Recognition of a Need or Want ■ Stage 2—Search for Information ■ Stage 3—Evaluating Alternative Decisions ■ Stage 4—Making a Choice ■ Stage 5—Evaluating the Decision Made ■ For an Individual Buyer—It Depends

REASONS FOR CONSUMER LOYALTY

DEMAND CHARACTERISTICS AND MOTIVES OF INDUSTRIAL PURCHASERS
Different Market Traits ■ And Just What Are Their Motives?

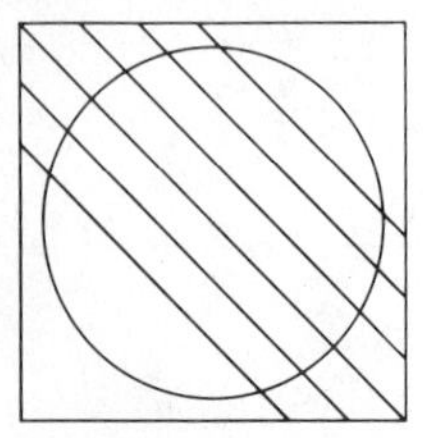

It is a universal truth that favorable consumer attitudes are prerequisites to marketing success.
LOUIS E. BOONE

Here's what you should be able to do after studying this chapter:

1. List and describe six important factors that influence the buying behavior of consumers.
2. Summarize the motivational theory of Maslow.
3. Restate in your own words the phrase "felt needs motivate."
4. Describe the effect of culture on consumer behavior.
5. Describe the effect of attitudes on consumer behavior.
6. Explain how social classes affect consumer behavior.
7. Explain how perception affects consumer behavior.
8. Describe how the purchase decision process affects consumer behavior.
9. List the factors that tend to cause consumers to patronize a particular firm regularly.
10. Cite the principal demand characteristics and buying motives of industrial purchasers.

Have you ever analyzed why you bought a particular product—say an automobile? Were your motives purely *rational* or was there some degree of *emotion* involved in your decision? Did you buy a simple economy car with few accessories or was it a luxurious vehicle with air conditioning, bumper-to-bumper stereo sound, a built-in cellular portable telephone, and an electronic digital instrument panel? Did you absolutely *need* the model you bought, or was it more in the nature of a *want* or *desire?* Did you think only in terms of your own needs, or did you consider what your friends and associates might think of your purchase? When your friends asked why you bought that particular car, did you tell them the real reasons or did you make up reasons that sounded more rational—that more closely fit the personal image you wished to convey?

It's important to understand needs and wants since they motivate us to behave in specific ways in order to satisfy them. Why does a person make a decision to buy a particular product? Usually to satisfy a *felt need* or *want.* An understanding of the underlying causes of consumer motivation can enable salespeople to sell and serve their customers more effectively. This chapter should help you to gain an improved awareness of why and how consumers make their typical buying decisions.

THE CAUSES OF CONSUMER BEHAVIOR

No simple explanation tells us everything about why people buy products and services. Each person has a unique set of reasons for purchasing specific products. Your own motives for buying a particular product or service are likely to be quite different from another person's. Some individuals, for example, might want a product because of the feelings of status or self-esteem it provides. Others might want the same product because of specific safety features. And still others might desire the product because they believe it to be an economically sound purchase.

Wanted—Part-Time Selling Psychologists

Creative salespeople are, in a sense, part-time psychologists. They should understand why consumers buy some goods and services and not others. Of course, since salespeople are not professional psychologists, they should be cautious in applying incomplete knowledge. Nonetheless, as a salesperson, you should attempt to learn as much as possible about human behavior, especially the types of behavior that motivate consumers to purchase products. Now let's move into an examination of six important factors that tend to influence the buying behavior of consumers. They are:

What influences buying decisions?

1. Needs and motives
2. Culture
3. Attitudes
4. Social class
5. Perception
6. Purchase decision process

THE NATURE OF NEEDS AND MOTIVES

Everybody has needs and wants that affect their buying decisions. When you already have something, then you don't really need it. When we refer to the term **need,** we'll mean the condition of *deprivation;* that is, the idea that *something is missing from a person's situation.* That "something" may be physiological (such as food), social (such as companionship), or psychological (such as self-esteem). The absence of food, for example, would tend to stimulate activity designed to satisfy that felt need: you would try to obtain some food. Stated differently, if you don't have something but you feel that you *must* have it, then you have a *need.*

Motives, too, are important to understand. A **motive** is a *feeling or condition that causes specific activity designed to bring about satisfaction.* The concept of motivation should become clearer as you progress through this chapter.

There are lots of things we could survive without, such as electricity or video camcorders, but we wouldn't survive for long without such basics as food, drink, adequate clothing, sleep, breathable air, and a satisfactory temperature; we *need* them. These are what psychologists call **primary needs**—that is, *basic* or *physical needs.*

"Everybody has needs, but not everybody tries to satisfy them in precisely the same fashion."

We humans also have a variety of **secondary needs**—that is, *psychological* and *social needs*—which also tend to motivate or drive us. Our secondary needs are often *learned;* that is, we learn to need or want additional things, far less basic than food or drink. These secondary needs motivate us to act in certain ways. Among these needs are the desire to feel secure, to be with other people, to have sex appeal, to be respected as human beings, and sometimes even to climb mountains or to parachute from airplanes. Everybody has needs, but not everybody tries to satisfy them in precisely the same fashion.

Nor does everybody have precisely the same needs. Not everyone needs the same number of hours of sleep nightly, for example. Also, needs exist in each individual in varying degrees. As a salesperson, you could miss the opportunity to make a sale if you tried to appeal to needs or motives that your prospects don't even have.

Felt Needs Motivate

Does a salesperson **sell** *or* **activate** *a buyer—or* **both?**

Some students of selling feel that salespeople don't actually sell; instead, they activate the wants and motives that already exist within the prospect. The primary focus, it is sometimes argued, should be on *buying* rather than *selling* since a person is not likely to purchase a product unless he or she *recognizes a need or want for it.* The salesperson, therefore, should attempt to uncover a need that may already exist since a need by itself will not necessarily motivate a person to act. The need must be *felt.* For example, assume you've discovered that the Toledo Marine Insurance Company, one of your prospects, could save as much as $400,000 a year on office expenses if it were to adopt a system developed by your firm. In a sense, in order to save the $400,000, Toledo Marine *needs* your product.

When you haven't eaten for some time, hunger pangs usually help you recognize the need for food by creating a certain degree of inner tension. This tension then motivates you to act. Your action accomplishes a goal (the elimination of your hunger pangs) and thus relieves your tension. The achievement of your goal leads to a feeling of satisfaction, at least until the next time tension arises (see Figure 5.1). Now you should be able to see how salespeople are in the position to assist customers in recognizing needs, relieving tensions, and achieving goals.

Satisfied Needs No Longer Motivate

As a person's basic needs become satisfied, the secondary or higher-order needs become increasingly more significant. For example, you must eat to live. If you are ravenously hungry, your first morsel of food might give you tremendous satisfaction. As you continue to eat, however, you may begin to experience what economists often refer to as "diminishing marginal satisfaction" from each additional portion of food. After a certain point (which varies with the individual) you discover that your basic need to satisfy your hunger drive has been met.

"As a person's basic needs become satisfied, the secondary or higher-order needs become increasingly more significant."

If you are extremely hungry *and* extremely tired, one of your drives or motives might be stronger than the other. For example, assume that you have not eaten or slept for $2\frac{1}{2}$ days and someone leads you into a comfortable room. As you enter, you see on one side of the room a perfectly broiled, juicy T-bone steak and a tender baked potato smothered in sour cream and sprinkled with chives. On the other side of the room you see a comfortable looking queen-sized bed. Which of the two intense drives will you satisfy first? You would probably favor your hunger drive. After satisfying yourself with a meal, you would probably find that the bed had begun to look increasingly inviting.

If you satisfy your basic needs, that is, acquire most of the food and adequate

Figure 5.1 Recognized Needs Result in Tensions and Action Designed to Bring Relief.

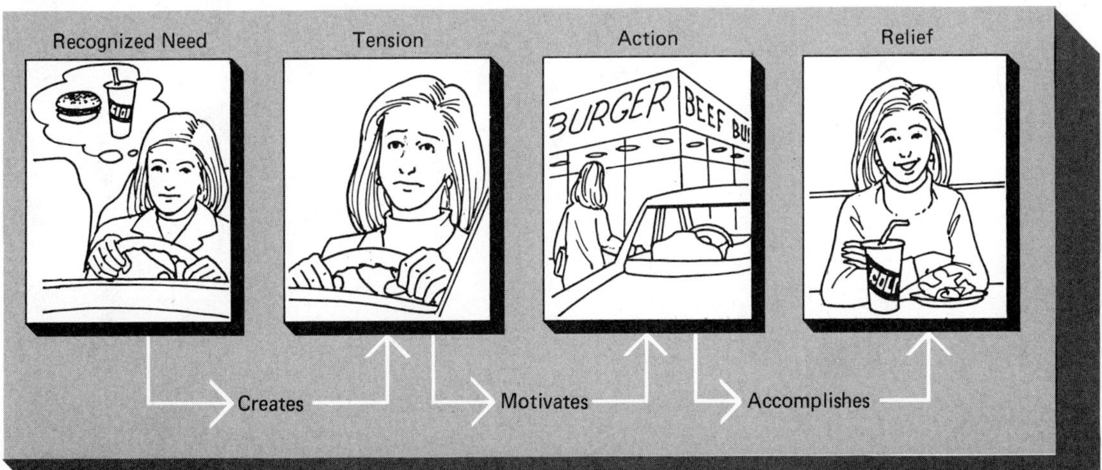

shelter you desire, other motives usually become more important to you. Perhaps *security* (a good retirement plan) or *social approval* (a home in a "good neighborhood"), or other factors become more significant. The point is this: as our basic, lower-order needs become satisfied, other needs—termed *psychological or higher-order needs*—increase in importance. This concept of priority or a hierarchy of needs was thoroughly developed by A. H. Maslow in his book *Motivation and Personality.*[1]

The Priority of Needs

Maslow suggested that human needs can be categorized into an *order of priority* (or a **hierarchy of needs**) and that each level of need has to be satisfied to some extent before the next level assumes importance. Maslow developed a concept that distinguished five levels of human needs (see Figure 5.2) ranging from *basic, lower-order needs to psychological, higher-order needs:*

1. Basic physical needs
2. Safety and security needs
3. Social needs
4. Self-esteem, self-respect, and status needs
5. Self-realization needs—the need for feelings of accomplishment

Figure 5.2 Maslow's Hierarchy of Human Needs.

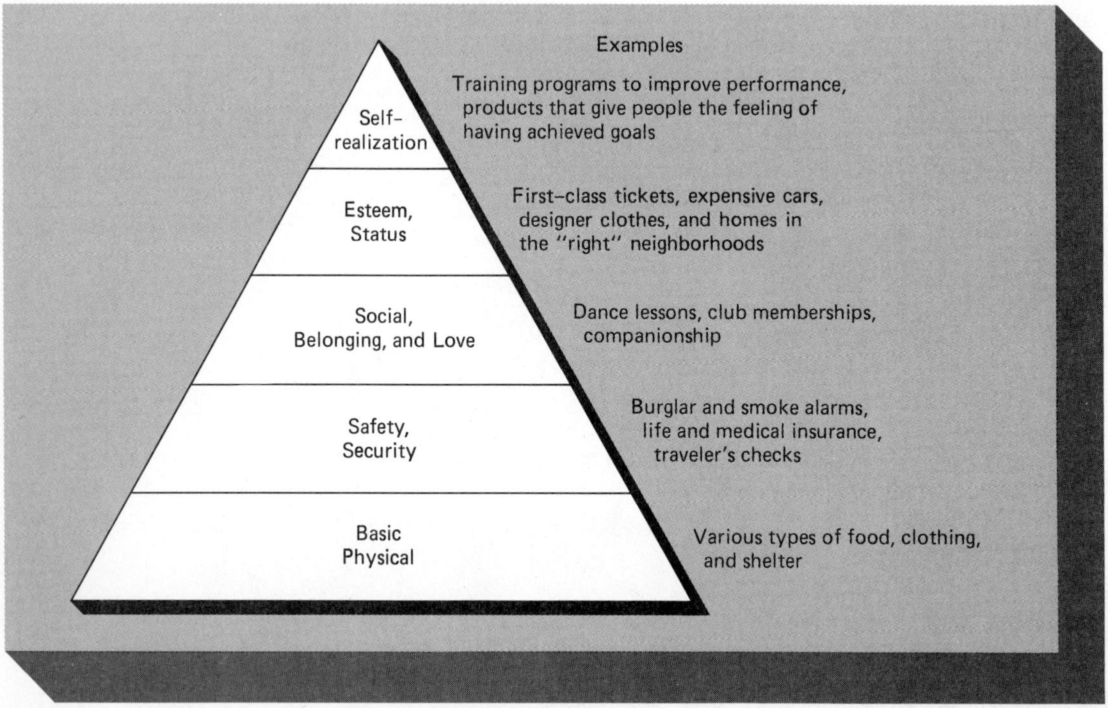

Examples

Self-realization — Training programs to improve performance, products that give people the feeling of having achieved goals

Esteem, Status — First-class tickets, expensive cars, designer clothes, and homes in the "right" neighborhoods

Social, Belonging, and Love — Dance lessons, club memberships, companionship

Safety, Security — Burglar and smoke alarms, life and medical insurance, traveler's checks

Basic Physical — Various types of food, clothing, and shelter

A cardinal point of the hierarchy-of-needs theory is that a *satisfied need ceases to motivate.* Lower-order needs don't become unimportant to a person, but higher-order needs achieve greater significance as basic needs are satisfied.

Take, for example, a manufacturer whose sales representatives sell thermostatic control devices for heating systems. The need for a satisfactory temperature is basic, but the salespeople might try to appeal to the psychological or high-order needs of company executives by appealing to their desire for *self-esteem.* Executives are accustomed to controlling organizational situations. They might also prefer to control the temperature of their own offices rather than have it controlled from a central location.

Airline representatives also might attempt to appeal to the higher needs of business travelers. Their approach is often something like this: "I'm sure that you would agree that your executives are of high caliber. If they *are* first-class executives, shouldn't they be traveling first class, rather than coach, on their business trips? If they are flying to an important conference where they have to face difficult situations, don't they need to arrive with the self-assurance and confidence that traveling first-class will help them maintain?"

Who . . . **Me** *scared?*

The need to feel secure or safe has become more important in recent decades, as indicated by some of the recent buying trends. Homeowners in the United States during past decades have installed "decorative bars" on their windows and bought guns and expensive electronic detection equipment to fend off unwelcome visitors. Automobiles have been fitted with electronic sirens and bells to discourage thieves. And some businesses subscribe to services that provide security personnel disguised as company workers whose function is to observe other employees.

Needs Are Not Mutually Exclusive

The implication you may get from our discussion of the hierarchy of needs is that it is like a stepladder; that is, as you lift your body past one rung on the ladder of needs, you are finished with it. Not true—needs are *not* mutually exclusive. For example, assume that you sell real estate to retired people in communities designed especially for them. The need for shelter—a house—is basic. But remember that people have higher-order needs as well. A retired couple may also have a *social need,* the desire for companionship with others of similar age and interests. Both types of needs may be important to them.

CULTURE AND CONSUMER BEHAVIOR

Someone once said, "We are what we eat"—and, in a sense, we all "eat" our environment. That is, we absorb mentally the various things we see and experience. This environment that we absorb is called culture. The term **culture** refers to the many environmental influences handed down from one generation to another that become a part of our present environment. Culture has a significant influence on what we see and do in a given situation. It also has a great influence on our needs

Pick a Picasso!

and wants. For example, children who are raised in households where books and paintings are a normal part of the cultural environment are more likely to purchase such items for their own households.

Culture does not include those things we do instinctively, such as eating and sleeping. However, culture does influence how we satisfy those instincts. For example, some families satisfy their hunger instincts by eating squid, snails, tripe, or even cow tongue. Other families, based on their cultural backgrounds, appear nauseated at the mere mention of such foods. They may prefer to satisfy their hunger needs by eating "good old steak and potatoes."

Yuk!

Yummie!

"Culture has a significant influence on what we see and do in a given situation. It also has a great influence on our needs and wants."

Changing Cultural Influences

Cultural factors are continually in the state of flux. For example, visualize the changes in the cultural value systems of college students since the 1960s. Their purchases, reflected by their values, have gone through numerous changes. Young people "dressed down" and adorned shoulder-length hair during much of the 1960s and part of the 1970s, after which "dressing up" and shorter hair became the cultural norms throughout the 1980s. Cultural values relating to sexual behavior also underwent substantial change during the same period as a result of fears of the dreaded diseases herpes and AIDS. Marketers of condoms took advantage of these changing values by increasing their advertising and promotion of condoms.

Changing cultural values and influences of all types are highly important to marketers since they significantly affect what they can sell to consumers. Some of the most important changes in cultural factors and value systems in recent years include:[2]

1. Evolving attitudes toward more equal roles of women at home and on the job

2. More conservative sexual attitudes

3. Prevalence of a singles life-style

4. Baby-boomers becoming middle-aged

5. Increased numbers of senior citizens

6. Desire for immediate rather than postponed gratification

6. Freer spending habits with increased use of credit

7. An increasing concern for physical fitness and health

8. Changing ethnic composition of the United States

ATTITUDES AND CONSUMER BEHAVIOR

In addition to needs, motives, and culture, another factor that influences buying decisions is **attitude,** which, simply stated, is how a person feels about something. Attitudes relate to the beliefs and feelings people have and the ways they behave toward people, objects, and ideas. Let's now examine some factors that tend to shape consumer attitudes and also learn about some forces that could cause such attitudes to change. We will also see how we can put customer attitudes to use in selling.

Reference Groups

Our attitudes aren't inborn; they're typically learned from our families, friends, culture, and personal experiences. There are certain groups, therefore, that we tend to identify with for various reasons. These groups are termed **reference groups** and are likely to have a significant effect in shaping our tastes, values, and attitudes toward a host of things, such as for whom to vote in an upcoming election or what brand of denims or walking shoes to wear to school.

To which group do you refer?

There are various types of reference groups. A **participational reference group** is one that individuals are integral members of, such as their families, clusters of friends, and their neighbors. A person's buying habits are often derived from these reference groups.

Does an individual have to be a member of a particular group to have his or her attitudes influenced by that group? Not necessarily. A group that an individual is not a member of but would like to belong to are termed **aspirational reference group.** For example, you might identify with a particular athletic team yet live thousands of miles from its home field. Many Raiders' football fans from the Oakland-San Francisco Bay Area continued to feel that the team was still theirs long after it moved from Oakland to Los Angeles. In other situations, there are individuals who may not be wealthy yet they identify with "the rich and the famous" and, as a result, tend to copy some of their buying habits.

Go Oakland Raiders!

Many producers are well aware of the commercial value of reference groups. Some apparel manufacturers, for example, have provided at no cost to Olympic athletes all of the sports garb they needed to compete in the games. The generous manufacturers hoped to extract economic gain from the publicity value of the gifts since people who identify with the athletes, it is believed, tend to purchase the clothing lines of the donating manufacturers.

Reference may not always be to a group; it can also be to an individual. For example, some individuals might be influenced to purchase a particular brand of toothpaste promoted by a famous movie star.

Even Popeye has been credited with enhancing children's consumption of spinach!

People are also influenced by **negative reference groups.** These are groups that a person doesn't want to identify with; therefore the person adopts attitudes *opposite* to those of the group. For example, why might some individuals choose to purchase a Honda motorcycle rather than a Harley-Davidson, or vice versa?

"In some cases, products or services have to be tailored to fit the attitudes of the consumer, while in other cases consumer attitudes themselves may be changed."

What Causes Attitudes to Change?

What could change attitudes?

Since consumer attitudes are so significant to buying decisions, a major problem for salespeople is to determine how they can influence existing attitudes so that individuals are more favorably disposed to purchase their products. Most psychologists feel that attitudes are highly resistant to change; consequently, in some cases, products or services have to be tailored to fit the attitudes of the consumer, while in other cases consumer attitudes themselves may be changed.

How do "significant experiences" modify attitudes?

What are some things that just might change consumer attitudes? For one thing, a *significant experience* can influence a person's present attitudes. Assume, for example, that Jesse Steinberg never felt that automobile seat belts were much good, in spite of a law requiring their use, and therefore seldom buckled them. Let's also assume Jesse has a serious automobile accident and is severely injured. Jesse is told that seat belts would have substantially lessened the extent of his injuries. After that, might he not change his attitude toward seat belts?

Here's another example related to a significant experience: Cynthia Cynique has always pooh-poohed some of the recent trends in stereo equipment, believing that many of the "new and different" innovations were more marketing gimmicks than real improvements in quality. A friend of Cynthia, Jason Johnson, invited her over for tea one day and played his new "150 watt integrated amplifier, 14-band graphic equalizer, quartz digital tuner, and precision compact disc player programmable up to 16 songs, with 3 beam laser accuracy." Cynthia couldn't believe her ears! That "significant experience" changed her attitude. She rushed out the next day to the nearest music equipment store, "Sounds Rad," and plunked down $1500 on a set just like Jason's. Can you think of any other significant experiences that could change a potential customer's mind?

How do expectations modify attitudes?

A person's *expectations* can modify attitudes, too. Let's return once more to our friend, Jesse, and his seatbelts. Jesse might change his mind toward seatbelts if he believed and *expected* that he would receive a traffic ticket from a law enforcement officer if caught without a seatbelt on. Our other friend, Cynthia, also had expectations that modified her attitudes. She *expected* to be able to enjoy the sounds of music more fully through the purchase of more modern stereo equipment.

Recognition of a want can also change attitudes. Let's assume that our same friend Jesse detests wearing neckties. In fact, he once exclaimed, "I'm my own man. I won't wear a necktie for anybody!" He might change his attitude, however, and be willing to wear a necktie if doing so were a precondition to getting a particular job that he strongly wanted.

Another factor that can alter a person's attitudes is a *shift in one's self-concept.* We all possess what is termed a **self-concept** or **self-image,** which means the way we see ourselves and the way we believe others feel about us. A distinction is sometimes made between the *actual self-concept* (the way we *really* see ourselves) and the *ideal self-concept* (the way we *want* to be seen or *would like* to view ourselves). A customer's purchases can be influenced by either. Assume, for example, that a person named Bernice Bayer is separated and in the process of being divorced from her husband, Barry. During her marriage, Bernice's **actual self** influenced her into developing relatively conservative tastes: she drove a maroon four-door hatchback automobile and wore dark, somewhat old-fashioned clothes. After her separation, something happened to Bernice's self-concept. Her **ideal self** became dominant. She became an eligible woman who wanted to make a favorable impression on potential companions of the opposite sex. She recently purchased a sleek sports car and some fashionable designer clothes, since these reflect the way in which she would *like* to be viewed by others—her ideal self. The way in which people perceive themselves, therefore, significantly influences their buying decisions.

Changes in a product or in the quality of a service can also change attitudes toward a product or company. A change in a product's design, for example, can change a person's attitude toward it. Or, a customer of an automobile repair shop may stop having her car serviced there because of a feeling that the service deteriorated when a new shop supervisor was hired.

Putting Customer Attitudes to Use

Attitudes can be significant clues to how a salesperson should approach a particular prospect. Let's assume that one of your customers, Mrs. Blanche White, is known to prefer conservative clothes. She probably could be approached more easily if you also displayed conservative tastes when you called on her. If Mrs. White has political attitudes significantly different from yours, you would also be wise to avoid discussing politics in her presence.

"When Peter talks about Paul, we often learn more about Peter than we do about Paul."

"I don't trust Paul" equals "Don't trust me."

You can often learn a lot about the personal attitudes of prospective customers by listening carefully to what they say about others. There is a fairly common tendency to attribute to others some of our own values and motives, a characteristic called **projection.** A Dutch philosopher, Spinoza, seemed well aware of this concept when he said, "When Peter talks about Paul, we often learn more about Peter than we do about Paul."

For example, you might ask your prospect—let's call him Mr. Leroy Carter—whether he is aware of a new system that your company recently installed for another company, the Ajax Sunburst Corporation. Mr. Carter might respond with something like: "No, but I'm not surprised. Ajax is quite a progressive firm. They always seem to be a giant step ahead of their competition."

From such a statement you might infer that Mr. Carter's attitude toward your products is quite favorable and that he could be a likely prospect for a purchase.

SOCIAL CLASS AND CONSUMER BEHAVIOR

"You mean that money won't put me at the head of my class?"

Does a social class system exist in the United States? As much as some Americans prefer to feel otherwise, sociologists generally contend that such a system does exist, although not as predominately as in some societies in the world. A **social class** is a group of people who have similar status in society. Their status, as perceived by the others in the community, is generally determined by their attained *educational level, occupation,* and by *where they live.*[3] Surprisingly, income is not considered a primary determiner of social class, although it certainly can have a significant influence on a person's ability to maintain a particular social standing. Figure 5.3 summarizes the principal categories of social class in the United States.

Class is not perceived by marketers as something either "good" or "bad," "better" or "worse," but rather as another method of segmenting markets. Marketers believe that the class with which individuals identify tends to influence their

Upper class, about 1 to 2 percent of the population, consisting of (1) established wealthy "old-money" families with inherited wealth (upper-upper) and (2) "new rich," owners of large businesses, certain professionals, and corporate executives (lower-upper). They tend to avoid mass merchandising, rather preferring exclusive types of goods and services. "Old-money" families tend to be less conspicuous in their consumption than the "new rich" and the upper-middle class.

Upper-middle class, about 11 to 14 percent of the population, consisting of moderately successful business owners and professionals. Purchases by this group tend to conspicuously reflect their successes. They tend to purchase quality products and be concerned about their own and their children's future.

Lower-middle class, about one third of the population, consisting of white-collar workers, small business owners, office workers, teachers, and technicians. This group is composed primarily of what is popularly considered "mainstream America," with traditional, conforming, and highly religious values. They tend to be more future oriented than the upper-lower class described below.

Upper-lower class, about 38 percent of the population, consisting of skilled and semiskilled workers, service employees, and factory production workers. They tend to be security minded, earn fairly good incomes, and live more for the present than do the lower-middle class mentioned above.

Lower-lower class, about 16 percent of the population, consisting primarily of unskilled laborers, chronically unemployed persons, certain ethnic immigrants, and long-term welfare recipients. They tend to make purchases that are necessities and that help them enjoy the present, rather than the future.

Figure 5.3 Principal Social Classes in the United States. [Adapted from Richard P. Coleman, "The Continuing Significance of Social Class to Marketing," *Journal of Consumer Research,* December 1983, pp. 265–280; E. Jerome McCarthy and William D. Perrault, Jr., *Basic Marketing* (Homewood, IL: Richard D. Irwin, 1984), pp. 209–212; and Dennis Gilbert and Joseph A. Kahl, "The American Class Structure: A Synthesis," in *The American Class Structure: A New Synthesis* (Homewood, IL: Richard D. Irwin, 1984).]

purchases far more than their level of income. The various classes frequently shop at different stores and purchase different types of automobiles even when their incomes are comparable to each other's.

"Marketers believe that the class with which individuals identify tends to influence their purchases far more than their level of income."

Various studies indicate that social class has a significant influence over consumer behavior as a result of differences in three major areas:[4]

1. *Sources of information.* Higher social classes tend to read different magazines and newspapers than do those in the lower social classes, the former preferring publications that emphasize current events rather than those that dramatize romance and gossip, which tend to be preferred by the lower social classes. Similar patterns hold true for television watching—the higher social classes tend to prefer current event programs and drama, the lower social classes tend to prefer sitcoms, quiz shows, and "soaps."

2. *Shopping patterns.* Many marketers attempt to cater to the different shopping patterns of the various classes. Some retailers, such as the Seattle-based chain of Nordstrom's stores, stress quality, snob appeal, and service in their sales promotions and advertising as a means of appealing to higher social class values. Other retailers, such as Gemco, attempt to appeal to a mass market of lower-class (lower-middle and upper-lower) values by stressing price and value, rather than snob appeal, in their advertising and promotion efforts.

3. *Leisure activities.* In general, members of the different classes tend to select different leisure activities. For example, the higher social classes tend to prefer their own facilities, such as private golf, swim, and tennis clubs, whereas members of the lower-middle class tend to be the greatest users of public recreational facilities. Although the major sports of football, baseball, and basketball appear to be enjoyed by all social classes, certain activities—such as boxing, bingo, bowling, and wrestling—tend to be favored more by the lower classes.

PERCEPTION AND CONSUMER BEHAVIOR

Salespeople should attempt to develop a sound understanding of the nature of perception, since what people see significantly influences their actions—whether they are in the process of selling or buying. Needs must be felt (perceived) before they motivate a person to act. And until a person feels (perceives) a need, he or she is unlikely to be moved to purchase a particular product.

"Needs must be felt (perceived) before they motivate a person to act. And until a person feels (perceives) a need, he or she is unlikely to be moved to purchase a particular product."

Is believing always seeing?

Take a look at Figure 5.4. What do you see? Most observers will see a woman. Approximately how old is the woman? Does she appear young, possibly in her twenties? Or does she look rather old, probably in her sixties? Or does she seem to be middle-aged? Make a decision before you read further.

About half of those who see this picture typically feel that the person is a young woman. Others contend that she looks quite old. A few will say that she appears middle-aged. Still others argue that there are *both* an old and a young woman in the sketch. Which did you see? Look at the picture again for a few moments and see if your original perception changes. If you saw the young woman, look for the older one. Did you see the older one first? If so, try to see the young one. *Both are actually there.* Take a long, hard look and you're likely to see both women.

If at first you observed only one woman, what might have been the reason? Could you have been mentally set to see only onc? Why did you see only the young (or the older) woman at first? The point is this: sometimes we don't see the

Figure 5.4 Approximately How Old Is the Woman in the Drawing?

entire situation immediately; accurate perception may take some intense effort or guidance. You might see your customers differently once you get to know them, and—equally important—they might need help in seeing you and your products as they really are.

Determinants of Perception

We've been using the term **perception.** Actually, what does it mean? *Perception* can be defined as *the way a person interprets a particular object, person, or situation.* We've already seen how *culture* can influence what we see and do in a given situation. The way we perceive is a fairly complicated process and can be influenced by a wide variety of factors. Our discussion in this section will be restricted to three important influences on perception, which are:

1. Snap judgments
2. Selective perception
3. Peer pressures

A brief discussion of each influence follows.

Snap Judgments

Don't confuse me with the fact . . . my mind's already made up!

Some people proudly believe that they can "size up a person right away." Unfortunately, their perceptions are often wrong. Many prospects (and salespeople) are guilty of making **snap judgments** before they have enough facts to come to valid conclusions. For example, they may feel certain that "your company doesn't provide adequate service," a belief that may be unfounded and based solely on a snap judgment. You should recognize that some prospects will make up their minds about you, your company, or its products with little factual evidence. And you may have to persuade them that your situation is different from the way they perceive it.

Selective Perception

You can expect to have to face numerous challenges as a salesperson, especially related to your attempts to overcome perceptual barriers. For example, there's the tendency for people (customers *and* salespeople) to see or hear what they want or are set to see and hear, and tune out any information that doesn't fit into their perceptual scheme. When people do this, they are engaging in what is termed **selective perception.** The following is an amusing illustration of this concept:

> A lady went up to a famous painter and said: "Mr. Aggigoni, will you paint me in the nude? I will pay any fee you wish."
>
> The painter thought for a while and then said: "Very well—but only if I can keep my socks on. Otherwise I shall have nowhere to put my brushes."

Do we want what we see . . . or see what we want?

Here's a selling application of selective perception: Let's assume that you've just explained to a potential customer that although the price of your product is somewhat higher than the prices of your competitors, your product actually costs less to operate. You also explained that these savings, therefore, result in lower costs and higher profits for the customer over time. However, your prospect may "selectively perceive"—that is, focus only on the higher-cost portion of your message—and completely fail to hear what you said about higher profits. In a later chapter on the important topic of communication, we'll discuss useful techniques for overcoming such perceptual problems.

Peer Pressures

Related to cultural influences is the effect that our associates have on what we see, think, and do, often referred to as the **peer effect.** Our perceptions and attitudes are often much different when we are in the company of others from what they are when we're alone.

Do people judge by the company they keep?

Some years ago, Solomon Asch conducted some experiments that helped to illustrate the apparent need people have to conform to the thinking of others.[5] Asch assembled several groups of eight people to participate in the experiments. The eight people sat around a table and were asked to judge the comparative lengths of various lines. Asch was sort of tricky, however. Only one person in each group of eight was a true subject; the others had been told in advance by Asch to conspire against that one by giving the *wrong* answers in a confident manner two-thirds of the time.

"Our perceptions and attitudes are often much different when we are in the company of others from what they are when we're alone."

The guinea pigs (the one innocent victim in each group) were always the last to make their choices. Almost 40 percent of the time, these people went along with the incorrect decision of the group, admittedly because they didn't want to look silly in front of the others and not because they truly believed the group's answers. The **Asch conformity studies** clearly brought out the effect of group pressure on the perceptions and attitudes of individual members of a group.

The peer effect can also work in selling. Assume that two salespeople, Jil and Hal, are interviewing one prospect, whom we'll call Ms. Fonce. They are involved with what is sometimes referred to as **team selling.** Jil, one of the two salespeople, speaks to her counterpart: "Hal, wouldn't you also agree that Ms. Fonce could really benefit from acquiring our model XLZ-102?" Hal responds, "There's no doubt in my mind, Jil. Ms. Fonce, how do you feel about it?" As brought out by the Asch conformity studies, there could be a human tendency for Ms. Fonce to want to go along with the group—the two salespeople. Inherent in the team approach, however, is the potential danger of appearing to "gang up" on the prospect. Selling teams should avoid such an appearance.

THE PURCHASE DECISION PROCESS AND CONSUMER BEHAVIOR

How do your customers go about making buying decisions? Marketers believe that the typical person goes through a series of five stages when trying to decide whether to make a purchase. These activities are considered more as a process than as individual steps and are termed the **purchase decision process.** The common stages that most purchasers are believed to go through in the purchase decision process are:

Stage 1—Recognition of a need or want

Stage 2—Search for information

Stage 3—Evaluating alternative choices

Stage 4—Making a choice

Stage 5—Evaluating the choice made

Let's now look briefly at each purchase decision stage.

Stage 1—Recognition of a Need or Want

Do you remember our discussion of needs and wants? As you should recall, an unsatisfied need or want tends to result in action designed to achieve relief or satisfaction. Let's now trace a typical example of the purchase process. Assume, for example, that a young man named Jeffery has a strong desire to own a compact disc player. Many members of his reference group (his friends) already have players. However, Jeffery also remembers that the tires on his automobile have 60,000 miles and are going to need replacing soon. He wonders if now is a wise time for him to buy the compact disc player or, instead, he should save the money for the tires. He must resolve this conflict before moving on to the next stage.

Stage 2—Search for Information

Jeffery believes that he really wants an improved sound system like his friends have, but he needs some information about the various units available for purchase. He has already received certain information in the past from newspaper and magazine advertising. He asks his friends for their opinions on different players. He also drops by SOUNDS RIGHT, a nearby electronics store, where he picks up some brochures describing some of the better units.

Stage 3—Evaluating Alternative Decisions

The next stage in Jeffery's purchase decision process involves evaluating some of his possible choices. One of the units enables him to select up to 16 songs with random-access programming from a remote control device for $300. However, for $100 more, he could obtain a player that allows him to select up to 32 songs, also with random-access programming, plus it has a 7-disc capacity. The lower-priced model houses only one disc at time.

Stage 4—Making a Choice

Now Jeffery must make a choice, the next stage in the purchase decision process. Jeffery discovered during his evaluation stage that he could obtain credit and finance either compact disc player, the lower-priced one at payments of $20 a month or the more expensive 7-disc player for $21 per month. "What the heck," says Jeffery to himself. "We only go around once. I've been working hard lately. I deserve a treat now and then." He also believes that by financing the player, he still will be able to afford his needed tires. He opts for the $400 set.

Stage 5—Evaluating the Decision Made

Depending on the purchase, many buyers develop certain attitudes after their purchase. They frequently question the wisdom of their decisions, especially those related to more expensive nonroutine purchases. Jeffery is actually quite pleased with the quality of the sound he gets from his new compact disc player. But he also feels an emotion that psychologists call **cognitive dissonance,** which is a form of stress caused by his uncertainty as to whether he should have made the purchase at this time. He now has an additional fixed expense each month that he would rather be without. And, since making his purchase, he has also learned that to obtain the maximum benefit from his new player he should buy a new set of speakers. However, his friends seem to be favorably impressed with his unit, and so he gradually begins to be pleased with his decision once again.

For an Individual Buyer—It Depends

Every purchaser doesn't necessarily go through every stage each time he or she buys a specific product. Stages may be bypassed altogether in certain situations, such as in routine and repeat purchases. Repurchasing your favorite toothpaste, for example, involves fewer stages than buying an automobile. Some products, therefore, especially lower-priced ones that are routinely bought without a lot of analysis, are termed **low involvement products.** More expensive products—those that are infrequently purchased and require more information—are termed **high involvement products.** The application of the purchase decision process, therefore, really depends on how much consumer involvement exists, which is influenced by the type of product, how frequently it is purchased, how much information is needed about the product, its cost, the extent of risk involved in the buying decision, and the perception of the buyer.

REASONS FOR CONSUMER LOYALTY

Up to this point we have been discussing why people buy particular products—some writers call these reasons **buying motives.** Another classification of motives—called **patronage motives**—is concerned with why people repeatedly and consistently buy from a particular company. This concept should be easier to understand if you think about why you patronize the same firm on a regular basis.

One somewhat general reason could be because of *past satisfaction* you have received from the firm. Students of learning theory point out that we tend to repeat experiences that please us. If we have had consistently favorable experiences with a particular store, for example, we are likely to return for more—not unlike a child who has discovered the secret hiding place of the cookie jar.

Why do customers keep coming back?

There are a number of reasons related to past satisfactions that tend to cause consumers to patronize a firm regularly. Most sellers strive zealously for consumer loyalty. How might the factors listed below positively influence buyers to return to the source of their original purchase?

1. A convenient location
2. Favorable attitudes and behavior of sales personnel
3. A positive public image or reputation, including appearance
4. The availability of service and credit
5. The speed of service
6. Price (high for snob appeal, competitive or low to appeal to economy motives)
7. A variety of goods available
8. An atmosphere that creates good feelings among those who deal with the organization

DEMAND CHARACTERISTICS AND MOTIVES OF INDUSTRIAL PURCHASERS

Household consumers, as we've learned, purchase products for a variety of motives, some rational but many of them emotional or psychological in nature. Purchasers for businesses and institutions also buy for a variety of reasons, sometimes rational and sometimes emotional, but the underlying motive for them typically relates to the opportunity to gain greater profits.

Different Market Traits

The traits of industrial markets vary considerably from those of consumer markets, and they significantly influence industrial buying motives. In general, six demand characteristics are unique to industrial markets:

1. *Demand is often derived* from another source. For example, an increased consumer demand for shoes would result in a **derived demand** for leather. Increased demand for automobiles would result in a derived demand for steel, glass, and other industrial products.

2. *Demand is generally more cyclical* than in many consumer goods industries. The demand for industrial goods tends to fluctuate drastically and is strongly related to current inventory policies and buyer expectations. For example, when shortages or rapid price increases are anticipated, forward buying (stockpiling) of goods often takes place. When expectations about future economic conditions are bleak, inventories are often allowed to be depleted and little effort is made to replenish them. Thus there is **cyclical demand.**

3. *Purchasing habits tend to be more rational.* In general, industrial purchasers are professionals with **rational buying motives.** They tend to be well informed as to the cost, quality, and availability of the products they purchase. Of course, some industrial purchases, such as a firm's purchase of an elaborate computer system it didn't really need, seem to be emotional or ego-related, but most are rational.

4. *Greater* **market concentration** *exists* in the industrial goods market. In the consumer goods field, large numbers of buyers are widely dispersed geographically. By comparison, there are relatively few buyers of industrial goods, and they tend to be more geographically concentrated. For example, the major portion of all manufacturing activity—almost 60 percent—takes place in only ten states: California, Texas, Michigan, Illinois, Ohio, Pennsylvania, New York, New Jersey, Indiana, and North Carolina.[6] Such clustering of industry makes personal selling more practicable than selling to widely dispersed retailers.

5. **Multiple buying decisions** are more common among industrial purchasers. Many buying decisions today are made by more than one person; sometimes they're made by established and formal **buying committees,** which are ongoing, established groups whose function is to determine the best sources for their organizational purchases.

   A related marketing concept is the **buying center,** which represents all the people who either directly or indirectly influence purchases. The buying center is not considered a formal group or place. Instead, it could consist of virtually any managers or employees scattered throughout the organization.

   In some instances, as many as 5 to 20 persons may be a part of the buying center and have to be "sold" before a final buying decision is made. Most of them are not typically a part of the purchasing department of the industrial customer. Instead, they might be production line personnel who are final users of the product, or they could be specific managers or employees who have been formally assigned final purchasing authority. They could even be secretaries and receptionists who are in the strategic position of being able to influence the flow of information to industrial purchasers with final buying authority. For example, a secretary could be more significant than the boss in determining which brand of word processor or software will be purchased. (See Figure 5.5 for a summary of types of individuals who may influence industrial buying decisions.)

6. **Custom production** is more common in industrial markets. Typically, a consumer good is manufactured, then put up for sale. Industrial goods, however, are quite often custom-produced. A set of specifications for a product are

1. *Users*—production line workers or their supervisors.
2. *Influencers*—engineering or R&D people who help write specifications or supply information for evaluating alternatives.
3. *Buyers*—purchasing agents who have the responsibility for selecting suppliers and arranging the terms of the sale.
4. *Deciders*—persons in the organization who have the power to select or approve the supplier—usually the purchasing agent for small items, but sometimes senior management for large purchases.
5. *Gatekeepers*—people who control the flow of information within the organization—possibly purchasing agents who shield users or other deciders. Gatekeepers can also include receptionists, secretaries, research assistants, and others who influence the flow of information about potential purchases.

Figure 5.5 Examples of Possible Industrial Buying Influencers. [Reported in E. Jerome McCarthy and William D. Perrault, Jr., *Basic Marketing* (Homewood, IL: Richard D. Irwin, 1984), pp. 232, 233, as having first appeared in Frederick E. Webster, Jr., and Yoram Wind, *Organizational Buying Behavior* (Englewood Cliffs, NJ: Prentice-Hall, 1972), p. 6.]

released by the potential customer and bids are tendered on the basis of these specifications. If a bidding firm is not awarded the contract, it does not manufacture the specific item.

And Just What Are Their Motives?

In general, industrial buyers are better informed and more rational than average consumers. As a result, the more rational the sales appeal, the more likely industrial prospects are to buy. Businesses cannot function for long without profits, and the sensitive salesperson realizes that the *profit motive* is of paramount importance in the buying decisions of industrial and commercial purchasers. As a result, many sales appeals relate to the profit motive, as discussed briefly below.

"In general, industrial buyers are better informed and more rational than average consumers. As a result, the more rational the sales appeal, the more likely industrial prospects are to buy."

Which do you prefer—dependability or price?

Price is an important factor in the purchase of many industrial products. However, the cheapest product is not always the item that a purchaser wants. More important than its price are two other factors: how it contributes to the total cost of the product the customer is producing and how it affects the total cost of operations. A higher-priced item can actually reduce the unit cost of production if it contributes toward greater efficiency in a firm's activities. Sometimes, for example, a purchaser will buy a product costing somewhat more than a comparable foreign-made product, but the certainty and dependability of the domestic supplier may be more important to the prospective purchaser than initial price.

If you were an industrial buyer, how important would you consider the appeal of *quality?* Generally, quality has quite a significant appeal, but would you necessarily purchase a product of greater quality than you really needed?

For example, if you were purchasing toilet tissue for employee rest rooms, would you buy the highest quality? Would your choice of tissue be different if you were a buyer for the Marriott hotel chain?

If you were a manufacturer, would there be much logic in purchasing a component part that would considerably outlast a final product? Often, it's far more important for a product to be of a *consistent* and *uniform* quality than that it be of a particularly high quality.

Industrial and commercial buyers are also motivated by a product's *salability,* a highly significant consideration. Assume that you are an industrial buyer. Try to think of an item you might purchase. Will it help you sell your own products? If not, will you be likely to buy it? Some purchased items can enhance salability while others might detract. Furthermore, a product that seems to improve salability during one period could be detrimental during a subscquent period if public attitudes or government legislation changed.

Fear also motivates. Although not a pleasant emotion, fear and the desire to feel more secure are strong motivating factors in the purchase of numerous industrial goods and services. The felt need for *protection* is a significant reason why such goods and services as safes, fire extinguishers, insurance policies, and patrol services are purchased.

Evidence of this desire for protection is apparent in the yellow pages of any typical telephone directory. "Guard dogs leased—24-hour radio dispatched" reads one. "Established to meet today's demand for a NEW security in commerce, education, industry, and property management" reads another.

The desire for *flexibility* is another motive in purchasing some products. An item that can be used for more than one operation is usually preferable to a less flexible one. For example, assume that a company is involved in international markets. Its office managers might prefer to purchase printers for their word processors that have the capability of easily making foreign language symbols and accent marks.

Industrial purchasers are also human beings; they don't hang their *emotions* on hooks outside their offices. As a result, not all purchases are the result of rational decisions. A purchasing manager, for example, may simply like a particular salesperson and buy strictly on the basis of friendship. As we learned in Chapter 3, some purchases may be made on *reciprocity* basis in the belief that it is sound business practice for a firm to buy some products from its own customers. The practice of "you scratch my back and I'll scratch yours,"—that is, reciprocity—could be an undesirable policy in certain instances, though, especially where a purchaser may not be obtaining the desired quality at a favorable price.

Also, industrial purchasers sometimes ignore rational buying motives and buy, for example, a particular make or model of automobile for company use strictly because of the *prestige* it affords its users.

SUMMARY

It is difficult in the relatively short space of a chapter to exhaust the possible reasons why consumers buy the products available to them. Our purpose has been merely to provide you with a framework of the principal causes of buying behavior—you can add additional motives and theories to it as you confront them.

Each person is a unique being and thus has unique motives for purchasing specific products. Significant factors that influence the buying behavior of consumers include needs and motives, culture, attitudes, social class, perception, and the purchase decision process.

Everybody has needs and wants. There is a significant relationship between needs and buying motives. For purposes of convenience, needs can be categorized as primary and secondary. However, they vary in importance and intensity with the individual and are not mutually exclusive of each other. A need must be felt if it is to motivate.

Culture, a concept related to the environmental influences handed down from one generation to another, also has a significant effect on consumer behavior. Marketers should be aware, however, that cultural traits are in a continual state of flux.

Understanding consumer attitudes can also aid marketers. Attitudes are significantly influenced by the reference groups with which a person identifies. Although attitudes also tend to be relatively fixed, they sometimes change because of significant experiences, expectations, a recognition of wants, changes in self-concept, and changes in particular products of company services. Attitudes can be significant clues to how a salesperson should approach a particular prospect.

Social class is also considered an important concept to marketers, since the various classes tend to have different tastes and buying habits.

The ways in which individuals perceive particular objects, persons, or situations strongly influences their buying motives. The major determinants of perception include snap judgments, selective perception, and peer pressure.

Most buyers are believed to go through five stages of activities—the purchase decision process—when considering a purchase.

An understanding of patronage motives is important in learning why people repeatedly and consistently buy from the same firms.

The buying motives and characteristics of industrial, institutional, and governmental purchasers tend to differ from those of ultimate consumers. Generally, the demand for industrial products is derived and somewhat cyclical in nature. In addition, industrial purchases tend to be more rational, markets generally more geographically concentrated, and multiple buying decisions and custom production far more common.

KEY TERMS

need
motive
primary needs
secondary needs
hierarchy of needs
culture
attitude
reference groups
participational reference group
aspirational reference group
negative reference groups
self-concept (self-image)
actual self
ideal self
projection
social class
perception
snap judgments
selective perception
peer effect
Asch conformity studies
team selling
purchase decision process
cognitive dissonance
low involvement products
high involvement products
buying motives
patronage motives
derived demand
cyclical demand
rational buying motives
market concentration
multiple buying decisions
buying committees
buying center
custom production

QUESTIONS

1. Evaluate the following statement: "One of the major purposes in learning about consumer behavior and motives is to enable a salesperson to manipulate potential customers."
2. What must occur before a need is likely to motivate a prospective customer to purchase a product?
3. List the five levels of needs that Maslow indicated exist in human beings. What are products that relate to each level?
4. Why is an understanding of motivational concepts especially important to salespeople?
5. List five products that would tend to appeal to a person's higher-order needs.
6. Explain why a satisfied need ceases to motivate.
7. How do cultural values affect the purchases of consumers?
8. What are some of the most important changes in cultural factors and value systems that have occurred in recent years? How do they influence consumer purchases?
9. What are *reference groups?* How do they affect the attitudes of consumers?
10. Even though attitudes are said to be highly resistant to change, what might be some factors that can influence and possibly alter a person's attitudes?
11. What are the differences among *participational, aspirational,* and *negative* reference groups?

12. What is meant by the term *self-image?* How does it relate to consumer purchasing?

13. How does a person's *actual self* differ from his or her *ideal self?*

14. Explain the following statement: "When Judy talks about Beatrice, we often learn more about Judy than we do about Beatrice."

15. What are the principal social classes that are said to exist in the United States? With which one do you identify? Why?

16. How does the concept of social class relate to consumer purchases?

17. From a marketing standpoint, evaluate the following statement: "A rich person is simply a poor person with more money."

18. Would your perception of a political speech that you had watched on television with three close friends be any different if you had watched it alone? How does this example relate to team selling?

19. How does the activity of *team selling* relate to the *peer effect* concept?

20. Evaluate the following statement: "A marketer should realize that every buyer goes through the *purchase buying decision process* in exactly the same manner."

21. What is the difference between *low involvement* and *high involvement* products.

22. What influences a customer to buy repeatedly from the same source?

23. What, in your opinion, might reduce the high degree of cyclical demand for industrial goods?

24. Industrial buyers are said to be more rational in their purchases than are consumers. What are some exceptions to this general rule?

25. Evaluate the following statement: "Purchasing agents buy for only one reason and that is to enhance the profit pictures of the companies for which they work."

26. Why wouldn't a manufacturer necessarily purchase the cheapest or the highest quality of materials?

27. The chapter discusses the concept of a *buying center* and how a variety of different individuals in an organization may influence industrial buying decisions. What might be some key questions that you as a sales representative should answer to correctly identify key organizational decision makers?

28. Explain why salability is an important consideration to an industrial buyer.

29. What is *reciprocity?* When might it be an undesirable business practice?

APPLICATIONS

5.1 AN EXERCISE IN NEEDS

Using Maslow's hierarchy of needs concept, which level of needs is reflected in the following excerpts from actual advertisements:

a. "Romance, sharing, devotion, memories, love. A diamond is forever." (DeBeers)

b. "Now there are two new places to feel like a fat cat in California." (Embassy Suites Hotels)

c. "When you are dealing with something quite extraordinary, price somehow seems irrelevant or even irreverent." (Johnnie Walker Black Label Scotch)

d. "$250,000 invested in Hanson Trust in January 1982 would now have grown to $1,100,000." (Hanson Trust)

e. "Learn how telecommunications and AT&T can help your small business become a big success." (AT&T)

f. "Flowers say I LOVE YOU." (Florists, Nurserymen & Landscapers Assoc.)

g. "Clarion makes beautiful eyes. Pure and simple." (Noxell Corp.)

h. "Friends are worth Smirnoff." (Heublein, Inc.)

i. "Train for success—A better job and better pay." (International Correspondence Schools)

j. "You've come a long way, baby." (Virginia Slims cigarettes)

k. "How your horoscope can bring you wealth, love, success, and happiness." (The American Astrological Association)

l. "The Sleep Saver Pillow—the ultimate for a good night's sleep." (Back-Saver Products Co.)

m. "Have you written your will? (If not, the state has written it for you!)" (Thos. Oak & Sons, Personal Will Kits)

5.2 POWER TO THE PURCHASER!

"The act of buying gives the normal person a sense of pleasure. There is a certain feeling of power in being able to acquire things, entirely apart from any anticipation of enjoying the products or services bought."

Questions

1. What is your reaction to the above statement? In general, do you agree or disagree with it?

2. If you agree, list three purchases you have made "apart from any anticipation of enjoying the products or services bought."

5.3 THE HEALTH-MOTIVE PURCHASES

Many individuals buy specific items because of a desire to maintain their health—both physical and mental. List ten products or services whose purchase is related to the health motive.

NOTES

1. Abraham H. Maslow, *Motivation and Personality* (New York: Harper & Row, 1954).

2. Adapted from William J. Stanton and Charles Futrell, *Fundamentals of Marketing* (New York: McGraw-Hill, 1987), p. 116; and Fred C. Allvine, *Marketing Principles and Practices* (New York: Harcourt Brace Jovanovich, 1987), pp. 116–126.

3. Stanton and Futrell, p. 118.

4. As reported in William H. Cunningham, et al., *Marketing: A Managerial Approach* (Cincinnati: South-Western Publishing, 1987), pp. 165–166.

5. Solomon E. Asch, "Effects of Group Pressure upon the Modification and Distortation of Judgments," in *Readings in Social Psychology,* edited by Eleanor E. Maccoby, Theodore M. Newcomb, and Eugene L. Hartley (New York: Holt, Rinehart and Winston, 1958), pp. 174–183.

6. "1985 Survey of U.S. Industrial & Commercial Buying Power," *Sales & Marketing Management,* April 22, 1985, p. 30.

PART THREE

THE NEED FOR BASIC SELLING SKILLS

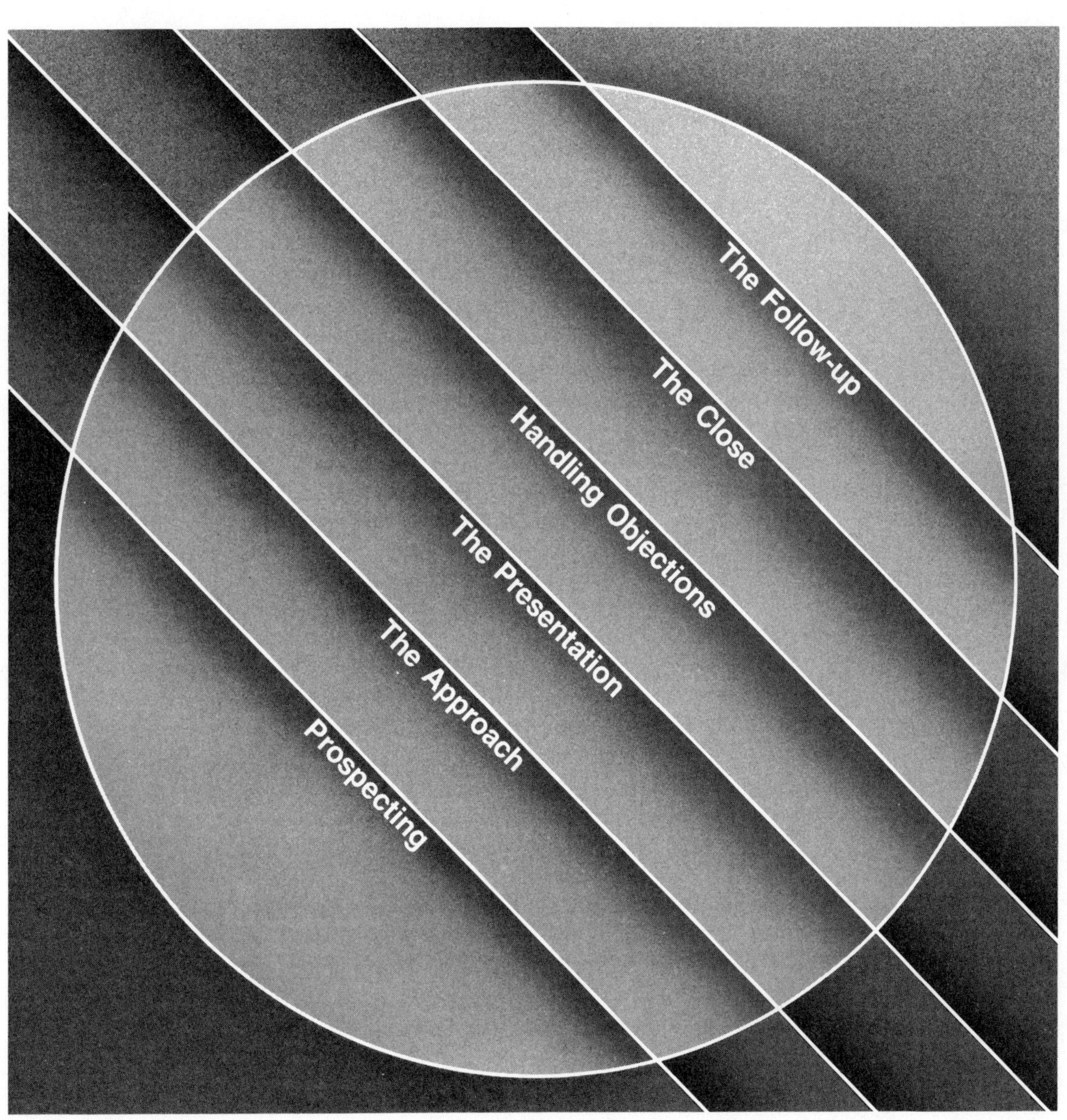

Preparation for Creative Selling

Know Thy Customers, Thy Company, Its Products, and Thy Competition

THE IMPORTANCE OF KNOWING THE FACTS

KNOW THY CUSTOMERS

KNOW THY COMPANY

Company History and Past Performance ■ Policies and Procedures ■ Service Facilities ■ Names of Company Personnel ■ Future Plans of Company ■ Socially Responsible Activities

KNOW THY PRODUCTS

SOURCES OF PRODUCT INFORMATION

KNOW THY COMPETITION

What You Need to Know About Competition ■ Why Information About Competitors Is Important

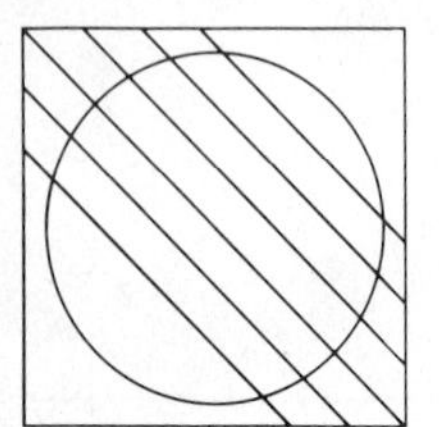

The modern professional salesperson is well informed. A glib tongue and an attractive personality cannot compensate for lack of knowledge.
BERTRAND R. CANFIELD

Here's what you should be able to do after studying this chapter:

1. Show how customer, company, product, and competitor information can facilitate the selling process.
2. Cite the principal types of company information a salesperson should learn.
3. Restate five questions relating to product information that salespeople should be able to answer about their own products.
4. Summarize the major factors relating to competitors' products and activities that can be turned into selling points.
5. Explain why information about competitors is important to salespeople.

If Socrates had been a sales manager, his advice would have gone beyond "know thyself." More than likely, he would have added, "Know thy customer, thy company, its products, and its competition." Today's selling activities allow scant room for the con artist, the hit-and-run type of salesperson, who is here today and gone tomorrow. To his or her customers, the salesperson *is* the company, and, as a result, must be amply prepared with facts *before* seeing customers. Wouldn't you agree that your customers have every right to expect you to be familiar with their organizations, your company, products, and competition?

How does such information facilitate the selling process? What are the facts you should know about your prospects, your company, its products, and its competition? Where can you obtain such information? These are the principal questions we focus on in this chapter.

THE IMPORTANCE OF KNOWING THE FACTS

Before reading the following list, try to develop some reasons of your own on how knowledge can assist you in selling activities. What specific reasons did you develop?

How many of the reasons listed did you come up with? Did you think of any not listed? All the better. The following are some of the major reasons why such knowledge is important:

How can having information help you?

1. When you are well informed, you can more readily develop self-confidence and enthusiasm in your selling activities.
2. If you radiate self-confidence and enthusiasm to your customers, your customers are more likely to have confidence in you.
3. When you have information, you can more easily confront customer objections and deal with competition more effectively.
4. You can improve customer service by knowing how to match your products with your customer's needs.
5. You are likely to be a more loyal employee when you are familiar with your company and products.
6. You are assisting your own self-development, an especially important factor if you want to advance in your company.

Most companies involve sales trainees in activities designed to help them become more familiar with prospective customers, with their own organizations, their products, and their competition. Let's turn to an examination of the various important types of information you should master in order to function effectively as a salesperson.

KNOW THY CUSTOMERS

As we'll observe regularly throughout this text, customers generally don't buy features; they buy goods and services intended to satisfy their needs and solve their problems. Therefore, as a creative and professional salesperson, you must absorb as much useful information as possible about your prospective customers' situations. The topic of understanding about **customer requirements** is so important that it will be covered in greater detail in upcoming chapters on prospecting and approaching customers.

KNOW THY COMPANY

Is the salesperson **actually** *the company?*

Although we have indicated that the salesperson *is* the company to customers, you should realize that, in fact, the salesperson only *represents* the company. Salespeople, for example, do not determine company policies; they carry them out.

Therefore, you have a responsibility to find out about your organization and its policies—this **company knowledge** can be useful in selling. Prospects are generally favorably impressed with representatives who are able to answer questions about their firms in an intelligent manner. In industries where your products are similar to those of competitors, your company's image is frequently a key factor in influencing a prospective customer's decision. You should, therefore, know the strengths and limitations of your firm. You would look rather foolish to a prospect if you accepted an order and later learned that your firm did not have the technology necessary to fill it.

"No one customer is likely to tax your entire knowledge of your firm, but you should attempt to anticipate potential questions about it."

What should you know about your company?

No one customer is likely to tax your entire knowledge of your firm, but you should try to anticipate potential questions about it. You should learn the following kinds of information about your company: its *history and past performance, policies and procedures, service facilities, names of key company personnel, future plans, and activities in the realm of social responsibility.*

Company History and Past Performance

Napoleon once said, "History is a fable agreed upon." Many of your customers might agree and couldn't care less about the **founders** of your organization. Nevertheless, a knowledge of company background information can sometimes assist you in your selling activities.

Where've you been?

A firm often reflects the **company philosophy and values** of its founders. An understanding of this philosophy can give you greater feelings of enthusiasm, loyalty, and concern for your organization. Such knowledge can help make you feel a part of your company rather than an "employed outsider."

There are numerous sources of information on companies. Some firms publish materials regarding their *historical development* (see Figure 6.1). Articles about specific firms and their past histories and performance are regularly printed in publications like *Fortune, Forbes, Business Week, Money, Black Enterprise,* and *The Wall Street Journal.*

"Customers usually prefer to deal with successful, sound companies whose supply of products is likely to be more dependable and stable."

What information about your company's *past performance* do you feel could prove useful as a selling tool? How about such factors as *financial soundness? Productive capabilities? Rank and reputation* in the industry? This information is highly desirable to know, not only as a positive selling point but also to help you overcome certain kinds of objections. For example, assume that a customer accuses your company of having engaged in undesirable business activities. You might draw on your company knowledge and say something like, "Mr. Stein, if we regularly

Company and Product Information

Companies frequently publish booklets designed to enable their own personnel and the public to become more acquainted with their organizations, activities, and products. Reproduced below are sample covers of materials developed by well-known companies. These merely illustrate the wide range of approaches employed by firms to inform others about their operations.

Figure 6.1 Company and Product Information.

engaged in the type of behavior that you mentioned, is it really likely that we would have attained our present position in the industry?" Customers usually prefer to deal with successful, sound companies whose supply of products is likely to be more dependable and stable.

Policies and Procedures

How do you do it?

In order to be an effective salesperson, one in whom your customers have confidence, you must also be familiar with the **policies** and **procedures** established by your organization. For example, you could put yourself in an embarrassing position if you promised a customer something that was outside your area of authority. You should also be acquainted with your company's procedures regarding price, discounts, credit terms, delivery of products, vacation schedules, and any other information likely to be needed during a sales interview.

Service Facilities

Will you do it?

The selling process is seldom completed when customers receive shipments of ordered goods. They must also be satisfied, or they will be unlikely to repeat their purchases. **Service facilities,** available in the event of product malfunction or difficulty, are also highly important to your customers. Prospective customers frequently want to know the extent and location of service facilities. Are replacement parts readily available? Or do they have to be ordered from a firm in another country? How long are replacement parts maintained in stock for discontinued items? These and many other questions regarding service are likely to be asked of sales personnel. Your best bet is to "be prepared," as the old Boy Scout motto goes.

Names of Company Personnel

Who are they?

Sales representatives who isolate themselves from company personnel generally feel less like members of a team. The *other members of your company* are there to back up your sales activities, and knowing their names and functions can prove helpful when problems or unusual circumstances arise. Furthermore, the more you know about your organization, the more confidence your customers are likely to have in you.

Future Plans of Company

Where are you going?

Plans are like road maps—they can guide you along specific paths. An understanding of the *future plans* of your company can help you along your sales paths. As a salesperson, you have the responsibility to find out about any changes planned by your company. Often such changes can serve as key points in your sales presentation. For example, your company might be planning an expansion of its service centers, a factor that could be extremely important to some of your customers. Or perhaps your company plans changes in product design or price—this information could also be significant to your accounts. In short, you should try to be familiar with any change likely to affect or influence your customers and their buying decisions.

Socially Responsible Activities

Do you really care?

Does your company have a policy of **social responsibility?** Is it involved in socially responsible activities, such as environmental or waste prevention programs? Craftsman/Met Press of Seattle previously disposed of its waste and scrap paper by burning it, an activity that contributed to air pollution. Company officials have since switched to a more responsible approach, one involving the recycling of waste paper. Goodwill has been gained at no cost, since revenues received for the scrap paper about equal the costs of the recycling program.

Metropolitan Life Insurance Company has always made available, free of charge, brochures with information on health and hygiene. Naturally, the longer people live, the longer they will pay insurance premiums to insurance companies. However, this factor need not detract from the social usefulness of such efforts.

Some firms have programs designed to assist handicapped workers; others are active in providing counsel to minority-owned businesses.

The point is that knowledge of activities in which your company is involved can frequently provide you with additional selling ammunition while also enhancing the public image of your firm.

KNOW THY PRODUCTS

Most everyone would agree that salespeople should be familiar with the products and services they offer. Disagreement arises, however, as to just how comprehensive such **product knowledge** should be. Some managers, for example, feel that salespeople don't really need extensive knowledge of their product. They argue that a salesperson's principal function is to sell, and that detailed product knowledge merely gets in the way of effective selling.

"Most managers . . . feel that salespeople who appear to have a good understanding of their product will be more highly favored by prospective customers."

How much product knowledge should you have?

Most managers, however, hold a contrary view. They feel that salespeople who appear to have a good understanding of their product will be more highly favored by prospective customers. Of course, a salesperson should guard against spending too much time talking about the technical features of a product; more important is focusing the sales presentation on the *needs* of the prospective buyer.

There may be instances when a sales representative does not have ample technical knowledge of her or his products. Some firms employ technical specialists, sometimes called **sales or marketing engineers,** who can be called upon to assist the salesperson with customers. A suggestion: never fake knowledge that you don't have. Instead, tell your customer that you will find out the information as soon as possible—and do it!

Any product knowledge that enhances your sales presentation can be useful. You are off to a good start if you are prepared to answer the five questions discussed below.

How does your product relate to the specific needs of your customers? Products should relate to customers. As an illustration, let's assume that you sell photographic equipment in a retail outlet. Cameras, like many products, are available in a wide variety of prices and models. Why does your prospective customer want a camera? For professional purposes? For personal enjoyment? A combination of both? An important point is that if you know the *needs* and *motives* of prospective buyers, regardless of what you are selling, then you can more readily determine which item in a line of products best suits their needs.

How might your product resolve some of your customer's problems? Continuing with the camera example, perhaps your customer has had difficulty taking pictures at the proper exposures, and, as a result, has wasted film in the past. A camera with automatic electronic features could be the solution to this problem. Once again, understanding how your product fits the situation of the customer is essential.

What are some of the principal uses and limitations of your product? Does your camera have real-time continuous autofocusing? Does it have average and spot metering with highlight and shadow biasing? Does it have AMPS plug program shift? Are these features important or merely a lot of technical gibberish to your customer? How close can pictures be taken? Is the lens interchangeable? Does it have a locking device to prevent accidental exposure? Will the camera function well in subzero temperatures? Be prepared to answer a variety of questions regarding the operation of any product you sell.

What are the service requirements of the product? Prospective customers may be interested in your product's necessary upkeep. What sort of maintenance or lubrication does your product require? Does it use batteries? How long do they last? Does the camera require special handling of any sort? What does the customer do if service is needed? What sort of guarantees or warranties are included with the product? To avoid embarrassing moments with customers, be certain to know in advance how a product works and what service it may need.

Is the product of too high a quality (and cost) for the needs of the customer? Based on the needs of your customer, would a lower-priced camera of lesser quality suffice? Is your prospect an amateur photographer? If so, would a lower-priced lens with less but satisfactory resolving power serve as well? You can sometimes create goodwill for yourself and your firm by talking a customer out of buying a product that is of greater cost and quality than is needed.

You should readily be able to see from the above discussion that the creative salesperson needs far more than a shoeshine and a smile to function in today's complex and competitive business environment.

SOURCES OF PRODUCT INFORMATION

Where can product information be found?

The motivated salesperson should have little difficulty getting product information since the sources are so numerous. New salespeople acquire much of their product information during company training programs. But a word of caution here: product knowledge can become outdated quickly, so it must be updated regularly. Up-to-date product information can be obtained at company sales meetings, through company correspondence courses, during tours of factories, from company manuals and sales literature, and from consumer publications. Other product information sources often accompany products, as in the form of owner manuals for appliances and stereos or product labels and hangtags on wearing apparel.

Product information can be acquired in unexpected ways, too, as in informal discussions with fellow employees. Even your customers or competitors might inform you of uses for your products that you had overlooked.

KNOW THY COMPETITION

Why should you be familiar with your competitors' products?

Familiarity with your own products is essential, but you also need to be familiar with the products and activities of your competitors. Competition is virtually a way of life for most salespeople. Whether you sell in a highly concentrated industry like aluminum or steel, with few firms, or are involved in an industry like insurance or vacation/business travel, with hundreds of firms, you cannot avoid competition. And since there are acceptable substitutes for the products of nearly every firm, **competitor knowledge** is essential.

"Competition is virtually a way of life for most salespeople. . . . And since there are acceptable substitutes for the products of nearly every firm, a knowledge of competition is essential."

What You Need to Know About Competition

Of course, you cannot know the minute details of every product and every activity of all the companies in your industry. There are, however, certain significant factors about the products and activities of your competitors that can frequently be turned into selling points. Among the more important comparison factors are the following:

What can you add to this list?

1. Distinctive strengths and weaknesses of competing products or services
2. Comparative position of competing firms in relation to sales volume, reputation, financial soundness, and research activities
3. Dependability of competitors in relation to consistent quality control, deliveries, performance, and service
4. Variety of competing lines regarding sizes, colors, and other special characteristics
5. Names and experience of competing salespeople
6. Price and credit policies of competitors
7. Methods of distribution
8. Future plans of competitors

Competitor information may be obtained from any of the following sources:

1. Sales training sessions
2. Sales meetings
3. Newspaper articles
4. Your own customers
5. Company literature and advertising
6. Trade journals
7. Annual reports

Why Information About Competitors Is Important

It should now be clear that there is a lot of information you should have about the products and activities of your competitors. Have you thought about why this information is so important?

Self-confidence, improved image, and better sales presentations

As with most knowledge, an understanding of the competition can help build *self-confidence* and thus help *improve your image* in the eyes of customers. In addition, you should be able to develop *better sales presentations* since you'll be able to point out to your customers the outstanding features inherent in your products but lacking in those of your competitors.

More skillful handling of objections

Furthermore, armed with relevant information about competitors, you should be able to *handle objections more skillfully.* For example, your customers may be quite familiar with the products of competing firms in your industry, but if you aren't, you could find yourself at a disadvantage during sales presentations. Some customers might even try to use another company to your disadvantage by saying that its products, prices, or credit terms are superior to yours, when in reality they are not. As a result, familiarity with your competition is essential to effective selling.

Enables product comparisons.

Finally, you may discover that your customers will frequently expect you to be able to make a **product comparison.** If you can supply the information, prospective customers may not bother to "shop around" on their own. An important point is to be honest in your comparisons or you are likely to lose the confidence of your customers. It should also be stressed again that you should never criticize your competitors since such actions may be insulting if your prospective customer uses and likes their products. A more desirable approach is to stress the advantages and benefits of your own company and products. In selling, a positive approach is usually far more effective than a negative one.

SUMMARY

To be an effective salesperson, you should develop reasonable familiarity with your customers, your company, your products, and the competition. Adequate knowledge in these areas is not only expected by customers but also helps you develop greater self-assurance and enthusiasm. In general, you will be able to perform your sales activities far more effectively when you are an informed salesperson.

Among the essential types of company information you should know are the history and past performance of your firm, its policies and procedures, the names of key company personnel, its service facilities, its future plans, and its activities in the area of social responsibility.

Product information is also important for you to know. More important than a highly technical knowledge of every facet of a product is an understanding of how it relates to the specific needs and problems of the customer.

You are also expected to be familiar with your competition. Such information builds self-confidence and helps in developing better sales presentations and responses to objections. And finally, knowledgeable salespeople are able to provide their customers with more complete information about the products that interest them.

KEY TERMS

customer requirements
company knowledge
founders
company philosophy and values
policies
procedures
service facilities
social responsibility
product knowledge
sales/marketing engineers
competitor knowledge
product comparison

QUESTIONS

1. Would you be at a disadvantage if you were hired as a salesperson by a firm that provided no sales training for new employees? Explain your position.
2. Assume that you are involved with training an employee who is new to the sales field. What persuasive reasons might you offer the person as to the importance of learning relevant information about the company, its products, and its competition?
3. Evaluate the following statement: "You can't *know* too much about your product; just be careful not to *say* too much about it."
4. How might an understanding of your company's history aid you in selling?
5. In what ways can information about your company's activities in the area of social responsibility be used as a selling point?
6. Assume that you sell portable laptop computers for an electronics firm. What do you feel you should know about your products in order to sell them effectively?
7. Why is an awareness of your competitors' products and activities so essential?

8. Do you feel that in addition to the topics discussed in the chapter, a salesperson should also be familiar with general and local business conditions, interest rates, availability of bank credit, and trends in consumer tastes? Explain.

APPLICATIONS

6.1 THE INQUISITIVE FIELD ENGINEER

Jim Johnson, an energetic field engineer with the Parameter Electron Company, a medium-sized electronics firm, was recently assigned to the Santa Clara territory. Located in the heart of Jim's territory was one of his chief competitors, the Push-Pull Generation Company.

About three weeks after Jim was assigned to the territory, he decided to call on Push-Pull and told the receptionist that he would like to see one of their field engineers. Shortly thereafter, Jim met Diane Darby, a field engineer for Push-Pull. Jim introduced himself, told Diane that he was a field engineer for Parameter, and asked her if she would like to go out for a cup of coffee and some conversation. Diane said that today wasn't a good day for leaving the office but invited Jim into her work area.

Jim asked Diane a number of open-ended questions and was amazed at how receptive she was. Within a matter of 25 minutes, Jim had learned the extent of Diane's territory as well as the names of her major accounts and was given the specification sheets for three of Push-Pull's new high-frequency oscilloscopes.

Jim then thanked Diane for the conversation and information and departed.

Questions

1. Do you feel that Jim acted unethically in probing Push-Pull for information that could assist him in his own territory? Explain.
2. What are some other ways of engaging in field intelligence (uncovering competitive marketing information)?
3. Do you feel that Diane did the right thing in revealing so much information to Jim about Push-Pull's activities and products?

6.2 LET'S GET IT BACK!

You represent an electronics firm whose products have traditionally been among the best in the industry. Your firm, in fact, pioneered many of the current developments. Recently, however, your company has begun to lose its hold on the marketplace. A new company offers a similar product for a comparable price and has begun to make a significant penetration into your market share.

Questions

1. What are some things that you might do to help regain your previous share of the market?
2. Do you feel that you should "knock" the new firm making inroads into your market? Explain.

6.3 THE CURIOUS PROSPECT

Assume that you have called on Mr. Edward Janco, an executive of the Heedlock Security Systems Company. Heedlock has never purchased your firm's products in the past. On your present visit Mr. Janco says to you, "I'm really quite impressed with what I've been hearing about your company lately, especially since it developed that new capillarity process last year. As a matter of fact, I've been seriously contemplating the purchase of some stock in your company. But before I contact my securities broker, could you give me some background information on your firm?"

Project

Choose a well-known firm with facilities in your community. Call on one of its company representatives—preferably someone in the public relations department—and request specific information that you feel would be of interest to Mr. Janco. Then develop an informational presentation that could be delivered to him.

7 Communicating with Customers

There's More to Communication Than Meets the Ear

THE NATURE OF EFFECTIVE COMMUNICATION
What Is Communication? ■ A Two-Way Process

TYPES OF COMMUNICATION

SAYING IT WITH WORDS—VERBAL COMMUNICATION
Words (and People!) Have Many Meanings

SPOKEN VERSUS WRITTEN COMMUNICATION
Spoken Communication ■ Written Communication ■ Some Tips on Improving Written Communications

SHHHHH!—NONVERBAL FORMS OF COMMUNICATION
Let's Face It—Bodies Speak! ■ Kind of Symbolic ■ The Sounds of Silence ■ Voicing Your Feelings ■ You Appeared, But How's Your Appearance? ■ I'm Sorry I'm Late ■ Touching—Handshakes and Hugs Communicate ■ A Few Words of Caution About the Nonverbal

MINIMIZING COMMUNICATION BREAKDOWNS
Use Face-to-Face Communication Where Possible ■ Develop Effective Listening Habits ■ Don't Be Overeager to Respond ■ Follow Through on Promises—Credibility ■ Choose Effective Times for Communication ■ Eschew Obfuscation—That Is, Avoid Wordiness

THE IMPORTANCE OF LISTENING

DEVELOPING ACTIVE LISTENING SKILLS
Listening Responses ■ Phrasing Questions ■ Listening Takes Practice

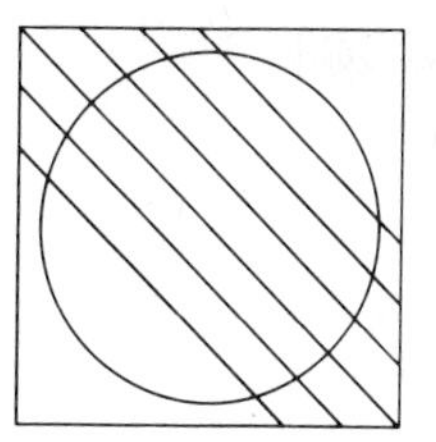

God gave us two ears and only one mouth. In view of the way we use these, it is probably a very good thing that this is not reversed.
CICERO

Here's what you should be able to do after studying this chapter:

1. Identify the essential ingredients of effective communication.
2. Describe the nature of verbal and nonverbal communication.
3. Contrast spoken with written communication.
4. Apply the precautions and approaches useful for minimizing communication breakdowns.
5. Cite the benefits of active listening habits.
6. Recognize the difficulties that may arise when salespeople don listening "earmuffs."
7. Employ five types of listening responses.
8. Contrast open with closed and alternate-choice questions.

Imagine being in a group situation and playing the silly little game of whispering a phrase or sentence into the ear of the person beside you, who then passes the message on to the next person, and so on, until the message has been transmitted to everyone in the room. The results could be startling. The message would probably be completely unrecognizable by the time it returned to you.

Such an exercise helps to illustrate an important concept: the act of communicating can take place in a variety of situations, but for communication to be *effective,* there must be *understanding.* One of the major causes of problems between salespeople and their customers is the lack of effective communication. The development of communication skills is essential to you as a salesperson if you are to maximize your results with prospects and customers.

In this chapter we consider some of the major facets of communication. In addition, we explore some of the significant aspects of verbal and nonverbal communication. We also examine some of the principal precautions and approaches that can aid in minimizing communication breakdowns. We conclude with some important concepts designed to improve the listening habits of individuals in the selling field.

THE NATURE OF EFFECTIVE COMMUNICATION

Have you ever thought about all of the various types of communication a salesperson has to compete with? Prospective customers are constantly bombarded by them during their daily activities. For example, in the San Francisco–Oakland Bay Area of California, television sets can receive at least 23 UHF and VHF TV channels (and up to 42 with cable TV), and the San Francisco newspapers list 72 AM and FM stations. All of these are technically classified as forms of communication.

"Communication, therefore, can be defined as a two-way process resulting in the transmission of information and understanding between individuals."

However, even when all of its power is on and an announcer is glibly chatting, a radio station isn't necessarily communicating. What is necessary besides power and station personnel? You may say, "This is obvious—the radio receiver must be tuned in to the broadcast." But being tuned in is still not enough. If communication is to be effective, one more ingredient is essential: an *understanding of the announcer's message.*

What Is Communication?

What are the essential ingredients for effective communication?

So, whether we are talking about a radio station broadcasting or about a sales representative talking to a customer, *three ingredients are essential* if effective communication is to take place:

1. A sender
2. A receiver (or listener)
3. An understood message

Communication, therefore, can be defined as *a two-way process resulting in the transmission of information and understanding between individuals.* If there is no understanding, or if there is a misunderstanding, the ideas have not been effectively communicated.

A Two-Way Process

Who's responsible for good communication?

Who has the responsibility for ensuring that effective communication takes place? Both the *sender* of the message and his or her *listener* share the responsibility. On the one side, the listener has to be tuned in to the message, as in the case of the radio station, before effective communication results. On the other, the sender has to aim the message—its tone, vocabulary, and so on—at the particular listener.

As a communicator, you have a considerable advantage over the broadcasting medium. You can, for example, discover immediately whether the receiver (your prospective customer) is tuned in. How? By attempting to get **feedback** from him or her. By asking certain questions, you can discover whether the receiver actually understood your message. If you are on the receiving end of the communication, you can restate what the speaker said and in this way determine whether you understood the message. Restating a customer's complaint will often help reduce possible misunderstandings about the particular problem.

Unfortunately, far too many salespeople are involved in **one-way communication;** they tend to dominate the sales interview and, as a result, frequently miss significant buying signals the prospect may be sending. To gain a real understanding of the needs and problems of customers, you must be involved in **two-way communication,** and this, of course, is a reciprocal process.

In a sense, both you and your customers are simultaneously *producers* (senders) and *consumers* (receivers) of communication. For example, assume that you are in the process of explaining a fairly complicated feature of a product to a customer whose facial expression suddenly turns confused. You were producing and sending to your customer a message about the product, but you were also consuming and receiving a message from your customer that could serve as a guide to your next message. Figure 7.1 graphically illustrates the two-way nature of communication.

TYPES OF COMMUNICATION

No one is predestined by birth to be an effective communicator. Newborn babies, it could be argued, certainly appear to arrive on the domestic scene with certain

Figure 7.1 Communication Is a Two-Way Process.

innate communication skills. At a typical 2 A.M. feeding, a tiny cherub leaves little doubt in its parents' minds about its message: "Waaah! Waaah! I'm famished! I want my milk—and I want it *now!*" This is a form of communication that we've already mentioned—the *one-way variety*—not quite the type recommended for the salesperson who is concerned with communicating effectively with customers.

We communicate with customers (or anyone, for that matter) in two different ways, *verbal* and *nonverbal.* **Verbal communication** involves symbols called words, not only those we use in face-to-face and telephone conversations but also those that appear in print. Even the sign language used by some people with hearing impairments is based on word symbols.

"A customer . . . may say one thing, such as 'I'm not really interested,' but his or her body language may indicate just the opposite feeling."

The sending of messages *without words,* or **nonverbal communication,** is just as important to understand—perhaps even more so—than verbal communication. A customer, for example, may say one thing, such as "I'm not really interested," but his or her body language may indicate just the opposite feeling. In the upcoming sections, we'll explore some of the major characteristics of verbal and nonverbal communication that affect you and your sales activities.

SAYING IT WITH WORDS—VERBAL COMMUNICATION

Although we don't typically *use* all the words we know in the course of conversation, you are likely to *hear* as many as 100,000 words during one of your usual days of fulfilling your responsibilities as a salesperson. Much of your daily communication is transmitted by word symbols. If you as a salesperson are to be understood, it would appear logical that you have to understand the meaning of words. We all know where we can look for the "correct" meaning of words: the dictionary, right? Wrong!! Most lexicographers (dictionary makers) contend that the book they've helped to prepare is merely a history book, one that shows how some words have been used at particular times and in certain contexts. You can probably think of numerous words used regularly in conversation that—although they are understood—are not in the dictionary.

Look it up?

Words (and People!) Have Many Meanings

Assume that you represent a fabric manufacturer and are making a sales presentation to a prospect whose native language is not English—a person who speaks English only as a second language. Let's also assume that during the presentation you enthusiastically explain that your fabrics are of high quality and that their colors are fast.

He: I haven't eaten anything for five minutes.
She: Wow, you're a fast faster!

Will your prospect necessarily understand what you mean by a *fast color?* Maybe, or maybe not. Do you realize how many meanings can be applied to the word *fast?* The word can imply motion, as in the case of a fast runner; or lack of motion, as in a fast color or in "She stands fast." This same word can also relate to eating habits, as in the case of a person who fasts or abstains from eating food. A person might even say, "He was too fast on the first date." A complete dictionary will offer at least 50 different meanings of the word *fast.* The same can be said for such words as *wind, wing, run, lie, air,* and many others. Is there any wonder misunderstandings sometimes develop between salespeople and their accounts? Since the true meaning of words is not always obvious, how can we determine it?

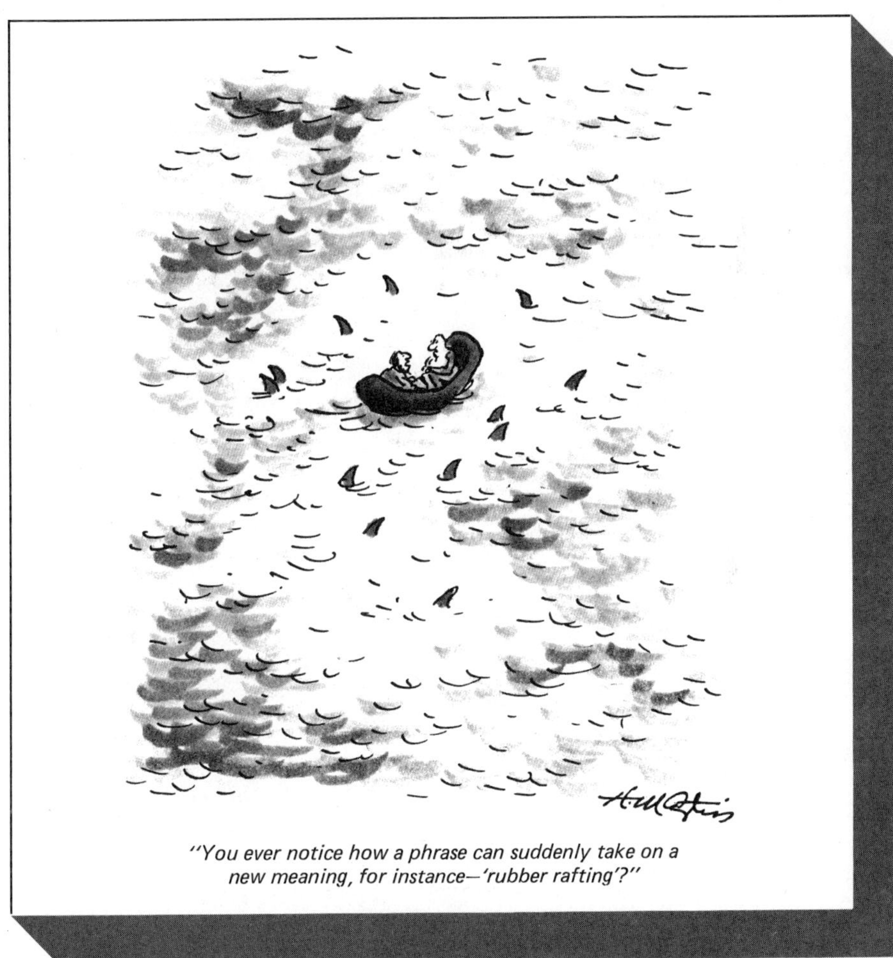

"You ever notice how a phrase can suddenly take on a new meaning, for instance—'rubber rafting'?"

Reprinted with permission from *Sales & Marketing Management* magazine; © 1985.

"Instead of wondering what the words in a message mean, a better approach is to wonder what the speaker means."

Where is the true meaning of a word?

First, you have to get it out of your head that words have inherent meaning. A word is not the thing it represents; a word is merely a symbol that represents different things to different people. The true meaning of a word is not in the word itself or in the way the listener interprets it but in the intention of the *sender.* There are believed to be about 600,000 words in the English language. An educated adult in daily conversation uses about 2,000, of which the 500 most commonly used have 14,000 dictionary definitions. Do you really think that you or your prospective customer can guess the right meaning every time? Of course not. If you are in doubt as to the meaning of a customer's words, the only way to be certain is to *ask what he or she means.* Instead of wondering what the *words* in a message mean, a better approach is to wonder what the *speaker* means. A corny story might help to illustrate this point: "Now," said the village blacksmith to the apprentice, "I'll take this iron out of the fire, lay it on the anvil, and when I nod my head, you hit it." The apprentice did so, and now he's the village blacksmith!

How can communication failures be lessened?

Two rules that can help lessen the chance of communication failure between you and others are (1) *never assume that everyone knows what you are talking about* and (2) *never assume that you know what others are talking about without first asking questions to make certain.* The blacksmith erroneously made the first assumption, and the imperceptive apprentice made the second!

SPOKEN VERSUS WRITTEN COMMUNICATION

Which are better for transmitting messages effectively—*spoken* or *written* forms of communication? Actually, both have their advantages and disadvantages, and salespeople generally have to use both types often. Let's look at them briefly.

Spoken Communication

I see *what you mean.*

One of the major advantages of spoken communication over written is that it enables you to receive *instant feedback,* whereas feedback may be delayed or even nonexistent with written communication. In face-to-face communication, for example, you can *observe* at a glance how your customer is responding to your message and thus alter your presentation if necessary. You can also *ask questions* to make certain that you've been understood or that you understand the other person.

"One of the major advantages of oral communication over written is that it enables you to receive instant feedback. . . ."

Another potential advantage of communicating orally is *speed.* With face-to-face or even telephone communication, you can usually transmit your ideas directly to others without having to take the time to write a memo, letter, or report. However, the tendency to "shoot the breeze" during oral transactions sometimes offsets the potential saving in time. And face-to-face communication with customers may also involve costs of transportation and lodging, which can be rather expensive these days.

Breeze shooting kills time.

Written Communication

Write on!

Written communication has an important place in organizations. One of its principal advantages is that it generates a *permanent record or reference.* Further, written communication typically is given *more thought* than oral communication. Written communication also serves as *evidence* of the transmitted message when proof is important.

Written communication isn't without its disadvantages. Many salespeople haven't developed the ability to write clearly and concisely. Instead, they tend to write in an *excessively formal, stiff style* rather than in easily read conversational tones. Further, written communication often has to be *followed up* with oral clarification. Another disadvantage is *cost.* Preparation can make a simple letter cost a good deal, sometimes more than it's really worth.

Some Tips on Improving Written Communications

You might find yourself writing letters or memos for a variety of purposes. Writing thank-you letters, for example, should be a routine part of your activities. You may also have to write occasional "bad news messages," as in reply to a customer who has made a request that you can't fulfill. Both types of letters will be covered in a later chapter on maintaining the goodwill of customers.

Another type of correspondence that you may have to deal with is the sales letter to prospective customers. This topic will also be covered in a later chapter that discusses the use of direct mail in selling.

Have you learned your CCCCs?

Virtually any letter can be improved by applying what we'll term "the four C's of letter writing." The four C's stand for Complete, Concise, Correct, and Conversational. Use the checklist in Figure 7.2 to help you determine whether your letters are likely to accomplish what you want them to.

"The creative salesperson today recognizes that much more goes into any sales interview than verbal symbols—that is, words."

SHHHHH!—NONVERBAL FORMS OF COMMUNICATION

Salespeople function in a world of words. You have probably noticed, however, that a great deal of communication can take place *without* words. You might even be surprised to learn of the research results of psychologist Albert Mehrabian. His

COMPLETE
Have you provided all the necessary facts?
Have you answered all of the customer's questions?

CONCISE
Have you avoided unnecessarily long and complicated words?
Have you said what you wanted in one page or less?
Are your paragraphs short and easy to read?
Have you avoided "hiding" important information, such as *where, when,* and at *what time* a meeting will be held?

CORRECT
Have you checked your correspondence for accuracy?
Are your commitments in agreement with company policy?
Have you checked your grammar, spelling, and punctuation?
Have you eliminated strikeovers and sloppy corrections?

CONVERSATIONAL
Have you written in a friendly, receptive manner?
Will your writing style evoke the response you want?
Have you avoided excessively complicated and flowery phrases?
Have you avoided words and expressions that will antagonize your reader?

Figure 7.2 The Four C's of Letter Writing.

I **see** *what you mean.*

studies suggest that feelings are communicated considerably less by the words a person uses than by certain nonverbal means. Mehrabian believes that the words in a given communication carry less than 10 percent of the meaning, while the speaker's voice and facial expressions carry most of the rest. The creative salesperson today recognizes that much more goes into any sales interview than mere verbal symbols—that is, words. Let's now briefly examine some of the more common nonverbal forms of communication.

Let's Face It—Bodies Speak!

Every **body** *speaks a language.*

"Your lips tell me no no, but there's yes yes in your eyes," are the insightful words of a "golden oldie" of the distant musical past. These lyrics significantly relate to your activities as a salesperson. Customers don't always say precisely what they mean. They may tell you, for example, that a purchase is out of the question—that they can't afford the product. However, their nonverbal expressions, the message of their eyes and facial muscles or the motions they make (or sometimes don't make) with their bodies may communicate a different meaning. **Body language,** therefore, is another important area for salespeople to understand.

The things people say with their bodies, either while sitting, standing, or walking, can often mean a lot to the observant salesperson. For example, the way your prospect is sitting may tell you whether he or she is really concerned with your sales message. These cues can suggest that it is time for you to provide further explanation, to be more convincing, or to attempt to close the sale.

The following is a list of some of the more important types of body language that salespeople should recognize:

1. Prospects *leaning forward intently, arms extended, eyes fixed on the salesperson or products*—typically a strong indication of an interest in buying.
2. Prospects *tapping their feet or fingers*—possibly an indication of impatience with, or being disturbed by, the salesperson.
3. *Folded arms*—often an indication of defensiveness or lack of receptiveness toward the sales message.
4. *Open arms*—typically an indication of receptiveness toward the sales message.
5. Sitting with *legs crossed* and *foot kicking*—possibly indicating boredom.
6. *Stooped shoulders*—possibly an indication that something is troubling the prospect.
7. *Erect posture*—often an indication of happiness and satisfaction.
8. *Cocked head*—an indication of strong prospect interest, possibly suggesting that the salesperson attempt to close.
9. *Resting chin on hand, elbow on desk*—frequently an indication of boredom and lack of interest.
10. *Stroking chin* or *hand on cheek*—possibly indicating prospect going through the purchase decision process.

Uh, huh. . . . I mean, huh?

Of course you should guard against becoming excessively preoccupied with body-language messages, since it is quite easy to misinterpret another person's motions. For example, if a customer nods his or her head, it would seem to indicate that listening and understanding are taking place. In reality, all it may mean is that the person hears your message but doesn't want to appear stupid by asking you what you mean.

Kind of Symbolic

How does space communicate?

Some types of **nonverbal symbols** can communicate special messages. For example, the use of *space* is a factor that can "say" something to you. In office situations, space may tell us something about the *patterns of authority* among the various employees. If you observe two purchasing managers, one with office space twice as large as the other, you might safely assume something about their relative authority within the organization.

"Any items that people perceive as significant can serve as symbols of status among organizational members."

What does height say?

Height also tends to "speak" to us. An executive suite is seldom found in the basement of an office building. In our culture, *higher* is assumed to be better than *lower.* Have you ever heard of a "bottom-notch" salesperson or of a person aspiring to "descend" the ladder of success?

What is a symbol of your status?

Status symbols are visible indicators of rank within an organization. Items that might appear trivial to an outsider can become important influences on the self-image of employees, such things, for example, as a telephone on or a wastebasket near an employee's desk. Some executives would rather have a rug on their office floors than a raise in pay. Any items that people perceive as significant can serve as symbols of status within organizations.

The Sounds of Silence

Assume that you are a conscientious salesperson, always cordial to the various employees you see in your customers' office. You seldom forget to say hello to anyone. However, one morning you wake with pressing problems on your mind, problems that demand your immediate thought and attention. Later, as you pass the receptionist in the office of one of your best customers, your mind is a million light years away and you hardly notice him. Have you attempted to communicate anything to the receptionist? No, not consciously; yet you might have communicated something. He may start wondering, "What's with the hotshot sales rep today? How come he didn't say 'Good morning' to me?"

How can you communicate through inaction?

Nonverbal communication might also include the failure to show appreciation to a customer for his or her time during a sales presentation. The customer might feel that the lack of a courteous "thank you" might be an indication that you don't appreciate the order you've received.

Voicing Your Feelings

Your voice is an important element of any sales presentation. Much of what your listeners interpret comes from the sound of your voice. In fact, that's the main thing a customer interprets when you use the telephone, and it is a critical part of any face-to-face communication.

Tone, volume, pitch, rate, and inflection all significantly influence whether you come across to customers in a sincere and enthusiastic manner or in a way that creates suspicion. Your voice tends to reflect your interest (or disinterest) in the customer's needs and problems.

Do you know how your voice comes across?

Typically, we aren't aware of the way our own voices sound to others. You can gain some personal insights by practicing your sales messages on a tape or video recorder—preferably by role playing with another person. Such activity can help you determine what voice changes you should attempt to make.

For example, as you listen to playbacks of your own voice, does it seem too loud and overpowering? Or is it too soft and difficult to hear and understand? Do you tend to speak in a dull monotone, or do you use adequate inflection and convey enthusiasm by your style of delivery? Attempting to sell a customer is far more difficult when you don't appear to be sold yourself. Is your rate of speech either too fast or too slow? Try to avoid coming across as a "fast-talking peddler," the type who tends to be distrusted. Too slow a rate of speech, on the other hand, tends to make it more difficult to hold the listener's attention. With an understanding of your existing strengths and weaknesses and by regularly practicing better techniques, you should be able to improve your vocal skills substantially.

You Appeared, But How's Your Appearance?

What do you usually notice first when you receive a letter in the mail? The appearance of the envelope? Probably so. If you were a purchasing agent, what do you think would usually be the first thing you'd notice when salespeople called on you? Undoubtedly their appearance and approach. Just as a carelessly typed envelope might cause you to form certain unfavorable impressions of the sender, so a slovenly appearance or approach by a salesperson might cause you to develop unfavorable attitudes toward him or her.

Some appearance guidelines seem to be plain *common sense.* However, common sense appears not to be as "common" as we'd like in many instances. Here are a few commonsense suggestions about appearance: Avoid wearing wrinkled, stained, or flashy clothing and jewelry. Keep your fingernails and hair groomed. Avoid the use of heavy cosmetics or colognes and deodorants with a lingering and noticeable afterscent. Guard against objectionable bad breath by brushing and flossing your teeth regularly to remove odor-causing particles. A sugar-free mint before making a sales call can be helpful when a toothbrush isn't handy.

A mint can really be a life-saver!

A person's appearance can be quite a controversial topic. "Why should society dictate to me how I should look or what I should wear?" may be a reasonable question. Many of your customers might even be completely unconcerned about the quantity of hair on your face or head (if you're a man) or the amount of makeup or the size of your earrings (if you're a woman). Realistically, however, there are certain standards of appearance in most industries and geographic regions that, when not followed, can affect your sales results negatively. Since your earnings and standard of living usually relate to your sales record, isn't it likely to be to your own personal advantage to learn and practice those standards of dress and grooming considered to be generally acceptable in your sales area?

Why create unnecessary obstacles?

I'm Sorry I'm Late

Don't be late for an important date!

Your attitude toward time also tends to communicate messages to your customers. Concerned salespeople, especially those who are well organized, seldom arrive late for appointments. Those who do arrive late often get off to a bad start with their customers. Prospective buyers, expecting you to arrive at specific times, will sometimes postpone other projects in anticipation of your visit. Any time spent waiting for you is wasted time for them—they could have been doing other things. To avoid this problem, plan to arrive at least ten minutes before an appointment; this allows time for possible delays such as those caused by traffic congestion. A struggle through highway traffic when you are already late for an appointment can create additional tensions and frustrations that can only detract from your sales delivery. Those who try to get to appointments precisely on time tend to be late since they often don't allow for those omnipresent "surprise factors."

"Those who try to get to appointments precisely on time tend to be late, since they often don't allow for those omnipresent 'surprise factors.' "

Touching—Handshakes and Hugs Communicate

Shake it, but don't break it!

We also send nonverbal messages when we touch each other. For example, handshakes are another way of communicating nonverbally. Americans are sometimes accused of being too ready to make snap judgments. Frequently, one hears the statement, "That person shakes hands like a fish." However, if you travel to different parts of the world, you will quickly discover that not all of the world's citizens shake hands like your fellow Americans. Nor do all Americans shake hands in an identical fashion. A point to remember is that some people will make judgments based on your handshake, which to them communicates something.

Don't touch me!

Other standards of touching also vary among cultures. For example, some American business people are embarrassed, and even shocked, while doing business with people from some Mediterranean cultures where "bear-hugging" is a common greeting practice. A Greek business person, for example, might feel offended by the lack of a warm hug by an American counterpart.

A Few Words of Caution About the Nonverbal

Could contact lenses be misinterpreted as the "look of love"?

As we know, there are numerous misunderstandings between people even if they speak a common language, such as American English. Remember that there can also be misunderstandings in the area of nonverbal communication. For example, have you ever had an experience whereby you felt that you were actually smiling at someone who then asked, "What's wrong? What did *I* do?" At times people will perceive what they are set to see regardless of what you might have intended them to see.

MINIMIZING COMMUNICATION BREAKDOWNS

Your sales messages are competing with literally hundreds of other types of communication for the mental attention of your prospects and customers. Imagine how many salespeople in your field alone want to present their messages to your accounts. In addition, salespeople in other fields, outdoor advertising posters, neon signs, theater marquees, company interoffice memos, and many others are all vying mightily for the attention of your customers. The competition for your messages, therefore, is gigantic.

Unfortunately, the general public is bombarded with such tremendous volumes of communication that they often resort to selective perception; that is, they hear or see the information they are set to hear or see and tune out most of the rest. Any person who has regularly attempted to convey information to others recognizes how difficult the process is. In most groups there seem to be some individuals who fail to get "the word." As a salesperson, you will find it essential to make sure that your messages are received and understood by your audience. Consequently, there are certain precautions and approaches you should take to minimize communication breakdowns. Among them are the following:

1. Use face-to-face communication.
2. Develop effective listening habits.
3. Don't be overeager to respond.
4. Don't create credibility gaps.
5. Choose effective times for communication.
6. Avoid wordiness.

Let's now examine each of these factors separately. (Also see Table 7.1, "Ten Commandments of Effective Communication.")

Use Face-to-Face Communication Where Possible

Why is face-to-face communication more effective than written communication?

Face-to-face communication, as we've already learned, is felt to be more effective than written communication because it enables the sender to receive immediate feedback and know whether understanding has taken place. The impersonal characteristics of a memo or letter can easily be misunderstood, especially when information of a negative nature is being conveyed.

While employed as a sales representative for an office equipment company, a person we'll call Victor Vendor discovered that *personal meetings* with his customers were more effective than impersonal written communications in resolving problems

TABLE 7.1 Ten Commandments of Effective Communication.[a]

1. Think with your brain before speaking with your mouth.
2. Know what you want to say and why you want to say it before you actually say it.
3. Adapt what you want to say to your present audience and situation.
4. Remember that the way you say something—inflection, choice of words, etc.—is as significant as what you actually say.
5. Realize that there's more to communication than meets the ear; your body also says something with facial expressions and gestures.
6. Say it with your listener's needs in mind, and the message is more likely to be remembered.
7. Get some feedback from your listener to make sure the message is understood and accepted.
8. Think in terms of the long-run effect of the message on your audience and organization.
9. Don't say it if you don't mean it; back up your words with some action.
10. Learn to be a good listener.

[a]Very loosely adapted from the American Management Associations' "Ten Commandments of Good Communication."

or conflicts that had developed. By *asking certain questions* and by *listening empathetically,* Vic regularly discovered that the problems and misunderstandings tended to diminish.

Develop Effective Listening Habits

Tense up!

Listening is anything but a passive activity. A relaxed listener is usually not an effective one. To be able to grasp what your customer is saying, you need some physical tension. Leaning your chin on your fist or routinely nodding your head while staring at your customer may make you appear to be attentive. Usually, however, a leaner-nodder's mind is miles away from the subject matter. Related to being an effective listener is the skill of asking questions. We'll look at more on the subject of listening, along with how to ask questions, in the concluding section of this chapter.

"A relaxed listener is usually not an effective one."

Don't Be Overeager to Respond

How do you feel about other people cutting off your sentences half way through? You probably don't like it, do you? Yet sometimes we do the same thing with others unthinkingly. We sometimes are overeager to respond to what the other person is saying. Related to being an effective listener is being a patient listener.

"I know that!"

Why do we sometimes appear to be overanxious to respond? It might be an ego problem in some instances. We may feel the need to be able to indicate to the other person that we already know whatever they are telling us, sort of a childlike, "I know that" response. We seem to need to make the speaker aware we are informed, not ignorant.

"I gotta get movin' on!"

Another reason for many salespeople's inclination to interrupt is caused by impatience. Salespeople are often high-achieving individuals who may feel long on work and short on time. Such characteristics tend to cause a preoccupation to move on to something else and not focus adequately on the present, which can create substantial barriers to effective communication with customers.

Try your best to convince yourself that hearing the speaker without interruptions is likely to pay dividends to you. Prospective customers will feel that you are sincerely interested in them and their needs. And you will learn far more about your customers' needs and attitudes by listening to what they have to say.

Follow Through on Promises—Credibility

One of the worst developments salespeople can encounter is the loss of their customers' faith. To prevent your customers from distrusting your communications, remember that *words do not substitute for action.*

"To prevent your customers from distrusting your communications, remember that words do not substitute for action."

Assume, for example, that one of your customers, Ms. Mary Anne Earnest, complains to you about the unordered goods that often accompany ordered items in her shipments. If you merely promise to take the problem to those responsible in your company but fail to do anything about it, you are likely to discover that Ms. Earnest will tend to disbelieve many of your promises in the future.

How might you lose your customer's faith in you?

Some salespeople seem to feel that a simple statement such as "I'll look into that problem" will placate their accounts. However, you should be aware that people frequently remember the promises you've made. The chasm of disbelief will widen with each failure on your part to deliver as promised. United Technologies offers some sound advice on the topic of "promises" in one of its public service advertisements (see Figure 7.3).

Choose Effective Times for Communication

When is the best time to convey important communications?

Optimum timing is as important as the choice of words in many situations, whether you are talking to your family, friends, superiors, subordinates, or customers. The best time to convey important communications is when your message is competing the least with other situations affecting the listener. A sales message is most likely to be considered and listened to when it appeals to your customer's buying needs and motives and does so at a time when these are uppermost in his or her mind.

Eschew Obfuscation—That Is, Avoid Wordiness

Does the use of a large vocabulary always make a favorable impression?

"I can readily comprehend your consternation, Mr. Harcourt. Although the enigmas of the recent counterproductive economic vicissitudes have caused explicit deleterious ramifications concerning our then-current financial position, especially as respects our liquidity status, it is with magnanimous profundity that I now can ecstatically and emphatically report to you, and anyone else with the most infinitesimal degree of interest, that conditions for the totality of our corporate enterprises have been copiously ameliorated." How would you react if somebody said that to you? Could you easily figure out what the person was trying to say? Couldn't it have been said more clearly with a simple "You needn't worry, Mr. Harcourt, our financial position has greatly improved since the recent recession"? The example is, of course, considerably exaggerated in order to make a point. But far too frequently both written and oral communications are prepared by individuals who seem unconcerned about clarity and understanding.

Say it with a K.I.S.S.?

A sales manager with a large insurance company once said that he believed all communications should be delivered with a K.I.S.S., which, he pointed out, means "*K*eep *I*t *S*imple, *S*tupid." Some people prefer the more tactful "*K*eep *I*t *S*hort and *S*imple." His approach has become known as the **K.I.S.S. concept.** Perhaps you should regularly ask yourself, "What is the major objective of any communication I want to make to others?" Since communication is not really effective unless there

Don't Promise What You Can't Deliver

"I'll have
your parts
in two weeks."
Four weeks later
the parts arrive.
"I'll put it
in your hand the
minute you walk
in the door."
But all you get
when you walk in
is a handshake.
"Dinner will be
at 6:00."
But as you dip
your spoon in the soup,
the clock
strikes 7:45.
"The doctor
will see you
in five minutes."
35 minutes later
you're greeted cheerfully:
"And how are we today?"
Avoid a lot of grief and
inconvenience for the
people you deal with.
Think before you
announce how long
something will take—
and then
deliver what you
promised.
On time.

Figure 7.3 A United Technologies Reprint from *The Wall Street Journal.*

is understanding (which should be a major goal of any communication), deliver your messages with a "kiss." Do not overcomplicate them. If there were a fire in your office, you probably wouldn't exclaim, "It is mandatory that we attempt to extinguish the portentous pyrogenation." You would be understood much more readily if you merely shouted, "Let's put out the fire!"

THE IMPORTANCE OF LISTENING

Listening uncovers needs and attitudes.

Most stereotypes of salespeople picture them as glib conversationalists, but few show them as good listeners. Yet many salespeople have learned that active listening is an essential skill, especially for discovering the needs and attitudes of prospective customers.

Salespeople are often under the pressures of time and quotas. As a result, they may feel that they just cannot find enough time to listen to their accounts. Some salespeople, however, know that time spent on effective listening can be as valuable as a capital investment and can save them a valuable resource—time.

"Having to engage in a less conspicuous activity, such as listening, sometimes affects or hurts salespeoples' egos, especially if they feel they have control of a situation only when they are doing the talking."

Effective listening habits are essential for sales representatives sincerely concerned with avoiding misunderstandings and maintaining good relationships with their customers. Unfortunately, too many salespeople have had no formalized training in the development of better listening skills and techniques.

Take off the earmuffs!

Judging from the frequency with which important communications are misunderstood, you might think that some salespeople wear earmuffs in face-to-face communication. Effective listening is not a simple or passive activity; it requires concentrated effort and a certain amount of tension. The **earmuff problem**—tuning out incoming communications—occasionally exists when a salesperson perceives her or his role as authoritative, one that involves guiding and controlling a sales interview. Having to engage in a less conspicuous activity, such as listening, sometimes affects or hurts salespeople's egos, especially if they feel they have control of a situation only when they are doing the talking. However, if you were to ask some satisfied customers what they like most about the salespeople who call on them, you will frequently hear: *"I like that salesperson. She listens to what I have to say."*

Less wear and tear on you and your customers

Effective listening by salespeople can be a form of **preventive maintenance.** Just as lubrication can prevent friction and the wear and tear of machinery, so can effective listening prevent friction and misunderstandings between customers and your firm. Occasionally you might find yourself greeted by one of your regular accounts with a barrage of negative comments about the service being received from your company. At first, it may seem that the customer plans never to do business with your firm again. However, for persons who have complaints or difficulties, merely finding empathetic listeners helps to "get things off their chests" and possibly allows them to see their problems more objectively. After the emotional release, especially if you don't interrupt, your customer might say, "I'm sorry about the barrage of complaints I threw at you when you arrived. I had some other problems pressing on my mind this morning, and I guess I took them out on you. Actually, I like your company. If I didn't, I wouldn't have given you so many orders in the past."

DEVELOPING ACTIVE LISTENING SKILLS

Active listening is not an inborn skill; it must be developed. Just watch the demanding behavior of a young child and you'll see that few persons are born listeners. Knowing how to make certain *listening responses* and how to *phrase questions* can greatly help you convey to speakers that you are interested, attentive, and wish them to continue. Let's first examine some effective ways to elicit responses from the other person.

Listening Responses

How can the use of listening responses assist you?

Listening responses should be made quietly and briefly so as not to interfere with a speaker's train of thought. As with any tool, responses can be misused, ineffective, and counterproductive. Responses are likely to appear manipulative and forced if they are not genuinely sincere. Responses are usually made when the speaker pauses. Five types of listening responses are:

The nod—nodding the head slightly and waiting

The pause—looking at the speaker expectantly but without doing or saying anything

The casual remark—"I see"; "Uh-huh"; "Is that so?"; "That's interesting"

The echo—repeating the last few words the speaker said

The mirror—reflecting back to the speaker your understanding of what has just been said: "You feel that . . ."

Often, using the mirror approach with disgruntled customers will cause them to reconsider their remarks.

Phrasing Questions

The way you ask influences **what** *you find out.*

Occasionally, a salesperson may notice that an account's volume of purchases has declined markedly. The ability to phrase questions effectively can often enable a salesperson to uncover the cause of the problem. Assume that you merely were to ask the customer, "Mr. Williams, I notice that your purchases have fallen off substantially in recent months; is there anything wrong?" This approach will frequently elicit a limited response, possibly a hasty and succinct no. There are far more effective ways of phrasing questions that increase the possibility of receiving more complete responses. Questions may be phrased as *open questions, closed questions,* or *alternate-choice questions.* Open questions usually generate better responses than do closed questions.

An **open question** is phrased in such a way that it *cannot* be answered with a simple yes or no. For example, "Ms. Carson, now that you've seen a demonstration of our product, what do you think?" If you ask an open question, exercise patience, and *say nothing until Ms. Carson finally responds,* you will discover more often than not that Ms. Carson will be more likely to express her feelings about the product and provide you with some positive clues as to the effectiveness of your sales presentation.

Psychiatrists and counselors regularly employ the open-question technique. Can you really imagine a psychiatrist saying to a patient, "Mr. Brown, do you have a problem?"

A **closed question** is phrased in such a way that it *can* be answered by yes or no. For example, "I've shown you how the product works, Ms. Carson, would you like to buy it?" Too frequently the answer will be a flat no. In general, closed questions should be avoided unless you are relatively certain that you'll obtain the desired response.

Practice formulating questions by using the open-question technique. You may be surprised and pleased with your results. The following is a list of key words that determine whether a question is open or closed.

Open	**Closed**
Who	Is
What	Do
When	Has
Where	Can
Why	Will
How	Shall

The **alternate-choice question** (sometimes called **forced-choice question**) is used by salespeople to get agreement from customers by making it easy for them to choose between two or more alternatives. For example, you could ask, "Which one of the two items I showed you seem to best fit your requirements, Ms. Shepherd?" Another example: "Well, Mr. Pappas, do you prefer the suit with the vest or the one without?"

Listening Takes Practice

Listening is a developed skill that doesn't come easily even though we've been provided with two ears and only one mouth, as Cicero so perceptively observed many years ago. Yet, it is a skill that can be developed with practice. There are at least five reasons why you should attempt to develop better listening habits:

Why learn to listen?

1. Most people like to feel important, and being listened to helps them feel that way.
2. Customers tend to be more responsive to sales presentations when they know their opinions and suggestions are listened to.
3. Listening can help to uncover small gripes and prevent them from blossoming into big grievances.
4. Salespeople who don't get the necessary facts often make poor decisions.
5. Salespeople who jump to conclusions lose the respect of their accounts.

The following are some important guidelines that can greatly improve your own listening skills:

Now hear this!

1. *Restrict your talking.* Can you really listen to the customer and talk at the same time?
2. *Try to put yourself into the customer's shoes.* Aren't you more likely to develop responses that relate directly to your customer if you attempt to understand the customer's problems, needs, and point of view?
3. *Ask questions.* If you're not clear on something that the customer said, wouldn't you be more likely to avoid embarrassment and greater confusion later on if you asked for immediate clarification?
4. *Don't interrupt the customer.* Does even a long pause necessarily mean that the customer is finished expressing a particular thought?
5. *Focus on what the customer is saying.* If you let your mind wander or if you aren't able to avoid distractions, will you really catch the meaning of your customer's statements?
6. *Use listening responses regularly.* Won't an occasional "uh-huh" or nod help to show that you're interested in the customer's comments? But if not used carefully and sparingly, mightn't such listening responses come across as superficial?
7. *Try to avoid becoming irritated by what the customer says to you.* Won't excessive emotion be likely to block your understanding of the customer's entire message and meaning?
8. *Hear the customer out before jumping to conclusions.* Is it realistic for you to assume that you know precisely what the customer means before he or she finishes talking?
9. *Practice listening more actively.* Since listening is a developed skill, isn't it likely that you can improve your listening habits with practice?

SUMMARY

Communication, a two-way process intended to result in the transmission of a message and understanding, requires a *sender,* a *receiver,* and *understanding* in order to be effective. Words facilitate communication, but they do not have meaning in themselves. They are like containers; their meaning actually lies in the *user.* When in doubt about the meaning of a word, ask the user what he or she meant.

The frequency of communication failures can be lessened by assuming neither that everyone knows what *you* are talking about nor that you know what *others* are talking about. Ask questions to make certain.

Both oral and written communication have their advantages and disadvantages, a knowledge of which should enhance a salesperson's effectiveness. Also significant are the nonverbal forms of communication, which include body language, nonverbal symbols (e.g., space, height, and status), silence, voice (i.e., tone, volume, pitch, rate, and inflection), appearance, use of time, and touching.

Face-to-face communication and effective listening habits can enhance a salesperson's effectiveness. Other precautions and approaches that can be taken to minimize communication breakdowns relate to not interrupting, the prevention of credibility gaps, selecting effective times for communication, and brevity.

In this chapter, we also explored the other side of the communications coin—*listening.* Skill in listening is not easy to acquire, even though most of us were born with two ears and only one mouth. However, the art of good listening can be developed with practice.

Much of our educational system has ignored the topic of listening. However, good listening habits can aid salespeople in their efforts to discover the needs and motives of prospects, prevent misunderstandings, and aid in maintaining good relationships with their customers. Time spent on effective listening can often save that valuable resource, time.

Skillful listening requires understanding the principal types of listening responses and knowing how to phrase questions effectively. Listening is an important skill that can be developed with practice.

KEY TERMS

communication
feedback
one-way communication
two-way communication
verbal communication
nonverbal communication
body language
nonverbal symbols
K.I.S.S. concept
earmuff problem
preventive maintenance
listening responses
open question
closed question
alternate-choice question (forced-choice question)

QUESTIONS

1. What is communication?
2. What is necessary for effective communication to take place?
3. True or false: If we want to know the "correct" meaning of a word, we should look in the dictionary. Explain.
4. Which is more effective—spoken or written communication?
5. Why is an understanding of nonverbal symbols important for salespeople?

6. Which of the body language examples cited in the chapter is probably most indicative of a readiness to make a purchase by a prospective customer?

7. How does "silence" communicate?

8. Evaluate the following statement:

   "I'm an individual. I dress the way *I* want for my sales calls. No one else has the right to control my tastes and desires. Besides, none of my customers has ever complained to me about my appearance."

9. Assuming that you are a salesperson, what might being late for a sales interview communicate to a prospective customer?

10. Is there anything wrong with hugging an established customer? Explain.

11. Why do some salespeople interrupt their customers? What can a salesperson do about the problem?

12. Explain the statement "Words do not substitute for action."

13. When is the "best" time to convey important communications to others?

14. Explain the *K.I.S.S. concept.*

15. Why do some sales representatives figuratively don "earmuffs" when their customers talk to them?

16. What are some of the benefits that result from the development of effective listening habits.

17. Give two examples each of open and closed questions. Why do open questions generally elicit a greater response from the receiver?

18. When might a salesperson use a forced-choice questioning technique?

19. Many people don't like to hear the words *sell* or *sold.* Why would you be unlikely to say the following to a friend? "Look at the beautiful new digital watch I was *sold* today."

APPLICATIONS

7.1 RECEIVED BUT NOT ORDERED

You are a sales representative for a wholesale firm, the Hardy Hardware Supply Company. Your major accounts are lumberyards, hardware stores, and paint and wallpaper retail outlets. Many of your accounts frequently place their orders by telephone. You have recently received a number of complaints about unordered goods going to your customers. Some customers are so disgruntled that they have threatened to cease doing business with your company.

After a detailed study, you discover that the major problem seems to be that incorrect information, such as wrong item numbers, quantities, and colors, was taken down by the inside employees on the telephone purchase forms.

Questions

1. What seems to be the major problem?
2. What might you recommend to the inside personnel to correct the problem?

7.2 WHAT'S A BODY GOING TO DO?

First, obtain a partner who also has an interest in the selling field. Next, review the ten important examples of body language cited in the chapter. Take turns acting out each body motion mentioned, and then develop techniques for responding effectively to each one.

7.3 WHAT'S YOUR L.Q. (LISTENING QUOTIENT)?

Your attitudes and actions are two factors that significantly influence the effectiveness of your listening. Here's a short exercise designed to measure these important factors and to help you find out how good a listener you actually are. Circle the number beside the question and underneath the heading that most closely reflects your listening habits. Then total the circled points. Remember to answer the questions on the basis of your *real* attitudes and behavior, not those you think you *should* have.

	Almost Always	Usually	Occasionally	Seldom	Almost Never
Attitudes					
1. Do you like to listen to other people talk?	5	4	3	2	1
2. Do you encourage other people to talk?	5	4	3	2	1
3. Do you listen even if you do not like the person who is talking?	5	4	3	2	1
4. Do you listen equally well whether the person talking is man or woman, young or old?	5	4	3	2	1
5. Do you listen equally well to friend, acquaintance, stranger?	5	4	3	2	1
Actions					
6. Do you put what you have been doing out of sight and out of mind?	5	4	3	2	1
7. Do you look at the speaker?	5	4	3	2	1

	Almost Always	Usually	Occasionally	Seldom	Almost Never
8. Do you ignore the distractions about you?	5	4	3	2	1
9. Do you smile, nod your head, and otherwise encourage the other person to talk?	5	4	3	2	1
10. Do you think about what the speaker is saying?	5	4	3	2	1
11. Do you try to figure out what the speaker means?	5	4	3	2	1
12. Do you try to figure out why the speaker is saying it?	5	4	3	2	1
13. Do you let the speaker finish what he or she is trying to say?	5	4	3	2	1
14. If the speaker hesitates, do you encourage him or her to go on?	5	4	3	2	1
15. Do you restate what the speaker has said and ask if you got it right?	5	4	3	2	1
16. Do you withhold judgment about the speaker's idea until he or she is finished?	5	4	3	2	1
17. Do you listen regardless of the speaker's manner of speaking and choice of words?	5	4	3	2	1
18. Do you listen even though you anticipate what the speaker is going to say?	5	4	3	2	1
19. Do you question the speaker in order to get him or her to explain the idea more fully?	5	4	3	2	1
20. Do you ask the speaker what the words mean as he or she uses them?	5	4	3	2	1

Total Score ________

Scoring:

90–100 = You're a great listener!
80–89 = You're a good listener.
65–79 = You're a fairly typical listener who could stand some improvement.
50–64 = You really need some practice and training in effective listening.
Under 50 = Are you listening?

PART FOUR

THE SELLING PROCESS

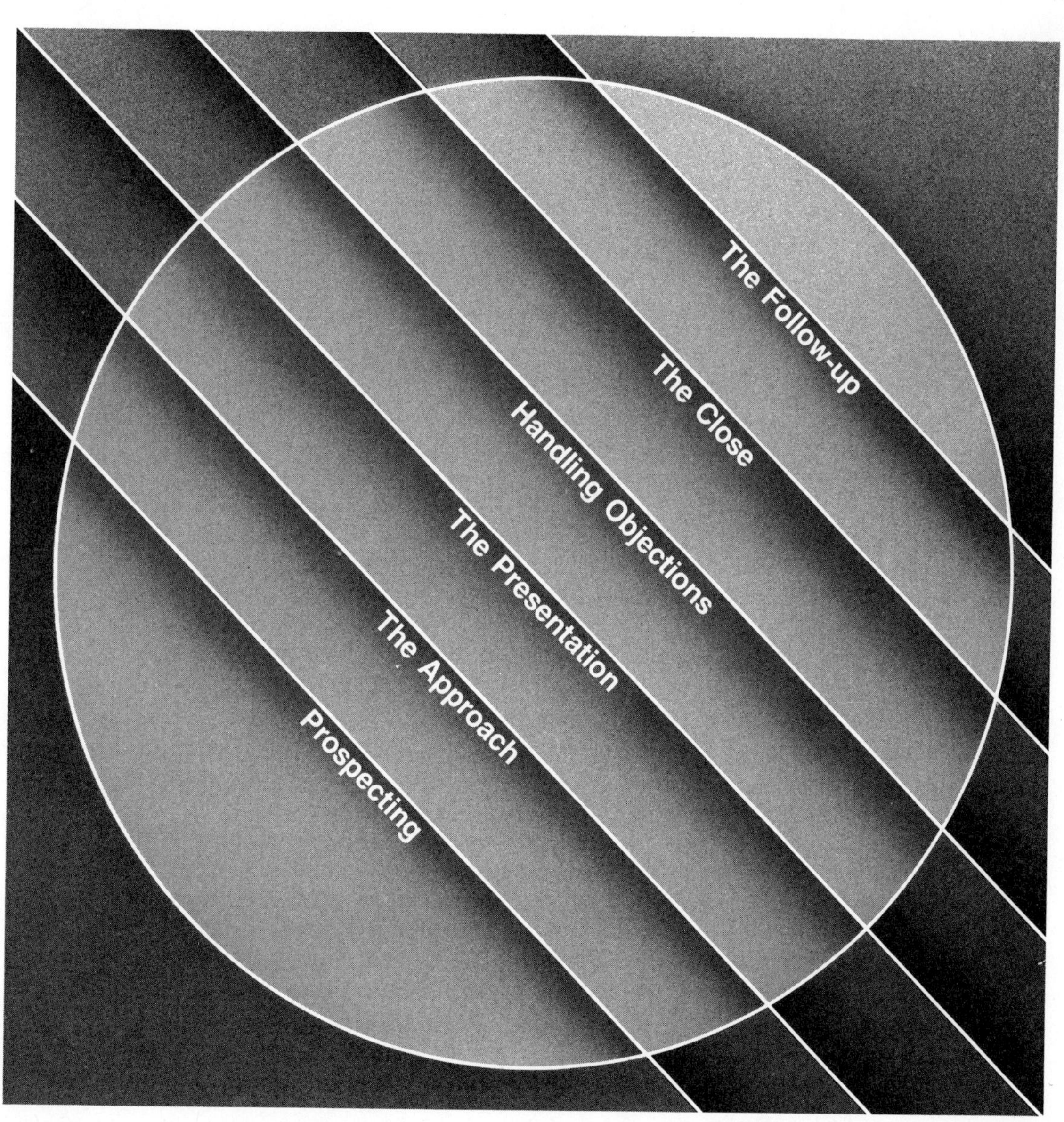

8 The Art of Prospecting and Preapproaching

There's Gold in Them Thar Hills!

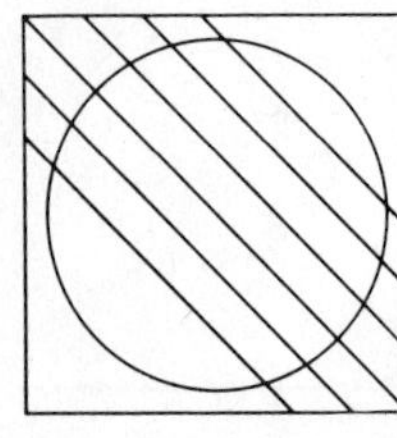

If companies are to grow, what they must have, and are often pressed to find, is new business.

WALTER J. ZIMMERMAN

Prospecting is essential for the salesperson's survival or growth. It also provides an excellent opportunity for the use of imagination and originality.

J. S. SCHIFF

Here's what you should be able to do after studying this chapter:

1. Cite the importance of the prospecting function.
2. Relate the preapproach activities to the function of prospecting.
3. State where to locate names of potential customers.
4. Summarize the technique for determining whether prospects qualify for the purchase of your products or services.
5. Describe the importance of maintaining adequate records and plans for prospecting activities.

Attached to the wall in the office of a small midwestern business establishment is a plaque bearing the inscribed words:

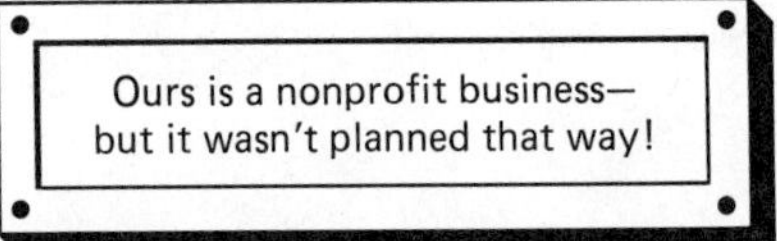

Ours is a nonprofit business—
but it wasn't planned that way!

Few private business concerns plan to be nonprofit organizations; they can't exist for long without the regular inflow of revenues in excess of their expenses. In many fields, salespeople have the key responsibility for generating such revenues. But the act of selling by itself is not enough; goods and services must be sold at a *profit.* In order to fulfill this responsibility, salespeople are expected to apply sound and proven concepts of selling to their activities.

In this and subsequent chapters we examine the **selling process,** which is presented in six steps (see Figure 8.1). This chapter focuses on the first step—the art of prospecting, including the preapproach—exploring such topics as why prospecting is important, where prospects can be found, how they can be qualified, and

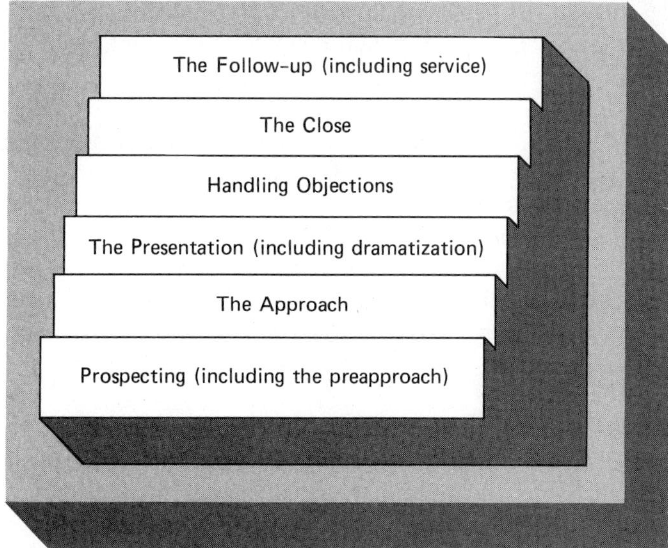

Figure 8.1 Steps in the Selling Process.

why planning and adequate prospecting records are essential for optimum prospecting and preapproaching effectiveness.

THE IMPORTANCE OF PROSPECTING

Do mice wait for the cheese to come to them?

Do you recall our story about building a better mousetrap? Although sales personnel in retail stores must ordinarily wait for customers to come to them, sellers of many types of "mousetraps" must actively seek out prospective buyers. For example, tremendous competition exists among producers of photocopying machines. Firms such as Xerox, IBM, Pitney Bowes, Minolta, and Canon seldom wait for customers to ask to purchase equipment. Instead, their sales networks are continually searching for new customers. This exploration for new accounts is referred to as **prospecting,** which can be defined as *the step in the selling process that involves locating potential customers.*

Prospects Versus Suspects

How does a **suspect** *differ from a* **prospect?**

In order to avoid wasting considerable time, it's extremely important for you as a salesperson to sort out so-called *suspects* from *prospects.* **Suspects,** also called **leads,** are considered to be any persons who might *possibly* buy your products or services but whom you've not yet placed into the prospect category. **Prospects** are what you hope your leads really are. These are individuals or organizations that can *benefit* from your product, can *qualify financially* to purchase it, and have the *authority* to influence or make buying decisions.

Virtually all those people you might contact can be considered to be suspects before you've uncovered certain qualifying information about them, since there is always the possibility that they might buy your products. *Possibilities,* however, aren't *probabilities*—every suspect isn't necessarily a prospect.

Is everybody a prospect?

To illustrate, assume that you intend to phone every person listed on page 143 of the local telephone directory. Will all of them purchase your product? It is possible, but is it probable? Your experience and wisdom should tell you that such an event is unlikely. You can waste considerable amounts of time if you assume that every breathing specimen of *Homo sapiens* is a hot prospect. On the other hand, you can also waste a disproportionate amount of time *overqualifying* prospects, that is, uncovering more information about potential buyers than is necessary.

Why Prospecting Is Essential

During the hustle and bustle of a typical day in your life as a salesperson, you might find it difficult to allot time for prospecting. However, an understanding of why prospecting for new accounts is so essential may help to motivate you into it. You should become aware that prospecting is one of the most important responsibilities you have as a salesperson. Why? Because the level of business in a particular territory seldom remains constant; it either grows or diminishes in volume. Without a consistent, planned prospecting program, the volume of business activity is likely to decline.

The following are some key reasons why sales volume tends to decline without a planned prospecting program:

No prospecting = declining sales volume.

1. Some accounts may stop doing business with your company.
2. Some customers may relocate and move out of your sales territory.
3. Some customers may go out of business due to bankruptcy.
4. Some customers may go out of business due to death, illness, or accidents.
5. Some customers may merge with or be absorbed by larger firms that have their own well-established suppliers.
6. Your buying contact with a particular firm may be promoted or transferred, may retire, or may resign.

Integrating prospecting with your other sales activities, therefore, is a must if your sales production is to grow rather than stagnate.

The Preapproach to Improve Prospecting Activities

A degree of advanced knowledge needed.

An activity that we prefer to include with prospecting is sometimes referred to as the **preapproach.** The preapproach is *an activity that involves obtaining as much relevant information as necessary about prospects before contacting them personally.* In simple terms, the preapproach is the process of separating "prospects" from "suspects." Among the principal types of questions that you as a salesperson should try to answer related to the preapproach process are:

1. Who actually is the customer? (Include who will influence the buying decision and would be likely to use the product or service.)
2. What does the customer need? (This information will aid you in developing a relevant sales presentation.)
3. What other information could be useful in approaching the customer? (For companies: background information on the firms, their past results and current financial conditions, and their products and markets. For individuals: personal information including hobbies, interests, and involvement in the community.)

Uncovering such information makes for a more effective preapproach and helps the salesperson in four major ways:

How does it help?

1. It provides relevant information and insight about potential customers to determine whether they qualify for purchase.
2. It helps determine effective strategy for approaching prospective customers and preparing sales presentations just for them.
3. It reduces the likelihood of making serious errors during sales presentations.
4. It helps instill more confidence in the salesperson, since it involves prior planning for sales interviews.

An amusing story helps to illustrate the importance of developing a sound preapproach process:

> A salesperson called a prospective customer and the phone was answered by what was obviously a young boy. "Is your mother or father home?" the salesperson asked. The child said no. "Well, is there anyone else there I can speak to?" asked the salesperson. "My sister," the youngster piped up. "Would you get her please?" requested the salesperson. There was a long silence, then the salesperson heard the little boy's voice again. "I'm sorry," he said, "but I can't lift her out of the playpen."

PROSPECTS—WHERE TO FIND THEM

In order to be successful in achieving your sales goals, you must be continually on the alert for ways to maintain and increase your volume of business. To avoid wasting valuable time, you should have a *plan* for maintaining an effective and useful prospect list. Where do you locate names for your prospect record file? The answer varies, depending principally on the nature of the product or service you are selling. A life insurance salesperson, for example, would be unlikely to use a list of retired senior citizens as a source of leads. A sales representative for a steel manufacturing company would be unlikely to canvass a suburban neighborhood door to door looking for potential buyers of cold-rolled steel.

You should be careful not to scratch someone off your list or snub someone who

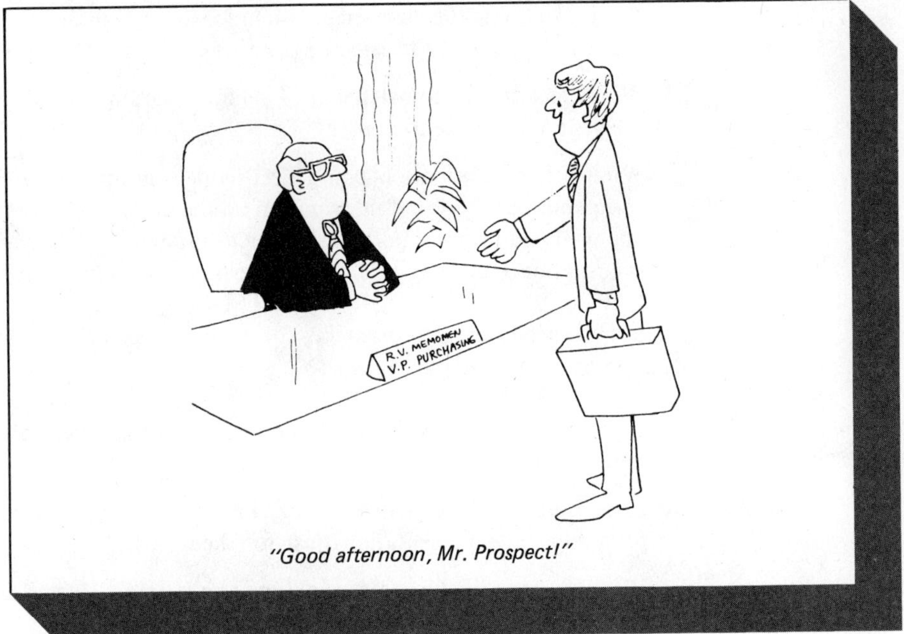

"Good afternoon, Mr. Prospect!"

might either become a prospect or refer you to one. Sometimes, for example, in addition to purchasing agents or managers, secretaries and assistants make significant buying decisions. We've already discussed in Chapter 5 the importance of recognizing the existence of a *buying center* in selling. It is essential, therefore, for you to find out who determines and influences what is purchased in an organization.

"You should be careful not to scratch someone off your list or snub someone who might either become a prospect or refer you to one."

What are your principal sources of potential customers? The main ones include:

1. Your own company
2. Your present customers
3. Former prospects
4. Friends, acquaintances, and neighbors
5. Other salespeople
6. Junior salespeople and bird dogs
7. Periodicals, directories, registers, and special lists

8. Personal observation
9. Cold canvass
10. Blitz technique
11. Trade fairs and exhibitions
12. Clubs and social groups
13. Group party plans
14. Surveys
15. Telephone and mail inquiries
16. Use of videocassettes

Let's now briefly examine each of these sources of potential customers for your product or service.

Within Your Own Company

How might your own company provide leads?

Your own company can sometimes be a valuable source of prospective purchasers. Some firms, such as Hewlett-Packard, advertise their products in specialized and technical publications. As a result, prospective buyers often *write or telephone for product information,* which can then be provided personally by sales representatives. Some firms offer free gifts in their advertisements as an inducement; these can be presented to prospective customers, along with creative sales messages.

Service or repair personnel within your company can also be a source of leads. A claims adjuster, for example, could give insurance agents the names of persons who, although insured with other companies, were pleased with the settlement of their particular claims. Or the service department of an auto dealership or office equipment company could be a source of names of individuals ready to replace their older equipment.

Your Present Customers

Easily overlooked but often a rich source of leads are your past and present customers. For example, they may be about to deplete their supply of items previously purchased from you and thus be in need of restocking. Or they may have recently realized that they have, after all, a previously unrecognized need for one of your products.

You should also attempt to employ with your present customers what is termed the **endless-chain method,** a process that simply involves *asking your existing customers for the names of prospective ones.* This approach, as illustrated in Figure 8.2, can provide you with a virtually endless supply of potential customers.

A related method, termed the **referral approach,** goes one step beyond the endless-chain method. In the referral method, the salesperson *obtains not only names*

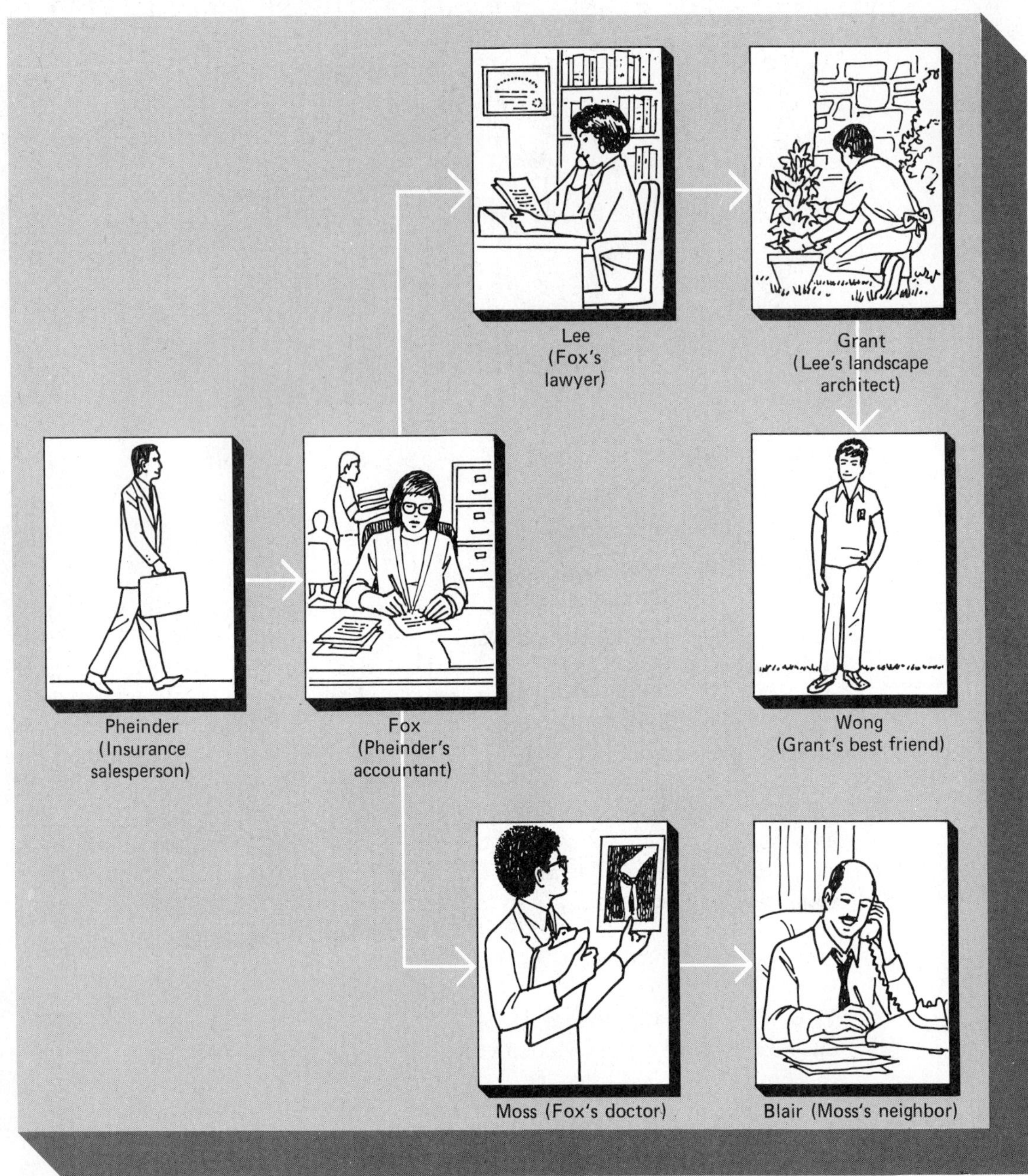

Figure 8.2 Endless-Chain Prospecting Method for a Hypothetical Insurance Salesperson Named Pheinder.

but also a personal note or letter of introduction. Your satisfied customers are generally quite willing to help you along these lines. Some salespeople even offer rewards, such as gifts and discounts, for referred leads.

Some customers are what is referred to as **centers of influence;** that is, they are well known in a community. Such individuals can be another aid to prospecting. Assume, for example, that you have insured the life of the mayor of the town. She or he may be willing to provide you with a **testimonial letter,** which is a sales tool indicating that the customer is pleased with you and your company's products and service. When customers tell you they're pleased with the way you've serviced their accounts, don't hesitate to ask them for referred leads and testimonial letters.

Former Prospects

Have you ever felt that you were positively disinterested in a particular product only to find later that you had changed your mind? If so, you have plenty of companions. As a salesperson you should recognize that, although individuals may not purchase your product when you first call on them, conditions frequently change. Prospects who have practically been written off as potential customers sometimes become dissatisfied with their existing sources. Occasionally structural changes in your industry cause your products to become more attractive from the standpoints of price, quality, or dependability. Or changing international currency values, newly imposed tariffs on imported goods, or shortages of competing products make your products less costly than those of foreign sources.

Should you ever give up on a former prospect?

Furthermore, over periods of time, your former prospects may become more aware of the advantages and uses of your products. Regardless of the reasons why former prospects change their minds, a creative salesperson recognizes that persistence in sales activities often pays off. You should be continually alert to any changes that might turn a former "suspect" into a full-fledged "prospect."

Friends, Acquaintances, and Neighbors

"I want all my customers to be my friends and all my friends to be my customers." As desirable a philosophy as this may appear, you should exercise caution when using friends as prospects. If you become "pesty" with your valued friends, you may discover that one day they are no longer friends. Some salespeople prefer not to do business with their friends, close social acquaintances, or neighbors, mainly because of unfavorable experiences with such contacts who expect special favors or discounts. Also some salespeople, almost unknowingly, develop the reputation of being the type who continue to push their wares every moment they are with friends or neighbors. Individuals whose friendship you value may begin to think when they see you: "Oh, oh, here comes that pushy sales one again!" The following story helps to illustrate what can happen when you run out of friends!

A seven-year-old boy named Jason decided to sell garden seeds to earn money to buy a bicycle. One day Jason's good friend, Jessica, saw him and the following conversation ensued:

Jessica How you doing with your seed sales, Jason?

Jason Great! I'm a fantastic little salesperson! I sold one to my mom, to my uncle Harold, to my cousin Bobby, my aunt Fannie, my dad, my neighbor, my sis, and my brother-in-law.

Jessica What's so great about that? If you're so cool, let's see you sell some seeds to a stranger.

Jason But Jessica—I'm only a child. I don't know any strangers.

Moral: For some salespeople—when they run out friends, they're in trouble!

"Some salespeople prefer not to do business with their friends or close social acquaintances, or neighbors, mainly because of unfavorable experiences with such contacts who expect special favors or discounts."

Should you "use" your friends?

This is not to say that friends and acquaintances *cannot* be good sources of sales and referred leads. In fact, business associations can develop into good friendships and friends often become good customers. Friends may be able to provide you with information useful for qualifying a particular prospect. You can maintain close personal relationships if you deal with your friends and acquaintances on a professional level.

Other Salespeople

How might other salespeople aid you?

An alert salesperson can obtain prospective customers from what might appear to be unlikely sources. For example, competing salespeople are occasionally generous with useful information and may unwittingly furnish you with leads or facts about a potential customer. Or a salesperson whose company doesn't produce a product you sell may generously volunteer the name of someone who could use your product. Always keep your eyes and ears tuned to sources of potential customers.

Junior Salespeople and Bird Dogs

Some firms employ **junior salespeople** (sometimes called **spotters**) whose job is to try to locate leads for more experienced salespeople. This approach enables more seasoned sales personnel to spend more of their time in actual selling.

"A creative salesperson, continually struggling to find new customers, should take full advantage of the numerous prospecting opportunities that arise."

A similar approach uses **bird dogs,** who are located by the salesperson rather than the company. Bird dogs, sometimes called **sales associates,** are typically individuals who have regular jobs with other companies but are in the position to discover leads for the salesperson. For example, an employee of a boat supply company could provide leads to a person selling boatowner's insurance. The bird dog is paid by the salesperson on the basis of successfully completed sales.

Periodicals, Directories, Registers, and Special Lists

A creative salesperson, continually struggling to find new customers, should take full advantage of the numerous prospecting opportunities that arise. These include an often overlooked but frequently lucrative source of prospects: *public information,* which is readily available to anyone interested. Among these potentially useful sources are the following:

1. *Current items in newspapers* (such as the opening of new retail stores or a change of ownership in established ones).
2. *New construction applications* (contractors may be prospects for your products or services).
3. *License applications* (such as business permits, boat and automobile registrations).
4. *Lists of recorded warranties* (these can indicate when individuals will be ready to replace their aging products).
5. *Voter registration lists* (these can be obtained from precinct captains).
6. *Professionally prepared lists* sold by list brokers (these include lists of subscribers of publications in all fields—boating, hiking, fishing, and so on).
7. *Lists kept by those whom you patronize* (such as your insurance agent, garage repairperson, or banker).
8. *Telephone directories* (including the white and Yellow Pages).

Personal Observation

The eyes **and** *the nose have it!*

Salespeople are continually "on the go." Creative salespeople, no matter what they're doing, are continually sensitive to potential sources of prospects. Sometimes a casual remark by an acquaintance or an item in a newspaper can alert the salesperson with a "nose for prospects." Some salespeople develop a keen sense for spotting potential customers in virtually any situation.

Here's a related anecdote Akio Morita, co-founder of Sony, is fond of expressing:

> Two shoe salespeople visit a lesser-developed country.
> One cabled his office, "No prospect for sales; nobody wears shoes here."
> The other salesperson cabled, "Send stock immediately; inhabitants barefoot; desperately need shoes."[1]

Cold Canvass

On what assumption does the **cold canvass approach** *work?*

Another method for finding prospects, termed the **cold canvass approach,** attempts to utilize the law of averages. Assuming that you have reasonable sales abilities and a useful product, then—based on the cold canvass approach—you are likely to sell a certain percentage of all those contacted; that is, the law of averages should work for you.

Prospects are not preselected for the cold canvass approach. Instead, you choose a specific group and then attempt to contact as many individuals in that group as possible. For example, you might call on every house in a particular area.

You should consider utilizing the approach followed by many professional salespeople who set aside a specific time to cold canvass for prospects. For example, you could plan to devote every other Thursday *exclusively* to the activity of making **cold calls,** that is, calling on prospects whom you've never contacted before. Planned prospecting days, such as these, help to eliminate the problem of procrastinating the all-important activity of prospecting for new accounts.

Far too frequently, a salesperson's efforts at prospecting go little beyond making the statement, "One of these days I've got to do some cold canvassing for new prospects." These words are analogous to statements like, "One of these days I'm going to start doing some stomach exercises." Often those "days" never come without a specific plan that has been followed through. The cold canvass approach is difficult and requires a substantial amount of self-discipline on the part of the salesperson, but it can be used with success by the persistent and patient salesperson.

Blitz Technique

A modification of the cold canvass approach is called the **blitz technique;** its purpose is to saturate a particular region or group in as short a time as possible.

For example, a team of sales representatives may be temporarily assigned to a particular territory to try to expand the number of outlets for their products. They might call on every retail store in a specific town, hoping to develop leads that they will then turn over to regular company salespeople in that territory for follow-up.

Trade Fairs and Exhibitions

Some firms display their wares at **trade fairs** and public **exhibitions.** Periodically presented in major cities are such events as boat shows, electronic equipment shows, computer fairs, and furniture shows, where product literature is distributed and products are described to visitors. Names of interested individuals are often obtained and given to company salespeople for follow-up purposes.

Clubs and Social Groups

For some products or services, **clubs** as well as **civic and social groups** can also be sources of prospective customers. **Computer user groups** and **bulletin board systems** are other types of special-interest groups that are especially good prospects for computer hard- and software products and services. Even if you are not a member of a particular group, you may know or meet someone who is a member and who could provide you with a list of prospective customers. Attending the meetings of such groups can also sometimes result in new leads. There is an ever-present danger, however, of your overextending your available time if you become too deeply involved in civic groups and clubs. Some salespeople have discovered, to their dismay, that they became active to the detriment of their jobs and families.

Group Party Plans

Some types of products—such as cookware, household cleaning agents, and cosmetics—lend themselves to being sold at **party groups.** These typically are gatherings at the home of a volunteer host who is responsible for inviting friends and acquaintances—potential customers for the demonstrated products. One German wine company, for example, sells exclusively in the United States through party groups at homes or offices where sales representatives present a wide variety of wines for tasting and, of course, purchase.

A significant advantage of group party selling is the opportunity for the salesperson to concentrate a relatively large number of prospects in one location.

Surveys

Surveys are another technique used to locate prospective buyers. This approach uses questionnaires to uncover potential needs of customers and thus pave the way for specific sales presentations. Unfortunately, the unscrupulous use of surveys by some salespeople have created attitudes toward them similar to those of marketing scholar, George W. Wynn:

> Surveys—I consider this method of finding prospects to be an out-an-out *lie.* How often has someone asked your opinion under the guise of a "survey," and you realized that he or she did not want your opinion but only wanted to sell you something. This method creates problems for actual market research projects, especially over the telephone. When I am approached by someone who wants to sell something under the guise of a survey, I will tell them that they are *lying* and I will never buy their product.[2]

The ethical use of surveys will be discussed in greater depth in Chapter 10.

Telephone and Mail Inquiries

A considerable amount of advertising today urges prospective customers to obtain additional product information either by telephoning a toll-free number (usually with an 800 prefix) or by mailing in a cut-out coupon or postage-free card. As a means of encouraging greater response, the readers are sometimes offered a free gift or brochure.

Telephone and mail inquiries are typically analyzed and screened for their potential as "hot prospects" and then turned over to local company salespeople for follow-up with a sales presentation.

Additional uses of the telephone as a sales tool will be discussed in Chapter 16.

Use of Videocassettes

A relatively new and novel method of obtaining new prospects related to mail inquiries is the use of **videocassettes.** For example, Soloflex, an Oregon-based body-building machine company, offered in its printed advertising a 22-minute video tape—either in Beta or VHS formats—that gave the viewer reasons for buying its exercise equipment. Soloflex drew 40,000 leads a month from the requests for the video tapes, which were free and didn't have to be returned.[3]

Could be Arnold S. on VHS!

There are some students of prospecting who feel that video tapes have their shortcomings, since the viewer must typically watch them from beginning to end. Unfortunately, there may be portions of the tape that are of no interest to the viewer. Regardless of this disadvantage, those who request the tapes by mail may furnish salespeople with useful prospecting leads.

ARE YOUR PROSPECTS QUALIFIED?

The importance of knowing your customers, your company, its products, and its competitors was discussed in a previous chapter. Equally important is for you to be familiar with the market for your products; such familiarity can help you differentiate suspects from prospects. As previously mentioned, virtually everyone is a suspect, but a "scattershot" approach—that is, treating everyone as a prospective customer—can waste a lot of your scarce and valuable time.

A reasonable familiarity with your products, their uses, and their limitations can help in **qualifying prospects.** For example, you would be unlikely to sell outdoor tropical plants, such as Canary Island Date Palms, to garden stores and nurseries in Butte, Montana, or Denver, Colorado. Your products would not be particularly suited to such intemperate climes. Likewise, there is little sense in trying to sell your products to those who have no need for them. It's useful to know for whom and for what your product is designed and to relate your sales presentation to the *needs* of your prospects.

"Virtually everyone is a suspect, but a 'scattershot' approach—that is, treating everyone as a prospective customer—can waste a lot of your scarce and valuable time."

The point is that you should get enough information to enable you to determine if your prospects *qualify* for the purchase of your goods or services. There are five important questions that you should attempt to answer when you are trying to determine good prospects:

How do you qualify prospects?

1. Does the person have a want or need that can be satisfied by the purchase of my products or services?
2. Does the person have the ability to pay?

3. Does the person have the authority to buy?
4. Can the person be approached favorably?
5. Is the person eligible to buy?[4]

Qualifying prospects in advance can actually save time later. Let's now turn to a brief examination of each of the above questions.

Is There a Need?

Find a need and fill it.

You may have developed a highly convincing sales talk, but you could be wasting valuable time if you're presenting it to someone who has no reason to want or need your product. We've discussed buying motives in a previous chapter. Does your product appeal to any of those motives? Is there some way in which the prospect will *benefit* from the purchase of your product? Is there an *actual,* rather than merely a *possible,* need for the product? A prospector for new customers, like a prospector for gold, must sort out the useful from the useless. "All that glitters is not gold," warns an old cliché, nor are all suspects potential buyers. As previously mentioned, most selling is not done on a one-shot basis. Customers who develop a genuine need for your products and are satisfied with them are likely to be consistent customers. And in many fields, it is the repeat sales that reap long-term benefits.

Can They Pay?

Cash or credit?

Would you appreciate someone trying to pressure you into purchasing an item you couldn't afford? Not likely. Your impression of such an approach would probably be unfavorable. As a salesperson, you should try to avoid overextending prospects by finding out during your preapproach if they can pay for your products.

Get the facts before assuming.

For example, if you were a real estate salesperson, would there be any point in your attempting to sell a $400,000 house to a family whose level of income and wealth would prevent it from qualifying for the necessary loan? However, a word of warning: don't assume, without obtaining adequate facts, that a person will not qualify for credit or a purchase. A person's outward appearance can frequently be deceptive. Many sales have been lost because of assumptions based on appearance alone.

"Many people may be involved in the buying process even though they lack official purchasing authority."

Is There Authority to Purchase?

Determining who has the specific authority to make buying decisions is sometimes a delicate proposition. Frequently, of course, merely asking your prospect for the names of those involved in the final buying decision can get you the necessary

Don't forget those with influence.

information. But be tactful. And at the same time, don't overlook the *influence* of those who lack actual buying authority. Many people may be involved in the buying process even though they lack official purchasing authority. For example, a supervisor's assistant may exert more influence than the supervisor when it comes to purchasing office equipment.

Can the Prospect Be Readily Approached?

"You mean to say that you went to the University of Washington, too?" "Sure did, College of Bus. Ad., class of '84."

"No kidding. Say, did you know Horace Houndstooth when you were at the U? Horace used to date my wife before we were married."

How do **similar** *backgrounds aid in prospecting?*

Have you ever heard a conversation like this? It serves to illustrate another important point related to prospecting: searching for new customers is far easier when you can approach your prospects under favorable circumstances. Although not always essential for effective results, some prospects are more easily approached if they have backgrounds and interests similar to yours.

Some sales managers feel that young, inexperienced salespeople have more difficulty approaching top management or older prospects. As a result, they often assign more experienced salespeople to key accounts and may even give them impressive titles—such as *account executive, sales manager,* or *marketing vice president*—as a means of adding prestige to their positions. Of course, without the skills to go with them, impressive titles mean little.

Proper timing is also essential in prospecting. If you approach a prospect when

campbell
"Never ask to speak to someone in authority."

Source: Reprinted from *The Wall Street Journal* by permission of Cartoon Features Syndicate, © 1985.

When is a bad time for prospecting?

she or he is obviously in a bad mood or deeply immersed in a sea of problems, you would be wise to make an appointment for another day. Or if you yourself are in a deeply depressed mood, you might do better to postpone your sales call. The founder of one large company used to tell his sales representatives that he would rather they sat on a park bench during such periods than create irreparable ill will toward their company.

Is the Prospect Eligible to Buy?

You might answer all of the above questions affirmatively and yet the prospect may still not be able to purchase your product. Our last question—Is the prospect eligible to buy?—must also be answered in the affirmative before a sale can take place.

For example, assume that you represent a life insurance company and have contacted Ms. Hattie Ferndowner regarding the purchase of life insurance. Hattie, the head of her household, has three dependent children. She wants an ordinary whole life policy, has ample income to pay for it, makes her own buying decisions, and is easy to talk to, but her doctor recently discovered that she has cancer of the esophagus. Because of this, you may not be able to get her the policy she wants, since insurance companies have health standards that must be met before they will issue life insurance policies. Perhaps your prospect would be eligible for a different type of policy. Can you think of any additional reasons why some individuals might be ineligible to purchase certain products?

Let's now conclude this chapter with a discussion of the need to plan and keep adequate records related to prospecting activities.

THE NEED FOR PLANNING AND THE MAINTENANCE OF ADEQUATE RECORDS

"Son of a gun! I *thought* there was someone I promised to call on yesterday. How did I ever forget to make that follow-up visit I promised to Mrs. Hotchkiss?"

"Successful prospectors generally first establish specific prospecting objectives and then develop logical plans for accomplishing them."

This is the plight that unplanned, disorganized salespeople are likely to find themselves in quite regularly. The need for planning has been stressed repeatedly throughout this text. Planning for prospecting activities becomes much easier when you maintain adequate records. An entire chapter will be devoted to the topic of planning in relation to territorial management. For now, let's examine some of the ways in which planning and maintaining useful records can help you in your prospecting activities.

Establish a Plan

Do you know where and how you are going?

Successful prospectors generally first establish specific prospecting *objectives* and then develop logical *plans* for accomplishing them. Asking yourself specific questions, such as the following, can also aid in planning:

1. Have you decided what prospecting techniques you are going to follow?
2. Have you allowed for flexibility in order to match your approach to the personality and needs of the prospect?
3. Are you going to send out prospecting letters or use the telephone before making personal calls?
4. How much time are you going to set aside for prospecting?
5. Have you actually planned specific times for prospecting rather than leave the activity to chance?

Any questions related to effective prospecting should be answered in advance to minimize wasting your scarce time.

Maintain Adequate Records

Why should you "woo" and "tickle" your prospects?

Effective salespeople usually develop a list of potential customers. A useful device for keeping track of this list for initial and follow-up calls is a **tickler file,** consisting of 3 × 5 index cards filed by date and serving as a reminder of when you plan to call or follow up on specific prospects and what you are going to discuss. (See Figures 8.3 and 8.4 for sample cards for householders and industrial purchasers.) In many fields, sales are seldom made during the first attempt; callbacks are frequently necessary. Prospects customarily have to be wooed by the salesperson. In effect, there may be what could be considered a "courtship period." But don't forget periodically to weed out the names of those who definitely are not prospects.

A growing number of salespeople are using computers—both desk- and laptop models—for prospecting and customer information. **Computer software programs** are available for salespeople that feature such elements as an integrated word processor, telemarketing, autodial, tickler system, call reporting, form letters and mailing labels, and notation space for account profiles.[5] The use of computers can save salespeople substantial amounts of time along with assisting them in the planning and organizing of their preapproach and prospecting activities. (Chapter 17 will discuss the use of computers in sales in greater depth.)

Rate Your Prospects

How do your prospects rate?

Creative prospectors often rate their prospects. After your initial visit, you may have a fair idea as to how receptive a prospect is to your message. You could rate prospects as "hot," "medium," or "cool" or use any other system that indicates to you how much additional effort should be expended on them.

Name: Spouse's Name:

Address: Phone:

City: State: Zip:

Type of Employment: Duties/Title:

Children's Names & Ages:

Prospect's Potential Needs:

Benefits to Be Discussed:

Proposed Date of Call:

First Call Date:

Results, Attitude, Benefits Accepted:

Follow Up? ____ Yes ____ No

If so, when?

Follow-up Requirements:

References:

Figure 8.3 Front (*top*) and Back (*bottom*) of a Sample Prospecting Form for Householder.

Why is it important for you to keep your "cool" when the prospect is "cool"?

Show Appreciation

Prospecting is tough work. It is an activity filled with rebuffs and disappointments. A prospect may not only be cool toward your message but also downright offensive toward you. Sound advice to follow is never to lower yourself to the position of the person who may have insulted or offended you. If you do, you may have reason to regret your actions at a later date. Some years ago Charles Reigner wrote an essay that relates to this concept:

Company Name: Product(s)/Service(s):
Division or Branch:
Address: Phone:
City State: Zip:
Key Contact Individual: Title:
Other Decision Makers: Titles:
Purpose of Call:

Prospect's Potential Needs:

Major Competitors:
Have you planned a sales presentation? _____ Yes _____ No
Benefits to Be Discussed:

Proposed Date of Call:

First Call Date:

Results, Attitude, Benefits Accepted:

Follow Up? _____ Yes _____ No

If so, when?

Follow-up Requirements Including Key Decision Makers to Contact:

Referrals:

Figure 8.4 Front (*top*) and Back (*bottom*) of a Prospecting Form for Industrial Purchasers.

> Life is too short to be little. Every one of us has his or her share of rebuffs and disappointments. When somebody says or does something that hurts us, our first impulse is to try to return the hurt. We want to fight back; but when we do so, we are just lowering ourselves to the plane of the attacker. When we exhibit littleness, we show that we have not attained maturity in our thinking and acting.
>
> It is those who are in love with their work who get the greatest measure of happiness and satisfaction in life. They are ready at all times to join hands with others in a good cause. Such individuals have passed the adolescent state of dependence or near dependence on others.
>
> Those who get worthwhile things done will have some people say cutting and unkind things about them. They will belittle their motives and question their actions. The worst thing they can do under such circumstances is to brood on the unkind things said about them.
>
> Because we play small parts in the scheme of things is no warrant for our ever being little in our attitudes. A friend of mine who was once unjustly attacked said, "I have enough pride not to give my attacker the satisfaction of knowing that what was said hurt me."
>
> Until people and nations actually mature in their thinking and acting, we are going to have tension and war. What can individuals do? Well, they can resolve not to be little themselves. They can act like mature persons, for life is too short to be little.[6]

A practice regularly followed by many creative prospectors is sending thank-you letters to every person contacted, an approach that can create substantial goodwill for you and sometimes be a factor in breaking the ice with your prospects.

SUMMARY

As you can see, prospecting is a complex but necessary set of activities for most individuals in the sales field. Because of normal changes, the volume of business activity in any sales territory seldom remains constant. Creative salespeople, therefore, continually plan prospecting and preapproach activities and experiment with a variety of techniques.

Prospecting involves locating potential customers. The preapproach involves separating suspects from prospects by obtaining as much relevant information as necessary about potential customers before contacting them.

A vivid imagination is helpful in obtaining names of prospective customers. Among the many sources of prospects are your own company, your present customers, former prospects, friends, acquaintances, and neighbors, other salespeople, junior salespeople, periodicals, directories, registers, special lists, and personal observation. Prospects are also obtained from cold canvass and blitzing activities, trade fairs, clubs, party groups, surveys, and through the use of the telephone, mail inquiries, and videocassettes.

In order to minimize wasting time, salespeople should also try beforehand to determine whether a prospect is qualified to buy their products or services. Planning and the maintenance of adequate records are essential for the success of prospecting activities.

KEY TERMS

selling process
prospecting
suspects (leads)
prospects
preapproach
endless-chain method
referral approach
centers of influence
testimonial letter
junior salespeople (spotters)
bird dogs
sales associates
cold canvass approach
cold calls
blitz technique
trade fairs/exhibitions
clubs
civic and social groups
computer user groups
bulletin board systems
party groups
surveys
telephone and mail inquiries
videocassettes
qualifying prospects
tickler files
computer software programs

QUESTIONS

1. Evaluate the following statement: "I really don't need to prospect. I have all the work I can handle servicing my existing accounts—they've got to come first. So prospecting, for me, would be a waste of my scarce time."
2. What advice would you give a salesperson who is not satisfied with his or her ratio of sales to total prospects contacted?
3. What are some advantages and disadvantages of being actively involved in civic organizations or service clubs?
4. What is the purpose of the preapproach?
5. Assume that you are a salesperson in the industry of your choice. From what sources might you obtain names of prospective customers?
6. The text gives an example of how the center-of-influence approach can be used by insurance salespeople. What other products or services do you feel could be sold by this same prospecting method?
7. How might you make use of testimonial letters when prospecting?
8. When should a name be deleted from your prospect file?
9. Should you use your friends as leads for prospective sales? Why or why not?

10. What is the major distinction between a "junior salesperson" and a "bird dog"? Evaluate their use.

11. In what ways might the cold canvass approach to prospecting consume more time than alternative prospecting techniques?

12. What is the principal advantage of the blitz technique of prospecting?

APPLICATIONS

8.1 QUALIFYING THE SUPERETTE

George Lee is employed as a sales representative for Far Afield, Inc., a food brokerage firm located in Los Angeles, California. George's territory consists principally of superettes (small supermarkets). Today, George has called on the Short Pause Market, a food store that recently changed ownership. George had poor sales results with the previous owners.

George has approached a middle-aged woman standing behind a checkout counter and politely says, "Good morning. My name is George Lee from Far Afield. Would you mind telling me where I could find the manager?"

The other person responds, "My name is Betty Fong, and I am the manager."

Questions

1. How might George determine whether Betty Fong is a good prospect for his food products?
2. What might George have done in advance of his cold call to qualify his prospect?

8.2 THE LETTER OF GRATITUDE

Write an example of a short letter that expresses your gratitude to a prospect for having seen and listened to you during a recent sales call. Assume that you did not make a sale.

8.3 WANTED—NEW OUTLETS NOW

The Carter Casualty Company, a national insurance company, has expanded rapidly since its founding by K. H. Pent in 1984. Dollar premium volume has increased each year by approximately 25 percent and profits have been satisfactory. One region, however, the Fresno/Bakersfield sales district, has not kept pace with the company's overall growth rate. The major problem has been an insufficient number of insurance agents in the area representing Carter. Lyle Brigham, Sales Manager for the Northern California Division, has decided to assign his own sales representatives temporarily to the weak territory for the purpose of obtaining as many new prospects as possible during a one-week period. Names of prospects will be turned over to the local service office at the end of the week.

The following is an informational bulletin sent out to participating sales representatives by the division sales manager:

May 8, 1990 Northern California Division

Project: Team Prospecting

It has been decided to prospect both Fresno and Bakersfield at the same time and really open up the whole area. The teams will be paired as follows:

Bakersfield:

Dodd	Niles	Smith
Lunstrum	Viau	Scurry

This team will use the company cars: Dodd, Niles, and Smith.

Fresno:

Schwab	Babler	Brigham	Hand
Hilferty	Carson	Lauck	Williams

This team will use the company cars: Hilferty, Carson, Lauck, and Williams.

All personnel are requested to attend a meeting in the Fresno Service Office at 7:30 P.M. on Sunday evening, May 21. Arrangements have been made for all visiting reps to stay at the Town Villa Motel that evening. The Bakersfield team will move to Bakersfield on Monday morning, May 22. Mr. Lauck and Mr. Smith, the local manager, will make motel arrangements in advance for the group in Bakersfield.

Each group will conduct a meeting each night at 8 P.M. to review the day's results. The Bakersfield group will meet in Mr. Lunstrum's motel room, and he will be in charge of these meetings. The Fresno group will meet in the Fresno Service Office at the same time.

On Friday, May 26, everybody will meet again at the Fresno Service Office to review the net result and to conclude the project. All planned prospecting should be completed at this time. We will meet at 12:30 P.M.

Your actual agency calls will be preceded by a special letter to the prospect over Mr. Lauck's signature. This will go out several days in advance of your call.

Each team will receive an agency prospect form for each call. These will have the name and address of the agency the team is to call on and, if possible, a list of the companies now represented. This form should be completed in as much detail as possible for future reference.

The following is the schedule of transportation for the visiting team members:

Mr. Carson's car—Betty Schwab will go with him. They will arrange their own schedule.

Mr. Dodd's car—He will arrange to pick up Mal Viau, John Scurry, and Lea Hand. They too will arrange their own schedule.

Mr. Nile's car—He will arrange to pick up Bernice Babler, Lyle Brigham, and Dick Lunstrum.

You will note that two of our new sales representatives, Jim Hilferty and Susan Williams, have been included in this program. It was felt that this would be very valuable experience for them and a good local assist for the project.

Again, please study the *Agency Development Manual* that was passed out at the April sales meeting. There is some very important information here on agency prospecting. This is a very important project. If we do a good job, we can set a chain reaction in motion that will have long-lasting results for our Company. We need good agents, and we especially need them in this district. This project can go a long way in taking care of a vital need.

Lyle E. Brigham

Sales Manager

jg

Questions

1. What type of prospecting technique has been planned in the above case?
2. What is your specific reaction to the approach to be followed by the Carter Casualty Company in the Fresno/Bakersfield district?
3. What sort of information on prospective agents should be turned over to the local service office sales department?

8.4 SEARCHING FOR PROSPECTS

Assume that you are a sales representative for a real estate firm in your community. Develop an actual list of 25 potential buyers and sellers of homes and then attempt to sell your prospect list to a local realtor. How will you go about developing a list of names?

NOTES

1. "Please Send Shoes," *Sales & Marketing Management,* December 1986, p. 16.
2. Extracted from a review of Stan Kossen's *Creative Selling Today,* 2nd ed. (New York: Harper & Row, 1982).
3. "This Foot in the Door's on Tape," *Sales & Marketing Management,* May 14, 1983, p. 102.
4. Carlton A. Pederson and Milburn D. Wright, *Selling—Principles and Methods* (Homewood, IL: Irwin, 1976), p. 217.
5. "Reach Out and Touch a Buyer on Your PC," *Sales & Marketing Management,* October 8, 1984, pp. 108, 110.
6. Reproduced from the article "Mature Thinking," by the special permission of the author, Charles G. Reigner, President of The H. M. Rowe Company and by the corporation, The H. M. Rowe Company, 624 North Gilmor Street, Baltimore, Maryland, business education textbook publisher since 1867.

Approaching Prospective Customers

Getting to Know You

GETTING OFF TO A GOOD START

Appointments—To Make or Not to Make ■ Butterflies in the Tummy ■ Your Shoes Are Showing ■ I'm Sorry I'm Late ■ Behavior with Intermediaries ■ Bypassing the Receptionist ■ How Long to Wait ■ Create a Receptive Atmosphere ■ The Need for Self-Assurance

HOW TO GAIN THE ATTENTION OF YOUR CUSTOMERS

Compliment the Customer ■ Appeal to Curiosity ■ Question the Buyer ■ Provide a Free Service ■ Present Useful Ideas ■ Present Customer Benefits ■ Solve Customer Problems ■ Use "OK Names" ■ Offer Samples and Gifts ■ Product Approach ■ Use Referrals ■ Use Surprise and Shock ■ Use Showmanship

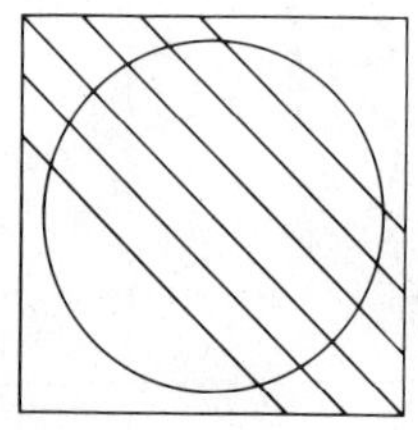

If you look outdated, people tend to wonder if your business skills are outdated. If you look too fashionable, you won't be taken seriously.
RITA GOLDBERG

Regardless of how good a product is, nothing really happens until the product is sold.
ANON.

Here's what you should be able to do after studying this chapter:

1. Create the favorable conditions that are important in approaching buyers.
2. Apply the major approach methods for gaining the attention of prospective customers.

A timid-appearing young insurance agent entered the office of a dynamic sales manager, shyly approached the desk, and then softly uttered, "You don't want to buy any life insurance, do you?" "No!" snarled the manager. "That's what I was afraid of," sighed the embarrassed agent, starting to leave. "Just wait a minute," demanded the aggressive manager. "I've been dealing with salespeople all my life, and you, without a doubt, are the worst I've ever seen. Don't you realize that you have to inspire confidence, and that to do it you must have confidence in yourself? To help you gain that confidence to make a sale, I'll sign for a $100,000 policy." As he signed the manager advised, "You have to learn some effective techniques for approaching customers and then use them." "Oh, but I have," replied the young agent energetically. "I have an approach for almost every kind of businessperson. The one I just used on you was my standard approach for sales managers!"

This anecdote, although grossly exaggerated (we hope!), helps to illustrate the need for developing creative and imaginative techniques for approaching prospective customers. Startling as it may seem, there are some salespeople whose sales approaches regularly consist of little more than the following: "Good morning, Mr. Green. I'm with the 6L Company and happened to be in the neighborhood. You don't need any supplies today, do you?" Such salespeople may then hear, "My name is Brown, not Green, and you're right—I don't!" So they respond, "Sorry, Mr. Brown. Okay, then, thanks anyway. See you next time I'm in the area. So long."

Salespeople whose styles are consistently no more imaginative than this one generally discover that they need to develop more creative approaches. Those who fail to make this discovery tend to have short-lived careers in the field of selling.

We've already discussed the importance of developing an effective preapproach (uncovering relevant information about prospects) and developing a sound prospecting plan (finding customers). Now we arrive at another important step in the selling process—the **approach**—which involves arranging for interviews and establishing rapport during your initial face-to-face contacts with customers. A major purpose of the approach is to enable you—the salesperson—to gain the attention of prospective buyers so that you will be able to interact with them more favorably. A good start helps to motivate your prospects into wanting to hear your sales message and, especially important, into making affirmative buying decisions.

Getting off to a good start results in a good finish.

GETTING OFF TO A GOOD START

The approach is the step in the selling process that enables you—the salesperson—to get to see your prospective customers and deliver a planned sales presentation to them. A sound approach, therefore, relates to those activities that help you get off to a good start with customers.

Yours may be an outstanding product, one designed especially to meet the needs of your customers. But don't be surprised to discover that having a good product doesn't always guarantee that you'll have buyers. You also need to develop a sound approach that will motivate prospects to want to see you. Some prospects tend to have a natural suspicion of strangers—and to a great many prospects, that's exactly what you are: a stranger.

Getting off to a good start with an imaginative approach can be tremendously helpful to you in the selling process. Your sales record is likely to reflect the skillfulness of your efforts in this area. The following section presents some of the more significant factors that should be considered when approaching prospective customers.

Appointments—To Make or Not to Make

Should you always make appointments before a sales call, or can you ever simply drop by to see a customer unannounced? Generally, normal courtesy dictates that appointments be made, either by telephone, letter, or prior personal contact. However, in some types of selling, such as house-to-house selling, making appointments in advance is often impractical. Furthermore, prospects unfamiliar with you or your products are sometimes hesitant to agree to a specific appointment. And prospects contacted for the first time find it relatively easy to refuse attempts at making appointments over the telephone.

"Some prospects tend to have a natural suspicion of strangers—and to a great many prospects, that's exactly what you are: a stranger."

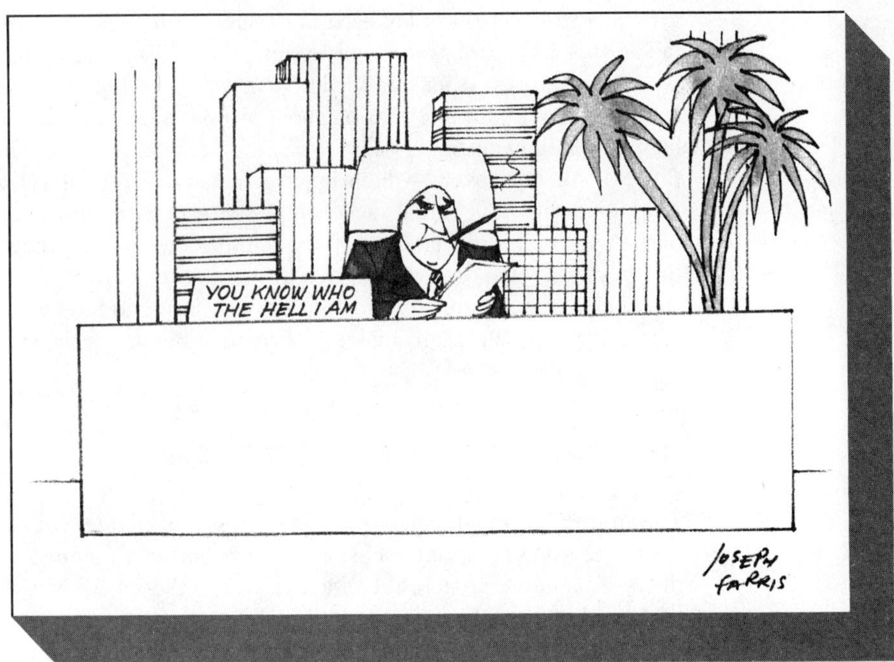

Reprinted with permission from *Sales & Marketing Management* magazine; © 1986.

Some customers rarely object to your dropping by without an appointment, especially if you have something useful to offer. However, you should not make a call unless you do have something to say or show that can truly benefit your customer. Most customers do not appreciate your dropping by merely to "shoot the breeze."

Why are scheduled appointments desirable?

One of the major advantages of having an advance appointment is that you are likely to *gain more complete attention* from your customers, since they generally will be mentally set to see you and thus more receptive to your message. Contacting customers without an appointment, when they are preoccupied with other activities, leaves your sales message competing for their attention.

When asking a prospect or customer for an appointment, always make it as easy as possible for him or her to make a decision. Inexperienced salespeople might ask something like, "Ms. Hoffman, when might be a good time for me to call on you?" Ms. Hoffman, in this instance, has nothing specific to grab onto, and it becomes easier for her to respond negatively to the request.

How should you ask for appointments?

A more effective approach would be, "Ms. Hoffman, I'm going to be working in your area next Tuesday. I have some information that will be of interest to you. I could see you at 9:30 A.M., or would 1:30 P.M. be better?" You have made it easy for Ms. Hoffman to make a decision, and if she indicates that she is busy at both times, you could ask, "When would be a more convenient time for you?"

Some sales representatives find it helpful to send a letter or postcard to the prospective customer as a reminder of the upcoming appointment.

Butterflies in the Tummy

Do butterflies ever get "people" in their tummies?

Your moods and attitudes, which are a part of your overall appearance, are extremely important when you make your first calls on accounts. Salespeople, especially before making their first calls in the morning, sometimes feel as though they were marching off to a perilous battlefield. Take the example of Bonnie Dewar: Bonnie, a representative of a large garment manufacturing firm, is about to make her first sales call of the day on the buyer of a medium-sized department store. It is Monday morning. Her weekend was enjoyably spent with her family, and she was in high spirits when she left home this morning. Bonnie has driven to within three blocks of her customer's store, and suddenly she feels some frightening changes in her emotional state coming over her. The rate of her heartbeat has jumped from the normal 72 to nearly 140 beats per minute. Her breathing rate has quickened, and her mouth feels as though her salivary glands had gone on a wildcat strike. Bonnie's mouth is so dry that she feels as though its roof and floor were about to fuse. Her sweat glands, working overtime, seem to be making up for the loss of activity in her salivary glands. Her forehead, palms, and underarms are moist with perspiration. Bonnie wonders if maybe she shouldn't have kept her job as a fry cook in a fast-food restaurant.

"A certain amount of tension or nervousness, especially before your first call of the day, is not only natural, but even somewhat beneficial."

Is nervousness always undesirable?

How can you rid yourself of those butterflies?

Although perhaps a bit exaggerated, Bonnie's emotional reactions are typical of what salespeople occasionally feel to one degree or another. You might find it consoling to realize that a certain amount of tension or nervousness, especially before your first call of the day, is not only natural but even somewhat beneficial. Such emotional feelings are likely to be evidence that you have a sincere concern for your performance. And concerned sales representatives are generally far better prepared for their sales presentations than those who are indifferent toward their activities. *Excessive nervousness,* however, could be the result of insufficient experience in selling or inadequate preparation for a specific sales call. With *greater experience and more effective planning,* you should find that your tensions lessen and your confidence increases. But don't be particularly concerned about occasional feelings of anxiety—it's unlikely that they'll be eliminated completely. Experienced salespeople realize that they "go with the territory" and learn to accept and live with such feelings.

Your Shoes Are Showing

In an earlier chapter, we discussed how a salesperson's appearance communicates various messages to prospective customers. There are enough hurdles for you to overcome when approaching prospects without beginning with the handicap of an appearance that is unacceptable to your customers. Rational or not, many people do tend to form first impressions of a salesperson based on his or her wearing apparel and grooming. As the Queen of England once wrote to her son the Prince of Wales:

> Dress gives one the outward sign from which people in general can, and often do, judge upon the inward state of mind and feelings of a person; for this they *can see;* while the other they *cannot see.* On that account, clothes are of particular importance. . . .[1]

Wearing apparel and grooming are only part of the *total impression* that salespeople make on prospective customers. Something as seemingly insignificant as a business card can affect your image before a prospect. For example, you're probably off to a bad start if you hand the prospect a crumpled or grimy card instead of a neat, fresh one.

Your sales aids also contribute toward the total impression you are making. You've probably lost some ground with your prospect if your sales aids are shopworn and tattered looking. Even your appointment book makes an impression. Is it bulging with disorganized looking scraps of paper, or is it neat and nondistracting to the prospect?

And finally, how about the seats and floor of your car? Are they littered with messy odds and ends? When you take your prospect somewhere in your car, do you generally have to apologize for the mess while you attempt to hurriedly straighten it up before you can drive on.

Appearance counts!

Remember that *everything* you wear, carry, and do influences the prospect's perception of you and your company. Appearances that may seem insignificant do have an effect on the total impression you make on your prospective customers.

I'm Sorry I'm Late

Don't be late for an important date!

Concerned salespeople, especially those who are well organized, seldom arrive late for appointments. Those who do arrive late often get off to a bad start with their customers. Prospective buyers, expecting you to arrive at specific times, will sometimes postpone other projects in anticipation of your visit. Any time spent waiting for you is wasted time for them—they could have been doing other things. To avoid this problem, plan to arrive at least ten minutes before an appointment; this allows time for possible delays, such as those caused by traffic congestion. Struggling through highway traffic when you are late for an appointment can create additional tensions and frustrations that can do little but detract from your sales delivery.

Behavior with Intermediaries

Is Mr. Scallopini in?

When making a sales call, you ordinarily will not see the prospective purchaser immediately. More typical is an initial greeting from an intermediary, such as an assistant, secretary, or receptionist. Curtness or lack of tact and consideration toward such individuals can sometimes result in lost sales. We discussed the important concept of buying centers in an earlier chapter. You recall that a buying center consists of everyone in an organization who participates or influences buying decisions. Intermediaries, who frequently are a part of the buying center, can have far more influence with their bosses than you realize. Study the ground rules below. They should be considered when dealing with intermediaries in order to avoid hurting your chances of securing a favorable interview with the actual buyer.

How should you treat the buyer's assistants?

1. Try to make a favorable impression on the intermediary. Introduce yourself and your company, possibly presenting the intermediary with your business card and some of your company literature.
2. Have a positive, courteous attitude, and don't forget to smile!
3. Don't waste the intermediary's time with idle chatter or flirtation. He or she also has jobs and responsibilities.
4. Don't waste your own time. Waiting can give you an opportunity to catch up on certain activities, such as planning, studying company literature (either yours or your prospect's), or preparing sales reports.
5. Be businesslike while waiting. Idly daydreaming or restlessly tapping your shoe on the linoleum floor is likely to create anything but a favorable impression.

Bypassing the Receptionist

When might it be okay to bypass the receptionist?

Office protocol generally assumes that outsiders who call on organizations will first check with the receptionist. Some salespeople feel that dealing with receptionists can waste time, especially when the customer is well known and friendly. But any salesperson who bypasses formal channels should be certain to know his or her customers well and avoid the practice in situations where it might be considered rude.

How Long to Wait

Occasionally you may have an appointment for a specific time, but your customer makes *you* wait. Above all, try not to display impatience or anger while waiting. However, the question sometimes arises as to how long you should wait. Your time is also valuable, and time spent waiting is time not spent selling.

Many sales managers advise their sales force to use sound judgment, but under most circumstances do not wait much longer than 10 to 15 minutes. If your prospect hasn't seen you within 15 minutes, there is a possibility that he or she has forgotten about you. Rather than continue waiting and wasting your selling time, you could inform the receptionist that you have another appointment and ask how soon your customer will be available. If the customer will be occupied for some time, you could request another appointment. Sometimes, of course, waiting is necessary, especially when an important buyer is unavoidably detained. As with any situation in selling, you should use your judgment in determining how long to wait for a specific customer. In any case, since you are destined to spend portions of your working day waiting, you could make effective use of this time by planning future activities or studying.

Why just wait when you have to wait?

Create a Receptive Atmosphere

Let's assume that you are a manufacturer's representative for a printing products company. You have called upon Black and Blue Ink, Inc., a dealership in your territory that purchases a variety of items for resale in the printing trades. The person responsible for prospective purchases is Henry Senefelder, an affable individual who was recently promoted to his present position with Black and Blue.

Those first few moments with your prospective customer, Mr. Senefelder, are extremely important, since they will set the tone for the entire sales interview. Remember that he's probably been thinking of everything but your mission. So if your presentation is going to be received and understood by Senefelder, you are going to have to get him into a frame of mind that wants to listen to your message.

"Those first few moments with your prospective customer . . . are extremely important, since they will set the tone for the entire sales interview."

A certain amount of small talk related to the buyer's interests and hobbies can sometimes serve to break the ice, but you should be careful not to appear phony or to be talking merely for the sake of talking. Your immediate goal should be to create rapport with Senefelder. This part of the interview becomes quite natural when you have a sincere interest in your customers.

Did you ever hear the one about the . . . ?

A few "should nots": you should not attempt to establish rapport by telling ethnic jokes. Even if your prospect positively is not a member of an ethnic group, he or she may have strong concerns in this area and feel that you are somewhat offensive. To be on the safe side, some managers advise that you avoid telling any jokes. If your joke "bombs," you place your prospect in the awkward position of having to feign a laugh in order to humor or be polite to you. Nor should you assume that all of your prospective customers are interested in sports just because you are. Politics is another subject that can result in unwanted differences, and possibly animosity, between prospects and you. A better approach is to ask probing questions, which can aid you in uncovering your prospect's true interests. Most people enjoy talking about their own interests and activities. You may bore them, however, if you talk only about your own interests. And you may anger them with your expressed political point of view.

The Need for Self-Assurance

How does being "confident" differ from being "cocky"?

You certainly don't want to appear cocky or arrogant during your approach; nor do you need to appear apologetic for taking a portion of the prospect's time. Some sales representatives unthinkingly open with such comments as, "I'm sorry to bother you, Mr. Angerame." One prospective buyer confronted with this approach wryly retorted, "Well, I'd hate to see you do something you are sorry for, so I'll see you some other time!"

Remember why you call on potential customers. You have products that can benefit them. You are there to serve and assist your customers with their problems and needs. If you sincerely see your responsibility as one of serving your customers, you are likely to discover that they see you the same way.

Foreign sales representatives, unfamiliar with American culture, have sometimes aroused undue suspicion in American buyers. For example, extreme politeness and humility are features of some cultures. And bowing, accompanied by humility, is considered normal within some groups. But Americans, typically unaccustomed to such behavior, sometimes feel uncomfortable in excessively formal situations.

When dealing with any market, you should try to tailor your approach and role to meet the style and expectations of the prospect. Acceptable behavior includes appearing reasonably confident, poised, and courteous.

HOW TO GAIN THE ATTENTION OF YOUR CUSTOMERS

What sort of attention do you want?

Let's assume that all has gone well so far. The receptionist has informed you that your customer will see you in a few moments. The curtain is about to rise and your debut to commence. Your opportunity to perform the skills of your trade has arrived at last. Now begins a crucial part of the approach phase of the selling process—*gaining the attention* of your prospective buyer. How you perform now will significantly influence the success or failure of your presentation. The attention you seek must, of course, be favorable and should make the prospect more receptive to your presentation. It certainly should not be merely attention for attention's sake.

One of your principal objectives at this stage of the selling process is motivating and guiding your prospect into making a favorable buying decision. Your prospect is unlikely to make a favorable decision, however, until enough information is received to justify one. And the information can't be received unless he or she pays attention to your presentation.

Sometimes getting the attention of the buyer is no trouble at all. In fact, you may be cordially greeted with something like, "Hello, you're just the person I was thinking about. I have an order here I'd like you to quote me some prices on." At other times, there may be numerous distractions competing for the buyer's attention. Here is where empathy on your part becomes significant. If you were in the prospect's shoes, what would attract your interest and attention? How have successful salespeople overcome this hurdle? Some of the proven methods used to capture the buyer's interest are discussed below. (See Table 9.1 for a summary of methods.)

TABLE 9.1 Approach Methods Used to Capture the Interest of Potential Buyers.

Compliment the customer	Use OK names
Appeal to curiosity	Offer samples and gifts
Question the buyer	Use the product approach
Provide a free service	Use referrals
Present useful ideas	Use surprise and shock
Present customer benefits	Use showmanship
Solve customer problems	

Compliment the Customer

Most people enjoy recognition and the feeling of self-esteem, so **complimenting customers** can be an effective way to capture a buyer's interest. If you have done your homework properly, you might know of significant achievements or events related to your prospects or their firms. For example, you may have learned that your customer's wife recently gave birth to a baby boy. You might say something like, "Casper, I hear you recently became the proud papa of a son. Congratulations! How much did he weigh?" Or perhaps the buyer's firm has developed a new product, received public recognition for a recent activity, or has an unusually attractive store layout.

Should you serve compliments with syrup?

A sincere compliment can often enhance your initial approach. But the compliment itself is not enough; it must be *sincere* and *believable.* You should avoid any compliments that will sound insincere to the prospect.

Appeal to Curiosity

Another approach used to gain attention relates to the human tendency to be curious. An action or an opening statement with **curiosity appeal** can pave the way to a more effective demonstration.

Curiosity killed the cat, but made the sale!

For example, a question that would probably arouse interest is: "Mr. Marner, if I could show you a system for reducing by twenty percent the cost of each letter mailed from your office, would you be interested?" Of course your prospect would be interested in saving money, and he'd probably be willing to give you some time if your approach seemed sincere and honest.*

Occasionally you may plan to use a visual aid, such as a portable videocassette player, in your sales presentation. If you do so, you can often arouse curiosity by not immediately saying what the visual aid is. Some salespeople, for example, arouse curiosity by placing the object, still in its container, on the floor beside the desk. The prospect often asks, "What's in the box?" The salesperson can then respond with a smile and say, "Filbert, I'm glad you asked. Inside this container is an idea that can eliminate one of your severest production problems."

Question the Buyer

Don't questions usually get you thinking?

Do you remember when your professor at college asked questions in class? Even if you weren't being called on, or the questions were merely rhetorical, didn't the quizzical sound of a question tend to draw you into the discussion? Effective speakers frequently use the **questioning approach** to create or maintain interest even when an answer isn't expected. In opening sales calls, probing questions are often used. For example, assume that you sent a letter to a prospect in advance of your visit. As an attention-getter, you might ask something like, "Ms. Clipson, what was your reaction to the plan discussed in the recent letter I sent to you?" Even if Ms. Clipson

*Not all salespeople agree with this approach. They feel that the "If . . . , would you . . . ?" approach puts the customer into a box since he or she has only one possible answer.

doesn't remember the letter, your initial question has paved the way for additional questions.

Provide a Free Service

Why would a free service arouse interest?

One of the most effective ways of opening a sales call is to offer a **free service.** This approach can serve as tangible evidence of your sincere interest in the customer and usually arouses his or her attention. 3M Company sales trainees are advised to use the service approach in this fashion: "My reason for calling on you today, Mr. Brown, is to check on the inventory control system we set up for ordering your 3M products." Salespeople calling on retailers often use this approach—they offer to check inventory needs or to set up promotional displays as a service to the buyers. Some representatives even offer to demonstrate their products—cameras or wall covering materials, for example—to the customers of retail outlets.

Present Useful Ideas

Got any good ideas?

Your customers are continually looking for new ideas. Ultimate consumers want to know how they can operate their households more efficiently. Businesses are interested in methods for reducing costs and increasing profits.

If you were a manager of, say, a retail store, wouldn't you be likely to be receptive to ideas that could help you in your operations? Most managers would be. During regular sales calls, salespeople are likely to learn of merchandising techniques and uses for their products that have proven effective for their customers. As a method of gaining attention, some of these **useful ideas** could be passed on to other customers during the approach. A favorable opening remark designed to develop the interest of your customers could be: "Mr. Hooper, the other day I came across an idea that resulted in a 10 percent increase in cash flow for a firm similar to yours. Here's how it works."

Present Customer Benefits

Related to presenting useful ideas is the **customer-benefit approach.** When using this technique, you would make a statement or raise a question that enables the prospect to realize how he or she can benefit from the purchase of your product or service.

For example, assume that you sell document transmission systems known in the industry as business facsimile machines. Yours is called the FAX-325i. It enables businesses to send and receive documents, graphics, and halftone photos anywhere over telephone lines.

What's in it for thee? Well, I'll tell you.

You might say something like this to your customer: "Mr. Replique, here's a significant benefit that the FAX-325i business facsimile unit provides: At the touch of one button, the FAX-325i can speed-dial up to forty-nine locations. Coded speed-dialing allows access to one hundred more. Its high-speed transmission capability sends crisp, clear, picture-perfect documents to their destinations almost instantly—twelve seconds per page—at the mere cost of a phone call. With this unit, your document transmission costs are cut to a minimum." (Of course, you would want to be certain that your prospect understood the terminology associated with document transmitting systems before using such jargon.)

Solve Customer Problems

Similar to the customer-benefit and questioning approaches is the **problem-solving approach.** Most prospects have problems. And it should be safe to state that most prospects would like to rid themselves of these problems. Prospects often don't perceive their actions as buying a particular brand of merchandise or service. Instead, their purchases are perceived more as an activity of creating solutions to specific problems.

Of course, you must discover what your prospects' problems are, which can be done through the skillful use of questioning and listening techniques. One effective method of getting prospects' attention during the approach, therefore, is to ask them to tell you what their biggest problem is. This approach will usually motivate most prospects, who generally are glad to talk about the problems with which they're currently wrestling. It also helps them to release some of their stress by "getting it off their chests." Later in your presentation you can show them how your product or service will solve their real problems.

Use "OK Names"

"George Washington slept here."

Some prospects are favorably impressed when they learn that well-known companies are using your products. The use of **"OK names"**—that is, names of firms that are known and respected by your prospects—can often favorably influence your own customers. Using **testimonial letters** is related to this approach and can help you secure your buyer's interest and attention.

Offer Samples and Gifts

Put a dab of **this** *behind your ear!*

In some types of selling, offering product **samples** or **gifts** is quite commonplace. For example, some salespeople open by saying, "Ms. Fisk, I have an appointment diary for you that I hope you will find useful." Salespersons with pharmaceutical companies generally pass out product samples and literature to doctors and pharmacists. Perfume company representatives often offer free miniature bottles of perfume to prospective buyers. Samples and gifts not only arouse interest and attention but are also useful as selling tools that appeal to a buyer's senses.

Product Approach

Here . . . try this for size.

Another method for arousing interest is the **product approach.** With this technique you simply hand your product or demonstration model to the prospective customer and wait for a reaction. In a sense, you're allowing the product to gain the prospect's attention and arouse his or her interest. After handing the prospect the product, say nothing—merely listen. The reaction that you get from the prospect will be a clue as to what your next actions should be. Questions from the prospect regarding price or product availability, for example, could be an indication of a sincere interest in making a purchase. The product approach is best used with products that have certain unique or appealing features likely to attract the prospect's attention.

If the product itself isn't available, brochures, merchandising pieces, cutaway models, or even a special part of the product can be used to capture the prospect's attention and interest. Be certain before your interview that your model is in good working order.

Use Referrals

"Knock twice, and tell 'em 'Joe sent ya!'"

"Mr. Larsen, last week I was talking to a friend of yours, Jim Murphy, and he told me that you might be interested in an idea that we put to work for him with astonishing success." This is an example of the **referral approach,** a technique that can be extremely useful for gaining the interest of your prospective customer, especially when he or she has great respect for the person giving the referral. Some salespeople also use **blind referrals**—for example, "Ms. Felps, a number of our customers have told us. . . ."

Use Surprise and Shock

Imagine the reaction of a prospect if you sold word processing systems and opened with the comment, "You, Mr. Harper, like everyone else, are concerned these days with rising costs. It seems as though the price of everything has soared sky high, and we're all looking for ways to cut costs. I would like to demonstrate a word processing system to you that is four times *more expensive* than any system you've purchased previously." Mr. Harper might first wonder if he had heard you correctly. The **surprise** or **shock approach** could be an effective attention getter. He might ask, "Did you say *four times more expensive?*" You could then explain that although the system is more expensive *initially,* its features would actually result in cost reductions because of more efficient operations, storage and retrieval capabilities, lower maintenance costs, greater flexibility, and a higher trade-in value.

How shocking!

Use Showmanship

A person selling an expensive line of porcelain dinnerware has successfully used what could be called a **showmanship approach** with customers. This salesperson places a delicate-appearing dish on the floor and asks prospects to stand on it to demonstrate its durability. As yet, not one dish has broken, and the prospects are generally fascinated by such an unusual approach.

Why don't you step on it!

These approaches are only some of the many that can be used to attract the attention of your prospects and customers. You should experiment with new techniques from time to time and vary your approach in order to avoid repetition with the same customers.

SUMMARY

The approach is the step in the selling process that involves doing whatever has to be done in order to see and deliver a sales message to a prospective buyer. A creative and planned approach can get you off to a better start with buyers and help you guide them into making affirmative purchasing decisions.

The concept of the approach is quite broad and involves making appointments, developing an awareness that some tension or anxiety before sales calls is natural, showing a concern for your appearance, arriving for appointments on time, and demonstrating courtesy and tact with receptionists and assistants.

The approach is also concerned with questions of whether or not to bypass the receptionist and how long you should wait to see a prospect or customer. Other aspects of the approach include the need for creating a receptive atmosphere and the importance of conveying a confident but not cocky attitude.

Effective and creative salespeople have developed specific techniques and methods for gaining the attention of their potential customers. Among the more common approaches are complimenting the customer, appealing to curiosity, questioning, providing a free service, presenting useful ideas and customer benefits, using the problem-solving approach, and using "OK names." Other attention getters include giving product samples or gifts, demonstrating product models, using referrals, using the unexpected, and engaging in showmanship.

KEY TERMS

approach
complimenting-customers approach
curiosity-appeal approach
questioning approach
free-service approach
useful-idea approach
customer-benefit approach
problem-solving approach
"OK-names" approach
testimonial letters
sample/gift approach
product approach
referral approach
blind referral
surprise/shock approach
showmanship approach

QUESTIONS

1. Why is it generally desirable to make appointments in advance of sales calls? Describe some of the circumstances under which prior appointments might be difficult or unnecessary.

2. Evaluate the following approach to securing an appointment:

   "Mr. Harcourt, I'm going to be working in your area next week. When might be a good time to see you to tell you something about our new line of products?"

3. What advice might be offered to a young salesperson who has explained to you that he is always nervous before making sales calls, especially before the first one in the morning?

4. Why is a salesperson's appearance—wearing apparel and grooming—so important to his or her sales accomplishments?

5. Why is it important for a salesperson to make a favorable impression on intermediaries, such as secretaries or assistants?

6. Evaluate the statement: "Arriving on time is not as important as having a good product and a well-organized sales presentation."

7. Assume that you have arranged an appointment with one of your regular customers for 10 A.M. You arrive at 9:55 A.M. and tell the receptionist about your appointment. The receptionist indicates that your customer is talking on the telephone at the moment, but should be able to see you shortly. The time is now 10:20 A.M., and you have not yet seen your customer. What should you do?

8. When, if ever, should a salesperson bypass the receptionist? What are the possible advantages and risks involved when bypassing occurs?

9. Even though a sense of humor is a desirable characteristic for a salesperson, what are the potential dangers in being a joke teller?

10. Should a salesperson ever engage in "small talk"? Explain.

11. Why shouldn't you appear apologetic for taking your prospect's time during a sales approach? What would be more desirable than an apology during such circumstances?

12. Offering a compliment is said to be effective as a means of "warming up" a customer. In what way should you be careful when employing this approach?

13. Assume that you are a representative for a telephone company selling yellow page advertisements to business concerns. Develop approaches related to the following:

- **a.** A prospect's curiosity
- **b.** Providing a useful idea
- **c.** The referral approach

APPLICATIONS

9.1 HOW DO YOU FEEL ABOUT THESE APPROACHING TECHNIQUES?

Below are listed three methods for approaching customers. Also presented are sample statements related to each approaching technique. First read and analyze each statement and then write a short comment related to how effective you feel each technique is likely to be.

Approach 1. Complimenting the Customer

a. "Good morning, Ms. Greene. You know, you're one of the cutest customers I have in my territory. Has anyone ever told you that you're a real knock-out?"

b. "Good morning, Ms. Greene. I hear that you were recently promoted to the position of head purchasing manager. That's quite an accomplishment for a woman."

c. "Good morning, Ms. Greene. I understand you were recently transferred to this office from Salt Lake. I think you're going to like it here. You have a fine group of people working with you in this office who should make your job a lot easier."

Evaluation of comment a: ______________________________

____

Evaluation of comment b: ______________________________

____

Evaluation of comment c: ______________________________

____

Approach 2. Questioning the Buyer

a. "Mr. Morinda, I was in the neighborhood so I decided to drop in. You don't need any supplies today, do you?"

b. "Mr. Morinda, how familiar are you with the line of products my company, the Faberoni Corporation, has to offer?"

c. "Mr. Morinda, what was your reaction to the information I recently mailed to you about our line of products?"

Evaluation of comment a: ______________________________

____

Evaluation of comment b: ______________________________

____

Evaluation of comment c: ______________________________

____

Approach 3. Customer Benefit

a. "The Peach-Tree IV Desktop Computer System that we offer will impress the heck out of any of your customers that walk in here."

b. "Our Peach-Tree IV Desktop Color System provides brilliant color displays."

c. "Small-business owners like yourself often find accounting work confusing, tedious, and time-consuming. You'll discover that the Peach-Tree System will enable you to manage your books far more effectively, which will translate directly into lower costs and higher profits for your business."

Evaluation of comment a: ______________________________

____

Evaluation of comment b: ______________________________

____

Evaluation of comment c: ______________________________

____

9.2 HI! MY NAME IS . . .

Many individuals—perhaps even you—are somewhat shy about initiating conversations with people they don't know. Yet the courage to do so is essential for the salesperson who is in the approach stage of the selling process. Salespeople continually have to strike up conversations with people whom they've never seen before. As a means of giving you experience and, therefore, enhancing your confidence, try this activity during the next five days: approach five strangers each day. Find out from each person his or her name, occupation or college major, career plans, and favorite flavor of ice cream. Plan your specific approach technique for each "prospect" before opening your conversation.

9.3 OOPS! WHAT A MESS!

You are on your way to meet with an important prospect, Ms. Dana Bandana. She is a key figure in making buying decisions for the Dragnet Security Systems Company. Your appointment is for 1:00 P.M. Driving to Ms. Bandana's office will take almost two hours, so you decide to stop for lunch about two-thirds of the way there. You take your presentation portfolio with you into a fast-food outlet to review it, since these are materials you intend to show Ms. Bandana during your sales presentation.

While eating, you accidentally knock over your coffee cup, and black coffee spills all over the place. What a mess! Your portfolio pages are stained with dark coffee spots. The left sleeve of your jacket is also stained. You don't have an extra sales portfolio or jacket with you.

You're not certain what to do now. You could phone Ms. Bandana and tell her that you have to attend an unexpected emergency meeting and won't be able to make it today. Or you might even go ahead with your presentation and say nothing. Maybe she won't even notice the stains on your clothes and portfolio if you don't make excuses for them. On the other hand, perhaps there is a better approach for you to take than either of these two choices.

Question

What should you do to salvage your call on Ms. Dana Bandana?

9.4 WE'RE A LITTLE BIT LATE, FOLKS

Assume that a week ago you arranged a breakfast meeting for this morning with Frank Battino, one of your best accounts. You were supposed to stop by Battino's office at 8 A.M. to take him out for breakfast. Unfortunately, you did not hear your alarm this morning, and you didn't awaken until 8:15 A.M.

Questions

1. What should you do about your plight?
2. Specifically, what would you say to Battino?

9.5 OBSERVATIONS OF A STUDENT

My name is Steven Kam, and I am a student in a sales class at a community college in Oakland, California. As part of my course requirements, I traveled with and observed the sales presentations of Michael Friedman, an account executive with Metro Communications Company, a firm publishing a variety of regional and specialized magazines. Among its publications are *Action Wrestling,* a combination program and magazine distributed at wrestling events, and several "in-flight" magazines that are distributed free to passengers of airlines.

Mr. Friedman, as an account executive, is responsible for selling advertising space for Metro Communications. I observed Friedman over a three-day period, accompanying him on twenty-three calls, of which three resulted in confirmed orders for advertising space. Friedman indicated that his sales results were somewhat typical of the industry since advertisement selling is a long-term process.

I was told that Friedman obtains a large proportion of his prospects from ads appearing in competing publications. Friedman refers to this technique as "competition research development," indicating that it's a fairly common industry practice for obtaining potential customers. Another source of leads results from inquiries to advertisements printed in business publications such as *Sales & Marketing Management.* Most sales calls are prearranged by telephone.

Prior to all initial sales calls, Metro's art department prepares sample layouts that relate specifically to the prospect. Although I learned that these layouts are seldom used by major clients, they do serve to get one's foot in the door.

During the initial meeting with a prospect, Friedman customarily opens by introducing himself and his company. He uses a portfolio to dramatize visually the previous and the expected accomplishments of Metro Communications.

I noticed that Friedman also used portfolios to show sample covers from recent publications along with circulation data and other demographic information.

One thing that interested me was that Friedman made no attempt to close a sale during a first call. Friedman told me that the purpose of the first call is to familiarize the prospect with Metro's advertising services. If it appears that the prospect has the potential to be a sizable and profitable account, a free advertisement in a forthcoming issue of a publication is offered. The sample offer includes a black-and-white ad as large as one full page. I was told that the free ad is not intended to obligate the prospect, but it seems to me that it does.

As I mentioned, no attempt to close is made at this point. And no return sales call is made until Mr. Friedman can show an actual copy of the magazine with the free ad in it.

During the second call, the previous presentation is summarized, specific recommendations are made, and an attempt is made to bind the prospective client to a one-year agreement.

I was told that the client isn't forgotten after the sale is made. Regular follow-up calls are made to ascertain that he or she is pleased with the service. In addition, all clients are put on a mailing list for Metro's in-house publication called *Update.*

Questions

1. Evaluate the approach followed by Mr. Friedman in the case.
2. Assume that you are an account executive for Metro. Develop five specific approaches that could be used to arouse and maintain a prospective client's interest.
3. What might be some sources of prospects for Metro in addition to "competition research development" and advertisements in business publications?

9.6 GROW YOUR OWN

An unknown philosopher is said to have advised:

Planting and cultivating,
not harvesting,
makes the crop.

Question

How does the above statement relate to the sales activity referred to as *the approach?*

NOTE

1. Mortimer Levitt, *The Executive Look and How to Get It* (New York: AMACOM, 1979), p. 10.

10 Preparing and Presenting The Sales Message

And Now . . . We Proudly Present. . . .

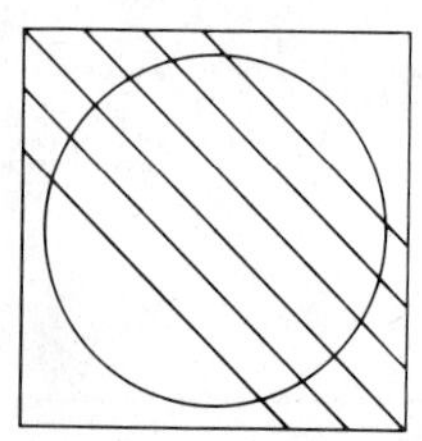

A benefit isn't a benefit unless it meets a specific need.
DENNIS HAWVER, PRESIDENT, RHR INSTITUTE

Selling is, for most of us, a continuous process of getting used to the things we hadn't expected.
R & R MAGAZINE, RESEARCH & REVIEW SERVICE

Here's what you should be able to do after studying this chapter:

1. Explain the purpose of planning and developing an effective sales presentation.
2. Utilize the major characteristics of a well-planned presentation.
3. Summarize the advantages and disadvantages of the four major types of sales presentations.
4. Resolve the major types of problems that tend to arise during sales presentations.
5. Develop an effective sales presentation of your own.

Let's assume that you've done a formidable job of prospecting, have uncovered necessary and relevant information about your potential buyer during your preapproach, and have developed an approach so powerful and persuasive that it would melt the icy heart of Ebenezer Scrooge, even convincing him to shout "Merry Christmas!" from the rooftops. Your appearance, of course, is impeccable—shoes shined, clothes pressed—and your prospect appears receptive and relaxed after a reasonable amount of informal conversation. You seem to have aroused a desired amount of curiosity for your product. In short, everything seems to be going precisely as you had hoped.

Suddenly, however, you're filled with fright. You're looking at the prospect, Ms. Anthrop, and she's looking expectantly at you. Ms. Anthrop suddenly exclaims, "Don't just sit there—say something!" You then realize that you forgot one "small" detail; you neglected learning about the next important step in the sales process: *preparing and communicating the sales presentation.*

All is not lost, however. Through the mystical powers of imagination we can extricate you from your plight and start you on a journey designed to get you to your sales destination. After your imaginary but harrowing experience with Ms. Anthrop, you should realize the importance of preparing a well-planned **sales presentation,** one that appeals to the needs and motives of your prospects and that helps you with that crucial step in the selling process: the *close.*

In this chapter we examine and evaluate some of the principal types of sales presentations, provide specific suggestions for improving them, and discuss a number of the more common obstacles or problems you may face when delivering your sales message.

THE IMPORTANCE OF PLANNED SALES PRESENTATIONS

Ask some sales representatives what type of sales presentations they use and you might be given a quizzical stare followed by, "What type? Heck, I don't have any fancy ivory-tower name for my sales presentations. I'll leave the labels to those college professors who don't have anything better to do. I just see my customers and sell, that's all!"

There may be some salespeople who have no planned presentations and merely "play it by ear." But in today's modern, competitive world, most well-managed organizations have highly organized sales training programs; in these, sales trainees study and practice some of the proven types of sales presentations in order to develop selling skills. Most sales managers today feel that without planned presentations, salespeople are likely to waste considerable amounts of their own and their prospective customers' time.

"Find a need and fill it," asserts a slogan affixed to the sides of trucks owned by the Kaiser Sand and Gravel Company. These words more or less summarize the major purposes of any sales presentation. As the Kaiser slogan implies, the primary purposes of any presentation should be:

Why make a sales presentation?

1. To arouse in the prospective customer a feeling of need or desire.
2. To show how your product can fill or satisfy the customer's recognized need or desire.

Stated another way, the major purpose of the sales presentation is to get prospective customers to realize how they *need* and can *benefit* from what you have to offer. There can't be too much stress placed on the importance of a focus on customer *needs* and *benefits.*

Why is the presentation really the heart of the selling process?

In reality, a sales presentation begins with the *approach,* the step in the selling process designed initially to get the prospect to want to see you and to arouse his or her interest and attention so that you can deliver your sales message. A planned presentation can help you *maintain* the buyer's interest. It also should help you *uncover customer needs.* Both can facilitate your major objective—creating a *desire* for your product or service. Buyer objections, which occur regularly during presentations, and techniques for closing sales are covered in separate chapters. Now let's move on to a description of the characteristics and types of sales presentations typically used by sales representatives today.

"Without prior planning and rehearsal, you will be less likely to make an effective presentation or to develop high-level selling skills."

CHARACTERISTICS OF EFFECTIVE PRESENTATIONS

A planned presentation should not imply inflexibility. In fact, experienced salespeople usually employ what can be termed **situational selling,** the process of drawing on past sales experiences and knowledge when confronting a prospective buyer while recognizing at the same time that each selling situation is unique. It is an activity, therefore, that requires flexibility and imagination.

Without prior planning and rehearsal, you will be less likely to make an effective presentation or to develop high-level selling skills. You should know in advance what you want to accomplish and how you intend to go about it. See Table 10.1 for a checklist for planning sales calls on commercial prospects. Before you can develop an effective sales presentation, however, you must be familiar with the essential elements of the typical sales message.

There are different ways of looking at what should go into a sales presentation. In this section we'll examine the following two concepts:

1. AIDA
2. FUN-FAB OPTIC

The AIDA Concept

A classic sales concept that most selling professionals are familiar with is the **AIDA concept.** According to proponents of AIDA, the salesperson should attempt to guide the prospect's mind through *four stages,* or steps, leading to a buying decision. The goal of each of these stages is to:

1. Secure *A*ttention.
2. Arouse *I*nterest.
3. Stimulate *D*esire.
4. Obtain *A*ction.

These stages are referred to as the AIDA concept, an acronym made up from the first letter of each goal. In effect, the salesperson guides the prospect through each of the four steps in order to make a sale.

"May I have your **attention?"**

The *first step* involves securing your prospect's *attention,* which should take place as early as possible during the interview. You can't get very far in selling a prospect something unless you have his or her attention. Undivided attention isn't always easy to acquire. Securing the necessary attention is going to be especially difficult if your prospect's mind is preoccupied with something else or burdened with

TABLE 10.1 Checklist for Planning Sales Calls on Commercial Prospects.

1. Company name and address of prospect.

2. Relevant information already known about the organization's operations.

3. Relevant information known about organization's buying policies and procedures.

4. Key personnel (and titles) to call on.

5. Purpose of sales call.

6. Previous calls (dates and results).

7. Competitors already positioned with this firm.

8. Advantages and disadvantages enjoyed by the competition.

9. Needs, wants, and problems existing in this firm that could be satisfied or solved by your products or service.

10. Opening technique planned to arouse customer interest.

11. Key points you intend to make in your presentation.

12. Proof for backing up your claims.

13. Principal types of objections anticipated.

14. Method for asking for order.

Adapted from Eugene M. Johnson, David L. Kurtz, and Eberhard E. Scheuing, *Sales Management* (New York: McGraw-Hill, 1986), pp. 67–68, having originally appeared in "Planning the Sales Call," *Sales Manager's Bulletin* (January 30, 1980), pp. 4–5.

problems or pressures. If you sense that you can't readily obtain a prospect's attention at a particular time, maybe you'd better make an appointment for another time when he or she will be more receptive.

"Your **interest** ***is my business."***

After you get your prospect's attention, the *second step* in AIDA is to try to arouse his or her *interest* in the meaning of your message. The previous chapter on the approach discussed various ways to gain both the interest and attention of prospects. You might gain interest through a sound choice of words or perhaps through graphic means, such as charts or other types of visual aids. As we'll see shortly, focusing on customer needs and product benefits is apt to arouse the prospect's interest in your message.

"Do you **desire action?"**

The *third step* in AIDA is attempting to stimulate your prospective customer into having a *desire* to do something related to your proposal. Without a desire—that is, the feeling of wanting something—the *final step,* getting *action,* is unlikely to follow. And it is *action—a decision to buy*—that you're attempting to influence the prospect to take. In summary, you've got to activate your prospect's *attention, interest,* and *desire* in order to get him or her to take *action.*

"Securing the necessary attention is going to be especially difficult if your prospect's mind is preoccupied with something else or burdened with problems or pressures."

Put Some FUN-FAB OPTIC into Your Sales Life

In training salespeople, one of the things professional sales managers and trainers usually try to discourage their trainees from doing is focusing primarily on a product's features during a sales presentation. As we'll see shortly, most salespeople are advised instead to incorporate into their sales presentations elements that we'll refer to as the **FUN-FAB OPTIC concept.**

As you can see in Figure 10.1, the FUN part of FUN-FAB stands for *F*irst

Figure 10.1 The FUN-FAB OPTIC Concept, Which Represents the Essential Elements of a Sales Presentation.

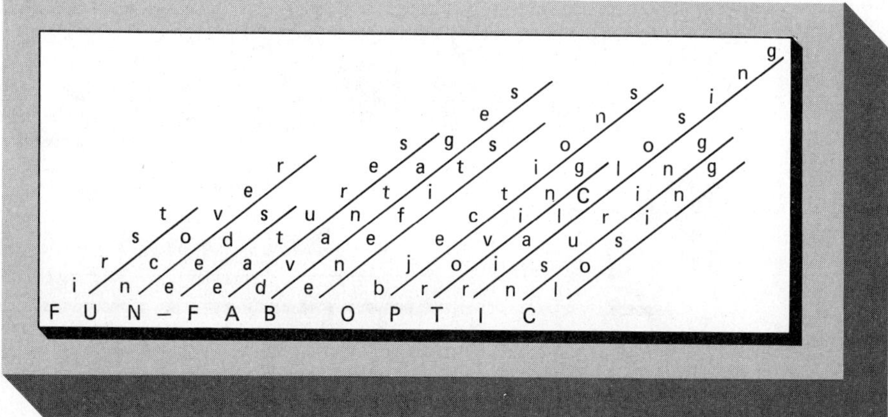

*U*ncover *N*eeds. The FAB stands for *F*eatures, *A*dvantages, and *B*enefits. The OPTIC represents *O*bjections, *P*roving, *T*rial closing, *I*nsuring, and *C*losing. The acronym FUN-FAB OPTIC gives you a mental handle that can help you to recall the essential features of a sales presentation. Let's now see if we can shed some light on all this alphabet soup.

Let's Have Some FUN

Why mightn't **features** *alone sell your product?*

One of the most common mistakes made by inexperienced salespeople is stressing the *features* and *advantages* of their products before they understand the prospective customer's *needs.* Let's pretend for the moment that we are observing a personable young sales representative—Mark Tyme is his name—who works for an audiovisual supply and equipment firm. Mark means well, but unfortunately he hasn't yet received adequate sales training. As we observe Mark, we see that he has already established reasonable rapport with his prospect, Ms. Dee Kline. Mark leads into his sales presentation by saying: "Ms. Kline, I want to point out to you what I believe is one of the outstanding *features* of this movie projector—its natural gray color. Our product developers feel that gray really enhances the appearance of the projector. I also want to emphasize one of the specific *advantages* that this projector has over many other projectors, namely, the ability to run at a slower than standard speed."

What did Mark overlook when he stressed how sold *he* was on the gray color and the advantages of a variable running speed? He failed to do something called **probing,** which basically is the activity of uncovering information related to the needs, desires, and attitudes of the customer.

What's in it for **your customer***?*

Will Mark's customer, Ms. Dee Kline, necessarily feel that the gray color is an outstanding feature solely because Mark feels that way? Does Ms. Kline have a recognized need for a projector that runs at a slower than standard speed? It's difficult for Mark to know for certain unless he probes. The important point to be remembered in the FUN part of FUN-FAB OPTIC is that before you stress something that may be irrelevant or unimportant to a prospect, you should carefully probe to uncover his or her needs and wants.

Let's now try to reinforce your understanding of the FUN segment. Think about the following:

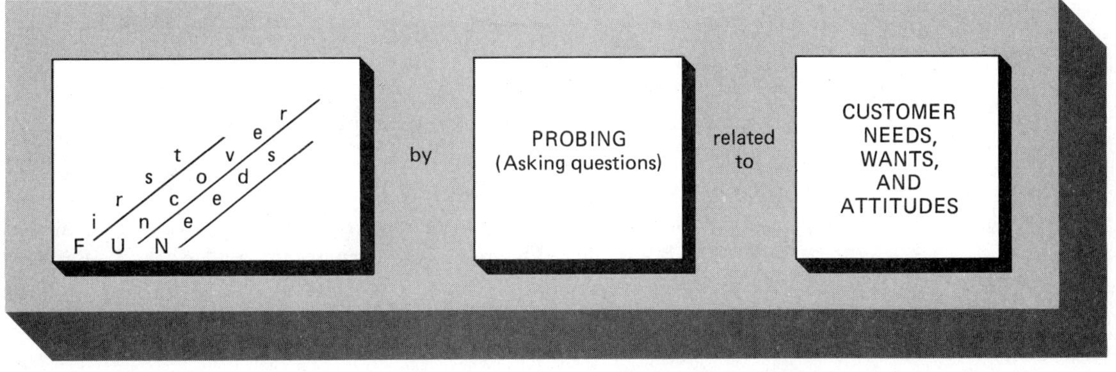

Here's an example of a probing question: "Mr. Training Director, what do you generally look for in a quality movie projector?"

Here's another example: "What are the major limitations of the projectors that you're currently using in your training programs?"

Make It FAB

Now comes the second part—FAB—of our acronym FUN-FAB OPTIC. Remember that FAB stands for *F*eatures, *A*dvantages, and *B*enefits. One of your main goals after you've uncovered the prospect's needs and attitudes is to convert your product's **features** and **advantages** into **benefits** that relate to the customer's **needs.**

For example, let's assume that you are an automobile salesperson. During the FUN phase of your sales presentation, you've learned that the prospect is on an extremely tight budget—and you have a car that should satisfy this need for economy. It *features* a four-cylinder engine. One of its *advantages* is that it can be driven farther than many others on a given amount of gasoline. How, therefore, might you convert those factors into customer benefits? Basically, they add up to the *benefit* of reduced operating costs. Which of the three factors is probably the most important to the customer—the engine *feature,* the *advantage* of greater mileage per gallon of gasoline, or the *benefit* of reduced operating costs? The latter, the reduced-cost benefit, would tend to be a major factor influencing the customer's buying decision. To illustrate:

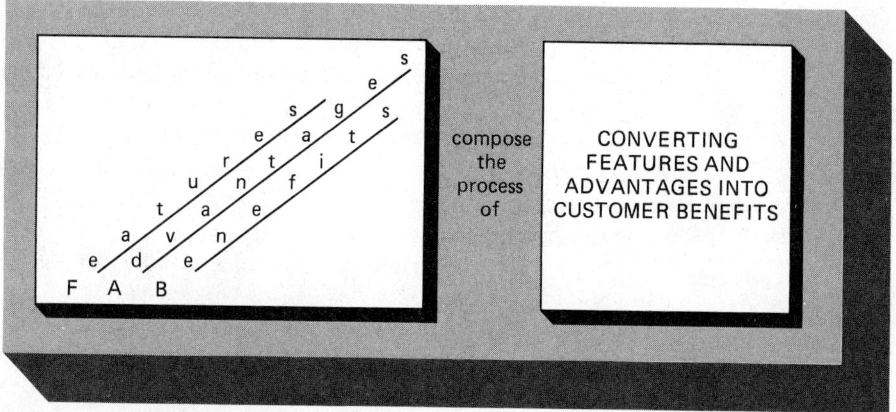

Convince with OPTIC

Now we're concerned with the last part of the FUN-FAB OPTIC memory jogger. As a reminder, OPTIC stands for *O*bjections, *P*roving, *T*rial closing, *I*nsuring, and *C*losing. Let's deal briefly with each factor.

"I object to your not listening!"

Objections, as most experienced salespeople have learned, are a normal and useful part of sales interviews. The prospective customer who doesn't offer any resistance to your sales message might not even be listening. The handling of objections is so important in any sales presentation that we will devote an entire chapter to this topic.

For now, keep in mind that objections are a lot like probes—they help you to learn more about the customer's reaction to your message and his or her present attitudes toward your product. Objections should be welcomed enthusiastically as opportunities to uncover more about your customers' needs, wants, and attitudes.

Proving is the factor in OPTIC that becomes necessary when a prospect seems skeptical of the merits of a benefit that you believe to be important to him or her. Proving basically involves using available evidence that substantiates the benefit claims you've already made.

For example, let's assume that you are a carpet salesperson and are in the process of making a sales presentation to a retailer who says to you: "Sure, all that sounds great, but how do I really know this fabric won't fade?"

"You can prove it by me!"

At this point, what the prospect really wants is *proof* of your product claims. You might say something like the following: "Mr. Retailer, you've brought up a good point, since no one wants a rug that loses its original luster. As you may know, rugs made of synthetic materials resist fading. In fact, recent research done by *Consumer Reports* compared the fastness of synthetics with that of natural materials and concluded that synthetic materials resist fading five times better than natural fibers. All of our rugs are made with synthetic materials, so you can rest assured that your customers will be satisfied with any of our products that they buy from you."

"Objections should be welcomed enthusiastically as opportunities to uncover more about your customers' needs and attitudes."

In general, proof statements are likely to be most effective when they are restatements of a previously mentioned benefit and when they offer credible evidence that substantiates your claims.

When should you try a close?

Trial closing is the next important element of OPTIC. The expression *trial closing* means an effort by the salesperson any time during the sales presentation to obligate the prospect to purchase a product or service. It's highly important to recognize that closing opportunities might occur *any time* during a sales presentation rather than only at the end of your message.

As a salesperson, you should continually look for **buying signals** that could suggest an opportunity to attempt a close. For example, let's assume that you're with a customer and have barely begun your sales presentation. In fact, so far you've discussed only one of your product's benefits. Your prospect, however—who has already agreed that the benefit you've stressed is useful—seems to believe your product claims. At this point, there's little need to discuss additional benefits or even make proving statements related to the agreed-upon benefit. Instead, merely begin your trial closing efforts.

Think sale!

There are a wide variety of closing techniques; these will be covered in a later chapter devoted exclusively to the topic of closing. Keep in mind, however, that an important ingredient of any closing efforts is the assumption that you have already made the sale. You might reveal your positive assumptions by saying something like: "Then, Ms. Shure, we've agreed that you need. . . ." If Ms. Shure offers no resistance to your trial closing efforts, then you could begin to write up the order. You might clinch the sale by asking: "How would you like to pay for this unit—in cash or on our credit plan?"

Your customer needs some **insurance.**

Insuring, the *I* segment of OPTIC, is another important element that you might have to employ at any time during a sales interview. To *insure* means "to make certain; to reduce, eliminate, or transfer risk." A safe generalization is that most customers don't like to make bad buying decisions. For some buyers, far more than time may be lost. Also at risk can be lost profits, damaged reputations, and bruised self-images.

As a result, you should continually be sensitive to the need for providing information and reassurance showing how the prospect's risks are minimized by purchasing your product. Methods for reducing prospect risk include stressing product quality, explaining warranties and guarantees, and discussing service and repair facilities.

Time to close!

Closing, that all-important element of OPTIC, significantly influences your future with your company as well as your own standard of living. Closing is the attempt to motivate a customer into making an affirmative decision regarding the purchase of a product or service. In short, the purpose of the close is to get the order. We'll hold off a detailed discussion of the close until a later chapter.

Guidelines for Making Good Presentations

Table 10.2 presents a checklist of essential characteristics of good sales presentations. Consider each of these factors when you prepare a sales presentation. Can you see how they relate to AIDA and FUN-FAB OPTIC concepts? A well-planned sales presentation generally includes most of the characteristics in Table 10.2.

TYPES OF SALES PRESENTATIONS

Companies throughout the world have developed a variety of techniques and approaches for presenting their sales messages. Regardless of the names assigned to them, most planned sales presentations are a variation or a combination of four basic types:

1. The standard *memorized* presentation.
2. The *outlined* presentation.

TABLE 10.2 Guidelines for Making Good Sales Presentations.

Well-planned sales presentations generally should:

1. *Arouse and maintain the interest* of the prospect.
2. Show how your product or service can *provide a solution* to a specific problem or *satisfy a specific need or want.*
3. *Motivate* the prospect into *action.*
4. Be *credible.* If you make outlandish claims about your product, you are likely to find your prospect becoming skeptical of you.
5. Be *clear.* Speak at an intelligible rate and in terms your prospect will understand. Don't assume that the prospect is familiar with all of your technical jargon.
6. Involve *two-way communication.* If you fail to ask questions that will uncover the buyer's needs and don't listen to his or her responses, your presentation may wander down blind alleys.
7. Describe the potential *benefits to your customers,* not to you or your company. Most customers do not buy solely because you might win a trip to Tahiti.
8. Be *flexible.* You should be able to adapt the presentation to the needs, wants, and interests of the prospect.
9. Be as *complete* as is necessary to guide the prospect into making a favorable buying decision.
10. *Provide opportunities for trial closes.*

3. The *programmed* or survey presentation.
4. The *audiovisual* presentation.

Each has its advantages and disadvantages.

The Standard Memorized Presentation

Should a sales presentation be memorized? You are likely to find sales managers disagreeing on this point. Some are completely against a "canned" approach, while others argue that a **standard memorized presentation** ensures that salespeople will deliver the most complete and orderly presentation possible. Still others feel that a partially memorized presentation is helpful, particularly for less experienced salespeople.

Should a presentation be memorized?

The memorized approach is said to have been started back in 1894 by John Patterson, who was then president of the National Cash Register Company. Patterson studied the presentations of his most successful sales representatives and developed what he called a "primer," a booklet containing a standard sales presentation. He then required all National Cash Register salespeople to memorize its contents and employ identical presentations in their selling activities. Due to increased sales volume, the results seemed indisputably successful, so other business firms were quick to adopt similar techniques. The assumption was that success would be relatively automatic if all salespeople presented their sales messages the way the more successful salespeople did.

". . . not everyone agrees on the merits of the memorized approach. If used, it should be employed in a natural, sincere way and allow for flexibility and two-way communication."

The standard memorized approach is still used extensively in house-to-house selling, in the selling of life insurance, and in combination with other presentations. As already mentioned, less experienced salespeople often find this method useful, at least until they have developed their own styles of presentation. Among the key advantages of the standard memorized presentation are that:

What are the arguments in favor of the memorized presentation?

1. It is often the result of highly planned and proven activities.
2. It tends to be complete and is less likely to overlook key points.
3. It can be developed to anticipate and overcome typical buyer objections.
4. It is helpful for the less experienced salesperson.
5. It can result in a more orderly, logically flowing presentation.

On the other hand, as already noted, many sales managers discourage the use of a memorized presentation. Their arguments generally are:

All those opposed?

1. It can seem excessively canned and mechanical, thus coming across as artificial and insincere.
2. It can create embarrassing moments for the salesperson who is interrupted. Lines can be forgotten, and—like the young child selling cookies door-to-door—the salesperson may have to start over at the beginning.
3. It makes it harder for situational selling to take place, since communication tends to flow in only one direction.
4. It is difficult to use when a salesperson is handling many items or fairly complex products.

In short, not everyone agrees on the merits of the memorized approach. If used, it should be employed in a natural, sincere way and allow for flexibility and two-way communication.

The Outlined Presentation

Situational selling is a concept that has been stressed repeatedly in this text. Each prospect is a unique being, and a "canned" or memorized approach sometimes fails to take this factor into account. Some memorization, however, is not only inevitable but also desirable. As you deliver any type of sales message regularly to a large number of prospects, you are likely to develop a particular and consistent pattern of presentation.

What is an outlined presentation?

A technique that helps to overcome the potential artificiality of pure memorization is the **outlined presentation.** This type of presentation is sometimes partially memorized. One of its major advantages is flexibility. The outlined presentation is typically an outline of key points that can serve as a memory jogger. The outline may be part of a sales aid, can be memorized, or may consist of key words or letters.

Of course, there are both advantages and disadvantages to the outlined presentation. Among its principal advantages are that:

What are the arguments in favor of the outlined presentation?

1. It allows for a greater two-way flow of communication than the memorized presentation.
2. It seems more natural and extemporaneous—less artificial.
3. It has greater flexibility, thus allowing for a more direct appeal to the needs and buying motives of a specific prospect.
4. It makes it easier to get back on the main subject when the speaker is interrupted by questions or latecomers to the interview.

The following are generally considered as disadvantages of the outlined presentation:

And the shortcomings of an outlined presentation?

1. This technique makes it easy to get sidetracked onto unrelated topics.
2. Relevant and key sales points may be inadvertently overlooked.
3. The presentation may not be as carefully prepared or as complete as a memorized one.
4. It may not fit the personality of a salesperson who has not developed skill in extemporaneous speaking.

All of these disadvantages can be overcome with experience and practice, however. Some salespeople rehearse their presentations on video- or audiotape recorders or in front of managers, selling classes, peers, spouses, and even their German shepherd dogs.

The Programmed or Survey Presentation

Another presentation method, which is sometimes used in conjunction with either standard memorized or outlined presentations, is the **programmed or survey presentation.** More than one sales call is typically required for the programmed method. The first call usually requires the salesperson to sell the prospect on the need for an in-depth probing analysis of his or her problems and needs—both present and future.

Take the facts, analyze them, and return.

After carefully examining and analyzing the prospective customer's specific problems and needs, the salesperson develops a "tailor-made" program or system to fit them. The actual sales presentation usually combines a written proposal containing technical and price information with an oral sales message. These are delivered on second or subsequent visits with the prospect.

The programmed method may be highly complex and require a great deal of study and analysis; it may also be simple enough to be prepared by an office worker or a computer that has been supplied with the necessary information. This technique is often used by people selling insurance, office products, accounting systems, and industrial equipment.

The Equitable Life Insurance Society trains its sales agents to utilize a combination of the three types of presentations discussed so far. For example, Equitable agents use the programmed approach by probing for necessary information during their initial visits with prospects. Agents also combine the memorized with the outlined techniques, utilizing what is called the "IDA BIRD EFGHE memory jogger." "IDA BIRD EFGHE" is an acronym that agents memorize to help them remember the key types of information that must be obtained from prospects. This technique helps to give the impression that agents want to talk in a conversational manner with prospects, since they use no written materials during their calls.

Like any type of presentation, the programmed sales presentation has advantages and disadvantages. Among its principal advantages are that:

What are the advantages of programmed presentations?

1. It stresses the buyer's needs because of the investigative nature of the survey.
2. It makes the prospect feel you are sincerely interested in his or her problems and needs.
3. It can be an impressive and more professional-appearing technique.

Among the major disadvantages of the programmed sales presentation are that:

And the cons?

1. It can be costly and time-consuming because of the necessity to probe deeply for information.
2. It may be distrusted by some prospects because of past experience with salespeople who used the survey approach as a gimmick or in an unethical manner.
3. Some salespeople may not be qualified or experienced enough to prepare programmed presentations.

The Audiovisual Presentation

An increasingly common method of delivering sales messages to prospective customers is the **audiovisual presentation.** This technique makes use of equipment that either separately or in combination utilizes elements of sight and sound. The equipment ranges in sophistication from relatively simple overhead projectors to highly advanced videotape or disc players.

The audiovisual presentation is sometimes referred to as an automated presentation because, in general, the equipment rather than the salesperson relates the product's features and advantages to customer benefits. The key advantages of the audiovisual presentation include the following:

Key advantages?

1. It tends to hold the prospect's attention without interruptions.
2. It delivers what it has to say in a limited amount of time.
3. It doesn't miss any major product benefits.

On the other side of the coin, the audiovisual presentation also has some key disadvantages:

And disadvantages?

1. It may not allow for two-way communication until the full message has been delivered.
2. It may cause some salespeople to feel subservient to a machine.
3. It may develop mechanical problems that can create embarrassing moments for the salesperson.

Because of the extensive use of audiovisual equipment by many marketing organizations today, we'll examine their nature and use in greater detail in the following chapter.

PROBLEMS, PROBLEMS, AND MORE PROBLEMS

Planning + problem solving = sales.

A sales manager once asserted, "You've got to learn to live with problems. Where there are no problems, there's no business!" There is a certain element of truth in that statement. The creative salesperson has learned, however, that the frequency and intensity of many problems can be reduced with effective planning. Nonetheless, even the best-organized salesperson will occasionally experience difficulties. Some are just impossible to avoid. The following section is intended to guide you through the maze of occasional difficulties experienced by salespeople during the presentation. It is hoped that you will profit by developing a greater awareness of some of the more common ones and will therefore be better able to avoid them. Table 10.3 summarizes the principal types of problems that may crop up during sales presentations.

What—Another Interruption?

Interruptions during sales interviews are usually extremely frustrating to the salesperson who is trying to deliver a sales presentation with a reasonable degree of continuity. Most interruptions are caused by *telephone calls,* the *prospect's assistants,* or *other company personnel.*

TABLE 10.3 Guidelines for Handling Major Types of Problems Faced by Salespeople During Sales Presentations.

Type of Problem	Recommendation
Interruptions	Ask client to hold interruptions. Request that all key people be present.
Short on time	Suggest another meeting.
Lack of ample knowledge	Don't bluff; check on needed information. Follow up with necessary information.
Maintaining interest	Use established techniques for maintaining interest.
Not being understood	Use language understood by client.
Maintaining control	Use questions to guide interview.
The "roadblock"	Maintain cordial relations. Try to contact other members of buying center. Write letters to key decision makers.

"Would you mind holding all calls during the next 10 to 15 minutes?"

A relatively simple solution to the problem of interruptions is to tell your prospect that your presentation will be far more useful and meaningful if it has continuity and then to ask whether the assistant or receptionist could be asked to hold any interruptions for ten minutes or so. Most prospects don't seem to object to such requests, especially if you've established a positive relationship with good rapport during your approach.

How do you handle latecomers?

Often interruptions are caused by latecomers. Assume you're in the process of delivering a sales presentation and Mr. Oscar Override, the assistant buying manager enters the room. Oscar, you have learned, shares purchasing authority with your prospect. What do you do? Your solution to the problem depends on how far into the presentation you are. If possible, give Oscar a quick recap and include him in the balance of the sales presentation. Or, if you feel that your original prospect would be bored by restating the initial part of the presentation, you could tell Oscar you'd like an opportunity to drop by his office a bit later with the complete story. The frequency of this sort of problem can be minimized if you request in advance that all key personnel—that is, those who influence buying decisions—be there during the presentation.

"The creative salesperson has learned . . . that the frequency and intensity of many problems can be reduced with effective planning."

The Squeeze Play—Short of Time

Assume you have a well-planned presentation requiring a minimum of 20 minutes to deliver and your customer says, "I'm really quite anxious to hear what you have to say, but all I can give you right now is about five minutes. I've got a luncheon appointment with Hattie Hathook, one of our suppliers, at noon. What did you want to talk to me about?"

Twenty into five equals "no sale!"

It is inadvisable to try to squeeze a 20-minute presentation into 5, and such a request places you in an awkward and tense position. Usually, when customers indicate they have less time than you need to make an adequate presentation, you would be wise to suggest another meeting—tactfully, of course. You might even offer specific choices of times. But above all, don't lose your composure or temper because you can't deliver your presentation as intended.

The Unknown Answer

Sometimes a customer may ask you a question that you can't answer. Although a salesperson should strive to be well informed, no person can know everything about his or her company and its products. You should never bluff your answer or offer incorrect information. Instead, you are better off if you admit that you don't have the answer to a specific question. You might say something like, "Mr. Waxbyrd, that's something that hasn't come up for a while. I want to make sure I give you the right answer to your question, so let me check on it, and I'll let you know first thing in the morning. Will that be all right?"

"I'll tell you the truth whether I know it or not!"

To avoid potentially harmful credibility gaps between you and your account, it's extremely important that you fulfill any commitments you make. Be certain to follow up and give the account the information as promised. Sometimes it's easy to make excuses for not following up, especially when you've been busy or preoccupied with other pressures and activities. You might feel, "Aw, he probably didn't expect me to return the information anyhow." But Mr. Waxbyrd just may be waiting anxiously for that information. He may feel that since you made a commitment to him, you intend to fulfill it. As a salesperson, you should develop the habit of following through on your promises; otherwise, your accounts might think, "I can't really trust that person. In the future I'm going to deal with a salesperson I can trust."

Keep your promises!

Maintaining Attention and Interest

An anonymous albeit sagacious French philosopher once advised, *"L'esprit peut seulement absorber ce que le posterieur peut endurer."* Freely translated, this means: "The mind can only absorb what the rear end can endure!" This bit of profundity brings us to another potential problem faced by salespeople: the problem of maintaining a prospect's attention and interest during the sales presentation.

What can you do to hold a customer's interest in your story? Examine the following guidelines—they've been useful for many individuals in sales.

How can you maintain the prospect's interest?

1. Keep your presentations to a *reasonable length.* If you have empathy and sensitivity for the feelings of your customers, you should be able to sense when their interest is waning.
2. Allow for ample *two-way communication.* Your prospect's interest is more likely to be maintained if he or she is directly involved and actively interacting with your presentation. Asking probing questions; then, as you listen to the response, you will be helping to create customer involvement.
3. Wherever possible, *appeal to the prospect's five main senses:* feeling, seeing, smelling, hearing, and tasting.
4. Use *audiovisual aids* such as flip charts, graphs, reprints of advertisements in national publications, films, and even the product itself when applicable.
5. Use *third-party references* (testimonials). They help to create a more favorable image of your product or service.
6. *Sell the sizzle*—not the steak; that is, be careful in your choice of words. For example, which sounds better to you, a product that is "flimsy and cheap" or one that's "light and economical"?
7. Relate your product's features, advantages, and benefits to the *needs* of the customer.

Not Being Understood

Ugga, ugga, boo; Ugga, boo, boo, ugga. Huh?

The common downfall of some salespeople is their assumption that they're being understood when, in reality, they are using jargon that is too technical for their customers. Use language that is clear and understandable. For example, if you are selling insurance and are talking to a prospect with scant knowledge of the field of insurance, guard against saying something like, "Mr. Risque, this CPL policy has a single limit for BI and PD and includes VPD at no extra charge. Furthermore, the company has the right to cancel on a pro-rata basis, but you suffer short-rate penalties if you cancel." In short, be certain that you are understood. Probe, if necessary, to find out whether your customer really understands you.

Maintaining Control of the Interview

How can you "control" a sales interview?

Who should control a sales interview? Most sales managers would contend that a good salesperson always controls the interview but allows customers to feel that they are the dominant force. Control is a subtle skill that tends to develop with experience. You can use probing questions to help guide the interview. Also, you should maintain control of your sales aids so they don't compete for your prospect's attention.

In the space limitations of a single chapter, we can barely scratch the surface of the myriad problems and unusual situations that can confront salespeople during their daily activities. With experience and training, you will discover that a pattern

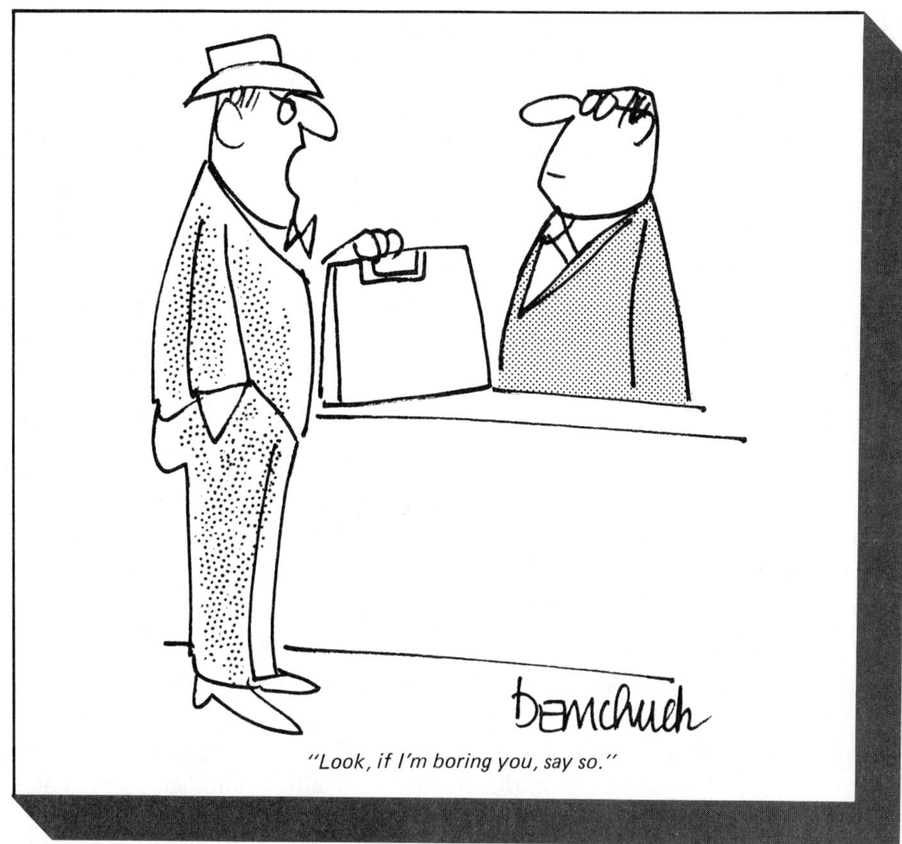

"Look, if I'm boring you, say so."

Reprinted with permission from *Sales & Marketing Management,* February 4, 1985, p. 70; © 1985.

seems to develop, with certain situations recurring regularly. Occasionally however, you may confront new and unique problems that require the use of situational selling. After any interview you should analyze the way in which it was handled; if you are not pleased with the results, you should develop and practice improved techniques for future use.

"Most sales managers would contend that a good salesperson always controls the interview but allows customers to feel that they are the dominant force."

The Gatekeeper

"May I see your I.D.?"

Occasionally, one of the decision makers in a "buying center" acts as a roadblock in your path to speaking with all relevant decision makers. Often referred to as **gatekeepers,** these are individuals who determine what information is received by key decision makers. They may or may not actually be decision makers themselves;

they could be secretaries or assistants to those with buying authority. Gatekeepers can prevent your establishing contact with critically important decision makers.

Gatekeepers essentially screen information and decide on their own what is worthy of being passed on to others. They may even suggest that you not meet with other key individuals who ordinarily would be involved with buying decisions.

What can you do when confronting a roadblock? Losing your temper might be satisfying but not too productive. You should try your best to maintain a cordial relationship with the person, hoping that his or her attitude will become more receptive. Even if the person continues to feel the need to be a roadblock, it is advisable to let other members of the buying center know that you are willing to meet with them. Doing so, however, is not without some risk. You might anger your gatekeeper. Yet, it is unlikely that you would be in any worse situation than you already were; you probably wouldn't have made a sale anyhow without seeing the other key decision makers.

Some salespeople overcome the roadblock created by a gatekeeper by writing sales letters to key people stressing the advantages and benefits of their products. A letter is also sent to the gatekeeper so that he or she will feel included in the communication.

SUMMARY

Each step in the sales process is like each link in a steel chain. It's an essential part of the whole. In this chapter we examined another essential part of the sales process, the *presentation.*

A sales presentation, like any responsible activity, should be planned, or it will lose much of its effectiveness. A planned presentation has two major purposes: (1) to arouse in prospective customers a feeling of need or desire for products or services and (2) to show how products or services can fill or satisfy the recognized needs of customers.

The AIDA concept shows how a buyer may be guided through four stages of activity: attention, interest, desire, and action. FUN-FAB OPTIC is an acronym intended to assist salespeople in recalling and applying the essential ingredients of most sales presentations. An understanding of the nature of good presentations can help you in developing your own sales interviews.

The major types of personal sales presentations vary in style from standard memorized to outlined to programmed, although, in reality, most are variations or combinations of these. A fourth technique—the audiovisual presentation—leans more heavily on mechanical devices. However, it too generally requires a salesperson to *close* the sale.

Each style has advantages and disadvantages. Since presentations seldom go exactly as intended regardless of the style adopted, salespeople should continually strive to engage in situational or flexible selling.

Salespeople should also anticipate potential problems during sales presentations. Among the more common difficulties are interruptions, insufficient time for presentations, not having answers to prospect questions, maintaining the interest of the prospect, not being understood, maintaining control of the interview, and the gatekeeper.

KEY TERMS

sales presentation
situational selling
AIDA concept
FUN-FAB OPTIC concept
probing
features
advantages
benefits
needs
objections
proving
trial closing
buying signals
insuring
closing
standard memorized presentation
outlined presentation
programmed or survey presentation
audiovisual presentation.
gatekeeper

QUESTIONS

1. Evaluate this statement: "A structured sales presentation is not only unnecessary but highly undesirable. An effective salesperson waits until he or she is face to face with the prospect to determine how the product will be presented, rather than being locked into a rigid plan."
2. Can a salesperson employ both a planned presentation and situational selling simultaneously? Explain your answer.
3. What is meant by the statement, "An effective sales presentation allows for two-way communication"?
4. What does the acronym FUN-FAB OPTIC represent? How can the concept be of use to salespeople?
5. Under what circumstances might a standard memorized presentation be applicable? What are some of its potential pitfalls?
6. Which type of sales presentation—standard memorized or outlined—would probably be more desirable for the sale of a farm tractor? Explain.
7. Which type of presentation generally allows for more interaction between the salesperson and the prospect, the standard memorized, the audiovisual, or the outlined? Why?
8. How does the survey or programmed presentation relate to the standard memorized and outline types of presentations?
9. What are the major purposes of the programmed sales technique? How might it be misused?

10. Evaluate the following statement: "There's really no reason why salespeople shouldn't welcome with open arms the opportunity to use audiovisuals in their sales presentations. Salespeople have everything to gain and nothing to lose by using them."

11. Are you ever justified in blowing up or getting angry at a customer?

12. Assume that you have an appointment with a prospect who seems to be continually interrupted by telephone calls and her staff. What can you do to lessen the frequency of this type of problem?

13. What are the dangers inherent in attempting to squeeze a 25-minute presentation into only 5 minutes?

14. The minds of prospects may wander during sales presentations, especially long ones. What can you do to reduce the likelihood of this problem?

15. Why shouldn't you guess the answer when a prospect asks you a question you are unsure of? What should you say when this does occur?

16. How can you discover whether the language you are using during a presentation is too technical for your customer?

17. Assume that you are demonstrating a working model of your product and your prospect takes it from your hands, examines it, but seems to be paying little attention to your presentation. What can you say to regain his or her attention?

18. Assume that you've discovered that there are a number of other persons in a buying center who should hear your sales message, but one person seems to feel that there is no reason for you to make contact with the others. You feel that it is essential for the success of your sale to explain your product's benefits personally to the others. What can you do about the "gatekeeper"?

APPLICATIONS

10.1 CAN YOU SELL THIS BOOK?

Assume that you are a salesperson for Harper & Row, the publisher of this text, *Creative Selling Today,* Third Edition. Your principal responsibility, let's assume, is to convince instructors of courses in selling that they should adopt *Creative Selling Today,* Third Edition, rather than competing sales texts, for use in their classes.

Where possible, apply the AIDA and FUN-FAB OPTIC concepts discussed in this chapter and complete the following forms. Then develop an outlined sales presentation for delivery to another person whom you will select to play the role of a selling instructor. Since you probably haven't read the chapters on handling objections and closing, you might want to return to this assignment to sharpen your responses after you've studied later chapters.

Planned Sales Presentation

Name of organization (school):	Names of competing texts:
Name and title of person to contact:	Number of prior calls made:

Purpose of this call:

Opening statements you intend to make (complete this section only after finishing balance of form):

Attention/Interest/Desire factors to be used (complete this section only after finishing balance of form):

Customer needs:	Features and advantages related to needs of customer:
1. ________	1. ________
2. ________	2. ________
3. ________	3. ________

Benefits to customer:	Proof of benefits:
1. ________	1. ________
2. ________	2. ________
3. ________	3. ________

Possible customer objections and your responses to objections:

1. Objection: ________

   Response: ________

2. Objection: ________

3. Objection: ________

   Response: ________

4. Objection: ________

Response: ______________	Response: ______________

Trial closing statements:

1. ______________

2. ______________

Insuring statements:

1. ______________

2. ______________

Closing statements:

1. ______________

2. ______________

In the following space, prepare your outlined sales presentation:

10.2 THE DAMPENING COVER PRESENTATION

Frank Fisk, a sales representative for the 3-Plate Printing Products Company, has made a prearranged sales call on Bob Burns, the production manager of Proof Press, Inc., a print shop located in Del Rio, Texas. The following is the conversation that developed between the two men during the sales interview.

Frank Fisk Good morning, Bob. I appreciate your seeing me this morning. I know you have a busy schedule. By the way, I saw the writeup in the Herald about your company's results over the past five years. It certainly seems to be headed in the right direction. I guess that says something for the management of your organization.

Bob Burns Yes, Frank. We're pretty proud of our results, but it hasn't been easy. We have our problems like everyone else.

Frank What sort of problems have you been having, Bob?

Bob Well, mainly we've been experiencing too much downtime on our presses.

Frank What seems to be the cause of your downtime?

Bob One reason is the poor quality of the dampening sleeves we've been getting, not only from Ajax, one of your competitors, but from your company as well. Those darn sleeves just don't last. Seams have been tearing, lint gets into the ink, and who knows what else?

Frank I can understand how you feel, Bob, and I'm glad you brought that problem to my attention. It's actually one that has been quite common in the industry until recently. In fact, it's one of the reasons I called on you today. The problem you mentioned shouldn't occur any more because we have recently developed a completely new and modern 3-Plate brand dampening sleeve for people with problems like yours. Have you heard about it?

Bob Can't say as I have.

Frank I assume you know Fred Filbert over at Paragon Press on Third Street. Would you say that his operations are somewhat the same as yours?

Bob Yes, in general. Why?

Frank Well, I was talking with Fred last month, and he told me that the average life of his wraparound paper dampening cover was only sixteen hours. He said that because of cracking, bubbling, and unraveling, the press was stopped on the average of once every other shift to change covers. Is this the type of problem you've been facing?

Bob I would say so, yes.

Frank At my suggestion, about four weeks ago, Fred decided to try the 3-Plate dampening sleeve. He discovered that—thanks to the one-piece seamless construction—he not only eliminated cracking, bubbling, and unraveling but is still using, after one month, his first 3-Plate dampening sleeve. Fred has also found that because he hasn't had to change covers, his press downtime has been reduced enough to pay for the 3-Plate dampeners.

Bob Sure, that's the same old story I always hear from you peddlers. I suppose the price is a lot higher too.

Frank Let's talk about price after I tell you something about this, Bob. Honestly, the 3-Plate sleeve is a revolutionary new product. It's an entirely new concept in dampening covers. It's perfectly round and especially constructed of rigid fiber tube. It's completely seamless—that will eliminate the problem you've been having. In fact, the 3-Plate sleeve is actually stronger wet than dry. Have you been using paper sleeves exclusively?

Bob Of course, they're a heck of a lot cheaper than cloth.

Frank They may be cheaper per unit, but they're far more costly over time. For example, the 3-Plate sleeve will not crack, wrinkle, stretch, or shrink as your paper ones do.

Bob How about mounting?

Frank I've got one with me. Let's go over to your press and try one. (They move to a press and greet the press operator.)

Bob, note how easily the sleeve mounts; you simply slide it onto the roller. You know how with some dampening systems you need elaborate or extensive mechanical control devices? Not so with this sleeve. It doesn't change the basic dampening design of the press one iota.

Although this sleeve is higher in unit cost, you actually save money by being able to change colors without washing the sleeves. They don't dry out like paper during short shutdowns. Why don't you leave that sleeve on the press—a gift from 3-Plate—and let's go back into your office where it's a bit quieter. (They return to Mr. Burns's office.)

Bob, let me summarize some of the advantages of the 3-Plate dampener sleeves. First of all, they give you cleaner printing and absolutely no lint. You can change colors without changing or washing covers. You won't find any pattern or seam marks on your work, and no resetting or readjustments are necessary.

You worried about cost, didn't you. With 3-Plate sleeves, you have no expense for alcohol or special fountain solutions; they just won't be necessary. And you have no laundry expense. People who have been using this sleeve have found them to be more economical than anything they've ever used before.

Questions

1. What is your reaction to the manner in which Frank made his sales presentation?
2. What specific elements of effective presentations did he seem to employ?
3. Assume that you are Frank. What should you say to Bob in order to get an order for 3-Plate dampener sleeves?

10.3 "SELL MORE COBRAS, OR WE'LL LOSE THE LINE!"

Stan Carlson, a sales representative for Outlet Consumer Product Distributors, Inc., a wholesaler, has the responsibility for calling on retailers located in the Seattle/Tacoma area. His form handles a line of various consumer products that it offers to retailers. Most of the manufacturers whose products Outlet sells have established minimum sales quotas for their lines. If Outlet doesn't meet or exceed the specific quotas on a regular basis, it stands to lose the right to continue selling particular products.

One day Stan's boss, Martha Mercury, called him into her office, where the following conversation ensued:

Martha Stan, you've been doing an excellent job selling most of our lines, and I want to tell you that I'm quite pleased, in general, with your results. There is one problem area, however, and it's an important one. I'm referring to what's happening with our line of American-made video camcorders—the Cobras.

Stan I was afraid that you were going to mention our Cobra line, and I've got to admit you're right. But the main problem I've been facing is the low-priced Korean-made video camcorders that are selling so well now. I'm sure you know that we can't come close to them in price, even though Cobras have been recognized from the beginning as being of as high a quality as anything the Koreans or Japanese have ever produced.

Martha I can understand the price competition you're facing, Stan. But you yourself just admitted that Cobras are noted for being among the world's finest video camcorders. The service network is more extensive than that of any of our competitors. We don't have much choice, however. Just the other day, Mr. S. N. Akely, Cobra's national marketing director, informed me that if we don't have more success with Cobras within the next six months, he'll start looking for another wholesaler to promote the line. We don't want to lose the Cobra line, Stan. It's been one of our most profitable items in the past, so please try to improve your results soon, okay?

Project

1. Develop an outlined sales presentation that could help Stan increase his sales of Cobra video camcorders.
2. Develop at least three benefit statements that could appeal to retailers' needs.
3. Develop an approach that you feel Stan could effectively utilize.

10.4 IF ONLY I HAD MORE TIME

Assume that you are a salesperson at one of the retail outlets of Orange Seed International Computer Stores, Inc., and a prospective customer, Ziggy Maslow, has just entered your store. He says the following to you:

> "Good morning. My name is Ziggy Maslow. I run a small management consulting firm, and I feel that I have a real need for one of the smaller personal computers, like your Orange Seed line. Quite frankly, I don't know anything about computers, but would like some information. Unfortunately, I have only about five minutes before I have to leave to meet someone. Can you help me?"

Question

Since your presentation ordinarily takes at least 30 minutes, what should you say to your prospect?

11 Dramatizing, Showmanship, and the Use of Selling Aids

Step Right Up, Ladies and Gentlemen!

THE IMPORTANCE OF DRAMATIC DEMONSTRATIONS

POSITIVE RESULTS OF SHOWMANSHIP

Maintains Attention and Interest ■ Substantiates Sales Claims ■ Appeals to the Senses ■ Makes Selling Points Easier to Understand ■ Facilitates Selling of Complex Products and Services ■ Shows How to Use Products ■ Makes Sales Presentations More Orderly

THE USE OF SALES AIDS

Products ■ Facsimiles ■ Photos and Illustrations ■ Advertisements ■ Charts ■ Graphs ■ Portfolios ■ Catalogs ■ Kits ■ Guarantees and Warranties ■ Product Data Sheets

THE USE OF PORTABLE AUDIOVISUAL AIDS

Can Increase Sales Call Productivity ■ Can Assist in Overcoming Objections ■ Can Take the Salesperson's Place ■ Can Take the Product's Place ■ Can Facilitate Add-On Sales ■ Can Assist in Opening up New Markets ■ Can Be Used in Trade Shows and Fairs ■ Can Be Used to Reach Ultimate Consumers

HOW TO DELIVER EFFECTIVE DRAMATIZATIONS

Be Certain That Your Product or Sales Aid Is in Good Working Order ■ Choose a Good Setting for the Dramatization ■ Recognize the Individual Nature of Each Customer ■ Appeal to the Senses ■ Involve the Prospect in Your Dramatization ■ Speak as Though Your Sale Depended on It ■ Maintain Control over Your Demonstration and Sales Aids ■ Keep Your Dramatization Fresh, Short, and Lively

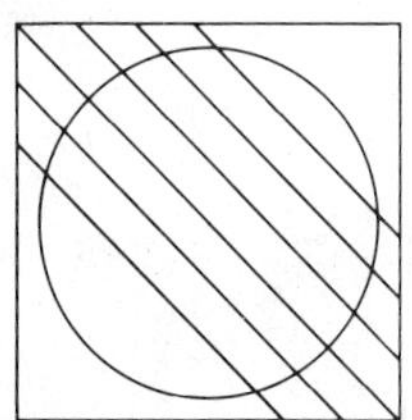

If one picture is worth a thousand words, then one dramatization is probably worth a thousand pictures.
MARVIN W. HEMPEL

Here's what you should be able to do after studying this chapter:

1. Explain the importance of dramatic sales presentations.
2. List and describe the positive results to be derived from the application of showmanship.
3. Employ the use of multiple-sense appeals when dramatizing.
4. Utilize the typical types of sales aids employed by today's salespeople.
5. Summarize the major reasons why the use of audiovisual aids can assist you in developing more effective presentations.
6. Demonstrate the use of the major guidelines for delivering effective dramatizations.

Your stereo is turned on. What a system it is! It's a magnificent PX2001e—a 2000-watt 14-speaker digital laser disc system. You're listening to one of your favorite music groups, Weeping Spruce and the Fig Neutrons, who currently have 5 songs on the nation's list of top 500 hits. Wow—do they ever sound *rad* to your ears. You've enjoyed the musical group since you were a senior in high school.

While listening to Weeping Spruce and the Fig Neutrons, you notice a newspaper on the coffee table; it's open to the entertainment section. Super! You see that Weeping Spruce and her group are going to be featured *in person* this Saturday evening in the annual Fiddlefeast Festival at the Fiddlefeast Fernwood Fairgrounds. You and a friend decide to go.

Afterward you think, "Was that ever an exciting concert!" You've been enjoying Weeping Spruce's music on records and discs for a long time, but seeing her group *in person* was a completely different and unique experience. In fact, you might even call it *dramatic!*

How does this incident relate to selling? Well, salespeople can come across like a record or disc, appealing solely to a customer's sense of hearing, or they, too, can be dramatic, appealing to the many senses and emotions of their customers. **Dramatizing** is an important sales activity that can turn an insipid presentation into an exciting and attention-getting experience.

We've been studying the various steps in the selling process. Now we're going to take a break. In this chapter we're going to explore the importance of dramatic presentations and discuss some of the typical sales aids currently used to dramatize sales presentations. We're also going to examine some of the proven methods for making your demonstrations more effective. Dramatizing is not a separate step in the selling process, of course. Instead, as you will see, it is an important activity that can take place anytime during a sales presentation.

THE IMPORTANCE OF DRAMATIC DEMONSTRATIONS

Seek aid from AIDA!

As a salesperson, you needn't be a frustrated actor or "ham." Yet think about what a good theatrical performance tries to achieve. Many of its objectives relate to the AIDA concept, which we discussed in Chapter 10. Actors do not rehearse hour upon hour solely for the sake of playing to the four walls of a theater. They hope to obtain the *A*ttention and *I*nterest of their audiences. They also want their audiences to *D*esire to view the entire performance and even to engage in the *A*ction, or activity, or recommending it to their friends. Thespians, too, utilize the classic AIDA technique.

"Dramatizing is an important sales activity that can turn an insipid presentation into an exciting and attention-getting experience."

So if you want to add some life and zest to your sales presentations and get your prospect's attention, interest, desire, and action, then you, like the polished performer in a play, can derive tremendous benefits from the application of showmanship. Some individuals react negatively to the idea of showmanship, but what they are probably reacting to is behavior that is ostentatious and insincere, not to showmanship per se.

Showmanship has long been used by high-volume salespeople in dramatic presentations. Basically, **showmanship** is the *act of vividly and dramatically demonstrating the features, advantages, and benefits of a product or service.*

For example, one packaging firm uses a highly dramatic example of showmanship in demonstrating the strength and protective features of one of its products. "Throw this box against the wall . . . then open" are the instructions on the shipping container holding one fresh egg. The egg is immobilized under a film of transparent plastic that is vacuum-drawn and heat-sealed to the inner surface of the carton. The potential customer opens the carton after pitching it against the wall and then reads a card insert that says, "Unless you have the arm of a major-league pitcher, we're betting our egg is still OK." This is a vivid example of dramatic showmanship. The

Batter up!

salesperson can involve prospects by letting them throw the carton. Far surpassing the effects of mere words, the unbroken egg is visual proof that the claims of the salesperson are valid.

POSITIVE RESULTS OF SHOWMANSHIP

Whether you sell consumer goods, industrial equipment, or services, there are positive results to be derived from applying showmanship. Let's briefly examine some of these benefits.

Maintains Attention and Interest

The mind of your customer can think far faster than you can speak. What, then, might your customer's mind be doing while you are delivering a straight verbal presentation?

Are you listening?

You've guessed it! Unless your prospect has had training in effective listening, there is a good chance that his or her mind will occasionally go "out to lunch." The human mind tends to wander from time to time when it is not actively involved with a conversation. One of the major benefits, therefore, of a dramatic and lively presentation is its tendency to help maintain the active interest and attention of the prospect for longer periods of time.

Substantiates Sales Claims

Do you remember our saying earlier that customers are often skeptical of sales claims? Probably they had good reason, since they've been exposed to many that were mere puffery. Prospective customers want proof, and a dramatic visualization of a product, such as throwing the packaged egg against the office wall, can be a highly effective means of substantiating sales claims.

Is this for real?

Take, for example, the case of an auto salesperson named Rosie. She can talk and talk and talk about the outstanding features of the all-new Belchmobile. But if Rosie takes her prospect out for a demonstration ride and gives the prospect an opportunity to feel and drive the vehicle, she'll find that her demonstration will be far more persuasive than any of her verbal claims.

Appeals to the Senses

See no evil, smell no evil, and hear no sales presentation!

Imagine, for the moment, that you are a salesperson of fine leather apparel, and one of your customers, Mr. Dan Banna, is seated behind his desk, his eyes covered with a blindfold. He informs you that his doctor requested him to rest his eyes this way each day for at least 45 minutes. That isn't all. Mr. Banna also has both hands bandaged as a result of an accident that occurred while he was lighting his barbecue last Sunday afternoon. To make matters even worse, he has a dreadful cold, which has significantly affected his senses of smell and taste. Nevertheless, Mr. Banna advises you: "Don't let my problems get in your way. Go ahead with your presentation."

"Words alone can be effective, but an appeal to a person's emotions and senses can result in clearer, livelier, and more meaningful presentations."

Can you see how your presentation might be handicapped? You would have lost one of the most effective means for dramatizing your sales message—the use of **multiple-sense appeals.** Unfortunately, many sales talks are presented as though each customer were suffering the same maladies as Mr. Banna. They lack showmanship and effective dramatization. Words alone can be effective, but an appeal to a person's emotions and senses can result in clearer, livelier, and more meaningful presentations.

Does this make **sense?**

Try, if you will, to describe solely with words the taste and aroma of a thick, broiled steak. You might be able to come up with a fairly good verbal description, but imagine how much more impact your description would have if your listeners could also see, smell, and taste the steak.

Makes Selling Points Easier to Understand

Do you **understand?**

The operation of a product that has been dramatically demonstrated is far *easier to understand* than if it had been described only by words. Imagine, for example, how different and much more difficult your presentation would be if it were to be given to a blind person. The combined use of sight and sound almost always has far more impact on the prospect than either medium used alone. As we have seen, showmanship can take advantage of a customer's senses and make presentations clearer, either by demonstrating the product itself or by using various selling aids.

Facilitates Selling of Complex Products and Services

Is this **clear?**

Certain products or services are quite complex and would be far more difficult to sell without creative showmanship. For example, one firm provides its salespeople with portable video recorders that can utilize either 8mm or VHS media. These audiovisual devices explain the company's complex circuitry in its electronic components in a $5\frac{1}{2}$ minute message. The audiovisual dramatization has proven to be so clear and effective that the usual need for supplementary presentations by engineers was eliminated, thus reducing the firm's selling costs. The point is this: a dramatic presentation can often make demonstrations of complex goods and services *far more meaningful* to the prospective buyer.

Shows How to Use Products

Showing is telling!

If customers are to be satisfied with your products, they must understand how they function. Another important application of dramatic showmanship is showing how a product can be used. A dramatization can use the product itself (as when a seller of chain saws cuts down a tree to show a prospect how it works), or it can use various types of selling aids.

For example, video systems have been used by the salespeople of medical products companies to dramatize "soft" contact lenses. The video equipment is sometimes provided to eye doctors to instruct them on the use of the product and on the proper care of the eyes. In some cases, doctors purchase the video equipment from salespeople but get the tapes free.

Makes Sales Presentations More Orderly

And that's an order!

A dramatic sales presentation requires planning and rehearsal. Therefore, the application of showmanship tends to result in more orderly and better organized presentations. For example, the use of sales portfolios, film transparencies, movies, or other visual materials tends to ensure a consistent presentation regardless of the mood of the salespeople during the interview.

In summary, then, we can say there are seven reasons why showmanship can help you in your selling efforts. Showmanship:

1. Maintains attention and interest
2. Substantiates sales claims
3. Appeals to the senses
4. Makes selling points easier to understand
5. Facilitates selling of complex products and services
6. Shows how to use products
7. Makes sales presentations more orderly

THE USE OF SALES AIDS

It has long been said that one picture is equivalent to at least a thousand words. If you subscribe to this old Chinese proverb, then you might agree that you have a lot to gain by not *telling* prospects something you can *show* them.

Visual aids, such as flip charts, graphs, and portfolios, have been used effectively by salespeople for many years. And an increasing number of companies have begun providing their sales forces with audiovisual aids, such as videocassettes and laser discs, which incorporate both sight and sound into sales presentations.

A medical doctor typically has many types of tools available to help in doing his or her work—examining and treating patients. A salesperson also has many types of tools—visual and audiovisual—to help in doing his or her work—selling. The salesperson, like the doctor, doesn't use every available tool or aid with every client. Both the doctor and the salesperson must use sound judgment to determine which type of aid can perform the desired task most effectively.

"Well-organized salespeople continually reevaluate their sales aids to make certain that they are not only up to date but also in good condition."

New types of aids are continually being developed. Well-organized salespeople continually reevaluate their **sales aids** to make certain that they are not only up to date but also in good condition. The following section summarizes some of the more typical aids employed by today's salespeople. (See Table 11.1 for a summary of these major types of selling aids.)

Products

Why not show them the real thing!

The most effective visual aid is the *product* itself. It adds clarity and interest to a presentation. Of course, other aids can be useful in helping a customer visualize your products, but nothing has quite the impact of a demonstration of the actual product.

Whenever possible, you should try to get the prospective buyer *involved* with your presentation. Using products in sales demonstrations is an excellent way to get your prospect to take an active part. Some products—automobiles, calculators, typewriters, cameras, and even surgical equipment—can be tested or operated by the prospect. Here's a specific example: The Auto Suture Company produces equipment for sale to hospital surgeons. Auto Suture's sales representatives encourage their customers to try the equipment. Surgeons are invited to laboratories where they can personally test the instruments on animals. Using the actual surgical equipment is thus far more meaningful to the doctors than mere words or pictures.

Products can also be used to help in substantiating sales claims. Unfortunately, product information is sometimes greeted with skepticism. But an actual demonstration of your product's capabilities—the show-and-tell approach—can help to break down sales resistance.

Facsimiles

Salespeople whose products are too cumbersome to demonstrate in prospects' offices sometimes use product **facsimiles.** These may be working models of the product or a cross section (a portion or cutaway) of it. Facsimiles can even be used to sell services. Insurance agents, for example, sometimes use specimen policies as a means of graphically pointing out coverages and exclusions.

Or at least something close to the real thing.

A working model, like the actual product, can give vivid support to your sales claims. When you are using facsimiles of your product, always tell the prospect what you are going to show, but be careful not to be too technical. Ask questions periodically to keep your prospect interested and involved. And remember to keep the presentation dramatic but relatively short.

TABLE 11.1 Major Types of Selling Aids.

Products	Portfolios
Facsimiles	Catalogs
Photos and illustrations	Kits
Advertisements	Guarantees and warranties
Charts	Product data sheets
Graphs	Portable audiovisuals

Photos and Illustrations

Proverb: One photo is worth a thousand trips.

Photos and illustrations are often used when a demonstration of the product itself is not possible. They can be especially helpful in clarifying what a salesperson is saying. Sometimes photos or illustrations are used to presell prospects. For example, assume that you are a real estate agent in Carmel, California, with an opportunity to sell a $670,000 house situated over 150 miles to the north in Piedmont, California. It would not be possible for you to show the house personally to each prospect who entered your Carmel office, but you could use photos and illustrations to give your prospects an initial impression of the house and to let them decide whether or not it suited their interests and desires. In this way, the aids can help in qualifying your prospects.

Advertisements

"As advertised in **Underwear Daily**"

Up-to-date **reprints** or examples of your firm's national or local advertising can be used in dramatizing your presentations. There tends to be a psychological benefit in using current advertisements. Attractive advertising helps to give your customers the impression that yours is a successful and dependable organization—sort of like the "name brand" concept.

Good examples of future advertising plans and activities can often favorably impress your wholesale and retail customers. They realize that an effective advertising campaign can help market merchandise purchased from your firm.

Charts

Flip *it . . .*

Charts are another aid in effective dramatization and can be used in a variety of ways. One common type of chart is the **flip chart,** which typically is a series of illustrations on individual sheets of paper or cards. Such aids have some key advantages as summarized in Table 11.2.

TABLE 11.2 Major Advantages of the Use of Charts in Sales Presentations.

Charts use visual as well as oral stimulation.
Charts help the salesperson deliver a more organized presentation in less time.
Charts help organize the sales presentation.
Charts help the prospect focus on sales presentation.
Charts help the prospect remember what has been covered.
Charts help explain the ideas visually for greater clarification and retention.
Charts help summarize and review what has been accomplished during the sales interview.
Charts provide the salesperson with an effective review device during and at the close of the sales presentation.

Source: Joseph J. Lane, "Data Sheets That Sell," *Sales & Marketing Management,* May 14, 1984, pp. 45–46.

and* slide *it . . .

Another type of chart used with favorable results is called a **slide chart.** Slide charts are aids, often of pocket size, with movable parts; they are used to show such things as product features, capacities, dimensions, and characteristics. They are also used to calculate, compare, and even solve mathematical and engineering problems. Some of them, for example, calculate automobile labor costs, determine return on investments, and show freight rates.

According to the Slide Chart Corporation, a manufacturer of such sales aids, one slide chart can provide 3497 answers to 39 different problems in 18 categories. Slide charts are often given as gifts or premiums to customers in order to gain their goodwill.

to get attention!

When using prepared charts, you should read the words clearly and add comments as you progress through the chart. Also, face your prospect rather than the chart as you read the words or make comments. Be certain that the chart is placed where it can be viewed easily by the prospect.[1]

Graphs

Or graph it!

Graphs are another type of visual aid used by salespeople. Typical graphs are *line graphs, bar graphs,* and *pictorial graphs.* They are often employed to show such factors as sales results, price trends, advertising schedules, profits, and comparisons with competitors.

Graphs tend to have great appeal to the visual senses by making statistical data easier to comprehend. For example, assume that you are a salesperson of SpinJAMMER flying discs and state to a buyer for a large chain of toy stores, "Mr. Jugar, you and I both know that Wham-O has 90 percent of the market for flying discs. However, I'd like you to take a look at this graph. (See Figure 11.1.) Look at how well the SpinJAMMER has caught on in the flying disc market. You can see by this graph that our sales have almost doubled each year since we first introduced the SpinJAMMER in 1987. Wouldn't you like to share in that growth by being able to offer your customers our product?"

When using either charts or graphs, you should keep a few tips in mind. Be sure to tell and show—that is, briefly explain to your prospect the purpose of the item. Plan in advance how you intend to use the sales aid. Be familiar enough with the chart or graph so that you can work with it skillfully and confidently. Recognize that not everyone feels at ease with graphs and charts, so use the sales aids at a pace that seems comfortable for the prospect.

Portfolios

Portfolio *it?*

Portfolios are visual aids that are often in the form of loose-leaf binders. A wide variety of materials is customarily included in them—photographs and illustrations of products, graphs, testimonial letters, and virtually any materials that can assist in graphically delivering a sales presentation. They may be large or small, elaborate or simple. Portfolios are used by many salespeople to add visual life to their sales messages.

American Airlines air freight division has used portfolios consisting of individual case histories of specific users of their services. Each case history is presented

Figure 11.1 Example of a Bar Graph Comparing Sales by Units Over a Three-year Period.

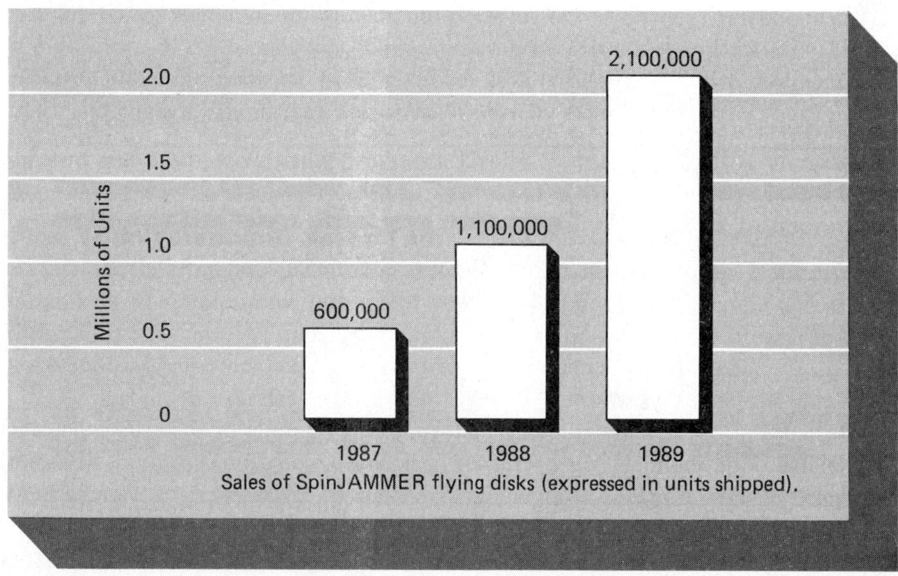

on a separate page and shows how American's air freight services have worked effectively for these customers.

Catalogs

Catalog *it?*

Most well-managed companies provide their representatives with **catalogs.** These are generally used more for reference than selling, although they can be used to show illustrations, specifications, prices, and terms of certain products. You should make certain that any catalog you use in selling is up to date and in good condition. You should, of course, be familiar with its contents.

Kits

Go try a **kit***!*

Many companies provide their sales representatives with **sales kits.** These generally consist of materials or samples that help in demonstrating a product. Attractively prepared kits bring variety and life to a sales presentation and hold the prospect's attention. They also help in organizing sales materials. As with any sales aid, be certain to rehearse how you intend to use your kit. Also, be sure to replace the aid *before* it becomes tattered and worn.

Guarantees and Warranties

It may **warrant** *a sale!*

Many consumers are concerned about what happens if something goes wrong with their purchases. Consequently, creative salespeople attempt to be as familiar as possible with their companies' **guarantees** and **warranties.** The actual documents themselves can also be used effectively as sales aids.

Product Data Sheets

You may have called on a prospective customer, delivered a stupendous sales presentation, but the prospect refused to make a buying decision on the spot. Such a situation is not unusual. However, after you've departed from the prospect's premises, then what?

It just keeps on selling!

A sales aid that keeps on selling long after you've left the prospect is a **product data sheet,** which is a document that provides the reader with technical information and specifications, dimensions, prices, cost savings, colors, efficiency, a review of major benefits, and performance data. A good product data sheet is an effective advertisement for your product as well. In fact, as much thought should go into its preparation as would in a good newspaper or magazine advertisement. Color photographs included in the data sheet showing what the product looks like and how it works can be especially effective for industrial and business products.

"A sales aid that keeps on selling long after you've left the prospect is a **product data sheet** . . ."

THE USE OF PORTABLE AUDIOVISUAL AIDS

Sales departments in a wide variety of industries use **portable audiovisual aids** to assist them in the marketing of goods and services. The numerous types of equipment have become increasingly sophisticated. Most are now considered as legitimate "tools of the trade" and not mere conversation pieces or gimmicks.

There are three principal types of portable media used by salespeople today. They are:

1. Videocassettes and discs
2. Slides
3. Filmstrips

Although state-of-the-art video systems tend to be the most popular, each medium has its advantages and disadvantages, as you can see in Table 11.3.

Because the use of portable audiovisual aids is becoming so prevalent in industry today, let's look briefly at eight specific reasons why their use can help you develop more effective presentations. Basically, audiovisual aids can:

1. Increase sales call productivity
2. Assist in overcoming objections
3. Take the salesperson's place
4. Take the product's place
5. Facilitate add-on sales
6. Assist in opening up new markets
7. Be used in trade shows and fairs
8. Be used to reach ultimate customers

Can Increase Sales Call Productivity

How can the use of AV get you more bang for the buck?

Many managers feel that the use of portable AV equipment can result in increased sales call productivity. The AV tools can often present a more complete, organized, and live-action story in less time than a salesperson can. Sales calls, as we have learned, are costly and time-consuming. During business recessions, especially, the productivity of a sales force is even more important. Therefore, any aid that can help make interviews more efficient should be used by today's creative salespeople.

Retailers also are in a position to increase sales productivity through the use of AV equipment. For example, one problem that retailers must often face is that of attempting to serve more than one customer at a time. Some retailers have resolved this problem by developing showrooms in which customers can observe an audiovisual presentation while waiting to be served. This arrangement not only helps

TABLE 11.3 Advantages and Disadvantages of Principal Types of Portable Audiovisual Systems.

Medium	Advantages	Disadvantages
Videocassettes and discs	Up-to-date and appealing Effective for demonstrating products that "move." Clients accustomed to watching video; many clients "reared on TV." Convenient to use with modern equipment.	Generally more expensive (equipment and production costs) than other types of media. Difficult to customize message for specific customers. Rapid obsolescence due to rapidly changing technology. Often used by salespeople for personal use, thus causing greater wear and tear on equipment. Much equipment lacks random-access capability.
Slides	Less expensive than video equipment. Can be computer-generated making slides cheaper and better than previously. Can be used with one or many customers. Can be customized for specific customers fairly easily.	Not as effective for demonstrations requiring motion. Greater breakdown possibilities; e.g., light bulb failure, etc. May appear to be outdated by some customers. Potential difficulty in synchronizing audio and visual components.
Filmstrips	Lightweight and compact. Less expensive to make copies than with other types of media. Copies easily transported or shipped.	Appears old-fashioned to customers. Difficult to customize message for specific customers.

Adapted from "Will It Be Video, Slides, or Filmstrips?" *Sales & Marketing Management,* January 1987, pp. 74–75.

to keep customers from becoming restless and possibly leaving but also helps to presell the product, thus reducing the amount of face-to-face selling time necessary.

Can Assist in Overcoming Objections

Well-produced films, videotapes, and videodiscs are often helpful in assisting the salesperson overcome objections. Assume, for example, that you sell business jets to private firms. Some years ago, if your prospects wanted to see your airplane, you had to take them down to the local airfield. Now you can, in effect, carry an airplane, a tractor—or any product or service—directly to your prospects. The skepticism of your prospective purchaser toward your product is often eliminated when he or she sees your product actually performing on film, tape, or disc.

Seeing is believing.

Can Take the Salesperson's Place

Not replaced—but restyled!

AV programs can sometimes be used to take the place of a sales call. Don't be alarmed! This is not to say that your sales job is to be eliminated. On the contrary; with AV, the sales function can become more efficient. You can, for example, send discs or videocassettes to your prospects, especially those located in areas so remote that a personal sales call would be too costly, and possibly close the deal over the telephone.

Here's another creative use of such aids. If your customer tells you that she doesn't have the time today to hear your sales message, you might say, "Ms. Juniper, I can really appreciate your shortage of time. How about if I leave this cassette with you, and when you have seven spare minutes, would you do me a favor and give it a listen? I think what you'll hear could save you far more than seven minutes. I'll be back in this area tomorrow morning to pick up the cassette, and I can get your reactions to the message then."

Retail outlets that sell computers typically have a computer display with a program continually running that demonstrates the computer and various programs. With such aids, a salesperson can be more productive, since he or she can be waiting on one customer while another receives a demonstration from the computer itself.

Can Take the Product's Place

He: *"What's in the box?"*
She: *"A tractor!"*

Some types of products don't quite lend themselves to product demonstrations, especially in a customer's office. (See Eiki/Bell & Howell's advertisement in Figure 11.2 for a vivid example.) Your product may be too large to fit on your prospect's desk top—or even in his or her office! Audiovisuals can come to your rescue in such difficult situations. AV units, not much bigger than an attaché case, can be used for selling anything from life rafts to life insurance, and they can make your presentation far more dynamic and alive.

Can Facilitate Add-On Sales

It all adds up.

Assume that you are in a prospect's office demonstrating your product, one that comes with a variety of attachments and accessories. Often it is not feasible to carry every possible attachment or accessory with you. Some salespeople contend that audiovisual aids can help you to make add-on sales (that is, sales of attachments and accessories). They believe that a prospect who can actually see videos of the accessories in action is more apt to develop an interest in them.

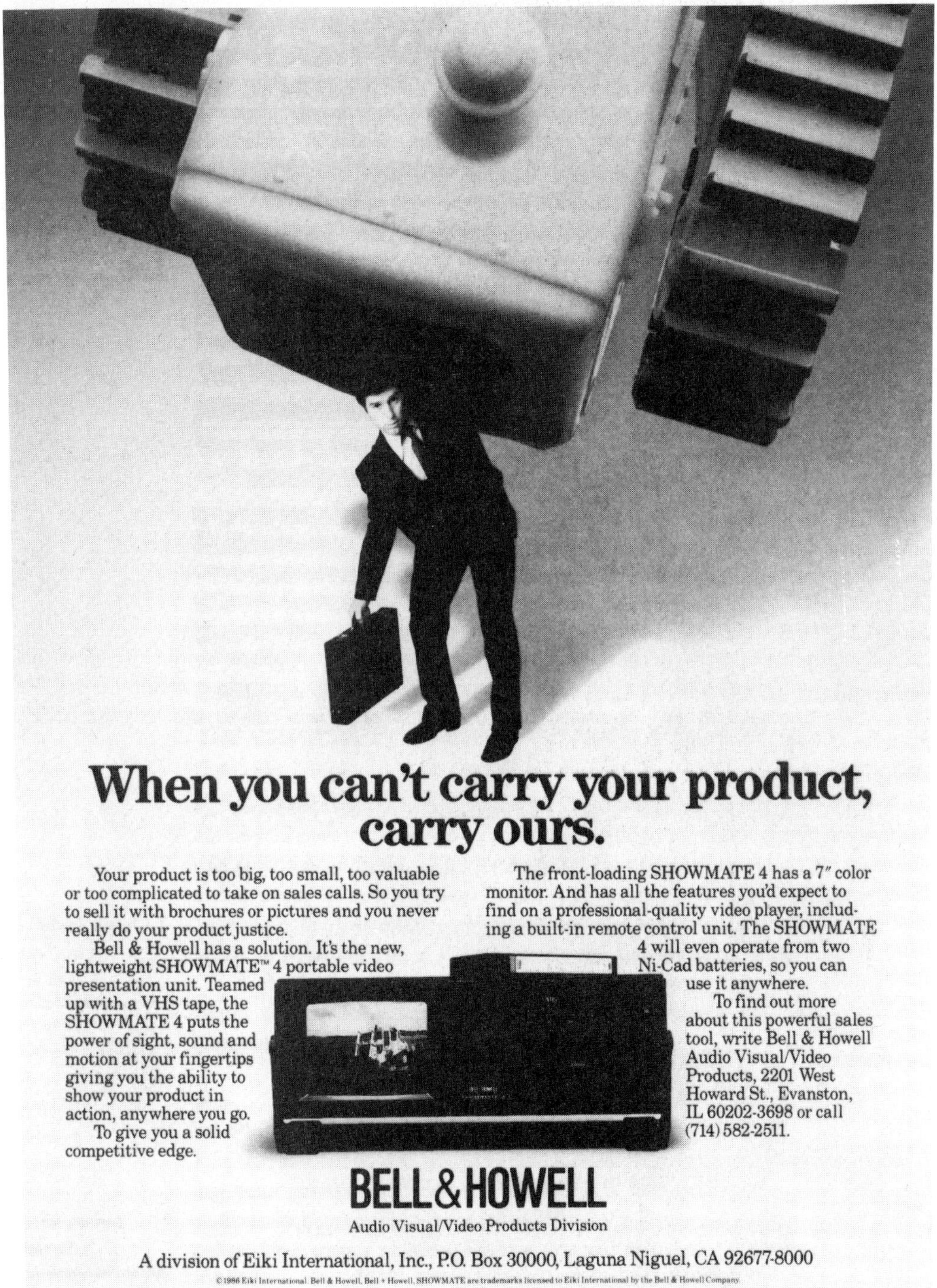

When you can't carry your product, carry ours.

Your product is too big, too small, too valuable or too complicated to take on sales calls. So you try to sell it with brochures or pictures and you never really do your product justice.

Bell & Howell has a solution. It's the new, lightweight SHOWMATE™ 4 portable video presentation unit. Teamed up with a VHS tape, the SHOWMATE 4 puts the power of sight, sound and motion at your fingertips giving you the ability to show your product in action, anywhere you go.

To give you a solid competitive edge.

The front-loading SHOWMATE 4 has a 7" color monitor. And has all the features you'd expect to find on a professional-quality video player, including a built-in remote control unit. The SHOWMATE 4 will even operate from two Ni-Cad batteries, so you can use it anywhere.

To find out more about this powerful sales tool, write Bell & Howell Audio Visual/Video Products, 2201 West Howard St., Evanston, IL 60202-3698 or call (714) 582-2511.

Audio Visual/Video Products Division

A division of Eiki International, Inc., P.O. Box 30000, Laguna Niguel, CA 92677-8000

Figure 11.2 Sometimes Products Don't Lend Themselves to Product Demonstrations. © 1986 Bell & Howell Company.

Can Assist in Opening up New Markets

AV equipment has been used successfully by some firms for opening up new markets. When you are introducing a new product or canvassing a territory for the first time, you can deliver effective, consistent sight-and-sound presentations to a large number of prospects in a relatively short period of time.

A real wheeler-dealer!

Here's one example: AV media played a big part in the promotion of the shopping cart. Sylvan Goldman, the inventor of the handy four-wheel carrier, had trouble at first convincing stores to buy his carts. So he developed a short silent film that was made in a supermarket. The film showed how carts could increase sales. Using the film and a projector on their sales visits, his salespeople found it much easier to gain the interest and attention of store managers. Within a relatively short time, Goldman had more orders for his carts than his small plant could produce.[2]

Can Be Used in Trade Shows and Fairs

Step right up, ladies and gentlemen!

Another common use of AV is in demonstrations at trade shows and fairs. People at shows and fairs seem to be naturally attracted to exhibits featuring sight-and-sound devices. In such situations, AV helps to lay the groundwork for future sales.

Can Be Used to Reach Ultimate Consumers

They're transportable!

Many salespeople who call on ultimate consumers in their homes or offices have found AV tools effective. These people have sold things like insurance and real estate. As already discussed, AV materials have been put to effective use in retail outlets as well.

HOW TO DELIVER EFFECTIVE DRAMATIZATIONS

An effective dramatization doesn't just happen; it takes considerable planning, rehearsal, and periodic reevaluation. Dramatizations that have proven to be most successful generally apply the following guidelines:

1. Be certain that your product or sales aid is in good working order.
2. Choose a good setting for the dramatization.
3. Recognize the individual nature of each customer.
4. Appeal to your prospect's senses.
5. Involve the prospect in your dramatization.
6. Speak as though your sale depended on it.
7. Maintain control over the demonstration and your sales aids.
8. Keep your dramatizations fresh, short, and lively.

Be Certain That Your Product or Sales Aid Is in Good Working Order

Excuse me, sir—got a light?

Something that should go without saying but is ignored so frequently it must be said anyway is this: *make certain that the product you intend to demonstrate or the aid you intend to use is in good working order.* Check any equipment *before* demonstrating it in front of your prospect. If you're using a projector, carry a spare bulb with you. A burnout during a presentation can be disconcerting and embarrassing if you aren't prepared for it.

Your products or aids should not only be functioning well but should also look good. We've already discussed in a previous chapter how a salesperson is judged by his or her appearance. The same holds true for equipment or sales aids.

Choose a Good Setting for the Dramatization

Avoid distractions.

Related to a well-functioning sales aid is the need for a good environment in which to demonstrate your product or use your sales aids. The product or aid should not be demonstrated in dirty, cluttered, or noisy surroundings—such surroundings will compete for your prospect's attention. Try to choose a place and time where distractions and interruptions will be minimal. If using an aid requiring special facilities, such as electrical outlets or water, be sure in advance that they're available. And keep in mind that the presence of an electrical outlet on a wall does not necessarily mean that electricity is going to flow through it.

Recognize the Individual Nature of Each Customer

Everybody's similar . . . but **different!**

We have already discussed the importance of focusing on the specific needs and wants of each prospective buyer when a sales presentation is being delivered. The same advice holds true for the dramatization, which is an integral part of a good sales presentation. In a sense, you should apply what could be called **situational dramatization,** in recognition of the fact that the type of dramatization that appeals to one prospect will not necessarily appeal to another. For example, one prospect may be impressed by your ability to apply showmanship, but another might be distracted or irritated by the same presentation. Be empathetic and sensitive during your delivery in order to ascertain whether you are gaining approval or disfavor.

Appeal to the Senses

The nose knows!

As we have learned, a sensory appeal is far more effective than words alone. Wherever possible, appeal to the prospect's senses of touch, sight, taste, smell, and hearing. Assume that you are demonstrating stereo speakers. Using only one tuner-amplifier, you could alternate between two sets of speakers to contrast their differences in quality and sound. The quietness of an automobile engine, the firmness of a mattress, the smell of flowers, the "mouth-watering goodness" of chocolate candy—all of these are examples in which sensory appeal can be used. Use them when possible, for they enable the prospect literally to "feel" your products.

"Wherever possible, appeal to the prospect's senses of touch, sight, taste, smell, and hearing."

Involve the Prospect in Your Dramatization

When demonstrating your product or using sales aids, always try to determine the effect the demonstration is having on your customer. Does it look as though your prospect is tuned in or, instead, is he or she mentally a thousand kilometers away? If the prospect's mind appears to be elsewhere, then perhaps you have not involved her or him enough in your demonstration.

"Would you mind plugging this in for me?"

Directly involving your customers as much as possible helps to maintain their attention. Such minor things as asking your prospect to plug a projector cord into an electrical outlet or turn a switch off or on can help maintain involvement. If you are demonstrating a product, having the prospect try to operate it, or at least help in its operations, can serve not only to involve the individual but also to back up any verbal sales promises you may have made regarding performance. And an important "must": ask regular questions to see whether the demonstration is being understood and accepted by your prospect.

Speak as Though Your Sale Depended on It

Lullaby . . . and good night!

In order to deliver an effective, dramatic presentation, you have to be understood. So why not speak as though your sale depended on it—since it does! Try to avoid monotony in your voice, or you might do an outstanding job of lulling your prospect to sleep. If possible, practice your dramatization with a tape recorder or—better yet—record an actual presentation and analyze it later for clarity and understandability.

Don't fizzle; sell the sizzle!

Don't forget to put inflection and variety in your voice, pausing at choice moments; vary your pitch where applicable. Also remember to choose your words carefully. Don't sell fried potato slices; sell crisp, crunchy, fresh potato chips. But don't let your efforts at creative showmanship make you forget why you're really there: *to fulfill the needs and help solve the problems of your customers.*

Maintain Control over Your Demonstration and Sales Aids

What can you do if the prospect takes your sales aid?

Many salespeople commit the cardinal errors of passing out sales literature at the beginning of their presentations or permitting their prospects to get hold of sales aids. Think about what can happen if you place a brochure or sales aid into the hands of your prospect. He or she may become so engrossed with the aid that your demonstration will receive scant attention. Visual aids are useful as sales tools, but you should maintain control of them as much as possible. If the prospect grabs the sales aid out of your hands, of course you don't want to become involved in a childish tug-of-war. Usually a polite remark, such as "I'll be glad to leave this brochure with you, Ms. Brash, but if you don't mind, I'd like to use it in my presentation." The prospect will generally accede to your request.

"Think about what can happen if you place a brochure or sales aid into the hands of your prospect. He or she may become so engrossed with the aid that your demonstration will receive scant attention."

Keep Your Dramatization Fresh, Short, and Lively

Ho, hum . . .

Have you ever heard a sales presentation that sounded as though it had been delivered no less than 5280 times by the salesperson? Effective showmanship avoids a stale, tired appearance. A key factor in making a demonstration interesting is to keep it fresh and lively, regardless of the number of times you've presented it. If you are showing a film with occasional humorous sections, laugh as though you've heard it only two or three times. Laughter is contagious and will spread to your audience. With practice and genuine enthusiasm, your reaction to any sales aid—regardless of the number of times it has been used—can seem natural, fresh, and sincere.

Dramatizations are often too long, and many attempt to cover too much territory. Discover the needs and desires of your prospect and deliver a presentation that discusses only what is necessary. An excessively long dramatization will not only fail to maintain the prospect's interest but can also hurt your chances for a successful sale.

SUMMARY

The delivery of an effective sales presentation is an art that requires sound planning and the creative application of your imagination. Some presentations appear monotonous, dry, and even sleep-inducing, while others seem original, dramatic, and attention-getting. The inventive use of showmanship and sales aids can go far to help you turn an insipid presentation into an exciting and lively experience.

Showmanship is the act of vividly and dramatically demonstrating the features, advantages, and benefits of a product or service. An effective dramatization appeals to the senses, is much easier to understand, makes complex products appear simpler, is useful in showing how a product works, and makes sales presentations more orderly.

Sales aids have long been used by intelligent salespeople as a means of appealing to the buying motives of prospects. Among the sales aids often employed are the product itself, facsimiles, photos and illustrations, advertisements, charts, graphs, portfolios, catalogs, kits, guarantees and warranties, product data sheets, and portable audiovisual equipment. The principal types of portable AV media used by salespeople are videocassettes and discs, slides, and filmstrips.

An effective dramatization utilizes equipment that is in sound working order, takes place in a suitable atmosphere and location, recognizes the individual nature of each customer, appeals to the senses, involves the prospect, and is clear and easily understood. Of course, a salesperson should also try to maintain control over any sales aids used in a sales interview and keep dramatizations fresh, short, and lively.

TERMS

dramatizing
showmanship
multiple-sense appeals
visual aids
sales aids
facsimiles
reprints
flip chart
slide chart
graphs
portfolios
catalogs
sales kits
guarantees/warranties
product data sheet
portable audiovisual aids
situational dramatization

QUESTIONS

1. In what ways does an effective sales presentation resemble a theatrical performance?
2. What is your response to the following comment: "I couldn't be a salesperson. Salespeople have to play all sorts of games and roles with customers. They're nothing but actors. They simply cannot be themselves in their jobs."
3. What are some specific examples of how dramatic presentations can help you maintain your customer's attention and interest?
4. Prospective buyers are sometimes suspicious of salespeople. How can showmanship help to overcome such customer skepticism?
5. List three examples illustrating the use of multiple-sense appeals in sales dramatizations.
6. How does showmanship coupled with the use of selling aids help a salesperson overcome normal ups and downs in moods?
7. How does the following statement relate to showmanship? "Our best salesperson is our product itself."
8. In what way can a recent reprint of your firm's advertising tend to enhance the prestige of your sales activities?
9. How can the use of portable audiovisual equipment result in increased sales call productivity?
10. Should audiovisual equipment ever be used to take the place of a sales call? Explain.
11. Explain how the concept of situational dramatization is important to the salesperson.
12. Why should AV equipment be regularly checked and maintained?
13. What sorts of locations or atmospheres might detract from the effectiveness of your product dramatizations?
14. Why is it important for you to maintain control over your sales aids during a presentation?

APPLICATIONS

11.1 LET'S GO, RITA!

Rita Respite is a marketing representative for the Let's Go Travel Agency of Pocatello, Idaho. She has been in the selling field only six months, enjoys her job, but hopes that things will be easier for her in the future than they have been thus far.

For example, last Friday morning one of Let's Go's long-time clients, Victor Vamos, telephoned the travel agency. He and his wife are considering a vacation in the Canary Islands next summer and are interested in getting information about the area.

Rita's boss, Ray Angier, suggested to Rita that she use the new portable audiovisual and promotional materials that were recently left off by Iberian Airlines to promote the Canary Islands. The materials consist of a slide projector with computer-generated color slides with synchronized audio plus some attractive travel brochures. Rita agreed that taking the materials was a good idea. Later that morning she drove to Vamos's office in downtown Pocatello. When she got there, the following conversation took place:

Rita Good afternoon, Mr. Vamos. I want to thank you for calling Let's Go. We have some information on the Canary Islands that I think you'll find interesting. I have a portable slide projector with a built-in screen in this case that should open your eyes to both Gran Canaria and neighboring Tenerife. I haven't had a chance to preview the materials yet myself, but they should be informative. Now if you don't mind, I'll just plug this cord . . .

Vamos Oh, I'm sorry, Rita, but that outlet doesn't work. I've called an electrician who should be here this afternoon. I didn't realize you'd need electricity for this. Wait a minute . . . there's an outlet on the light fixture in the bathroom. Stand by and I'll try to find an extension cord to plug into the bathroom receptacle. Then we'll be all set.
(Five minutes later.)

Vamos Sorry for the delay, Rita, but I didn't have an extension cord in the back room after all, so I ducked out and picked one up at the hardware store down the street. Okay, as your firm name states, "let's go!"
(Rita started the projector, but—alas—30 seconds later the projection bulb burned out.)

Rita Don't panic, Mr. Vamos. I, uh, I should have a spare bulb right here in my briefcase. Hmm, I thought I had one. Hold on. I'm sure I've got one in the car. I'll be right back.
(Five minutes later.)

Rita Looks like that hardware store down the street is doing better than I am today. I dashed down there to buy a new bulb. Now, let's go!

(After the slides were shown to Vamos, the following conversation took place:)

Rita I want to apologize for all that dust and hair on the lens. I certainly hope that Las Palmas isn't that dirty! Seriously, Mr. Vamos, what did you think?

Vamos Well, it looks like a delightful place to take the family on a vacation. I especially like the idea about supervised facilities for children during the day. As you know, we have two small children whom we love very much, but it would be nice to relax away from them for a while. How much extra is the child care?

Rita I'm not sure. It might be included in the package deal . . . and then again, it might not. I'll find that out for you when I get back to my office.

Vamos I have an appointment coming up in a few minutes, Rita. I wonder if you could leave me a pamphlet on the Canary Islands to show to my wife and kids tonight.

Rita I'd be happy to, Mr. Vamos. I have some right here in my briefcase. Hmm, I thought I had some. Wait just a moment. I'm sure I've got some in my car. I'll be right back.
(Five minutes later.)

Rita Whew, for a minute I thought I wouldn't find the brochures, but here they are.

Vamos If you wouldn't mind, Rita, would you write the approximate cost of the trip on the back of one of your business cards, and I'll give you a call regarding our plans early next week?

Rita I don't seem to have any business cards on me, Mr. Vamos. Would you please lend me a piece of paper and your pen, and I'll write it all down for you?

Question

Assume that you—an experienced salesperson—accompanied Rita on her sales call. Rita later asked you for suggestions on ways in which she could have improved her presentation. What advice would you give her?

11.2 A PROJECT

Contact the marketing departments of firms in your area until you locate one that uses visual aids in sales activities. Ask the manager if you could borrow one or two of the aids for a sales project. Then develop a presentation using the borrowed aids. If possible, deliver your presentation before a friend or to a sales class.

11.3 ANOTHER PROJECT

Visit at least three retail outlets, such as stereo equipment or personal computer stores, and ask the salespeople to demonstrate one of their products to you. After each presentation, prepare a summary of the specific techniques that the salesperson employed to dramatize the product. List and evaluate the specific efforts at showmanship that were used. Then develop your own product demonstration for the same products, utilize what you've observed, and add some additional aspects of showmanship that you feel would improve the demonstration.

11.4 THAT'S SHOW BUSINESS!

Steven Wong is a retail salesperson with the National Department Store located in Norfolk, Virginia. He works in the appliance department and enjoys demonstrating the various products that he sells. For example, a small portable washing machine with a power roller for squeezing out water is one of his favorites for applying a bit of sales showmanship. The washing machine is primarily purchased by individuals with cabins and those who enjoy camping but like to take some of their city comforts with them.

To show customers how gentle the rollers were on clothes and how they would raise up over buttons, Steven would put his fountain pen through the rollers. One day while demonstrating the model to a customer, Steven's pen split and ink spewed all over the clothes that were washing in the machine.

Questions

1. What is your reaction to Steven Wong's techniques of dramatizing his products?
2. If you were Steven Wong, what would you say and do now?

NOTES

1. Adapted from Homer Smith "Get Your Message Across—Communicating with a Flip of the Chart," *Sales & Marketing Management,* July 2, 1984, pp. 90.
2. "AV '77," *The Wall Street Journal,* September 12, 1977, p. 20.

Overcoming Objections

No Thanks . . . My Business Is Different

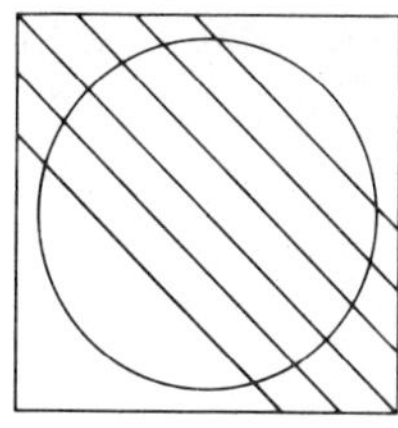

Never treat objections as a "No" answer. All they mean is "not yet."
"A SALES BULLET," *Economics Press*

An objection in a sales talk is like a small piece of eggshell in an order of soft-boiled eggs. When you run onto the shell, you remove it—and go on with the business at hand.
PERCY H. WHITING

Here's what you should be able to do after studying this chapter:

1. Summarize six principal types of buyer objections.
2. List and describe twelve techniques for overcoming objections.
3. Apply the major techniques for handling objections to given sales situations.
4. Recognize the importance of maintaining an objections file.

"I can't afford it right now." "I'm really not interested." "The one we have still works okay." "It wouldn't work for us; our needs are different." Statements like these don't surprise experienced salespeople. They know that objections are a normal part of the selling process.

As a salesperson, should you feel threatened if prospects resist your sales messages or react negatively to them? Not at all. In fact, prospective buyers who don't object may be thinking about a weekend skiing trip instead of listening to your presentation. So don't be afraid of objections—welcome them as opportunities for learning more about the prospect's attitudes toward you, your company, and its products.

Objections can be looked at as opportunities to convert resistance into sales. In fact, long-run success in selling hinges strongly on your ability to turn buyer objections into sales opportunities. Objections may arise at any time during a sales presentation, and you have to be ready for them. In this chapter we explore some of the proven techniques used for overcoming objections and then examine the more common types of objections you are likely to be faced with as a salesperson.

REASONS PROSPECTIVE CUSTOMERS OBJECT

Psychologists believe that resisting change is a natural human tendency. For many individuals, the old, familiar methods and products are better or more useful than

You are an opposing force.

the new ones, which are sometimes viewed as threatening or less predictable. As a salesperson, you are the force opposing a prospective customer's desires for stability and certainty. Your goal is to modify the behavior of potential buyers; therefore, every time you persuade them to purchase your products, you are an instrument of change.

The Desire to Be Persuaded

"I say it, but I really don't mean it!"

If you could get into the minds of prospective buyers, you might discover that frequently they have a genuine interest in your product, may even have the urge to make a purchase, but want to be convinced or at least reassured that their decisions will be right ones. Some objections that appear genuine are merely indirect requests for more information. When a prospect says, "I can't afford it," he or she may actually mean, "Tell me why it's worth that price." In some instances, objections are intended to test the salesperson's ability and knowledge. Objections, which are often used by prospects as protective shields, can be persuasively and gently removed by the deft activities of creative salespeople.

"Your goal is to modify the behavior of potential buyers; therefore, every time you persuade them to purchase your products, you are an instrument of change."

Common Types of Objections

Learn the typical types of objections you are likely to be faced with as a salesperson. By anticipating and preparing for them, you'll discover that you can develop the necessary skills quite rapidly. You may even find that you enjoy the experience of overcoming objections, an activity that can give you strong feelings of personal satisfaction and self-worth.

Let's assume that you've done your homework. You've done a good job of qualifying the prospect in advance and have called on someone who needs (whether recognized or not) your product or service. You are still likely to hear some objections, which typically fall into one of seven principal categories. These are:

1. Price
2. Product
3. Waiting for improved technology
4. Source and service
5. Salesperson
6. Poor time to buy
7. Inherent suspicion
8. Excuses

Understanding these types of objections can help you answer them more skillfully. A little later we'll discuss each of them in detail.

HOW TO OVERCOME OBJECTIONS

Is a stated objection necessarily a **real** *one?*

Resistance to any sales message is a somewhat natural tendency. In order to guide a customer into accepting your proposal, you need a tremendous degree of empathy: you must continually try to put yourself in your prospect's shoes. Try to classify your prospect's objections. Ask yourself whether they're genuine or merely a cover-up for other feelings. In developing methods for handling objections, you should carefully consider how your prospect really feels about your product or service. A prospect's stated reason for resisting your sales presentation could simply be a reaction to the changes you're trying to effect. Ask probing questions and listen—then you'll have a better idea of how to conduct your presentation.

Let's look at some of the techniques regularly used by professional salespeople to overcome objections. (See Figure 12.1 for a graphic summary of the major techniques.)

Figure 12.1 Techniques for Overcoming Objections.

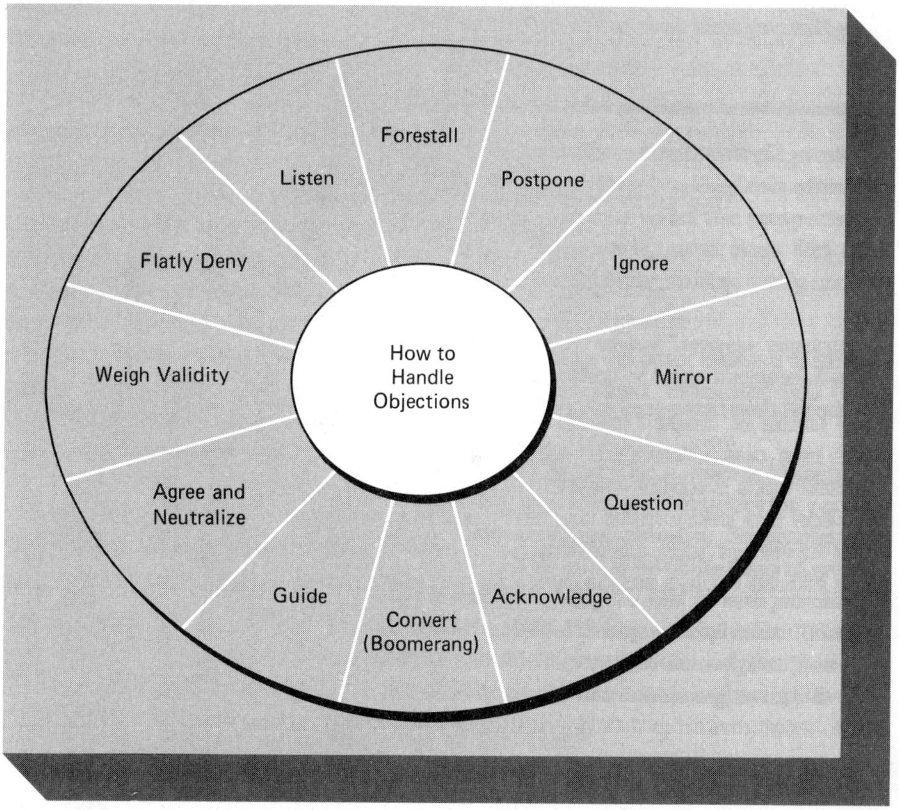

Listen to Objections

How does **listening** *help both you and your prospect?*

Although talking is a necessary ingredient to selling, during the early stages of your sales interview, **listening** is of far greater importance—particularly if you sincerely want to learn about your prospect's needs and attitudes. Effective listening, accompanied by creative probing, helps both you and your prospect. It helps you learn, for example, why your prospect may be resisting your sales message, and it helps the prospect get out into the open any negative feelings he or she might have.

Customers who are listened to are more likely to feel that you have a sincere interest in their needs and problems. When objections are brought out into the open, they frequently seem less real to the prospect. Also, people don't generally like to be contradicted. If you argue with or insult the intelligence of your prospect, you are almost certain to lose the sale—even if you win the argument. Your techniques should subtly guide—not push—your prospects into positive agreement. In Chapter 7 we discussed how to develop effective listening skills and how to phrase effective questions. Refresh your memory now by reviewing those concepts.

Forestall the Objection

How does **forestalling** *objections make selling easier?*

Although objections are not to be feared, the creative salesperson tries to anticipate specific objections and, in effect, answer them before they arise, an activity known as **forestalling.** By anticipating negative reactions, the salesperson stops prospects from being put in a position where they feel compelled to defend their objections. Customers don't have to bring up or defend objections that have already been covered to their satisfaction.

For example, you may have learned during your preapproach that your prospect, Ms. Schmidt, a buyer for a large janitorial service company, prefers to deal with firms that allow her at least 60 days to pay for purchases. Your company, however, requires payment within 30 days. During your sales presentation, you could forestall her objections to a shorter credit period by saying something like, "Ms. Schmidt, you can see that our supplies are not only of high quality, but are competitively priced, factors certainly of importance to you in your operations. As a businessperson, you realize that one of the ways we are able to offer and maintain reasonable prices is by operating efficiently and using businesslike practices, such as asking our customers for payment within thirty days. We've received few complaints on this policy since, by supplying better products at lower prices, we can help customers increase their profits."

Postpone the Objection

Part of your task as a creative, professional salesperson is to sort out real from stated objections, realizing, of course, that they are not always one and the same. You should not, however, regard any customer's objections as trivial, since to him or her they may be quite genuine and of great significance. In some instances, though, it's

What might be the advantage in **postponing** *an objection?*

better to postpone an objection, at least until you've had an opportunity to offer sufficient evidence of your product's value and its benefits to your customer.

One technique for **postponing** objections is to say, "Ms. Balsham, you've brought up a valid point. I'll be discussing that specific subject later in my presentation. If you don't mind, I'll just go on until then, at which time I think you'll find the answer far more meaningful."

"When you're involved in a field where repeat customers are desired, selling on the basis of price rather than value can be a costly mistake, even when your prices are generally lower than those of your competitors."

Sell on price and lose on price!

Price is one topic that many salespeople feel should be postponed until value and benefits have been established. When you're involved in a field where repeat customers are desired, selling on the basis of price rather than value can be a costly mistake, even when your prices are generally lower than those of your competitors. Say, for example, that you sell office supplies, including floppy disks for computer disk drives, and your floppy disks are $10 less expensive per 10-pack than the brand currently purchased by your prospect. If you try to sell the $10 savings, chances are you'll find later that another supplies salesperson took the business away from you, either by stressing quality or maybe even by having a price lower than yours. Instead of price, you should stress the quality and reliability of your disks in relation to the customer's needs.

Ignore the Objection

"You're ignoring me!"

A technique for handling objections that some sales managers feel may be dangerous to your selling health if not used with caution is the act of simply **ignoring** the objection. It certainly isn't a method you want to use frequently with the same prospect. Some salespeople use this method when they feel the objections are a bit weak. The salesperson may pass by the objection as though it didn't exist and move immediately on to the next point. However, it wouldn't be advisable to ignore the objection when the prospect restates it, since the restatement probably indicates that the objection is important to the prospect. You could respond to a restated objection with one of the other techniques for handling objections in your selling arsenal.

Mirror the Objection

"Mirror, mirror, on the wall. . . ."

In Chapter 7, you studied various listening responses. One of these, the *mirror response,* is the act of restating to the prospect what you think he or she has just said. **Mirroring** a response clarifies your own understanding and also allows prospects to reconsider their own words. Frequently an objection loses its apparent validity when it has been restated by another person. Ways in which you can phrase the mirror response include: "Mr. Prospect, are you saying that . . . ?" or "If I understand you, you're saying . . . ." or "Then you are worried about . . . ."

The mirror response may also provide you, the salesperson, with clues as to methods for overcoming the prospect's objections. For example, assume that the prospect states, "I really don't think I can use your product because it won't fit in my office." You might rephrase and mirror the objection with something like: "You mean, Mr. Prospect, that my product appears to be too large to fit in your office?" You then should pause and wait for the prospect to respond. Even if the prospect answers with a "yes" you now can proceed with answers to the objection, such as providing ideas on how the room might be rearranged or a different model be acquired as a solution to the size problem.

Question the Objection

Questioning objections can also be of considerable benefit in overcoming them. For example, assume a prospect says, "Based on what I've been hearing from my associates, I don't feel that I can depend on a regular supply from you people." You might respond with, "I'm certainly concerned about what you're implying. Specifically what have you heard about our shipments?"

What might the **question** *technique accomplish?*

In effect, by questioning the prospect, you are asking him or her to move from the general to the specific. When this method is used, especially when it's in conjunction with other techniques, the objection often appears less significant to the prospect. Let's look at another example:

Mr. Hitch (a prospect) I hear that Household Mutual doesn't pay its insurance claims.

Mr. Ouvert (insurance agent for Household Mutual) Household Mutual doesn't pay its claims (mirror)? Why do you say that (open question)?

Mr. Hitch Because I know of a man who had his insurance with Household three years and for *no reason* at all he was canceled.

Mr. Ouvert For *no* reason at all?

Mr. Hitch Well, that's what I was told.

Mr. Ouvert Is that the primary reason, then, why you feel you wouldn't acquire insurance from Household Mutual?

Mr. Hitch Well, yes.

Mr. Ouvert Wouldn't you agree, Mr. Hitch, that Household Mutual is in business to make a profit? We don't make it by *not* selling insurance. Mustn't there have been some good reason for Household to decide it no longer wanted to accept premiums from the person you've mentioned (closed question with likely affirmative response)?

Of course you must be careful to avoid appearing as though you were conducting an inquisition with the prospect, which would tend to create a defensive and counterproductive atmosphere.

Acknowledge the Objection

Why **acknowledge** *the objection?*

A low-key response to sales resistance is **acknowledging** the objection. This relatively soft approach can be used to show your prospect that you feel he or she brought up a logical point. In this manner, you show the person that you understand and sympathize with what was said. You aren't conceding anything, however, but are merely acknowledging that you understand the prospect's point of view.

Convert the Objection

A fairly common technique for overcoming objections is the **converting (boomerang)** technique; this involves converting objections into selling features. For example, assume that you work for the KaiCan Aluminum Company, and that your customer, Mr. P. C. Ristantz, has just informed you that his firm is no longer going to use your aluminum products. Mr. Ristantz has explained, "We've decided to discontinue the use of aluminum in our products in favor of other raw materials. We've discovered that we have to reduce the weight of our materials yet maintain strength. I really doubt that any of your products can meet our needs."

How does the **boomerang** *work?*

Your response could be, "Mr. Ristantz, I can certainly understand your needs for both reduced weight and adequate strength. Here's what we've recently done to overcome that problem. We have broadened our lower gauge limit from 0.020 to 0.008. This has resulted in a 60 percent potential savings in weight over the 0.020 sheet you presently use. And, it doesn't significantly alter the integrity or strength of your particular product. So you can see that our sheet aluminum eliminates your need to switch to raw materials you may not be as familiar with."

Guide the Objector

How can you **guide** *your prospect?*

Related to the conversion method is the **guiding** technique of handling objections. This method can be used when the prospect has made both positive *and* negative comments about your product. With this technique, you try to guide your prospect's thoughts toward those parts of your proposal he or she has already agreed with. For example, a prospect might say, "I can see several advantages of your photocopier over the one I'm leasing now, but I'm not sure if it's worth the extra cost." You could ask, "What are some of the advantages of our machine that you feel would be most helpful to you?" Through the use of the guiding technique, you can focus on the positive aspects of the interview and, in a sense, sidestep the negative portions.

Agree and Neutralize the Objection

A method long used by salespeople when facing objections has been termed the **agreeing and neutralizing** technique. Referred to also as the *agree and counterattack* or the *yes, but* technique, this method tends to disarm prospects, since the salesperson appears to be agreeing with their responses. The salesperson shows sympathy for their points of view, which relaxes them. At this point, however, the salesperson demonstrates that the objections are actually unfounded.

Don't **but** *me, fella!*

You must be careful with this technique also, since people generally don't like to be contradicted or proven wrong. If you appear contradictory, your prospect is likely to become defensive and to resist your efforts.

The 3M Corporation recommends that its sales personnel use a modification of the *yes, but* approach. 3M salespeople are advised to drop the "but" and in its place use a *pause.* For example, instead of saying, "I don't blame you for doubting that this procedure will work for you, but Mr. Dent at Arrowhead Offset . . . ," a salesperson might say, "I don't blame you (pause) . . . Mr. Dent at Arrowhead Offset. . . ."

Some salespeople use the word "however" instead of "but," feeling that it's a gentler term. For example, a customer might say, "That's one heck of a lot of money to pay for a car." The automobile salesperson then could say, "You're right. It is a lot of money. However, have you considered the low maintenance, high mileage, and extremely favorable resale price you'll get at trade-in time with this automobile?"

Some salespeople use the *agree-and-neutralize* technique by employing what they call the *3F's.* The F's stand for *feel, felt,* and *found.* Here's an example of the 3F method: "I understand completely how you *feel,* Ms. Block. Several people I've talked to in the past *felt* the same way. However, here's what they *found* after they tried. . . ."

Weigh the Validity of the Objection

On which side are there more kilos?

Assume that your prospect has made nothing but negative comments about your products. In such cases, you could use the **weighing** technique, a method that involves your listing on one side of a sheet of paper all the disadvantages cited by the prospect and on the other side the advantages. No product is perfect, but a visual comparison that shows how the advantages far outweigh the disadvantages can often overcome customer resistance. (See Table 12.1 for an example of the weighing technique.)

You should try to involve the prospect as much as possible with the weighing technique. For example, you might say something like, "Let's list all the reasons

TABLE 12.1 A Graphic Example of the Weighing Technique for Overcoming Objections.

Advantages	Disadvantages
1. Lower operating costs	1. Higher initial cost
2. Simpler to operate	2. Heavier weight than competitors' models
3. Higher resale value	
4. Greater flexibility	
5. Compatible with broad line of add-on accessories	
6. Local and dependable service facilities	

against your making a decision today." (Let the prospect list as many as possible without interference.) "Okay, let's now review some of the main reasons favoring your making a decision today." If necessary, you can add to the advantages list by stating, "Would you agree that (an advantage) would also be a benefit? Good, now let's count the advantages and disadvantages. Hmmm. It looks like the answer is fairly apparent, doesn't it?"

Flatly, but Politely, Deny the Objection

"That's right, you're wrong!"

The **denying** method for handling objections is another technique used by some salespeople. A major problem with this method, however, is that it can appear to be argumentative. The salesperson is hitting the prospect head-on with a contradiction. There are some instances, however, when a direct denial may be called for. For example, if a prospect has accused your company of engaging in unethical practices and you know that the charges are untrue, a definitive and sincere denial is a very convincing response. If the accusation about your company is true, however, your future credibility will be adversely affected by your denial.

See Table 12.2 for a summary of the major techniques for handling objections.

TYPICAL BUYER OBJECTIONS

After a few years of experience in sales, you might find yourself actually wishing that customers would develop some new and more challenging objections. You might even begin to feel that you've heard the same old patter so often that you can handle it easily with the polished responses you've developed. Earlier we saw that objections generally fall into one or more of eight categories. Let's examine those categories now.

Price Objections

How might a higher price be justified?

One of the most common objections concerns *price*. Frequent comments of resistance are: "I can get it cheaper elsewhere." "Your price is too high." "I think I'll wait until the price drops." Price objections can often be overcome by proving that your product is worth the price being asked. For example, you might justify price by stressing such features as higher quality of materials, better quality control, improved design, guarantees, service facilities, and prestige factors as well as by using third-party references. The *agree-and-neutralize* method of overcoming objections could also be put to good use in such cases. For example, you might say, "Mr. Parsimony, you're absolutely right. Our product is not cheap. Before we get too hung up on price, however, let's take a look at what you will be getting for your money."

Sometimes when customers complain about price, they really mean that they feel they don't have the money to buy the product. Common excuses related to this are: "I just don't have the money," or "I can't afford it right now; maybe later."

TABLE 12.2 Major Techniques for Handling Objections.

Technique for handling objections	Purpose of technique	Sample response or explanation
Listening	To enable prospect to air feelings; should be used in conjunction with questioning techniques.	Show interest in prospect's feelings through sincere use of listening responses.
Forestalling	To overcome known objections *before* they are stated by a prospective customer.	"In spite of high interest rates, now is an excellent time to purchase a house. Let me explain why, Mr. Capister."
Postponing	To avoid even greater buyer resistance that might result from an immediate response.	"You ask how much it costs? Far less than you might think, Mr. Parsimoni. First permit me to show you how these features can actually reduce the costs of operating your business."
Ignoring	To sidestep a prospect's objections when they appear flimsy and without merit; must be used with caution.	Prospect may later recognize the triviality of the ignored objection.
Mirroring	To clarify your own understanding of the prospect's feelings and to enable prospect to reconsider his or her own words.	"You mean that you don't expect *any* reduction in costs as a result of our proposed equipment installation?"
Questioning	To move prospect's objections from the general to the specific so that the salesperson can understand and deal more effectively with them; relates to the mirror technique.	"You feel that this product would be too harsh on delicate fabrics? What types of fabrics did you have in mind, Mr. Synique?"
Acknowledging	To show prospect that you understand and sympathize (not necessarily agree) with what he or she has said.	"You're right, our prices, like everything else, have gone up again recently."
Converting (Boomerang)	To convert an objection into a reason for buying.	"The fact that you say you're too busy is all the more reason why you should hear how this system can save you substantial amounts of time."
Guiding	To support favorable remarks the prospect has made about the product and thus guide the prospect away from negative feelings.	"Let's return to some of those product benefits we discussed earlier. Which ones seem to be most appealing to you?"

Technique for handling objections	Purpose of technique	Sample response or explanation
Agreeing and neutralizing	To "disarm" prospects by appearing to recognize the merits of the prospect's objection yet returning to your own position with renewed vigor.	"I agree that it's frustrating when children's plastic swimming pools become brittle and crack apart after one season. However, we are now using a manufacturing process that eliminates this problem."
Weighing	To show how advantages of the product outweigh any disadvantages.	"Let's weigh the advantages versus the disadvantages of this product and I think you'll then agree that. . . ."
Denying	To refute an untrue accusation made by the prospect toward you or your company.	"I'm afraid that someone gave you incorrect information. We have *never* canceled a person's insurance 'for no reason whatsoever.' "

Classifying objections is especially important when the objections are based on price. Is the prospect really telling the truth or merely giving you an excuse because he or she doesn't recognize the need for your product or service? Or is the prospect using price and lack of ample funds as a ploy to get you to lower your price? Some buyers are skilled negotiators and have no intention of paying your asking price.

A sale on need is a sale indeed!

Additional methods for overcoming price objections include pointing out how the prospect may actually save money as a result of purchasing the product (economy motive), explaining how little a product actually costs by showing how much it costs per day or per application, or suggesting the use of credit terms. If a prospect wants to postpone buying until the price goes down, you can remind the prospect how projected inflationary trends may make purchase of the product even more difficult in the future. Those in real estate sales often mention price trends to counter price objections.

Product Objections

What are some types of product objections?

Another common type of resistance relates to the *product* itself. You may hear objections such as, "Your product is too new; it hasn't been on the market long enough." You can agree with the prospect that your product is new, but raise the question, "Weren't all of today's well-known products—the radio, television, pocket calculator and videotape recorder—previously 'too new'? Newness, Mr. Prospect, should be utilized, not feared." In this case you might also use third-party references, show specific research results, and demonstrate the effectiveness of the product itself.

Let's assume that a retail customer says that she's satisfied with her present line of products. What might you say? You could ask her to check how many of her present products she had five years ago. There undoubtedly would have been a significant change in the types and brands of products on her shelves. You could point out that she kept up with change in the past and that she'll be able to do so in the future if she obtains your products.

How would you handle some of these other common types of product objections? "I don't like the design." "It doesn't have all the features I want." "I'm overstocked with that type of item." "There's no demand for it."

Waiting for Improved Technology

We currently are in a rapidly changing and highly technological era. New models of electronic equipment for both householders and businesspeople have been appearing in the marketplace with mind-boggling frequency. We've already learned that buyers vary greatly in their motives. Some individuals like to be on the leading edge of *improved technology* by being among the first to acquire a "new and different" product. Others, on the other hand, generally are hesitant to purchase the early models of an item. They frequently contend something like, "I'm sure that by next year there undoubtedly will be newer models available that will be much faster, more efficient, and with substantially more capacity. I'd rather wait for the technological improvements."

They'll **always** *be* **something** *new and improved!*

The hesitant type of prospect often offers similar comments after the "new and improved" model hits the market, since there certainly could be additional technological improvements made to the product the following year.

You, the salesperson, who confront such attitudes face the challenge of convincing the prospect that there is value in obtaining the product now rather than waiting for improved technology. For example, you might explain to the prospect how much savings in operating costs would have resulted if the product had been acquired a year ago. You can also show the prospect how the savings resulting from greater efficiency is greater than the purchase price of the item.

Some customers prefer to "trade up" their acquisitions before they become obsolete. Perhaps your firm offers customers such opportunities, which can be a method for countering the "improved technology" objection. For example, leasing a product for a specific period of time may be possible. The customer may then have the option of either buying or leasing a new model at the end of the leasing period.

Source and Service Objections

Another fairly common type of objection relates to the *source and service* facilities of the product. For example, a consumer may resist buying in certain stores because of unfavorable reports about them. Or a person may shy away from a particular brand of automobile because of negative feelings about the way the manufacturer assembles it or the way that dealers service the vehicles. Or a prospect may not be familiar with a particular company or its service facilities and therefore have insufficient confidence in the firm's financial stability, dependability, and so on.

"When you're faced with source or service objections, ask probing questions to find out whether the prospect's feelings are based on fact or rumor."

How can you forestall source and service objections?

Source and service objections can frequently be forestalled by the salesperson who has ample knowledge of his or her company's operations and accomplishments. Ways of forestalling or overcoming such objections include discussing the financial capability of your firm as well as its age, size, personnel, policies, and service facilities. Using charts and other visual aids can also be helpful.

For example, one swimming pool salesperson—faced with selling in an industry with a damaged reputation brought on by some unethical or underfinanced builders—maintains a sales portfolio with tearsheets taken from the Yellow Pages of the local telephone directory. He shows his prospects the names of pool companies that were in the telephone directory ten and five years ago. He then compares those pages with a new directory, which no longer shows many of the earlier pool companies. He uses this technique as a means of stressing that his company—unlike many others—will still be around "tomorrow" in the event a customer has a problem that requires service. He also uses the fact that his company is listed on the New York Stock Exchange as evidence of his firm's "financial strength and stability." In his sales presentations, he stresses, "We're not a here-today, gone-tomorrow type of company. We'll be around in the future for you to sue, if need be."

Here today **and** *tomorrow!*

When you're faced with source or service objections, ask probing questions to find out whether the prospect's feelings are based on fact or rumor. When valid, don't deny them. Instead, try to stress the offsetting benefits of purchasing your products.

Objections to the Salesperson

In some cases, a prospect may refuse to do business with a firm because of a personality clash with a specific *salesperson.* Customers may not always openly reveal their true feelings or sentiments, but such attitudes can often be sensed by the alert salesperson.

If you seem to rub a prospect the wrong way, you might try to find out why and then see what aspects of your personality you could change in order to come across more favorably. Are you behaving in a cocky, overly aggressive manner with the prospective buyer? Does he or she find certain mannerisms objectionable? If you're not certain of the real reason for the personality clash, ask the prospect point blank. You might say, "Ms. Contraire, I feel that there's something about my style of presentation that bothers you. That's certainly not one of my intentions. Would you mind telling me what it is?" If all efforts to resolve the personality clash fail, then, rather than lose the account entirely, a technique called the **T.O. method** might be necessary. The T.O. method means *turning over* a difficult customer to another salesperson. In some instances, of course, the T.O. method won't be feasible. Then you'll just have to make the best of what appears to be an undesirable situation.

When all else fails, then what?

Typically, however, objections are generally not of the salesperson. Instead, customers merely have sincere questions that they want answered. Salespeople should continually remind themselves that they personally are not necessarily the object of the objection.

The Poor-Time-to-Buy Objection

Another common buyer objection relates to timing. This type of objection also is commonly used to "brush off" the seller. Probing to determine the validity of such objections is essential.

"On your bike, mate!"

Typical *poor-time-to-buy* objections include: "Now isn't the best time." "I have to think it over." "I have to discuss it with my partner (wife, husband, assistant)." "I think I'll wait until the price comes down (or the new models are unveiled, or until I can afford it)." To counter such objections, salespeople who have done their homework can show their customers how costly such delays can be.

Frequently, this type of objection is merely a stall. You might ask the prospect which parts of your discussion require clarification and then review them. Perhaps the prospect didn't understand certain aspects of your sales presentation but doesn't want to appear dumb. Try to make it as easy as possible for the prospect to act now, not at a later time.

Inherent Suspicion

Some objections are more psychological—that is, they are related more to the mental attitudes of prospective buyers than to the product, firm, or salesperson. One need only look at the growth of the security industry in the United States to have evidence of what appears to be deteriorating trust and *inherent suspicion* among members of our society. Homeowners in America during recent decades have installed "decorative bars" on their windows and bought guns and expensive electronic detection equipment to fend off unwelcome visitors. More and more American citizens no longer dare to take leisurely strolls at night. Automobiles have been electronically equipped to discourage thieves. Some businesses even employ security personnel disguised as company workers to spy on employees.

Who's that knocking on my door?

"It is in this unhealthy atmosphere of distrust, where individuals tend to be apprehensive of all their associates, that today's salesperson must function."

It is in this unhealthy atmosphere of distrust, where individuals tend to be apprehensive of all their associates, that today's salesperson must function. Should you be surprised, therefore, to discover that your prospective buyers are suspicious and distrustful of what you are trying to accomplish? Looking your customers directly in the eye and providing them with honest responses helps in overcoming inherent suspicion. We stress, once again, the importance of a sound *approach,* that step in the sales process where you significantly influence the extent of trust you are likely to receive from customers.

Excuses

Some prospects are loaded with excuses as to why they can't make a current buying decision. An important characteristic to identify is the difference between an *excuse* and an *objection.* Gus Kotoulas, professor of selling at Morton College, has this to say about the importance of making the distinction between an excuse and an objection.

> I use some strong language to differentiate between an excuse and an objection. I tell my students that an excuse is a lie, and that they must be able to ferret out the real objection before they can continue their presentation. An example might be when a prospect states, "I have to talk it over with my wife." The statement may be true, but it also may be an excuse to extricate himself from the sales presentation.
>
> I tell my students to use the following phrase: "Is that all that's keeping you from buying today?" If the customer says "yes," I tell the student to call his bluff and ask "Why don't we call your wife?" If the prospect's statement was the real objection, he will usually go along with the salesperson's request. If it's merely an excuse, the prospect might come up with another excuse. I tell my students to keep asking "Is that all?" and calling the prospect's bluff until they uncover the real objection.[1]

As Professor Kotoulas emphasizes, the salesperson must get through the excuses and work on the real objections in order to make a successful presentation and sale.

MAINTAINING AN OBJECTIONS FILE

Keep track of flack!

We've covered some of the more common types of objections likely to confront those in the selling field. We've also discussed some of the frequently used methods to overcome them. Overcoming objections is a skill that comes only with practice. Many creative salespeople keep track of the types of objections they receive on the job. Some salespeople write them on cards and develop answers for them (see Figure 12.2 for a sample form). Well-developed responses can be practiced on co-workers and sales managers, or they can be taped. Experiment with a variety of methods until the techniques become a basic part of you. Always show sincerity when answering objections. If you can maintain enthusiasm for your job and products—along with a good sense of humor and ethical behavior—you should find that handling objections is one of the most enjoyable activities you'll experience during the selling process.

SUMMARY

In this chapter we discussed some of the proven techniques for overcoming objections. In selling, an objection is considered a negative response to a sales proposal. The skillful handling of objections by a sales representative can be likened to the coordinated activities of a shortstop fielding ground balls or a tennis player adroitly backhanding tennis balls. Whether the activities be athletic or a part of the selling

Product ______________________	Objection No. ______________________
Type of Customer ______________________	
Objection or Question	Appropriate Response

Figure 12.2 Objection/Answer Reference Form.

process, the individuals involved can receive tremendous personal satisfaction from using the skills they develop as they master their specialties.

Salespeople who attempt to understand their prospects can often anticipate potential objections and overcome them early in the presentation. Professional salespeople have developed a variety of techniques for overcoming objections—most of these have been discussed in this chapter. Although seasoned salespeople may feel that they've heard every possible objection, they still, at times, must engage in situational selling when an unexpected objection is presented.

KEY TERMS

listening
forestalling
postponing
ignoring
mirroring
questioning
acknowledging
converting (boomerang)
guiding
agreeing and neutralizing
weighing
denying
T.O. method

QUESTIONS

1. Why is listening one of the most significant and effective techniques for overcoming objections?

2. How can you, as a salesperson, benefit by forestalling objections?
3. Evaluate the following: "Some objections are merely lame-brain excuses for not buying. The best technique when confronting flimsy excuses is to ignore them."
4. Under what circumstances might it be advisable to postpone a prospect's objections?
5. Why should a salesperson welcome rather than fear objections?
6. In what way does mirroring an objection tend to soften its impact?
7. What technique might be the most effective if you were trying to determine whether an objection was valid or merely an excuse? Explain.
8. Which technique for handling objections might be most effective when a prospect has made both positive and negative comments about your product? Explain how it can be used.
9. In what way might the *yes, but* technique for handling objections tend to make prospects defensive? In what way might the *yes, but* method be improved?
10. What is a major danger inherent in the direct-denial method for overcoming objections? Under what circumstances might it have merit?
11. Should you ever reduce your prices for prospective customers? Explain your position.

APPLICATIONS

12.1 EXERCISE IN HANDLING OBJECTIONS

Develop effective responses for the following situations:

a. You have delivered a sales presentation to the head of purchasing, who says, "I'm really impressed with your product and can see how it could fit our needs. But I think I'll wait until I get a chance to discuss the proposal with my assistant, Mrs. Mason. She'll be back from her vacation in about two weeks."

____

____

____

b. You have just explained how your brand of tires is safer than most others, and your customer, Mr. Pomelo, says, "Of course, safety is important to me, but how do I know that your tires are as safe as you claim?"

____

____

____

c. You have started your sales presentation to Ms. Pima but have not yet had the opportunity to point out the benefits of your product. Ms. Pima interrupts by demanding, "How much is this unit?"

d. Your prospect, Mr. Findley, explains, "Your accounting people have been rude and offensive in their dealings with me. Their letters have been insulting and tactless, and I'm not sure I want to do business with your firm in the future."

e. Your prospect, Mrs. Triton, has made a misinformed statement about the service capabilities of your firm. You have attempted to correct her misunderstanding, but she has become even more irritated.

f. Your prospect, Mr. Edwards, says, "I'm a bit apprehensive about doing business with your company again. We really got stung by you guys back in '85, and I don't want that to happen again."

g. Your prospect, Ms. Owens, says, "Some of my associates have heard some pretty negative things about your packaging."

h. Mr. Brookdale, your prospect, says, "Oh, I'm sure you've got a good product, but it wouldn't work for us. You see, our business is different."

i. Your prospect, Ms. Polvo, says, "Yes, it's a beautiful compact disc player, but it looks awfully complicated to me. I'd need to be an engineer merely to figure out how to turn it on!"

____

____

____

j. Your prospect, Mr. Pulpa, objects, "I can't stock my shelves with blenders that expensive. My customers are just average working folks, not business executives."

____

____

____

k. You sell shoes in a retail store and your customer, Ms. Zapato, says, "I think you've got a good-looking product, but I'm afraid it's a bit out of my price range."

____

____

____

l. You sell pocket-sized dictating machines and your prospect, Mrs. Angosto, says, "It looks like a handy little gadget, but I notice the cassette is smaller than the standard ones. I think I'd be better off sticking with the regular-sized cassette recorders."

____

____

____

m. You sell batteries at an automobile parts outlet, and your prospect, Mr. Pila, says, "I've heard that you don't really stand behind your warranties when something goes wrong with a battery."

____

____

____

n. You are a retail clerk in the radial and table-saw section of a large retail store, and a customer seems to dislike you for a reason unknown to you. He appears to be highly upset and begins to swear at you.

____

____

____

o. You sell quartz digital watches to jewelry and department stores, and a retailer says, "I don't care to stock up on those right now. I've been hearing that prices on those watches are headed down. I don't want to get stuck with an overpriced inventory, so I think I'll hold off buying any now."

p. You sell brushes house to house, and you have no idea why a particular prospect seems so suspicious toward you. How might you overcome this problem?

q. You are a new-car salesperson with a prospective buyer, Mrs. Trava, who has just said, "I really like the practical design of your new Hoo-go .5-liter car, but I don't think it's large enough for my husband and me. We like a comfortable car with lots of room."

r. You sell computers in a retail outlet and your customer, Ms. Dee Lay, says, "I can see the need for a computer with spreadsheet, data bank, and word processing capabilities. But I think I should wait until they're improved. I'm sure that next year's model will have much more memory and capabilities than the models you've shown me.

12.2 A LONGER LIFE—MILK IT FOR WHAT IT'S WORTH

The firm you work for has recently developed a new packaging process for dairy milk. The packaged product is called *StretchLife* milk. The milk keeps without refrigeration for at least three months because it has been heat treated to seal in the freshness. Once opened, the milk must be refrigerated.

The process has long been used in Western Europe, where it has been marketed successfully. North Americans, on the other hand, tend to be conditioned to believe that a dairy product must always be refrigerated to maintain its healthful characteristics.

A significant cost advantage to the grocery store is the lack of expense for refrigeration. Storage costs are also lower, since the milk carton is rectangular and measures only $6\frac{1}{2}$ inches tall, $3\frac{3}{4}$ inches wide, and $2\frac{1}{2}$ inches deep. The product will keep its freshness on store shelves for at least three months. A major benefit to consumers is their ability to stock up on milk without having to worry about spoilage. For example, a case of 10 cartons could be purchased, stored, and be readily available for use without having to "run to the store" for a carton of milk.

The product has been test marketed in regions of the country that are similar to your territory. *StretchLife* has been selling at double the rate of your firm's standard milk products. As a result, your sales manager has asked you and all members of the sales team to begin bringing in large orders in the local sales territories as has been done in the test markets in other regions.

At the moment, you are visiting Larry Leche, owner of Leche's 24-hour Superette. Leche seems to like the advantage of *StretchLife* heat-treated milk but acts somewhat hesitant to give you a order.

Question

What should you say to Leche to obtain an order for *StretchLife* milk?

12.3 "BUT YOUR *PRICE* IS TOO HIGH!"

Joe Desaliento has been in the selling field for only three months. He has become somewhat discouraged lately because of an objection that he consistently receives from his prospects. He is regularly told that his products are typically higher priced than those of his competitors. Joe has begun to fear even mentioning price when he tries to close sales. He likes his company and the people he works with and doesn't want to give up yet. Joe wonders what he can do about the price problem.

Question

What advice would you give Joe if you were his manager?

12.4 EXERCISE IN IMPROVING OBJECTION RESPONSES

Assume that you observed salespeople make the following responses to customers' objections. What is wrong with the responses, and how might you improve them?

a. "We know it works. We'd like you to try it."

b. "Don't you agree that this is the product for you?"

c. "You're wrong. This product is cheaper than you realize."

d. "You say your business is different? That's what all my customers say."

NOTE

1. Gus Kotoulas, extracted comments from a review of Stan Kossen's, *Creative Selling Today,* 2nd ed. (New York: Harper & Row, 1982).

Closing the Sale

Which Would You Prefer?

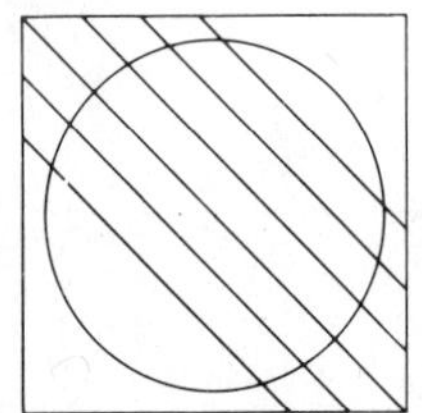

Salespeople who cannot close sales are not salespeople; they are merely conversationalists.
CHARLES ROTH

Here's what you should be able to do after studying this chapter:

1. Describe why some salespeople experience difficulty in closing sales.
2. Explain the importance of recognizing buying signals.
3. Recognize the various types of buying signals that suggest it's time for a trial close.
4. Demonstrate the major techniques for closing sales.
5. Engage in the types of behavior that result in a smooth post-sales-interview period.
6. Explain the purpose of the postcall analysis.

What truly measures a salesperson's skill? The number of prospects seen? The fluency of the sales presentation? The deft manner of handling objections? These and every aspect of the selling process are, of course, essential, but they are of little value unless the salesperson has developed another key skill—the ability to close the sale. The **close** is the attempt by the salesperson to motivate the prospective customer into making an affirmative decision regarding the purchase of a product or service. This is a fancy way of saying that no sale takes place until the salesperson gets the order.

This chapter discusses reasons why some salespeople experience difficulty with this important sales step. It also discusses the need to recognize buying signals and examines some of the proven techniques for closing the sale. The chapter concludes with suggestions for postclosing activities.

REASONS FOR CLOSING DIFFICULTIES

The close is probably the most important step in the selling process, yet it's the one that seems to be the greatest stumbling block to many salespeople. Some individuals, especially less experienced salespersons, make outstanding presentations and handle objections with consummate skill, but then they fail to recognize those all-important signals that urge them to attempt a trial close. Salespeople, for a variety of reasons, often dread asking for the order, yet they can't remain salespeople for long unless they overcome this significant obstacle. Most sales managers want more than glib conversationalists on their sales teams.

Let's examine some of the common causes of closing failures. Studying them should help you develop useful countermeasures and become a more effective closer. The principal causes of closing failures include:

1. Fear of being turned down
2. One-way communication
3. Lack of training
4. Poor planning
5. High-pressure selling
6. Lack of enthusiasm

Fear of Being Turned Down

Should* fear *be* feared*?

Franklin D. Roosevelt once asserted, "We have nothing to fear but fear itself." Nothing could be closer to the truth for individuals in sales, yet it is *fear itself,* mainly the fear of personal rejection, that is a major cause for muffing sales interviews. Like almost everybody else, salespeople don't like to be rebuffed: the word *no* can be unsettling and bruising to a tender ego. Experienced salespeople usually learn that their own attitudes toward their jobs and customers influence how they react to rejection. They realize that no salesperson closes 100 percent of the time. They realize that buyer resistance is a normal part of selling. They also realize that they personally aren't being rejected—only the propositions they have made. Improved proficiency in closing activities, which develops with experience, helps to reduce the intensity of a person's natural fears.

"Salespeople, for a variety of reasons, often dread asking for the order, yet they can't remain salespeople for long unless they overcome this significant obstacle."

We're OK, they're OK!

We stated earlier that an effective salesperson must be sensitive to his or her prospect's needs yet strong enough to withstand the continual rebuffs inherent in the selling field. You must convince yourself not only that you are okay but that your product is okay and so are your prospects, even when they flatly say no. You must learn to handle such rejection without becoming negative yourself. (See Figure 13.1 for some inspirational comments on the topic of failure.)

Some salespeople also fear that their attempts to close may seem pushy. Naturally, you want to avoid such an appearance, but if you have an air of confidence, have answered the customer's objections satisfactorily, and enthusiastically believe in your product or service, there is no reason why you cannot be an effective closer.

Don't Be Afraid To Fail

You've failed
many times,
although you may not
remember.
You fell down
the first time
you tried to walk.
You almost drowned
the first time
you tried to
swim, didn't you?
Did you hit the
ball the first time
you swung a bat?
Heavy hitters,
the ones who hit the
most home runs,
also strike
out a lot.
R. H. Macy
failed seven
times before his
store in New York
caught on.
English novelist
John Creasey got
753 rejection slips
before he published
564 books.
Babe Ruth struck out
1,330 times,
but he also hit
714 home runs.
Don't worry about
failure.
Worry about the
chances you miss
when you don't
even try.

A message as published in the *Wall Street Journal*
by United Technologies Corporation, Hartford, Connecticut 06101

Figure 13.1 A Public Service Advertisement. Courtesy of United Technologies.

One-Way Communication

Whom do you hear when you *are talking?*

Another cause for failure in closing often develops when the salesperson talks excessively during the presentation, fails to ask probing questions, doesn't listen and isn't alert to buying signals coming from the prospect. A presentation that is primarily one-way doesn't allow for interaction with the prospect. You should continually be alert, listening to and observing clues that indicate a trial close is in order. There will be more on buying signals later in this chapter.

Lack of Training

Practice!

Successful closes require knowledge, training, and practice. Unfortunately, some individuals in sales have never studied the closing techniques that have been employed by other, highly creative salespeople for years. Learn the proven closing methods; then *practice, practice,* and *practice* again. Recognize the typical customer buying signals. Learn how to obtain a series of agreements throughout your presentation. With increased experience and experimentation, you should discover that closing becomes one of the most challenging and satisfying steps in the sales process.

Poor Planning

Have you done your homework?

The close, like all the steps in selling, is merely a link in the chain of activities leading to an order. The strength of your closing attempts, therefore, will be highly dependent on how well you plan all of your sales activities. Do you qualify your prospect? Is your approach made under favorable circumstances? Do you probe for customer needs, wants, and problems? Do you anticipate how your product could help to satisfy these needs and resolve your prospect's problems? There tends to be a direct relationship between effective planning and a high closing ratio.

High-Pressure Selling

Try to force one to buy now *and hear them say, "Bye now!"*

If you were taking a tour through the Louvre museum in Paris, how would you like the tour leader to conduct your visit? As you stopped to appreciate the masterpieces of some of the greatest artists the world has ever known, would you like the leader to place her hands forcefully on your back, push roughly, and snap, "Let's keep moving; we've got a lot of paintings to see, and we have to be back at the bus by 2 P.M.!"

Most tourists prefer a more comfortable pace, one where they don't feel pushed. In short, they prefer being guided, not goaded. Wouldn't the same apply to customer attitudes? The creative salesperson guides prospects—not through museums, but easily and as comfortably as possible through the process of making buying decisions. High-pressure closing techniques generally have counterproductive results. Selling authority George Lumsden warns against the use of pressure when a prospect hesitates to buy. He states:

> Hesitations aren't refusals. Put pressure on a hesitation, and you're likely to get some backpressure. Nudge it a little, and you're likely to get agreement. And it's agreement that closing is all about![1]

Lack of Enthusiasm

Hip hooray! Not blasé.

In Chapter 2 we discussed the importance of enthusiasm as a necessary personal characteristic of salespeople. It is the lack of this trait that often costs salespeople closing opportunities. As stated earlier, an enthusiastic attitude tends to influence customers in a positive manner. It puts them more in the mood to make affirmative buying decisions.

Enthusiasm, in effect, is infectious and tends to make the salesperson's job much easier. Prospects have more difficulty feeling confident about buying your products or services if you don't appear to be excited about them.

RECOGNIZE BUYING SIGNALS

A **buying signal** is *an expression, either physical or verbal, of a prospect's desire to make a buying decision.* It may be as subtle as taking off one's eyeglasses and sitting back in a chair or as obvious as the statement, "When can you make delivery on these items?"

Because buying signals don't always jump out at you, you must be continually attentive to the buyer's body language, comments, and questions. A good time to make a trial close is whenever you see what appears to be a buying signal. Don't be afraid. You haven't made the sale yet anyway, so you have far more to gain than to lose by attempting a close.

Questions as Buying Signals

Buying signals, as already indicated, can be physical or verbal. Watch for them. Here are some specific examples of questions a prospect might ask that could be a clue for you to attempt a close:

1. "Could I try it out one more time?"
2. "Is it available in blue?"
3. "How soon can I get delivery?"
4. "What sort of credit terms can I get?"
5. "Would you consider my old one as a trade-in?"
6. "What sort of a guarantee do you offer?"
7. "Is it available without accessories?"
8. "Should we move to the dining-room table where we'll have more room to work?"
9. "Could I please take a look at the contract?"

"Because buying signals don't always jump out at you, you must be continually attentive to the buyer's body language, comments, and questions."

Statements as Buying Signals

Sometimes a buying signal is more subtle than the listed queries and may be couched in statements like the following:

1. "That really looks good."
2. "I guess I can afford it."
3. "These leather seats are really comfortable."
4. "I've always wanted one like this."
5. "A friend of mine has one of these, and he says you can't beat it for dependability and economy."
6. "Yes, I think it could work for me."
7. "It's okay with me; what do you think, dear?"
8. "My accountant has recommended a plan like that."

Body Language as Buying Signals

Chapter 7 introduced body language, which is an even more subtle way of communicating buying signals. Interest in making a purchase may exist when:

1. The prospect shows signs of agreement by nodding.
2. The prospect's facial expression changes to one of greater receptivity.
3. The prospect takes off his or her glasses and leans back comfortably in a chair.
4. The prospect appears generally to be more relaxed and intent on hearing your message.
5. The prospect intently studies the sample or sales material.
6. The prospect performs calculations on scratch paper.
7. The prospect pulls out a checkbook or credit card (not very subtle, but a sure sign that you should close!).

Buying signals, as you can see, are not always too apparent. Far more obvious is the need for you to attempt to close sales when buying signals aren't apparent. Let's examine some of the commonly used techniques for closing sales.

TYPES OF CLOSING TECHNIQUES

Many years ago, those in sales believed that there was one—and only one—right time or psychological moment to close; they felt that if it was missed, the chances of making a sale were nil. Over the years there has been a change of attitude. Today,

When is the "right" time to close?

most sales managers hold the opposite view. They believe that good opportunities for trying a close can come at any time during a sales interview. Some managers even suggest that their salespeople employ the "ABCs of closing"—that is, they should *A*lways *B*e *C*losing.

The close can sometimes be practically automatic, as when a young woman runs up to the salesclerk in a sporting goods store and hurriedly exclaims, "Give me a can of Sterling tennis balls—quick!" The salesclerk needn't go through a sales pitch on the merits of the product or delay the obviously hurried customer by attempting to demonstrate another. The close, in this instance, comes at the opening. Other closes may take place at any time during a first or even a subsequent sales interview.

Close early, close often!

Experienced salespeople are usually familiar with a variety of closing techniques, which, in essence, are merely different ways of asking for the order. We can't stress too often the necessity of not being afraid to try the close. After all, since your prospect knows you are a salesperson, should he or she be surprised when you try to sell your products?

". . . good opportunities for trying a close can come at any time during a sales interview."

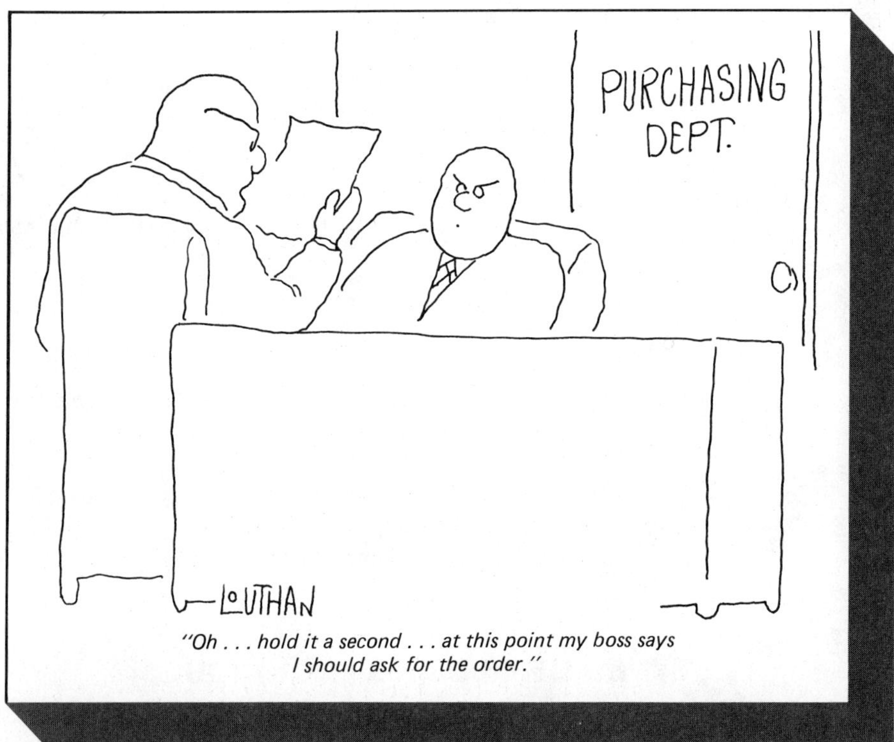

"Oh . . . hold it a second . . . at this point my boss says I should ask for the order."

Reprinted with permission from *Sales & Marketing Management,* December 28, 1985 © 1985.

We are now going to examine some of the best-known closing techniques. Look first at the major closing techniques in Table 13.1.

Assume the Sale

Of all closing techniques, the one referred to as the **positive-assumption close** is the most basic and should be incorporated into all your selling activities. When using this technique, you're simply assuming that your prospect wants to buy your goods. You maintain a positive attitude, one that assumes a purchase is virtually a foregone conclusion. This attitude is easy if you've done your preliminary homework. Let's assume that you have. Then you already know that the person is a qualified prospect. You also know that a need or want exists. Furthermore, you've shown your prospect how you and your products can satisfy these desires, so what's stopping you? Now is the time to assume! If not yet ready to buy, your prospect will let you know. Little is to be lost if you assume, in a tactful and nonpressured fashion, that your customer is ready to purchase your product. As a creative salesperson, you have plenty of sales ammunition in reserve, so you're not likely to lose the battle.

You can use the positive-assumption close by asking such questions as, "Will this be cash or charge?" or "Would you care to have it delivered?" Your choice of words should avoid the use of "I" whenever possible and should convey the impression that an order for your product is virtually understood.

A word of caution: Be alert to appearing to exert pressure with this or any of the closing techniques to be discussed. If the prospect seems upset by your efforts, modify them along softer lines. Some of the following methods can appear high-pressured if your prospect has not been convinced of your product's benefits.

Give More Than One Choice

An excellent way of attempting a trial close is to assume that your prospect is sold on your product or service and then ask a question that calls for a choice. This method, referred to as the **forced-choice close,** gives the prospect a choice between something and something, not something and nothing. When used, this technique enables you to know immediately whether you've made a sale or if, instead, you must provide additional proof of how the product's features can benefit the prospect. Examples of this close include: "Shall we start with one dozen or two?" and "Will you need delivery by Monday, or would Wednesday be all right?"

If you were to ask, "Do you wish to buy this car?" it would be quite easy for your prospect to respond with a flat no. But by asking, "Which model seems to fit your needs best, the two-door or the four-door?" you are providing your prospect with the opportunity to make a positive choice between two alternatives.

"An excellent way of attempting a trial close is to assume that your prospect is sold on your product or service and then ask a question that provides a choice."

TABLE 13.1 Summary of Major Closing Techniques.

Closing technique	Activity	Sample statement
Positive-assumption close	Assume the sale is a sure thing.	"Please put your name right here where I've indicated with an X."
Forced-choice	Provide a choice between two positive alternatives.	"Will this be cash or charge?"
Open-question-and-pause close	Ask a question and wait for the answer.	"How do you feel about this proposal?" (pause)
Multiple-acceptance close	Obtain a series of agreements leading to a final close.	"Then you like the way this car handles? And you say you like a lighter color? Then you prefer only an FM radio? How much of a down-payment would you like to make?"
Minor-point close	Obtain agreement on a minor point to check receptiveness of prospect.	"As you've indicated, you could move in by the first of the month. Is that correct?"
Contingency close	Make a promise based on a promise.	"If I can get the color you prefer by Wednesday, then do we have a deal?"
Future-event close	Suggest buying now before something unfavorable occurs.	"An order placed before the fifteenth of this month will avoid the impending price increase and save you 10 percent."
Special-offer close	Provide an added inducement to buy.	"We'll give you a free carwash with every purchase of 10 gallons or more."
Trial-order close	Ask the prospect to test the product with little risk.	"Why don't you try this computer in your office for two weeks and then decide?"
Suggestion close	Relate to previous point that suggested a purchase should be made.	"Based on the problem you've been having with their service, I'd like to suggest that you try us, and I think you'll notice the difference right away."
Counselor close	Advise customer what to buy.	"What we'll do is place some of these items at eye level so that shoppers can see them right away."

Closing technique	Activity	Sample statement
Last-chance close (SRO)	Use when supply is limited.	"This is the last time we'll be able to offer it at this price."
Summarize-the-benefits close	Review features, advantages, and benefits related to prospect's needs.	"Coupled with social security, this plan will provide you with the income you and your spouse will need during your retirement."
Direct-request close	Ask for the order.	"How many cases do you need?"
By-the-way close	Appear to have "given up," then try one more close.	"By the way, I just remembered that this is the last year you can obtain a tax credit on purchases of this nature. Wouldn't you like to save something on taxes this year?"

Some salespeople misuse this method by giving the prospect too many choices. For example, one computer manufacturer currently offers nine different models of its portable computer. Any prospect relatively new to the computing field who was given a detailed explanation and demonstration of all nine computers would probably be so thoroughly confused that he or she might say, "Er . . . thanks a lot for explaining all those models to me. I believe I'd better think it over for a while." A better technique is to first uncover your prospect's needs or wants, and then narrow the choices down to a reasonable number—say, two or three models at the most.

Ask an Open Question and . . . Pause

Another method for determining whether or not your customer is ready to buy is the **open-question-and-pause close.** Assume that you have converted the major features and advantages of your product into benefits related to your prospect's needs. However, you're not quite certain as to your prospect's willingness to buy. By asking an open question and then waiting—and the waiting part is especially important—you can often discover whether the prospect is ready to make a purchase. You might ask something like, "Bill, you've seen what this product can do. What are your reactions?"

You can also use this method in conjunction with the forced-choice technique. For example, you could say, "Mr. Fernhopper, you and I have examined your needs and have looked at two models of our portable computer, the model T1000 with a 512 KB storage capacity and a battery life up to 4 hours, and the Model T1100 Plus with a 640 KB storage capacity and a battery life up to 8 hours. Which of these two models do you feel best suits your computing needs and desires?"

In effect, what you are doing with this method is placing the responsibility for making a buying decision squarely on the shoulders of the prospect. When you use the open-question-and-pause technique, *it is essential that you remain silent and wait for your prospect to make the first statement.* To you, 20 seconds of silence may seem like 20 minutes. To the prospect, the pause provides him or her the opportunity to formulate an answer. If you interrupt the prospect's train of thought instead of waiting silently for a response, you may fail in your closing attempt.

Obtain a Series of Acceptances

Another technique that helps in securing an order is called the **multiple-acceptance close.** This involves asking the customer a series of questions likely to elicit favorable responses. When this method is used, the buyer is guided along a receptive path that makes answering the big question—asking for the order—far easier. Here is an example of how a "paper-flow analyst" for an office machines company might employ the "multiple yes" technique:

Salesperson Have you ever noticed that there are only eight hours in a business day but a lot more than eight hours of work?

Prospect Yes, I sure have.

Salesperson Would you agree, as have many of our customers, that paper handling has been an activity taking a disproportionate share of those eight hours?

Prospect Yes, I would say so.

Salesperson If I could show you how to turn much of your paper handling into a process we call "paper-flow," thus freeing people in your office to do more important work and reducing your costs, would you be interested?

Prospect Of course.

Agree on a Minor Point

A modification of the multiple-acceptance close is the **minor-point close.** Salespeople who employ the minor-point method try to get agreement on a relatively minor point, which can indicate whether or not the prospect is willing to make the major decision—the purchase. For example, a person selling earth moving construction equipment might state, "Based on what you've told me about your current financial situation, Mr. Cornfield, you would probably prefer to lease rather than make an outright purchase. Is that correct? An agreement from Mr. Cornfield could be an indication that he is ready to buy. Other types of statements implying agreement on a minor point could start with: "We've agreed. . . ." or "As we've seen. . . ." or "As you've indicated. . . ."

The minor-point close seems to be especially effective with prospects who tend to be indecisive—those who feel more comfortable making smaller decisions.

If I Can . . . Will You Agree . . . ?

A technique called the **contingency close** is involved when the salesperson agrees to do something provided the prospect agrees to make a purchase. This method is especially useful for the customer who is having difficulty making a buying decision. An example of this close is, "If I can get the color and model you prefer, do we have a deal?" Another example is, "I know that time is important to you during the current holiday season, Ms. Dior. If I promise to get the material to you by next Tuesday, will you place the order now?"

Order Now Before It's Too Late!

The **future-event close** is a technique that can be used in a variety of situations. Basically, it motivates customers to buy now in order to avoid the greater losses that might, in the future, result from the postponement of purchases. This technique relates to specific impending events. For example, shortages of certain products could develop due to strikes, political activities, international conflict, or bad weather. Or prices may be expected to rise rapidly during inflationary periods. Salespeople might use the future-event close by saying something like, "With the rapidly deteriorating political relationship between our country and Checkmatania, we don't know how much longer we're going to be able to supply you with our line of imported hand-carved ferndock spreaders. So I would suggest that you stock up now to prevent your being caught short over the Easter holidays." Of course, such comments should be truthful, or you will ultimately lose far more than you will gain.

Let's Make a Deal!

Salespeople must remember that they are hired to sell—not give—their products away. A tendency of less experienced salespeople, especially when they're confronted with difficult prospects, is to offer to reduce their prices or to let the prospects try a product for a period of time without charge. In general, most firms feel that salespeople should avoid giving away merchandise unless doing so is virtually certain to result in greater profits.

There are situations, however, when it is simply sound business practice to make certain concessions to customers. A technique referred to as the **special-offer close** is based on this thinking. It involves providing the customer with an added inducement to make a purchase.

The special offer may take a variety of forms. It may be a *sharing of costs,* as when a manufacturer offers to share advertising expenses with retailers for certain periods if the retailers purchase minimum amounts of merchandise. Sometimes the special offer may be in the form of an outright *gift,* or it may be in the form of *special discounts* for purchases over a certain amount, or it may be *tied in with purchases,* as when a chemical firm representative makes the following special offer: "Harry, let's place an order for twenty-five gallons. We'll ship twenty-six to you. You use the first bottle free, and if you're not satisfied, return the remaining twenty-five to us for full credit."

You should, nevertheless, be careful about offering special concessions. Some shrewd buyers never plan to accept original prices. Instead they haggle and bargain, acting as though no deal is possible without reduced prices. In reality, however, the price-haggling approach may merely be a ploy. After all, a prospective buyer has nothing to lose by trying to get a special deal. The astute salesperson, however, should be alert to customers who want something for nothing. A final warning on special offers: you could be breaking the law if you make certain concessions, since there are price statutes designed to eliminate price discrimination in marketing.

Why Don't You Try This for Size?

A closing technique related to the special-offer method is the **trial-order close.** Sometimes used when all else has failed, it involves asking the customer to test the product on a limited scale. For example, you might encourage your prospect to place an order for a quantity far less than your usual minimum order. You can point out how your prospect has risked little, and, if pleased with the product, can later place a larger order.

Sometimes there is no charge for the trial order. For example, a word processor or other article of office equipment may be lent to a prospect for a trial period with the proviso that, if satisfied, the prospect will order a specified number of the items.

Based on . . . I'd Like to Suggest. . . .

Another form of close designed to gently nudge the prospect into making a positive buying decision uses the key words, "Based on . . . I'd like to suggest. . . ." With this technique you refer to a point previously discussed by you or your prospect and then suggest—based on that point—that the prospect place an order. You can use the **suggestion close** in conjunction with a third-party reference and say, "Joe, *based on* the outstanding success that Major Motors has been having with our components, *I'd like to suggest* that you start with 50 X3Cs."

Here's another example of this method: "Harriet, based on the enthusiasm you and all of our accounts have shown for our new fall line, I'd like to suggest that you place an order for 150 dresses, which should enable you to have an adequate stock right through the back-to-school season."

Be a Counselor

Once you have developed a sound, trusting relationship with your customers, you will find that they tend to look to you for assistance and advice. After you have earned their respect, one close that can be used beneficially is the **counselor close,** which simply advises the customer how and what to buy.

Assume, for example, that you are a travel agent who has been discussing vacation plans with a prospective client. You might counsel as follows: "In view of your desire to be completely free during your Tahitian vacation, we're going to book you on our package based on a completely new concept of South Sea island travel.

We'll provide you with a round-trip air ticket and a packet of prepaid hotel vouchers covering the number of nights you choose to spend in French Polynesia. We'll arrange your first night's hotel reservation and provide on-the-spot orientation. After that, you're completely on your own to island hop where and when you want. If you need help, we have consultation service available to you on the islands. Unless you have further questions, I'll book you on this plan. Which have you decided on—the 8-day or the 13-day plan?"

Did you notice that more than one technique was combined in the above example? Can you spot the positive assumption, the multiple-yes, and the "based on . . ." closes blended with the counselor close?

Only One Left

Have you ever noticed how intensely you wanted something you couldn't have? Have you also sometimes felt you would like to have an item owned by someone else? Our next closing technique relates to these natural feelings. It's termed the **last-chance** or **SRO** *(standing room only)* **close.** This close involves an honest statement made by the salesperson as to why the customer should buy now. If the purchase is delayed, the item may not be available later. Real estate salespeople use this technique when there are only a few houses left in a new development. Automobile salespeople also use the SRO method, especially when closing out last year's models just before the new ones are introduced. They might say something like, "We have only a few of these models left. When they're closed out, you'll only be able to obtain the new model, and at a much higher price. To save money, I'd advise you to pick up one of these while you can."

Don't misuse the last-chance technique, as have some disreputable salespeople who implied that there was only one of an item available when they had shelves packed with them. You will open up gigantic credibility gaps between you and your customers if you use this technique unethically.

Summarize the Bennies

One Safeco Insurance Company sales training director feels that among the most effective ways to close a sale is to **summarize the benefits,** especially those relating to features that seem important to the prospect. The training director refers to this method as "summarizing the bennies."

The summary close can be incorporated into most sales presentations. In it you relate the key features of your product to the buying motives of your prospect. This method not only reminds the prospect of the product's desirable features but also helps the salesperson to see whether any additional information needs to be covered. When summarizing, you should avoid discussing benefits not previously agreed upon. If you don't you might find yourself having to overcome new objections. Focus, instead, on the benefits that most attracted your prospect's interest. Don't bring up previous objections. Merely guide the prospect into making a positive buying decision by blending your summary of benefits with one of the other closing techniques already discussed.

"When summarizing, you should avoid discussing benefits not previously agreed upon. If you don't, you might find yourself having to overcome new objections."

Why Not Merely Ask for the Order?

Another technique for closing, so obvious that many salespeople overlook it, is the **direct-request close,** which simply asks the prospect for the order. Sometimes an outright "May I have your order?" will be sufficient to budge the prospect into buying. This technique can be especially useful if there is a relationship of trust between your prospect and you. The prospect may have already made up his or her mind to buy but not yet decided on when to place the order. Some salespeople, as we have mentioned, hesitate to ask for an order. A more positive and direct method would be to assume that your prospect wants your product and ask directly for the order: "Clarence, how many boxes do you want us to ship?"

By-the-Way Close

There may be times when a prospect may strongly resist any attempts by you to close. A technique used successfully by some salespeople to overcome such resistance is called the **by-the-way close.** With this technique you give the impression of having given up attempting to make a sale, which tends to relax the highly resistant prospect. As you begin to leave, you casually pause and then mention another benefit or an old one described differently. You then attempt once again to close. You could say something like:

> (Moving toward the door.) By the way, Mr. Duro, I just recalled that the new investment tax credit statute enables you to write off 100 percent of the purchase price of this product during the first year. How would you feel about Uncle Sam paying a good proportion of your investment?

You have little to lose by attempting this technique, since your opportunity to close the deal during the visit with the prospect would have been over once you went out the door.

Practice Makes Performance

Obviously, you can't use every type of close in every sales situation. And perhaps the list of different closing techniques seems a bit overwhelming. If so, study and practice only two or three of them until they seem natural and a part of you. Then test them out in real selling situations. After you've mastered these, learn a few more, try them out, and see which methods work best for you. Continue learning new techniques until you discover those with which you feel most comfortable. Any of the methods could be useful under certain circumstances—another good reason to apply *situational selling* when attempting a close. A technique that works effectively with one prospect might result in disaster with another.[2]

THE CRITICAL POST-SALES-INTERVIEW PERIOD

Once you've convinced your prospect of the need for your product, you ordinarily don't merely utter a magical word or two and disappear from the premises. In fact, your behavior after the close is important from the standpoint of the image you create for yourself and for your firm. In most instances, the selling process isn't complete merely because the customer has stated that he or she will buy your product or service. Regardless of your customer's previous feelings toward your company, your actions at the time of your departure and thereafter will significantly influence your long-run success and that of your firm.

Why is the **departure** *sometimes awkward?*

The **departure,** that is, the process of leaving the customer's premises, is sometimes a surprisingly awkward activity. If a sale has been made, you may feel either excessive excitement or even an anticlimactic letdown. If a sale hasn't been made, you might feel discouraged and despondent. In either case—sale or no sale—your behavior at this stage is important from the standpoint of the image you are creating for yourself and your firm. Let's look at some ideas that can help you with your postinterview activities.

Don't Dig Yourself into a Post Hole

Yeeow! I mean, thanks.

Do you remember the tensions we indicated earlier as being normal emotional reactions for salespeople? A successful sale, accompanied by a sudden release of tension, can sometimes result in weird behavior on the part of some salespeople. To illustrate, assume that you are relatively inexperienced in the sales field. You have just completed a sales presentation and obtained a fairly sizable order. You may suddenly feel so ecstatic over your success and thankful the interview is over that your emotions are about ready to run wild. Now, however, is *not* the time to "lose your cool." If you do, you could lose the sale. Although you certainly should show gratitude and appreciation for the purchase, don't let your emotions get out of control. Try to retain the appearance of a competent salesperson, one who is accustomed to closing sales. Behaving in a semihysterical fashion is likely to cause your customer to lose confidence in you as a salesperson.

"Once you've convinced your prospect of the need for your product, you ordinarily don't merely utter a magical word or two and disappear from the premises."

Stick 'Em Up!

Come back. It's only a pen!

After your customer has agreed to buy from you, be certain you've taken the order correctly. Don't place your trust in memory. It's easy to forget specific items or colors in the hustle and bustle of a busy day. Put all relevant information in writing. Where applicable, get the buyer's signature and determine credit arrangements. Something that seems routine but that can actually frighten some prospects is using a pen. Don't whip out your pen as though it were a "Saturday night special." Have your pen and order form out in the open during the entire presentation so that they don't suddenly appear like an invading force from outer space. Some firms help in this respect by supplying order forms that are both sales aids and order blanks. Your pen, too, can be a sales aid during your presentation. You can, for example, use it to point to parts of a diagram in a sales portfolio or to key points in testimonial letters.

Reassure the Buyer

"I'm sure you'll be pleased with your choice."

Do you remember the concept of *dissonance* discussed in Chapter 5? It relates to something all of us have to some degree: feelings of insecurity. Your customer, who has just made an important decision, is also likely to have some uncertainties about his or her buying decision. This feeling of doubt is sometimes called **buyer's remorse.** The postclosing period is a time when you can reassure your buyers, informing them that they have made wise choices. In doing so, however, be both sincere and cautious. You don't want to dig yourself into a postclosing hole that might cause the customer to reconsider.

Hit and Run?

Should you exit immediately after the sale?

Some salespeople believe that the *least* said after a sale has been made the *better.* They feel that many good deals have fallen through because a salesperson became overtalkative when he or she thought the sale was final. They argue that a better technique is to take the order, thank the buyer, and depart as soon as possible. Of course, whether or not to leave the premises immediately depends primarily on your customer. Some purchasers are busy individuals with many pressures and responsibilities, people with little time or inclination for idle gossip after their purchases have been made. Others enjoy an informal rap session or a trip out for a cup of coffee. You should use sensitive judgment in each situation.

Will You Be Welcomed Back?

¿Bienvenida?

After making a sale, you should never depart in such haste that you appear unappreciative of the order. Always be courteous to your customer and anyone else associated with the organization. Whether or not a sale was made, you should express your thanks for *their* time, especially since you want the welcome mat to be out for you the next time you call. Your postclosing activities significantly influence the extent of goodwill created for your company.

A Time for Self-Analysis

Why a postcall analysis?

As soon as possible after you've left your customer's premises, you should do a **postcall analysis.** This is a careful and objective examination of your sales interview made to help you improve future sales techniques and customer relations and improve your closing ratio. A useful method for analyzing your sales call is to ask yourself certain questions, such as those listed in Figure 13.2.

1. What were my precall objectives? ______________________________
____
____
2. Did I achieve these objectives during my sales interview?
Yes _____ No _____
3. If not, how am I going to alter my activities during the next call? ________
____
____
____
4. What were some of the weaknesses in my sales presentation and in my manner of handling objections? ______________________________
____
____
____
5. Which objections did I handle poorly? ______________________________
____
____
____
6. How might I improve my responses to those objections? ______________
____
____
7. When should I make a follow-up call? ______________________________
8. What information regarding customer needs or competition did I uncover that should be reported to my management? ______________________
____
____
____

Figure 13.2 A Postcall Analysis Form.

SUMMARY

The step in the selling process termed the *close* is probably the most important in selling. Unfortunately, it is also the one that many salespeople find the toughest. There are a number of reasons why some salespeople find closing the sale difficult. Among these are fear of rejection, lack of effective two-way communication, lack of sales training, poor planning, and the use of excessive sales pressure.

The ability to recognize buying signals and a sensitivity toward prospects' needs can both help the salesperson in this vital step. A *buying signal* is an expression, either physical or verbal, of a prospect's desire to make a purchase. Buying signals may take the form of questions, subtle statements, or body language.

The opportunity to close a sale can occur any time during a sales interview. There are a variety of methods used for closing sales. Every technique, of course, cannot be used in each sales situation. The alert salesperson will use the technique that best suits the situation at hand.

Your behavior immediately following a sale is also significant. Guard against appearing overanxious or excited as a result of the sale. Try to retain the air of a counselor and reassure the buyer that his or her decision was the right one.

KEY TERMS

close
buying signals
positive-assumption close
forced-choice close
open-question-and-pause close
multiple-acceptance close
minor-point close
contingency close
future-event close
special-offer close
trial-order close
suggestion close
counselor close
last-chance (SRO) close
summarize-the-benefits close
direct request close
by-the-way close
departure
buyer's remorse
postcall analysis

QUESTIONS

1. Why is the close considered to be one of the most important steps in the sales process?
2. How might salespeople overcome their fear of attempting the close?
3. How does two-way communication between a salesperson and the customer play an important role in the process of closing sales?
4. What forms of body language not discussed in the text could also serve as buying signals?
5. Evaluate the following statement: "There is one—and only one—*right* time during a sales presentation to close. If you muff that opportunity, your chances of making a sale are nil."
6. Is it considered high-pressure to assume an affirmative buying decision has been made before a prospect has actually agreed to buy your product or service? Explain.
7. Why is it considered more effective to give a prospective buyer a choice between something and something rather than between something and nothing?
8. Assume that you are a sales clerk in a sporting goods store and have described the merits of two types of tennis racquets to a customer. Prepare a closing statement using the open-question-and-pause closing technique.
9. What is a likely psychological advantage of obtaining a series of acceptances during a sales presentation?
10. Give examples of the minor-agreement, contingency, and future-event closes.
11. What are some potential dangers inherent in the special-offer and the trial-order closes?
12. Give an example of the suggestion closing technique.
13. What ingredient is essential for the counselor closing technique to be effective?
14. Why might some prospects distrust the last-chance (SRO) close?

15. Why, when summarizing benefits, should you focus only on those that seem to appeal to your prospect?

16. Should a salesperson ever directly ask for the order? Explain.

17. In your opinion, what could be a danger associated with the use of the by-the-way close?

18. Why is the postpurchase period, in some respects, as important as closing the sale?

19. What influences how long a salesperson should remain with a customer after a sale has been made?

20. What is the principal purpose of the postcall analysis?

APPLICATIONS

13.1 THE BAIT AND DISC SWITCH

The At-Pac Sound System, Inc., is a nationwide chain specializing in the retail sale of electronic sound equipment. At-Pac's salesworkers tend to to be quite eager to close sales since their incomes are directly related to their sales volume.

Jason Shire is a retail salesworker at the Morton Village store. One Friday morning Nat Ross entered the store and told Shire that he was in the market for a new compact disc player. Ross had already decided that he would choose a player in the $300 to $350 price range. He noticed one on display that he liked for $299.50.

Shire explained some of the major features of the compact disc player to the satisfaction of Ross, who then asked, "What is the best price you can give me on this model?"

Shire immediately responded, "I could sell it to you for $275." Ross said that he would take it, and the sales order was prepared. Shire said that the unit would be brought to the counter within a few minutes, thanked Ross for the order, and went to the storeroom.

About a minute later Shire returned and the following conversation ensued:

Shire Nat, I'm terribly sorry, but we are completely out of the model you wanted. I think our Westwood Creek store might have one in stock. It's only about twenty-five miles from here. Would you like to drive out there and pick up the unit?

Ross I don't have time to drive way out there. Can't someone in Westwood Creek bring the unit here?

Shire I'm afraid no one is coming in this way today. I think we'll be getting a new supply of the model you want on Monday, so you could pick it up then at this store.

Ross Damn it! I had my mind set on picking this up today. I'm having a party tomorrow night and wanted to have the new player by then. Why did you sell me something you don't have?

Shire I'm sorry, but I wasn't aware that we were out of that model.

Ross It may not be your fault, but I'm upset. I could have bought the same unit elsewhere today. The heck with it. Cancel the purchase order and give me my money back.

Questions

1. Shire immediately lowered the price of the player when Ross asked about the "best price" available. What is your reaction to his price-cutting technique? What technique, other than reducing the price, might he have employed?
2. Ross has requested that the purchase order be canceled and his money refunded. What should Shire do now?

13.2 IT'S TIME TO CLOSE

Charlie Nugget is a sales agent for the Litmus Life Insurance Company. Two weeks ago Charlie made a sales call on Harriet Houso, a widow with two small children, to uncover her insurance needs and develop a life insurance program for her. Now Nugget has returned to his prospect's house to discuss the proposal he prepared. Nugget has already explained the features and benefits of life insurance to Houso and now wants to get her to agree to purchase the policy. During the interview, the following conversation takes place:

Nugget Good evening, Ms. Houso. I appreciate this opportunity to talk with you again. As I promised, I developed a program of life insurance benefits for you. Would you mind looking over this proposal to see if the names are spelled correctly?

Houso I'd be happy to.
(After a short pause.)

Nugget Do you have any further questions, Ms. Houso?

Houso Well, I'm wondering if. . . .

Nugget What I'm really interested in is your reaction to this proposal. What do you think? Isn't it the best way for you to guarantee security for your children if you die, and at the same time assure something for yourself if you live?

Houso It does seem as though. . . .

Nugget What about the amount we've discussed, Ms. Houso? Do you think it's enough? Do you think it's about right—an amount that won't be a strain on your budget?

Houso Everything looks about right, but I really feel as though I should think it over a bit longer.

Nugget I'm a bit surprised, Ms. Houso. You're a grown woman who should be able to make decisions when they have to be made. Now is the time to buy this plan. I went to a lot of work developing this program, so the least you could do for me is make your decision now. I don't know when I'll be able to return. I'm really quite a busy person, you know.

Houso Yes, I'm sure you are, Mr. Nugget, but the more I think about it, the more I feel I'd better hold off buying your insurance. Thank you for your time. If I change my mind, I'll give you a call.

Questions

1. What is your reaction to the way Nugget handled the above situation? What do you feel he did wrong? Be specific.
2. Using the multiple-acceptance process and the positive assumption technique, develop what you feel to be a more effective closing presentation.

13.3 WATCHING FOR BUYING SIGNALS AND CLOSES

Take the opportunity to make three or four sales calls with an experienced salesperson. Carefully observe both the prospective customer and the salesperson and then answer the following questions.

Questions

1. What specific buying signals did the prospects give?
2. Did the salesperson seem to notice the prospect's buying signals?
3. If so, what techniques of closing did the salesperson employ?
4. Was the salesperson successful in closing the sales? Why or why not?

13.4 CLOSING PRACTICE

Choose one or more products or services that you would be willing to sell. List the products or services in the indicated spaces below. Then list at least five specific closing techniques that could be used to sell the items you've chosen. Finally, develop closing statements that apply to each of those techniques.

Closing Practice 1

Product or service ______________________

Closing technique ______________________

Closing statement ______________________

____

Closing Practice 2

Product or service ______________________

Closing technique ______________________

Closing statement ______________________

____

Closing Practice 3

Product or service ______________________

Closing technique ______________________

Closing statement ______________________

____

Closing Practice 4

Product or service ______________________

Closing technique ______________________

Closing statement ______________________

____

Closing Practice 5

Product or service ______________________

Closing technique ______________________

Closing statement ______________________

____

13.5 MAKE A CLOSE CALL

As a salesperson, you should attempt to recognize buying signals that come from your prospects, since they suggest a favorable time to try to close a sale.

Some typical buying signals follow. Read each one and select the one you feel would be most likely to lead to a sale. (The prospect's words are in italics.)

1. *What are your terms?*
   a. Twenty percent down and the balance in 30 days.
   b. We would have to arrange that after you decide on the purchase.
   c. What sort of terms are you interested in?
2. *What will it cost me?*
   a. About $20 per hundred.
   b. Less than you think.
   c. For what quantity?
3. *Is it available in earth-tone colors?*
   a. Oh yes.
   b. It's available in red, green, tan, brown, beige, and yellow.
   c. Are earth tones your preference?
4. *Is there a minimum purchase quantity?*
   a. Yes.
   b. No.
   c. How many units were you considering?
5. *Do you gift wrap?*
   a. Yes.
   b. There is a slight charge for gift wrapping.
   c. Your choices of wrapping paper designs are on that wall. Which do you like best?

(Answers can be found following the notes section on this page.)

NOTES

1. George Lumsden, "Closing" (Chicago: The Dartnell Corporation), 1986, pp. 14, 15.
2. For a thorough discussion of closing techniques, see the special report, "Closing the Sale," (New York: Sales & Marketing Management), 1977.

ANSWER TO APPLICATION 13.5

The best response for all five examples is *c.* Can you explain why?

PART FIVE

THE IMPROVEMENT OF SALES EFFECTIVENESS

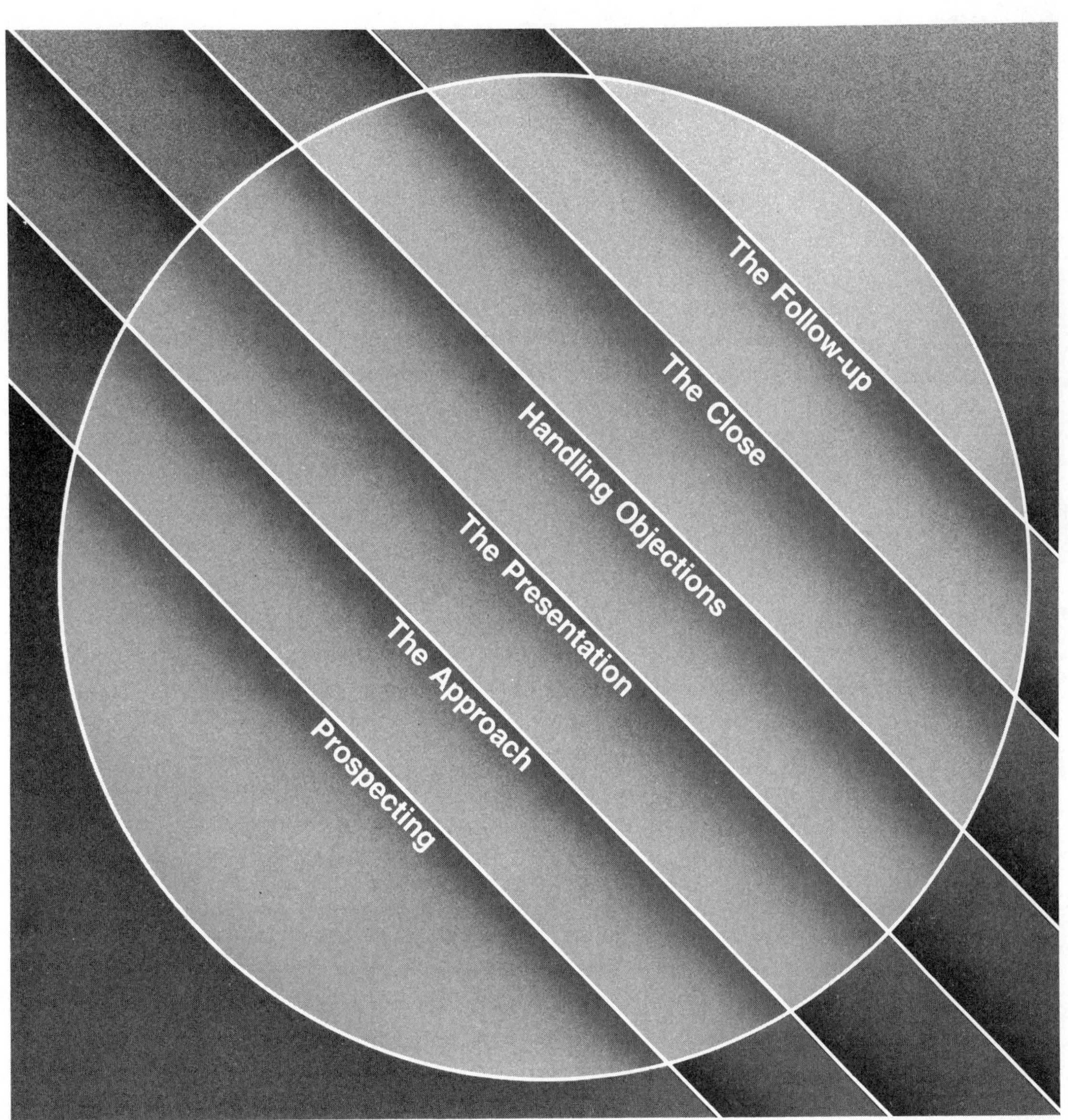

14 Following up and the Maintenance of Goodwill

We've Only Just Begun

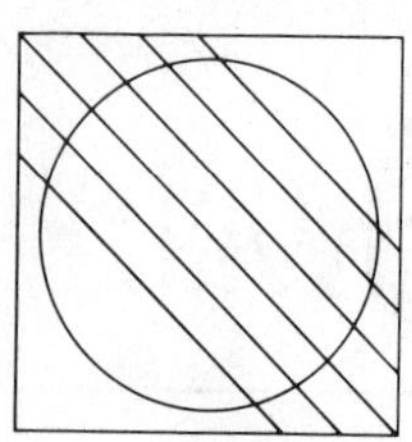

Never forget a customer, and never let a customer forget you.
LEE SHAKLEE

We make a living by what we get, but we make a life by what we give.
WINSTON CHURCHILL

Here's what you should be able to do after studying this chapter:

1. Recognize the importance of determining the extent of follow-up necessary for each customer.
2. Review the major types of follow-up and customer-service activities.
3. Identify some of the more common warning signs of deteriorating customer relations.
4. Restate the significance of maintaining the goodwill of customers.

"Ah . . . ," you smugly say to yourself. "I made the sale, the customer seemed satisfied, my sales manager will be delighted, and most important—*I feel good!* After I return to my white-picketed bungalow tonight, I shall kiss my collie on the tip of her tender nose and then celebrate by carving another notch on the butt of my gold-handled cane. I'll be able to relax a bit, and then start planning for the next sale."

You ponder for a few moments. "Hmm, wait just a minute," you think, "Is this really the end—or merely the beginning? I've only just left the office of my customer, Mr. Herring. In fact, the ink is hardly dry where he signed the purchase order. I'm not in this business to make sales on a 'one-shot basis.' In fact, my earnings and my company's survival are dependent on long-term repeat business. I spent a lot of time with Mr. Herring . . . didn't even sell him until the third sales call. My company might not even make any money on this account unless there's some repeat business. Maybe I'd better be concerned with goodwill-building activities, or this **post-sales-call period** could become a postmortem period instead!"

These hypothetical musings relate directly to the concepts discussed in this chapter. In most instances, the selling process is not complete merely because the customer has stated that he or she will buy your product or service. Throughout the entire selling process, the maintenance of goodwill is important, but it's even more so *after* the purchase or sales call. Regardless of your customer's previous feelings toward your company, your actions at the time of departure and thereafter will significantly influence your long-run success and that of your firm. In the previous chapter, we discussed some of the critical factors associated with customer relations immediately after a sale is closed. In this chapter, we examine some important methods for cultivating and maintaining the goodwill of your customers—methods that are part of the follow-up process.

"Throughout the entire selling process, the maintenance of goodwill is important, but it's even more so after *the purchase or sales call."*

THE FOLLOW-UP

A major life insurance company reveals that in nearly 60 percent of all life insurance lapses, the policy terminates after the second premium payment. The same company points out that after a policyholder makes four premium payments, lapses are negligible. What is the significance of these data? Customers must remain convinced that their buying decisions were correct or repeat purchases are likely to go down the drain.

"Customers must remain convinced that their buying decisions were correct or repeat purchases are likely to go down the drain."

You, through the final step in the selling process—the **follow-up**—can influence the satisfaction your customers derive from their purchases. And isn't customer satisfaction the basic concern of goodwill-building activities?

Extent of Follow-up

Assume that there exists in your territory a customer whose purchases have been nominal during the past year—almost the smallest amount bought by any of your accounts—and they are not likely to increase significantly in the future. Also assume that you have a highly profitable account whose purchases amount to nearly 23 percent of the total volume in your territory. What sort of follow-up and service should you provide to each? Naturally the larger, more profitable, account would be entitled to greater attention on your part.

What determines how extensive your follow-up should be?

For all customers, you should analyze how extensive your follow-up should be. For most semidormant accounts, an occasional letter or telephone call should suffice. For more active customers you might have to make in-person calls every week or two. Customers who have made *or are likely to make* large purchases at some time in the future certainly deserve the utmost in service you can provide.

Don't assume, however, that it is only the larger accounts that demand the most attention. Often a smaller account requires considerable amount of service yet has the potential to be a highly profitable account in the future and, therefore, warrants the investment of your time now. In addition, some larger accounts neither need nor want a lot of contact with their vendors. George W. Wynn, head of the marketing department at James Madison University, emphasizes such beliefs in the following manner:

> Do not let size alone dictate time spent with a customer. A very large account may not want a lot of attention. One of my *giant* customers accounted for more than 95 percent of a particular product line. The customer told me on the first call, after the business had been secured, to treat his firm like any *good* account, and not to treat it like it amounted to more than 50 percent of my entire business volume. His statement was made voluntarily, apparently after certain other sales representatives literally "ran over" my customer.[1]

Many salespeople have noticed that about 80 percent of their customers provide them with only about 20 percent of the total sales volume in their territories. Conversely, about 80 percent of total sales volume comes from only 20 percent of their customers. So prevalent is this tendency that a concept called the **80/20 rule** is regularly bandied about among sales managers.

Importance of Follow-up

Your principal responsibility as a salesperson is to sell products or services profitably. This should be your rule of reason when servicing accounts. Your time is limited, but time spent with customers is often an investment in greater sales and profits for the future. Even accounts that are semidormant or lacking in potential might become high-volume purchasers if service and follow-up activities can change their attitudes toward you and your company. Furthermore, the follow-up can provide you with excellent opportunities to obtain referrals from your existing customers.

TYPES OF FOLLOW-UP ACTIVITIES

Follow-up activities vary substantially by industry and product. At one extreme, it is unlikely that a Girl Scout selling cookies house to house during her annual fund-raising drive will make any follow-up calls during the year. On the other hand, a retail merchant buying household products for resale may require regular assistance with such things as inventory maintenance, merchandise displays, and cooperative advertising programs. Let's look more closely at some of the goodwill-building activities that can be a part of the follow-up.

Maintaining a Good Relationship

You are much more likely to get repeat orders if you develop an amicable relationship with your customers. Any activity that helps to cement this relationship, from a simple "thank you" to hand-delivering a rush order, can benefit both you and your customer. A simple goodwill builder, but one far too frequently overlooked, is sending a **thank-you letter** or card soon after a sales call has been made. Figure 14.1 is an example of a thank-you letter.

Why might thank-you letters create favorable impressions?

Writing thank-you letters should be a routine part of your activities. You can develop a few formats and then modify them to suit each specific customer. The cost of postage and the time expended are minimal compared to the goodwill that letters or cards can create.

"Writing thank-you letters should be a routine part of your activities."

Another company provides its sales representatives with thank-you and congratulations cards for sending to customers. One life insurance agent in Berkeley, California, even sends Thanksgiving Day cards to all of his clients. He says, "My competitors usually send Christmas cards to their clients, so I thought I'd be a bit different." An Arizona agent sends birthday cards to remind policyholders to check the expiration dates of their drivers' licenses, so the birthday card helps to maintain goodwill and keeps the agent's name before the clients. Some salespeople also make a practice of sending get-well cards to their customers. All of these follow-up activities can be summarized by two words: "Be thoughtful."

Remembering the Names of Customers

Have you ever noticed how you tend to feel more friendly toward individuals who use your name during a conversation? Names are important to most people; they are a form of self-identity. As a salesperson, you should especially attempt to remember the names of your customers and use them in conversation. Such activity tends to soften some of the natural sales resistance in many customers.

Q.: What's in a name?
A.: A lot!

For most people, remembering names is not automatic; it's a developed art. Study the guidelines in Table 14.1 and you should find that remembering your customers' names is a lot easier in the future.

In-Person Delivery

In some instances, you might be able to develop more satisfied customers by delivering your product in person. For example, life insurance agents frequently deliver policies in person as soon as the contract is prepared and returned from the home office. Five major reasons for this type of in-person delivery are:

Why in-person delivery?

1. To review the features of the policy
2. To reassure the client that a wise purchase was made

Diversified
Coffee Service

Division of
dePaul Services Inc.
2182 Paragon Drive
San Jose, CA 95131
(408) 435-0575

June 22, 1989

Mr. Peter F. Welch
dePaul Services, Inc.
2375 De La Cruz Blvd.
Santa Clara, CA. 95050

Dear Peter:

Thank you for giving me the opportunity to provide your company with our finest coffee service. We are confident that you will be happy with the manner in which we will be handling your account. It is now our goal to provide your firm with the best of service. By doing so, we believe that you will have no reservations about referring others to us who might have needs similar to your own.

Respectfully yours,

Judith Vella

Judith Vella
Field Representative

JV:jp

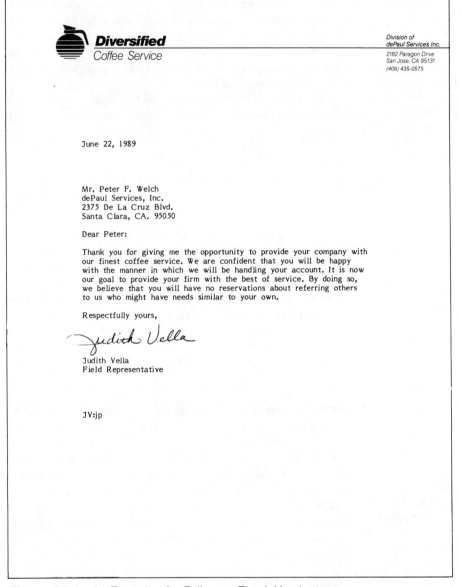

Figure 14.1 An Example of a Follow-up Thank-You Letter.

3. To remind the client when the next premium is due so as to help make the sale stay sold
4. To promote the sale of additional life insurance in the future
5. To solicit referred leads

TABLE 14.1 Guidelines for Remembering the Names of Customers.

When someone is introduced to you:
1. Ask the person how the name is spelled if you are not certain.
2. Say the name regularly during the conversation.
3. Try to associate the name with something that helps you to remember.
4. Develop the practice of greeting your associates by name.
5. Don't hesitate to ask people to repeat their names if you forget them.

As a means of building goodwill during the in-person delivery of the policy, for example, agents of one life insurance company are advised to make commitments like the following to their clients:

> Mr. Lyons, today I'm making two very important commitments to you, and I would like you to make two to me. First, I stand ready to advise you, whenever you wish, on social security or tax changes that may affect your overall life insurance program. Second, I will be personally available to review your insurance program at any time you request—and I will contact you periodically to remind you of the advisability of such a review.
>
> Will you promise that you will contact me whenever you have questions and welcome me into your home to review it? Second, you will come in contact with many life insurance agents through the years. You'll never have time to talk to all of them, so will you just hand them my business card and tell them that I handle your life insurance? If they have anything they think you should have, tell them to get in touch with me. If I think that it will be to your benefit, I'll certainly recommend it. I'll keep my commitments. Mr. Lyons, will you keep yours?[2]

Builders and real estate brokers can also make good use of a follow-up after a sale. N. Richard Lewis, president of Lewis & Associates, an advertising and public relations firm, has said:

> There's a double reason for after-sale selling. First, the existing buyer is, and always has been, a great referral source. Second, a builder (or broker) makes friends before he needs them when he keeps selling after the sale. The third-person testimonial to a builder's code of conduct by an existing buyer is an extremely powerful sales tool in today's climate of uncertainty.[3]

Postpurchase Service and Assistance

Even if the product is not delivered in person, a telephone call or an in-person visit may enable you to help your customers with the proper use of your products. Customers who don't know how to use a purchase may blame you or the product for their frustrations and problems. Besides instructing your customers on the

What sort of postpurchase service can you provide?

"proper care and feeding" of your products, you may also be able to point out additional uses for the items. And sometimes there may be minor repairs or adjustments resulting from faulty installation that you can correct or arrange service for. In some cases, you may create goodwill just by checking with customers to make certain that their orders were filled and delivered as directed on purchase orders. Table 14.2 offers some specific suggestions regarding follow-up activities.

Don't Make "Waste-Time" Calls

When you make in-person follow-up visits, be sure they aren't "waste-time calls." Before making the call, ask yourself, "How is my customer likely to benefit from this call? What do I want to achieve?" As we have indicated, some small talk is acceptable, but remember that the typical customer is under pressure and probably has little interest in merely killing time.

"Rather than being something to dread, a properly handled complaint can serve as a means for the salesperson to cement relations even more firmly."

Handling Customer Complaints

No company is perfect, including the one you work for. As a result, complaints are fairly likely to occur, at least occasionally. Follow-ups may be necessary when customers have complaints—whether legitimate or not—about a product or service. Perhaps the order was damaged in shipment, the delivery delayed for some reason, wrong quantities or colors sent, or defective products shipped.

Often you—the salesperson—are the one who will receive the brunt of the complaint and be responsible for resolving such difficulties. As suggested in Figure 14.2, complaints can actually be opportunities in disguise. Rather than being something to dread, a properly handled complaint can serve as a means for the salesperson to cement relations even more firmly. Table 14.3 offers some specific suggestions for handling customer gripes.

TABLE 14.2 Some Useful Suggestions Related to Follow-up Activities.

1. Make a follow-up goodwill-building visit to your customer within a week after delivery of the product to make certain that the order was filled properly.
2. Make certain that the product is satisfactory and being used properly.
3. Offer suggestions to the customer on ways to make more effective or additional use of the product.
4. Use the follow-up visit as an opportunity to obtain new prospects; i.e., ask for referrals.
5. Handle any complaints or misunderstandings as soon as possible and with a positive and courteous attitude.

IN COMPLAINT HANDLING

Why is it so few persons like to handle complaints? Perhaps it's because the atmosphere is tense, the customer is angry and it's a "no-win" situation no matter what. Yet it's a fact that some of the greatest opportunities of your career lie in wait behind that next phone call, that next complaint. Here are some examples:

Opportunities to solve a problem. Did you ever start working on a problem and then suddenly find the hours whizzing by? For many people, problem-solving isn't an unpleasant chore but rather a very interesting way of spending time at work. Far more interesting certainly, than not having any variety at all, or doing the same thing day in and day out. And problem-solving not only beats boredom, but it's the mark of the professional in every walk of life!

Opportunities to be creative. Not everybody can write a book, paint a picture or compose a symphony. But people who work with customers can be just as creative -- in some cases more so -- in receiving complaints and calming down irate customers, in deflating complaints by helping customers let off steam, in helping resolve claims before they escalate. For dealing with people is an art in itself, and it takes special skills and ingenuity -- and the opportunity to develop those skills and ingenuity.

Opportunities to gain recognition (and rewards!). We've said it before, every complaint situation *seems* negative, but it's also an opportunity to gain recognition for your department and for yourself . . . and for your company. Not all customers write angry letters; in fact a review of any firm's correspondence files will show a fair number complimenting an individual -- often a Customer Communicator -- on the way a complaint was handled, and a major problem averted . . . and a customer saved. Letters like that going to the top management of a firm bring tangible rewards in the paycheck, too, as well as opportunities for promotion!

Opportunities to improve your skills. The majority of complaints usually represents a new and different type of situation. The challenge to creativity, mentioned above, is also an opportunity to develop new skills and to perfect existing ones. Every time you have contact with a customer, every time a new problem is dumped in your lap, you have a new opportunity -- a new opportunity to learn, to deal with new technology, to find out more about customers' businesses, to perfect your skills as a "diplomat," to broaden your own horizons both as an individual and as a Customer Communicator. It's called "experience," but it's far more than that: it's the opportunity to grow in your job . . . to become more valuable because your skills *have* improved, and to get the more interesting assignments.

Opportunities to make an economic contribution. When you resolve a problem for a customer, reduce a complaint into tangible action that keeps that customer as a customer, you're also making a profit contribution for your firm. It's far less costly to *keep* a customer than to lose one and have to replace him . . . and your economic contribution shows up in improved share of market for your firm, improved profitability, an improved working environment, and the ability to continue to provide good working tools, attractive opportunities and good compensation for the increasingly important work you do.

Opportunities to win friends and enjoy yourself. The friend you win when you resolve a complaint and overcome a "crisis" is likely to be a friend -- of yourself and your firm -- for life. And far more friends are made by helping solve problems than by simply doing the routine, undemanding jobs anybody can do. And . . . it's much more fun making friends that way, too!

Figure 14.2 Opportunities in Complaint Handling. Reprinted from *The Customer Communicator* © 1980, Marketing Publications, Inc. Reprinted with permission of the copyright holder.

How do you handle a disgruntled customer?

TABLE 14.3 Guidelines for Handling Customer Complaints.

1. Don't postpone action. Frequently the problem is not as bad as you may have anticipated.
2. Don't be afraid to admit mistakes and to apologize.
3. Even when you believe that a complaint is unfounded, show the customer courteous attention and indicate that you will check out the problem.
4. Learn to listen to complaints. Often allowing customers to "get it off their chests" lessens the intensity of the gripes.
5. Investigate and probe for specific facts. Sometimes there's no valid complaint—the account merely feels irritable.
6. Never attack your customers. You will almost always come out on the losing end.
7. Don't pass the buck, mark, pound, ruble, or whatever, to your company. When you criticize or blame your company personnel, you are really saying to your customers that you don't have a well-run organization. And don't blame your electronic data processing equipment; it, too, is part of your company. Blaming others in your organization tends to cause your customers to lose confidence in your firm.

Sending Bad-News Messages

Regardless of how good a relationship you've established with customers, there will probably be certain occasions on which you may have to send them unpleasant information, or **bad-news messages.** Can you think of any reasons why you might have to send a customer a bad-news message? Some of the major ones are:

1. Refusal of an application (e.g., for insurance or credit)
2. A shipping or billing error
3. Unavailability of ordered products
4. Inability to comply with a customer request
5. An unexpected increase in prices
6. A change in company policy that adversely affects the customer
7. A customer complaint

Remember, your attitude is showing!

Probably the single most important suggestion to follow when writing bad-news messages is to be empathetic. Carefully reread any letter you intend to send to a customer and ask yourself, "How might I react if this letter were sent to me?" The attitude you convey in such messages goes a long way in influencing future relationships between you and your customers.

A bad-news message should contain at least four elements that we'll refer to in terms of the **BAD-C bad-news technique** in order to help you remember them. The four letters in the acronym BAD-C stand for:

*B*uffer

*A*nalysis

*D*ecision

*C*lose

Let's now look briefly at each of these elements.[4]

Buff—don't gruff it!

Buffer Although you don't want to mislead the reader of your bad-news message, you should attempt to begin your letter with a statement that tends to promote a receptive frame of mind. Remember that the primary goal of any bad-news message should be to convey a fair, reasonable, and concerned attitude in order to maintain positive relations with the customer. The buffer statement, for example, could be a simple *expression of thanks* or *appreciation for past orders,* or an *acknowledgment* of some sort, such as for the receipt of a customer's application for credit. It could even be an attempt *to resell* the customer, as in the case where an ordered model was discontinued or out of stock and you attempt to sell a comparable item. Other buffer statements could *compliment* the customer; express an attitude of *cooperation, empathy,* and *understanding;* or reveal certain types of *good news.*

Let them know **why***—tactfully.*

Analysis The second segment of a bad-news message expresses why you must do something differently from what the customer might have expected. In some instances—as in routine, confidential, or sensitive matters—stating a reason may be unnecessary or even undesirable. When used, however, the explanation should be presented *before* your actual decision is stated. The explanation should convey a sincere attitude and avoid hackneyed, insincere phrases such as, "We really would like to help you with this matter, but. . . ." Also, avoid using company policy as your scapegoat. Most customers are not placated by the statement, "It's against company policy." Instead, customers usually want to know *why*—that is, the reasons—"it's against policy."

"But what **can** *you do?"*

Decision Now comes the crucial part of your bad-news message: the decision. Try to convey your decision in a positive manner. Don't tell customers what you *can't do;* instead, tell them what you *can do.* For example, if delivery of a purchased product will be two weeks late, your analysis/decision segments of the bad-news message might state, "As you may know, Ms. Treat, the recent trucking strike created some challenges for people in our industry. As a result, your order for ten X-1400s will arrive on your premises no later than November 15 rather than the original November 1 date. We certainly hope that the new date will be acceptable to you." Try to avoid dogmatic sounding phrases like, "We must refuse . . ." or "We cannot allow. . . ." Since a bad-news message should also be considered to be a sales message, you might tactfully attempt to resell your customer on the benefits of your products and service.

Close Always attempt to end your message in a positive, sincere, and cordial manner. Your close might include some of the following elements:

A happy ending!

1. An expression of appreciation for past (or possibly future) orders
2. An invitation to offer suggestions, make future purchases, or submit future applications
3. A request to comply with your decision
4. A clear statement of what action, if any, the customer must take to comply with your decision
5. An expression of your continued interest in and appreciation of the customer

WARNING SIGNS OF DETERIORATING CUSTOMER RELATIONS

We have stressed how success in selling is generally the result of repeat sales to satisfied customers. Remember, however, that a customer who seems satisfied today may become disgruntled tomorrow. Just think about the many companies that were once giants but are nonexistent today. Because you work in a competitive world in which there are acceptable substitute sources for nearly every product or service, you should continually be on the lookout for any warning signs that your customers are switching their business to your competitors. See Table 14.4 for a listing of some of the most common warning signs of deteriorating customer relations.

Asking the Customer How Things Are

How do you feel about us?

Knowing how customers feel about your company can enable you to provide and maintain (or correct) the quality of the service expected by most customers. Some firms seem unconcerned or even defensive about the negative attitudes of their customers. More progressive companies, on the other hand, are exceedingly con-

TABLE 14.4 Common Warning Signs of Deteriorating Customer Relations.

You are hereby forewarned!

1. Changes in purchase volume
2. Increased frequency of complaints regarding your products, company, or service
3. Repeated comments regarding the merits of competing products or companies
4. A less cordial atmosphere during sales calls
5. Recently hired personnel who are neither familiar with nor sold on the merits of your products and service
6. The absorption of *your customer's organization* by a larger firm
7. The absorption of *your organization* by a larger firm

cerned. They realize that the replacement of customers is expensive. To illustrate, the American Management Associations has established the cost of selling a new customer at five times the cost of retaining that customer once the initial sale is made.[5]

One company, Grede Foundries, Milwaukee, Wisconsin, seems well aware of the need to know what its customers think. It has adopted a program well worth emulating. To keep on top of customer attitudes, Grede sends a detailed questionnaire to each of its 300 accounts' plants (see Figure 14.3). Each customer is asked to grade Grede on how well it does by comparison with its competitors. The customer has a choice of four rating categories: (1) not as well, (2) same as, (3) better, or (4) much better. Since Grede has positioned itself in the marketplace with a slightly higher-than-average selling price, it is keenly interested in maintaining above-average customer relations.

Jack Steele, Sales and Marketing Vice President, believes that it is important to respond to the customers' comments rather than merely to file the questionnaires away in the recesses of a file drawer. A number of customer-oriented changes have been made as a result of Grede's surveys.

The Not-So-Hidden Costs of Customer Alienation

We've already indicated that it usually costs substantially more to obtain new customers than to service existing ones. There are numerous other costs associated with having disgruntled customers.

Dissatisfied customers are seldom satisfied!

For example, the customer who has had good reason to develop negative attitudes toward your company is less likely to cooperate during situations that are beyond your control, as during strikes and resource shortages. The dissatisfied customer is likely to be far less accepting of even trivial problems, thus increasing the time that you—the salesperson—will have to spend trying to get things back to normal.

Disenchanted customers also may begin to generalize negatively about a variety of things associated with your company. For example, if customers feel that service is poor, they may begin to wonder whether production quality standards might not also be poor. Furthermore, unhappy customers are less apt to want to increase their volume of purchases, since they might feel that to do so will only amplify the unpleasantness of their dealings with your company.

"The dissatisfied customer is likely to be far less accepting of even trivial problems, thus increasing the time that you—the salesperson—will have to spend trying to get things back to normal."

THE IMPORTANCE OF GOODWILL

Sales − goodwill = lost sales.

Goodwill is a factor related to customer attitudes and sentiments toward you and your company. The loss of customer goodwill is, in effect, the loss of sales. Goodwill building is not automatic. It requires a deliberate, conscientious, and sincere concern

GREDE FOUNDRIES, INC.
CUSTOMER SERVICE SURVEY

Concerning Our Performance At

- ☐ Liberty
- ☐ Spring City
- ☐ Iron Mountain
- ☐ Reedsburg
- ☐ Milwaukee Steel
- ☐ Wichita
- ☐ Hartmann Mfg. Co.
- ☐ Short Run Specialty

When comparing Grede to other suppliers, how well do we.....	Much Better	Better	Same as	Not as well
SALES				
make use of sales calls to provide information you need				
respond on time to your requests for quotations				
respond accurately to your requests for quotations				
respond to your emergencies				
use telephone and mail to provide your requested information				
keep you informed of overall business activity				
TECHNICAL SERVICES				
provide technical information				
provide educational programs and/or seminars				
provide engineering assistance on design				
furnish technical field service				
provide cost saving ideas				
MANUFACTURING				
provide quality castings (internally sound, meet size specifications, surface appearance)				
meet metallurgical specifications				
ship castings on time				
ship castings in Quantities requested				
respond to your emergencies				
respond to corrective action requests				
provide "Customer Service" through visits of our quality and manufacturing personnel to your plants				
GENERAL ADMINISTRATION AND MANAGEMENT				
plan and forecast to meet your casting requirements				
respond to capacity needs				
accurately invoice for price and quantity				
accurately and efficiently handle debits, credits, etc.				

In general, how well does the foundry industry perform on delivery and quality compared with other purchased commodities.				

Please use reverse side for any comments or suggestions.

Figure 14.3 An Example of a Customer Survey Form. Courtesy: Grede Foundations, Inc.

about customer interests and needs over extended periods of time. Virtually every step in the selling process has an influence on goodwill.

Goodwill is not concrete—you can't put your finger on it or measure it accurately in dollars. Nevertheless, goodwill is of significant value since it helps the salesperson in making initial and repeat sales. Furthermore, customers with favorable attitudes toward your company and its products are also excellent sources of referral business.

SUMMARY

Businesses that are profitable in the long run are typically businesses that have developed sound relationships with their customers. Repeat business—the key to the long-run profitability of most companies—comes only from satisfied customers.

The maintenance of goodwill is an important sales activity, one that is necessary throughout the entire selling process. Virtually every sales activity—from the initial approach to postpurchase service—influences customer relations. Alert salespeople are continually on the lookout for warning signs of deteriorating goodwill. They recognize that goodwill is not something that develops automatically; it must be earned and maintained.

KEY TERMS

post-sales-call period
follow-up
80/20 rule
thank-you letter
bad-news messages
BAD-C bad-news technique
goodwill

QUESTIONS

1. How can goodwill be measured?
2. What do you feel are some significant reasons why customers fail to make repeat purchases?
3. Since, as a salesperson, your time is limited, what are some criteria for determining the extent of your follow-up activities with specific customers? Should your *sales volume* be the main criterion?
4. What are some ways in which salespeople can show appreciation to their customers?

5. What are some techniques that can be used to aid you in remembering the names of people whom you meet?

6. What are some advantages of the salesperson's in-person delivery of a product? Why isn't such an activity always feasible?

7. What are some of the ways in which you should handle customer complaints? How should you treat the customer whose complaint is unfounded?

8. Evaluate the following statement: "Customers are a fickle lot. One day they're with you and the next day they're against you—and there's not much you can do about it."

9. What is a major reason for avoiding the blaming of your company or its inside personnel for problems that develop with customers?

10. What is the purpose of the buffer portion of a bad-news message?

11. What is goodwill? How can it be developed and maintained?

APPLICATIONS

14.1 THANK YOU VERY MUCH

Write a short letter expressing your gratitude to a prospect for seeing you and listening to your presentation during a recent sales call. Assume that you did not make a sale.

14.2 LATE BACK-TO-SCHOOL

Assume that you are a sales representative for a nationwide garment manufacturing company that sells various types of clothing apparel to retail stores. This morning you received a fax message from your manufacturing facility indicating that because of a shortage of denim, an order of blue jeans for one of your retail customers will be delivered four weeks later than you promised. Your customer was anxious to receive the ordered items on time because they were purchased for the back-to-school sales period. Any delays in delivery will result in substantial losses of sales revenues to your customer, since the garments will have to be marked down in price in order to be sold after school starts. You're quite concerned about the problem, especially since it took a fairly long time to cultivate this account.

Questions

1. What are some specific things that you might do to prevent a deterioration of your customer's goodwill?

2. Assume that you will not be able to arrange any solution to the delivery problem at this time. What might you do in the future to regain your customer's lost goodwill?

14.3 COLOR MY FACE RED!

Assume that you are a sales representative for the Craftspeople Press Company, a large printing firm located in Minneapolis, Minnesota. You recently acquired a new customer whom you had called on for six months without getting an order. About a month ago, however, the customer, Dewey Fishbeck, owner of a large mail-order merchandise house, became dissatisfied with his former printers. As a result, you took a large catalog printing order away from your competition.

Unfortunately, a problem has developed. Your secretary took a call from someone at your customer's office who asked that a color change be made on the catalog's cover. Nothing was received in writing to authorize the change. The order was delivered to your customer this morning. This afternoon your telephone rings. You answer it and are greeted by the highly emotional voice of Mr. Fishbeck who shouts, "What in heck is going on at your plant? I never agreed to the color magenta appearing on my cover. I'll be darned if I'll pay for something I didn't order. You promised me better service than I was getting from Acne Press—but so far, I'm not too impressed!"

Questions

1. What should you say and do now about this misunderstanding?
2. What can you do to prevent such problems from recurring?

14.4 A HARD ACT TO FOLLOW UP

You've always believed, let's assume, that following up after making a sale is essential for building and maintaining customer goodwill. However, you have one customer in your territory, Ray Zhist, who doesn't seem to share your philosophy. You sold Zhist some equipment about four months ago, and each time you try to get an appointment with him, he seems to make a halfhearted excuse for being unable to meet with you. You just telephoned him again to attempt to get an appointment, and this is his response: "For the life of me I can't understand why you keep pestering me with phone calls. I bought your equipment; what more do you want?"

Questions

1. What should you say to Ray Zhist at this time?
2. Why is making follow-up calls important to both you and your customers?

14.5 A "GOOD-NEWS" MESSAGE—YOU'VE GOT TO GIVE THEM CREDIT!

Figure 14.4 is an adaptation of an actual letter sent by a major bank to its credit card holders. Study the letter and then answer the following questions.

Questions

1. Could the Good Cargo Blaster card letter be considered a bad-news message? Explain.
2. What portions of the letter contained a buffer? What is your opinion of the way in which it was written?
3. What portions of the letter contained an analysis/explanation? What is your reaction to it?
4. Did the letter contain a decision? Explain.
5. What is your reaction to the manner in which the letter concluded?
6. If you were a customer who had received the letter, what would be your overall reaction?

14.6 "I'M BAD . . . I'M BAD!"

Project

Develop an idea for a BAD-C bad-news message, and then write one to a real or hypothetical customer. Attempt to include the major elements of a BAD-C bad-news message in your letter. Then have someone else in your class read and critically evaluate your letter.

NOTES

1. Extracted from a review of Stan Kossen's, *Creative Selling Today,* 2nd ed. (New York: Harper & Row, 1982).
2. *Equitable's National Sales System* (New York: The Equitable Life Insurance Society, 1973), p. 5.3.
3. "Powerful Sales Tool Neglected," *Oakland Tribune,* May 25, 1975, pp. 1C, 4C.
4. For a more detailed explanation of bad-news messages, see Herta A. Murphy and Charles E. Peck, *Effective Business Communications* (New York: McGraw-Hill, 1980), pp. 261–327.
5. "One Way to Beat the High Cost of Selling," from a special report entitled "Managing Costs for More Productive Selling," *Sales Marketing & Management,* December 8, 1980, p. 12.

GOOD CARGO BANK
NATIONAL ASSOCIATION/MEMBER FDIC

We appreciate having you as a Blaster card customer. We are making some necessary changes to your account. . . but, *we are not charging an annual fee.*

Dear Customer:

You'll be pleased to know that Good Cargo is not instituting an annual fee for your Blaster card. Due to the increased costs of providing credit card services, together with federal credit restraints, many banks have increased their credit card interest rates and fees. We, too, find certain changes are necessary.

We want you to pay for your Blaster account *only* when you use it. As in the past, we expect you'll turn to your Good Cargo Blaster card to take advantage of special purchase opportunities, and for those occasions when you find your Blaster card more convenient to use than cash or a check. However, when and how you use your card are still matters for you to decide.

Please refer to the enclosed notice for a detailed description of the following changes that become effective if you use your card after July 15, 1989:

The *Monthly Periodic Finance Charge* rate is being increased to 1.67% (20% Annual Percentage Rate). The current rate is 1.5% (18% Annual Percentage Rate). The new rate reflects our increased cost of lending money to our Blaster card customers.

A new *Purchase Activity Charge* of $2.00 will be applied to your account in each billing period when one or more purchases are posted to your account. This means you'll pay for the convenience of purchasing goods or services on your Blaster card account *only when you use it.* This new charge reflects the increased costs of maintaining and operating our credit card services.

The *Minimum Monthly Payment* is being increased to $40, or 4% of your outstanding balance, whichever is greater. Currently, the minimum is $20, or 2%.

The *Cash Advance Transaction Charge* will be 3% of the amount of the advance, with a minimum charge of $25. The present charge is $10 per advance.

Please give special attention to the options for using your Blaster card account described in the attached notice. *If you use your card on or after July 15, 1989 the new terms automatically apply to your account.* You also have the choice of paying off your balance under the existing terms and conditions. Of course, which option you choose and how you use your card are *entirely up to you.*

We appreciate having you as a customer of Good Cargo Bank. It remains our goal to keep the use of your Blaster card account as convenient as possible, and we hope you will continue to look upon it as a valuable financial service.

Sincerely,

J. Shuck

J. Shuck
Senior Vice President
Credit Card Division

JS/ah

Figure 14.4 An Adaptation of an Actual Letter Sent to Bank Card Holders.

15 Telemarketing and the Use of the Telephone in Selling

Dialing for Dollars

THE NATURE OF TELEMARKETING
Prospecting ■ Making Appointments ■ Inbound Marketing ■ Outbound Telemarketing ■ Taking Orders ■ Maintaining Goodwill ■ Notifying Customers of New Products and Special Offers ■ Providing Service and Handling Complaints ■ Recharging Less Active Customers ■ Maintaining Contact with Marginal Accounts

THE ADVANTAGES OF TELEPHONE USE IN SELLING
Saving Time ■ Saving Money ■ Greater Convenience ■ Greater Flexibility ■ More Profits and Income

SHORTCOMINGS OF TELEMARKETING
Lack of Multisense Appeal ■ Easier to Say "No" ■ Higher Telephone Bills ■ Possible Creation of Ill Will

REQUIREMENTS FOR EFFECTIVE TELEPHONE USE
Plan Your Telephone Sales Talk ■ Develop Good Prospect Lists ■ Engage in Postcall Activities ■ Guidelines for Effective Telephone Use

TRY AIDA ON FOR SIZE
Get Your Prospect's Attention ■ Develop Interest in What You Have to Say ■ Create Desire for Your Product or Service ■ Get Action or Agreement

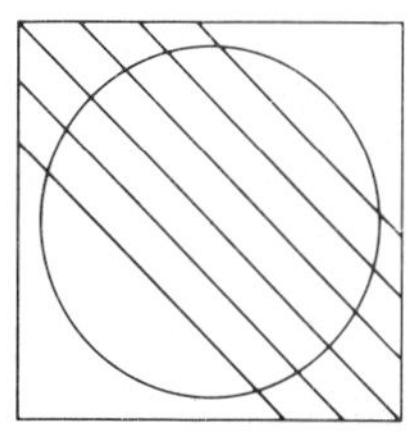

With the telephone, you're selling something the customer can't see, and your success depends on how well you "show" the benefits of your product or service all verbally, of course.

KATHLEEN PHILLIPS SATZ

The phone is just a phone until you learn how to use it!

S. F. DAMKROGER

Here's what you should be able to do after studying this chapter:

1. Describe the principal uses to which the telephone can be put by salespeople.
2. Explain five advantages that can result from effective telephone use.
3. Recognize the limitations of the use of the telephone in selling.
4. Summarize ways in which the use of the telephone can be made more effective.
5. Relate the AIDA concept to the use of the telephone in sales.

"Telemarketing—you mean trying to sell by telephone? That may work in some fields, but my business is different. The *only* way I can sell effectively is through personal contact with my customers."

Such utterances as these have not been uncommon in the past. However, they seem to be less valid, if they ever were, for an increasing number of salespeople today. It is estimated that 80 percent of Fortune 500 companies use some form of telemarketing in their contacts with customers.[1]

Some busy salespeople frequently complain that they never have enough time to service all of their accounts adequately. Many of the more effective salespeople, however, have learned how to use a valuable supplement to their regular sales activities—the telephone.

In this chapter, we examine how salespeople can benefit from the effective use of the the telephone. We shall also explore the various uses that salespeople can make of this electronic marvel in the activity of telemarketing. Nothing is perfect, so we will also take a brief look at some of the major shortcomings of telephone use. Then we shall look at some useful procedures that successful salespeople have applied to telephone use. And finally, we shall see how the concept of AIDA can be applied to telemarketing.

THE NATURE OF TELEMARKETING

Telemarketing is much more than selling by telephone. **Telemarketing** is a set of activities that involves the use of the telephone to support and, at times, to serve as a substitute for personal face-to-face selling. Telemarketing is a process that serves to make the total sales process more effective. Among the principal applications of telemarketing are:

1. Prospecting
2. Making appointments
3. Inbound telemarketing
4. Outbound telemarketing
5. Taking orders
6. Maintaining goodwill
7. Notifying customers of new products and special offers
8. Providing service and handling complaints
9. Recharging less active customers
10. Maintaining contact with marginal accounts

A brief discussion of each of these uses follows.

Prospecting

Insurance, real estate, securities, magazine/newspaper subscriptions, office products, and automobiles are only a few of the fields that utilize telemarketing in the attempt to develop new customers. You ought to review the concepts discussed in the chapter on prospecting before attempting to prospect by telephone. They are as applicable to telephone prospects as they are in attempting to prospect by face-to-face contact. Of course, as with any prospecting, closing ratios will tend to be far more successful when the names of firms chosen for telephoning have been carefully and logically selected.

Brrr . . . It's cold out here!

RACO Manufacturing and Engineering Company makes use of telemarketing to develop prospects for its Chatterbox, a talking temperature-monitoring device that calls the manager of a farm when critical temperatures threaten crops. The product also enables the farmer to call the Chatterbox from any telephone to find out about current temperatures in the field. RACO sends prospecting letters to potential dealer customers and runs advertisements in several agricultural publications inviting interested readers to telephone its "24-hour demonstration hotline." Prospective customers can then hear a sample Chatterbox in operation and leave their names, addresses, and phone numbers with the telephone answering device. This technique has proven successful for RACO in developing leads for its Chatterbox line.

Making Appointments

"I'm here—surprise!"

"Another surprise—Get out of here!"

An excellent time saver is the use of the telephone for *making appointments.* Dropping by unannounced on prospects or established accounts can waste considerable amounts of your time when the customer is occupied or out of the office. Furthermore, some customers do not appreciate "surprise" sales visits. Figure 15.1 suggests a method for securing appointments after a prospecting letter has been sent to a prospective buyer.

Confirming or rescheduling previously arranged appointments is an additional time-saving use of the telephone. For example, assume that you are unavoidably detained with one customer, a situation that is likely to cause you to be late for an appointment with another. A simple phone call informing your customer of your difficulty will usually help you to avoid the creation of ill will. It helps to show your account that you are sincerely concerned about the delay.

Inbound Telemarketing

You're "bound" to reduce costs.

Prospecting can be an expensive activity. Telemarketing can aid in reducing these costs. An activity termed **inbound telemarketing** is a technique that many firms now utilize to reduce the cost of acquiring leads, one that contributes substantially to sales efforts.

Inbound telemarketing relates to the various services available through the telephone system that assist salespeople in obtaining prospects. Toll-free 800 numbers, for example, are available and can be included in company advertising and promotional materials to encourage readers to call the firm for product information or company literature. Such leads can be utilized by telemarketers or followed up personally by field representatives.

Outbound Telemarketing

Many organizations today successfully apply telemarketing to their sales activities. The activity of contacting prospective customers by telephone for the purpose of closing sales is termed **outbound telemarketing.**

For example, various telephone companies throughout the United States employ telemarketing representatives who regularly call householders and businesses for the purpose of promoting the purchase of additional telephone service. Banks have used telemarketing in conjunction with direct mail to promote the purchase of certificates of deposit (CDs). Magazine and newspaper representatives frequently solicit by telephone. Funds for colleges, churches, and social causes are often raised through telephone solicitation. Even the textbook that you're reading at this moment was telemarketed to various college professors throughout the United States and Canada after they had received sample examination copies.

Some sales managers disagree on whether attempts should be made to actually sell the *product itself* or, instead, only an *idea* or *concept* (such as a future appointment) over the telephone. Many salespeople employ the telephone solely to arouse a prospect's interest in hearing more about the product or service. They are principally interested in qualifying prospects and obtaining appointments for personal interviews. However, there is no reason for not attempting to close sales over the

Try These Four Steps:

1. *Ask.* Assuming you've already sent a letter to your customer outlining the benefits of your visit, he or she is expecting your call. Announce yourself, identify your company, and ask for the appointment. (If the customer should ask "why" rather than saying "yes," proceed to the next step.)	"Mr. Vendido, this is Keith Compra of the Calidad Company. I wrote you a letter a few days ago telling you I would phone—and why. I'd like very much to see you today if your schedule will permit. Would ten o'clock be all right or would two o'clock be more convenient?"
2. *Tell.* Answer the question in as few words as possible. Include a benefit or advantage the customer will get from your visit. Ask again for an appointment. (If the customer still resists, you should promptly go to the next step.)	"My letter outlined a way for you to increase your profits by using our line of products. May I stop in and see you this morning at ten or would this afternoon be more convenient?"
3. *Sell.* Point out to your prospect what your appointment will mean to him or her. Sell the prospect on the value of your visit at this time, not your product. Ask again for an appointment, phrasing the question so it's easy for your prospect to say "yes."	"I understand Mr. Yendido that your sales operations cover the entire midwest area. There's considerable building going on in this area at present. Our product fits right into that picture—at a profit to you. But it will be easier to explain if we could get together, say ten o'clock? Or would you prefer sometime this afternoon, say two o'clock?"
4. *Thank the prospect* for the appointment.	"Thank you, Mr. Vendido. I'll see you at two o'clock then."

HINT: When there's a secretary between you and the prospect, ask to speak to the prospect in a confident and pleasant tone. If the secretary asks why, give the reason but not in too much detail. If your call has anything to do with company policy try this: "I wanted to talk to Mr. Vendido about a matter concerning company policy." Usually, this will get you through to the person you're calling. Develop a reason why you prefer not to tell your whole story over the phone this time, such as a model you want to show—a floor plan, a drawing, etc.

Figure 15.1 Suggestions for Making Appointments by Telephone. (Adapted from training materials previously furnished by The Bell System, no date.)

telephone if your product or service lends itself to such telemarketing and if you experience consistent success in telephone closing.

Have you sold yourself on telephone selling?

Guard against the pitfall of assuming automatically that your product or service doesn't lend itself to telemarketing. Instead, try to develop the positive attitude that with imagination, training, and diligent effort, you, too, can put the telephone to effective use, as have many imaginative salespople before you.

"Some sales managers disagree on whether attempts should be made to actually sell the product itself *or, instead, only an* idea *or* concept *(such as a future appointment) over the telephone."*

Taking Orders

For customers to place orders by telephone is not uncommon in some fields. A fairly obvious advantage exists when customers do so: much time and expense is saved. Some consumers, for example, do substantial amounts of their shopping with department stores by telephone. Office managers, too, place many of their unsolicited orders for office supplies by telephone.

A tremendous opportunity, therefore, exists for the alert and skillful telemarketer when unsolicited orders come in by the telephone. The salesperson, while writing up the orders, can serve as a counselor of sorts to the customer and remind him or her of other potential needs that might exist. Or perhaps a good value exists on a nonrelated product. The customer might appreciate the information, make a purchase, and the telemarketer has added to sales volume with a minimum of time and effort expended.

Maintaining Goodwill

How can the telephone aid you in maintaining goodwill?

We've already devoted considerable space in a previous chapter to the importance of developing and maintaining goodwill. Have you thought about how the telephone can aid you in accomplishing some of your goodwill goals? A technique used by many successful salespeople is to follow up with a telephone call a few days after they've made personal calls on a customer. Sometimes the telephone call is made after the product has been delivered to a customer, at which time the salesperson might say something like: "Hello, Ms. Stapletacker. This is Cindy Ashe of the Wizard Ball and Roller Bearings Company. As you recall, you placed an order with me about two weeks ago. I'm calling to express our appreciation for the order and to make certain that the shipment arrived as you requested. Was everything received as expected?"

Through a simple and relatively inexpensive telephone call, Cindy has shown a concern for her customer. Can you think of some additional ways in which you could use the telephone for goodwill-building activities? Here are a few suggestions that have been utilized by others: You could use the telephone to find out whether the products purchased by your customer are functioning properly. Or you might ask your customers if there are any ways in which you might assist them in the use of your products, as in training employees. You could also remind customers of the need for maintenance service, notify them of special sales, and even congratulate them for recent achievements such as awards or promotions.

Don't be a "T.P." (telephone pest).

Your sound judgment should warn you not to make a "telephone pest" of yourself. Your intentions may be purely honorable, but if you appear to be telephoning without any specific purpose—merely to engage in idle chatter—you may create ill will rather than goodwill.

Notifying Customers of New Products and Special Offers

"Have I got something to tell you!"

Another common use of the telephone by salespeople is for notifying customers of new products and special events. For example, a computer store salesperson could contact a former purchaser when new types of software or other equipment are introduced. An automobile salesperson could keep a list of former buyers and contact them when their cars are about ready for a trade-in and trade-up. Or a salesperson in a quality clothing or department store could contact good customers personally to notify them of an upcoming sale. Or an insurance agent could telephone prospects whose policies are about to expire to let them know about newer and improved types of policies. With imagination, salespeople can find a myriad of reasons to contact customers by telephone.

Providing Service and Handling Complaints

Many items sold these days are highly technical and complex. Buyers sometimes have difficulty understanding certain aspects of the equipment that they've purchased and may require outside assistance. A customer tends to have good feelings about your company and products when he or she knows that help is a mere telephone call away.

Reach out and help someone!

Occasionally, various problems, such as shipping or quantity errors, may develop in your sales territory. Frequently, a mere telephone call can resolve the difficulty in a relatively short period of time. The resolution of the problem may take some effort on your part, but through the use of the telephone, you can demonstrate to your customers that you sincerely intend to deal with their problems quickly.

Recharging Less Active Customers

Why not recharge by telephone?

Every sales territory, for various reasons, tends to develop some accounts that seem to go dormant or inactive, those that submit few and infrequent purchase orders in the direction of your firm. Dormant or excessively small accounts are costly for your firm to maintain. They often receive (or request) the same mailings, catalogs, promotional materials, and other company literature as do active accounts, but their low volume of purchases may not even cover the cost of these items. Here, again, the telephone can be an excellent and efficient tool for attempting to revive or recharge some of your less active accounts. Often you can ask some leading questions in order to discover the causes of the customer's inactivity. The information uncovered can aid you in developing future plans and strategy with the account. The same things frequently can be accomplished by telephone as with a personal call at much less expense. Figure 15.2 provides some suggestions on recharging inactive accounts.

Maintaining Contact with Marginal Accounts

Most territories have some customers that are **marginal accounts;** that is, they can't be given much of your time because they don't provide a lot of income for your company nor do they seem to have much potential for increased purchases in the

Try These Seven Steps:

1. *Identify* yourself and your firm. Briefly explain the purpose of your call. Address the customer by name.	"Good morning, Mr. Terco. This is Peter Porfia of the Polvo Corporation. I've become quite concerned, since we haven't heard from you for quite some time."
2. *Pause.* The customer probably has a good idea why you're calling. Pause, and he or she will probably volunteer the information.	Pause.
3. *Ask* leading questions (if reasons were not volunteered) to uncover inactive customer's reason for not buying. Listen. Don't argue.	"I was wondering, Mr. Terco, if there might have been something unsatisfactory about our last shipment of Polvo Powder or the terms involved?"
4. *Admit* mistakes made. Show your sincere desire to correct past irregularities.	"I'm terribly sorry about that last shipment. I'll send out a replacement order immediately" (or whatever action is necessary) . . . or if nothing was wrong, "Well, I'm glad that everything is all right."
5. *Sell.* Resell the need for your products or services by stressing their benefits.	"Then you're still using Polvo Powder, Mr. Terco? By the way, Mr. Terco, we have a special offer this month on case lots of Polvo Powder. You'll save $75.00 by ordering by the case."
6. *Ask* the customer to buy.	"How many cases will you need?" (Pause) "They'll be delivered first thing Monday morning."
7. *Thank* your customer for the order. Show appreciation.	"Thanks for your order, Mr. Terco. It was really good talking with you once again. I hope that we hear from you often from now on."

Figure 15.2 Suggestions for Recharging Inactive Accounts. (Adapted from training materials previously furnished by The Bell System, no date.)

But they are *worth something.*

future. Personal, face-to-face sales calls would be excessively expensive for these accounts.

Once again—Ma Bell, eh . . . MCI . . . or is it Sprint? to the rescue! Regardless of which telephone company you use, the telephone gives you the opportunity to maintain contact with the low-volume accounts, continue their goodwill, and who knows? Maybe one of these days they might surprise you with a big order!

THE ADVANTAGES OF TELEPHONE USE IN SELLING

Ever since Alexander Graham Bell, a Scottish-born American, invented it—the telephone—that incredible conveyor of electrical impulses over simple strands of wire, has been both used and misused by those in the selling field. Telemarketing is not easy. Some sales managers, as we've mentioned, argue that the telephone should never be used to attempt to close a sale—only to develop interest in the purchase of goods and services. Other sales managers, however—and an increasing number of them—make extensive use of the telephone in direct selling. Correctly used, the telephone can be effective not only in selling, but for a number of other purposes, as we've just seen in the previous section.

Assuming that you are still among the unconvinced, take a look at the several advantages that the effective use of telemarketing can provide. Among the more significant are:

1. Saving time
2. Saving money
3. Greater convenience
4. Greater flexibility
5. More profits and income

Let's now explore each of these advantages separately in order to see how you might personally benefit from the effective use of the telephone.

Saving Time

Care to save some time?

One of the principal advantages of the use of the telephone is that it is quick and therefore can result in substantial *savings in time* for the busy salesperson. Occasionally an account must be contacted immediately, especially in cases where there are shipping problems, where changes in price or product availability have occurred, or when a salesperson learns that a prospect is ready to make an immediate purchase. Ordinarily, you will find that not all of your accounts require the same amount of personal attention. New accounts, problem accounts, and some large and some medium-sized accounts typically need more direct salesperson involvement than do certain others, especially your well-established customers. For some customers, a telephone call will accomplish your major objectives and is usually far better than total neglect. The use of the telephone can also enable you to make contacts in out-of-the-way places.

"One of the principal advantages of the use of the telephone is that it is quick and therefore can result in substantial savings in time for the busy salesperson."

If your territory involves traveling from town to town, the use of the telephone can assist you in blanketing a much larger area and in freeing you for greater numbers of face-to-face interviews with customers who need more personalized service. (See Figure 15.3 for a summary of the nature of telephone use during **on-route calls.**) Basically, then, the use of the telephone can enable you to make more calls in the same amount of time.

Saving Money

Related, of course, to savings in time is another significant advantage of telephone use by salespeople: *savings in money.* Once you've learned how and when to use the telephone, you should discover that you are spending far less time on travel and thus incurring less expense for hotels and meals. Many salespeople have learned that the **call-ahead approach** can save them valuable time that ordinarily is spent waiting.

Dialing can save dollars.

1. When moving from one town to another, telephone rather than visit those prospects that are located in remote, less accessible areas.
2. Plan in advance so that you can blanket entire areas surrounding the key towns that you are selling in from your motel or hotel room.
3. You can extend your sales territory over a much larger area with on-route calls than you ordinarily would be able to cover.
4. On-route calls gives you greater flexibility in dealing with customers, enabling you to adjust personal visits to meet individual customer needs. You thus can service customers better, thus helping to maintain goodwill.
5. On-route calls help you to cover more territory, thus reducing your overall cost of sales visits and unnecessary travel expense.
6. On-route calls give you the opportunity to qualify a prospect's needs before you make a personal visit.
7. On-route calls help you to create more selling time on each trip, thus resulting in greater sales volume.
8. On-route calls are useful for covering the markets all around the key towns you're selling in.

Figure 15.3 Suggestions for Effective Telephone Use During On-Route Calls. (Adapted from training materials previously furnished by The Bell System, no date.)

Sales calls are expensive. By calling your prospects and customers in advance, you can make firm appointments with the people you want to see at the times you want to see them. Also, when you're making an important in-person visit to a customer, it's nice to be expected. And finally, you're likely to discover that calling in advance helps to avoid the loss of valuable time that occurs when the prospect fails to show up for the appointment.

"Once you've learned how and when to use the telephone, you should discover that you are spending far less time on travel and thus incurring less expense for motels and meals."

The costs of operating an automobile for sales purposes has soared over the years and has a significant effect on the profitability of a sales call. Although the telephone cannot entirely eliminate travel on the part of sales personnel, its effective use can reduce the amount of unnecessary travel.

Greater Convenience

You can use it with ease.

Another principal advantage of the telephone is its *convenience.* With a telephone, prospects are as close as your telephone dial. While others are waiting to see your prospects and customers, you can contact them without even making appointments or driving long distances.

Greater Flexibility

Try another!

Have you ever considered the *flexibility* that the use of the telephone affords? For example, if you telephone a prospect who isn't available at the moment, you can immediately call another with little time having been wasted. In what additional ways might the telephone provide you with greater flexibility in selling?

More Profits and Income

¡El tiempo es oro!

"Time," as the old adage says, "is money." And because the use of the telephone tends to result in more effective use of time and reduced expenses, you need not be a cost accountant to discern that this can mean *greater profits* for your firm and *more potential income* for you.

SHORTCOMINGS OF TELEMARKETING

All is not honey and roses in using the telephone. Although we've been praising the merits of telephone use, the handy little instrument is not without its limitations. Three major shortcomings are discussed below.

Lack of Multisense Appeal

Do you recall our discussion on buying signals in an earlier section, especially things like facial expressions and hand movements? One day in the not-too-distant future, an instrument combining television with the telephone is likely to be commonplace. An entirely new transmission technology, **Integrated Services Digital Network (ISDN),** will be installed in most major U.S. cities by 1990. It will enable phone users to transmit voices, video images, and computer data along the same line simultaneously. Without such devices, however, we must live with one of the principal drawbacks of telephone selling: you cannot observe your prospect's reaction to your sales message.

What you need is a smellephone!

Furthermore, until you can conveniently demonstrate a product over the telephone, your prospect will tend to experience more difficulty attempting to visualize what you are trying to describe. And, unlike with face-to-face selling, the telephone doesn't permit you to appeal to your prospects' senses of smell, touch, or—for most telemarketers—sight.

Easier to Say "No"

"I said 'No!' " Click!

If you were to compare prospects' telephone behavior with their behavior during face-to-face interviews with salespeople, you would be likely to discover considerable differences. Prospects generally find it much easier to say "no" over the telephone than in the presence of a salesperson. Confidence to resist sales efforts seems to build up more when the salesperson cannot be seen.

There are some prospects, however, who have trouble saying "no" to anyone, and thus find difficulty in turning down a salesperson even on the telephone. Unfortunately, the person who is too easily persuaded is often the person who cancels the order soon after hanging up the receiver, especially if pressure was felt during the telephone interview.

"A far wiser approach than reducing telephone use is to analyze the returns that result from telephone use."

Higher Telephone Bills

If the telephone is put to greater use, then it naturally follows that telephone costs will rise. Some managers respond to higher telephone bills with drastic economy campaigns or warnings designed to reduce telephone use and expense.

Couldn't higher costs also mean greater profits?

A far wiser approach than reducing the use of the telephone is to analyze the returns that result from its use. Although telephone expenses are likely to rise with greater use, other expenses, such as automobile, lodging, and meals may actually decrease by even greater amounts. A reduction in the use of the telephone, therefore, could be a false economy. Of course, those who use the telephone, especially for long-distance or toll calls, should learn how to use the telephone efficiently and in the least costly fashion, a topic to be discussed in the following section.

Possible Creation of Ill Will

Telephones have gotten a lot smarter in recent years, but they haven't yet developed consciences. They don't, for example, seem to realize when their high-tech nature can be irritating to some prospects when used in **programmable telemarketing.**

Some phones can now be programmed to memorize over 100 numbers so that telemarketers need dial just one or two digits to make a call. Other models are even more sophisticated and require no human being to be nearby. These models automatically dial a list of phone numbers and present a recorded sale message to the answerer. The recorded message may request that the prospects respond. Their statements are recorded and provide information that serves as leads for salespeople to contact later by telephone. Other models pass the calls on to a human being—a telemarketer—only when a human voice—a householder or business person—answers on the other end. "Smart" telephones can also be programmed to redial indefinitely when a line is busy.[2]

"My line's engaged!"

Although these high-tech phones can substantially reduce costs and increase productivity of salespeople (MCI Communications Corporation telemarketers average between 250 and 300 calls a day[3]), the use of programmed telemarketing has become bothersome to some householders and business people who feel that their privacy has been invaded. Some householders and business people have also complained that the automatic dialers tie up their lines so that emergency or important business calls might not be able to make it through. There has even been some public pressure intended to legislate programmed telemarketing out of existence. What are your feelings on the subject?

REQUIREMENTS FOR EFFECTIVE TELEPHONE USE

The use of the telephone in sales should never be left to chance. Telephone selling is a difficult art. To be effective, it requires training, practice, and patience. It also requires planning, utilizing good prospect lists, utilizing effective telemarketing tools, and engaging in postcall activities. We briefly examine the latter four requirements below.

Plan Your Telephone Sales Talk

What does planning help to avoid?

Effective use of the telephone in selling requires a well-organized plan. Your prospect is unlikely to strike up an interest in your presentation if you come across in a disorganized fashion. As with any technique of selling, you should attempt to know your product or service well before attempting to sell by telephone.

Be certain to practice your telephone presentation before making any calls. Record it on tape, preferably video, and then watch and listen to it critically. As a means of acquiring constructive feedback, rehearse your telephone approach in front of other sales representatives or make arrangements to deliver it over the telephone to them. Try to anticipate your prospects' potentially negative reactions or objections. (Figure 15.4 provides a list of suggestions for effective telephone use.)

1. Don't be sneaky; always **identify** yourself, your company, and your purpose at the beginning of the call.
2. Strive to **speak clearly** and at an **understandable rate**.
3. Try to make a **smile** come through in your voice; have a mirror in front of you so that you can observe your facial expressions.
4. Speak in a manner that **instills confidence**.
5. Be **courteous**, never argumentative or insulting.
6. Maintain a tone of **friendliness, enthusiasm**, and **confidence** in your voice regardless of how rough the going may be at times.
7. Be **realistic** in your goals.
8. Don't make undelivered **promises**.
9. If a trial close fails, try to get an **appointment**.
10. Take **notes** about what was discussed; it is easy to forget essential points.
11. **Evaluate** the likely results of each call; is a follow-up desirable? If so, when?
12. Vary your telephone techniques from time to time and **compare** results.

Figure 15.4 Guidelines for Effective Telephone Use.

Write out your plan on a step-by-step basis, making certain that no vital point is overlooked. A useful method is to develop a checklist of ideas and write them in the order that you plan to present them. Don't read or memorize the sales talk. Strive to develop a conversational, spontaneous-appearing style of telephone presentation. Always listen carefully for cues from your prospect, be flexible in your approach, and try to relate your presentation to the needs of the prospective customer.

Develop Good Prospect Lists

What's a good prospect list?

Related to effective planning is the need to develop a good prospect list. Contrary to your personal wishes, not everyone in the telephone directory is likely to be interested in your sales message. To save effort and time, attempt to develop a list of individuals who are likely to be in the market for your product. The more you can learn about your prospects, the easier it will be to develop proper opening remarks and effective sales appeals and—most important—the more likely you will be to close sales successfully.

Engage in Postcall Activities

It's easy to become preoccupied with other types of activities immediately after you've finished a telephone call with a customer. Doing so runs the risk of forgetting important details of your conversation. To avoid such problems, you should follow the four important recommendations below:

What next after your hangups?

1. Record all significant details of the conversation in the customer's file.
2. Determine and write down the date you intend to follow up with another telephone call.
3. Process the order you just sold or take care of the problem discussed.
4. Follow up at a later date to make certain the customer received the ordered goods and is satisfied with them.

Guidelines for Effective Telephone Use

As already stated, effective telephone use doesn't come about by accident—it takes considerable preparation and practice. Study and apply the list of suggestions in Figure 15.3 and you should find substantial improvement in your own telephone activities.

TRY AIDA ON FOR SIZE

In a previous chapter we discussed the AIDA concept of delivering sales presentations. As you may recall, this was a four-step method designed to guide sales presentations. Let's now see how the AIDA (Attention, Interest, Desire, and Action) method can also be put to effective use in selling over the telephone.

Get Your Prospect's Attention

May I have your attention?

In any type of selling, what is one of your initial objectives? Don't you want to gain your prospect's *attention* in as short a time as possible? You are, in effect, attempting to warm up the prospect, which is vital to the success of your telephone selling efforts. An obvious but often overlooked method for gaining the prospect's attention is to greet him or her by name and to use that name regularly during your telephone conversation. Furthermore, good telephone etiquette dictates that you introduce yourself immediately. Usually, a simple statement of your name, firm, and purpose is sufficient.

Develop Interest in What You Have to Say

Your customer's interest is your business.

To achieve your goals by telephone, you must also get your prospect's *interest.* Your statement for gaining the prospect's interest will depend upon your purpose for calling. For example, you might gain the interest of a previous customer by expressing your gratitude for the order. You might suggest some tips on promoting the items, which can lead into a new sales presentation.

Use your imagination for developing methods of obtaining your prospect's interest. Here are a few ideas: You might offer a *special service, congratulate the prospect* for a personal accomplishment, or you might be able to offer a *special price.* You could offer to *demonstrate your product* to the prospect. Or, if you have sent a letter or product brochure to your prospect, you might arouse interest by *referring to your recent mailings.*

Create Desire for Your Product or Service

Should you pop off like the cork?

The third step in the AIDA approach is the creating of a *desire* for your product or service. Here is where your voice has to do the selling. Champagne usually appears alive, sparkly, and effervescent. This may seem corny, but try to sparkle as would a bottle of bubbly California champagne. Use words that help your prospects to visualize your products and that appeal to their needs and wants.

Be careful not to monopolize the telephone conversation. Ask probing questions to discover the buying motives of your prospects, and then tailor your presentation to fit their desires and needs. Be certain to develop sound listening habits.

Get Action or Agreement

Create agreement, not antagonism.

The major purpose of your telephone calls is what? Isn't it to get prospects to *act* or *agree* on something of mutual interest both to you and them? You want some sort of affirmative response from any prospect. As with face-to-face selling, try to anticipate objections. Be prepared with effective responses to expected sales resistance. Never argue or antagonize your prospects or customers, even if they are curt or rude with you.

Typical objections that you might confront include remarks such as "I'm too busy to talk right now" (don't push—politely arrange for a more convenient time to call) or "I'm not interested" (stress additional benefits of the product).

You can't see buying cues over a telephone, but you should attempt to sense when the prospect is on the verge of making a buying decision. Sometimes a trial close is the best way to determine whether your prospect is ready to act. Employ any of the suitable methods for closing a sale discussed earlier. For example, you might *assume a sale* and say, "Then I'll write up the order on the basis we've discussed." Or you could give the prospect a *choice* by saying, "Which would be a better time for me to demonstrate our product, Monday or Tuesday evening?" The key point to remember is that there can be no sale if there is no agreement.

SUMMARY

Because of continually climbing costs of contacting customers face-to-face, telemarketing has grown increasingly important to firms. The telephone can be applied to a variety of business purposes by sales and other company personnel. Its major uses include prospecting, making appointments, inbound and outbound telemarketing, and taking orders. The telephone is also useful for maintaining the goodwill of customers, notifying them of new products and special offers, providing them with service, and handling their complaints. In addition, the telephone assists salespeople in recharging less active customers and maintaining contact with marginal accounts.

Telephone selling isn't easy, but the rewards can be substantial for the salesperson who masters it. Many salespeople have discovered that telemarketing has many advantages: it can save time and money, provide greater convenience and flexibility, and result in more profits for their firms and greater income for themselves.

Alex G. Bell never said his electronic and miraculous 1876 invention was perfect. In fact, Mr. Bell would probably agree that there are certain limitations that should be recognized by users of the telephone in selling. For example, it generally lacks multisense appeal (although this limitation is becoming more limited); prospects often find saying "no" easier over the telephone; telephone costs naturally rise with increased use; and there is the possible creation of customer ill will. These limitations, however, do not necessarily outweigh the telephone's advantages when it is used in a well-planned and effective manner.

Effective telemarketers do not leave the activity to chance. They plan their telephone presentations, develop good prospect lists, engage in proper postcall activities, and follow proven guidelines for optimum telephone use. The AIDA technique of selling can be applied to telephone as well as face-to-face selling.

KEY TERMS

telemarketing
inbound telemarketing
outbound telemarketing
marginal accounts
on-route calls
call-ahead approach
Integrated Services Digital Network (ISDN)
programmable telemarketing

QUESTIONS

1. Most salespeople consider time to be an important but scarce resource. What are some specific ways in which this valuable resource can be conserved through the use of the telephone?

2. Assume that you are a bit timid and apprehensive about using the telephone in your selling activities. How might you develop more self-assurance in this area?

3. Assume that you have developed a fair degree of success in using the telephone to maintain customer goodwill. However, your boss, Mr. Percy Penurious, has recently sent you a memo indicating that your telephone expenses are far out of line. What might you say to convince Mr. Penurious of the merits of continued telephone use in your activities?

4. Sales managers disagree on the feasibility of attempting to close sales by telephone. Choose a specific product or service and attempt to develop arguments, both pro and con, relating to its sale by telephone.

5. Develop an opening statement designed to interest your prospect in giving you an appointment for next Wednesday.
6. In what ways might the telephone make the management of your territory more efficient in terms of dealing with dormant or less active customers?
7. What would you say by telephone to an account who has not placed an order for nine months?
8. How does telephone selling significantly differ from face-to-face personal selling?
9. Assume that a regular customer places an order with you by telephone for five boxes of fan-fold computer paper. What specifically might you say to obtain a supplementary order for other supplies?
10. How might the shortcomings inherent in the use of the telephone be at least partially overcome?
11. Why is it essential for you to identify yourself, your company, and your purpose at the beginning of a telephone conversation with a prospect?
12. How would you handle a telephone prospect who angrily shouts the following? "You lousy peddler! I wouldn't trust you or any other crook who tried to push their wares to me over the telephone. I've been burned by hucksters before, and it's not gonna be your turn this time!"
13. There exists the inherent danger that an enthusiastic telephone user can become a "telephone pest." What can you do to avoid developing such an undesirable reputation?

APPLICATIONS

15.1 KEEP ON BUYING

The following is a telephone conversation that took place between Bobby Baronet, a sales representative from the Drofsnal Publishing Company, and his customer, Ms. Rita Random:

Bobby Hello, Ms. Random. This is Bobby Baronet of Drofsnal.

Rita Hello, Mr. Baronet. What can I do for you?

Bobby We received your order yesterday morning for our model 6900 overhead projector. Thanks very much.

Rita That's quite all right. We're pleased to do business with you.

Bobby Your order will leave our warehouse today by truck and should reach you by late this afternoon.

Rita That's great. Can't ask for much better service than that.

Bobby If at any time you have any questions or problems regarding the equipment, please let us know.

Rita Thanks, I certainly will.

Bobby By the way Ms. Random. We've noticed that many of our customers have found that our adjustable projection table has saved them a lot of headaches. You have probably noticed that finding a suitable place to set up a projector can sometimes be a serious problem. I've personally seen many damaged projectors that had fallen from their unstable locations.

Rita I guess that could be a problem. How much are they?

Bobby The regular price for our standard model is $149, Ms. Random. However, we offer a ten percent discount on the table when it is purchased with the overhead projector. Shall I send the table out with the projector?

Rita Hmm . . . It sounds like a pretty good idea . . . but I believe I better think it over for a while. Thanks, anyway, for the suggestion.

Questions

1. In general, what is your reaction to the telephone techniques employed by Bobby Baronet?
2. Describe the specific objectives of each step in Bobby's telephone conversation.
3. Why wasn't Bobby successful in closing the sale?
4. Develop an improved closing statement that would be more likely to sell the projection table to Rita Random.

15.2 HELPING OUT AT AUCTION TIME

Assume that you have volunteered to donate some of your time and selling expertise to a local public television station. Your responsibilities will include telephoning local merchants for the purpose of motivating them to donate products or services to the TV station for an upcoming fund-raising auction. Donated products and the names of donors will be shown over TV, thus resulting in "free" publicity for the merchants. Their gifts are also tax-deductible.

Study the checklist and evaluation sheet illustrated below. Then prepare an outlined telephone sales presentation that you can later role-play with another person. A third individual can evaluate your presentation on the basis of the following checklist of items.

Checklist and Evaluation Sheet for Telephone Selling

Checklist	Yes	No	Evaluative comments
Did the salesperson:			
1. Identify himself or herself and the TV station?			
2. Call the prospect by name?			
3. Establish rapport?			
4. Use an interest-creating comment?			
5. Probe to get information about the prospect, such as his or her familiarity with the auction and current use of TV advertising?			
6. Stress benefits over features in his or her sales presentation?			
7. Make a trial closing effort?			
8. Overcome objections effectively?			
9. Employ effective and proven closing techniques?			
10. Effectively wrap up the sales interview by confirming what will be donated and by making arrangements for obtaining donated items?			

NOTES

1. "Telemarketing in the Field," *Sales & Marketing Management,* May 1986, pp. 61–68.
2. "Telephones Get Smart," *Time,* March 30, 1987, pp. 36, 37.
3. Thayer C. Taylor, "MCI Mixes Computers and Motivation," *Sales & Marketing Management,* June 4, 1984, pp. 42–46.

Sales Promotion Activities

A Salesperson's Selling Partners

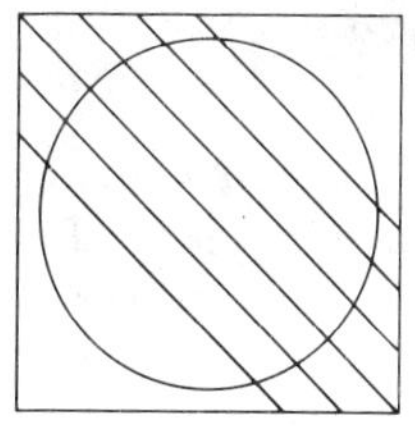

Sales promotion is the catalyst of business, big or small. It is the agent that gives direction to an advertising campaign, gives drive to a dealer organization, and gives enthusiasm to a sales force.

PROFESSOR ALBERT W. FREY

Sales promotions are mandatory today. You can play the price game, but after a while that wears thin.

RONALD G. SHAW, EXEC. V.P.,
PILOT CORPORATION OF AMERICA

Here's what you should be able to do after studying this chapter:

1. Distinguish sales promotion from other types of marketing activities.
2. Discuss the two principal ways in which sales promotion relates to company salespeople.
3. Recall the means used by some firms to stimulate their own sales forces.
4. List and describe the typical devices used by manufacturers to promote dealer sales.
5. Summarize the common types of sales promotion devices directed toward consumers.
6. Explain the ways in which the effectiveness of direct mail activities can be enhanced.
7. Describe the nature and use of three types of electronic sales promotion devices.
8. Review the major benefits derived from advertising for both you and your customers.
9. Recognize the advantages and limitations of the basic types of advertising media.
10. Describe the salesperson's role in relation to advertising programs.

Fortunately for you as a salesperson, you'll typically have a number of "partners" to assist you in arousing customer interest in your goods or services. Your partners are usually referred to as *sales promotion activities* or programs.

WHAT IS SALES PROMOTION REALLY LIKE?

Sales promotion is, in a sense, a fuzzy concept. Virtually everything a firm uses to foster the sale of its products can be considered a form of sales promotion. For example, the salesperson is a personal force attempting to promote sales. Advertising is an impersonal force attempting to promote sales. Publicity is another impersonal force, one that is often tied in to the public relations activities of a firm. Since favorable publicity can help enhance a company's image, it too can be considered as helping to promote sales. Are all three—the salesperson, advertising, and publicity—therefore considered forms of sales promotion? In a sense they are, since each promotes sales. This makes a precise definition of the term far more difficult.

There tends to be some disagreement on the precise meaning of *sales promotion.* It is typically defined as those marketing activities *other than personal selling, advertising, and publicity* that stimulate consumer purchasing and dealer effectiveness. It would thus include displays, shows and expositions, demonstrations, and other nonroutine selling efforts. In reality, though, many firms have promotional programs that frequently include certain types of advertising while also involving the salesperson in various aspects of the program. For our purposes, therefore, we'll use a somewhat broader definition: **sales promotion** refers to those marketing activities designed to inform, persuade, or remind potential customers about a company's goods or services.

You see, then, that sales promotion can cover quite a lot. You, as a salesperson, won't necessarily create the promotional materials yourself—modern firms typically have specialized sales promotion departments or sales promotion managers for this—but you *are* expected to know how to use such materials to your best advantage and that of your firm.

Advertising, a topic to be covered later in the chapter, has lost some ground to pure sales promotion in recent years, principally due to its cost. For example, a 30-second network-TV spot ad can cost between \$150,000 and \$300,000 (more than \$500,000 during Super Bowl games). Newspapers and magazines more than doubled their charges for reaching 1,000 readers during a recent 10-year period.[1] As a result marketers have turned increasingly to sales promotion devices as means of reducing marketing costs.

So far we have established the truism that sales promotion devices are designed to promote or stimulate sales. It's now time to become more specific. Who is affected by sales promotion programs? What is the nature of such activities? The answer to our first question is relatively simple. Basically, sales promotion is an activity aimed at three groups:

1. Sales force
2. Dealers and distributors
3. Ultimate consumers

Our second question, related to the nature of sales promotion activities, can be answered by examining how such programs are customarily used with each of these groups.

SALES PROMOTION AIMED AT COMPANY SALES FORCE

You are the one!

Although sales promotion departments or managers are responsible for the development of sound sales promotion programs, you, the salesperson, are a key figure in determining their success or failure. You may be the individual expected to explain and sell dealers on your company's sales promotion programs. Therefore, it is essential for you and other members of the sales team to be as enthusiastic about sales promotion activities as those who originate them. A sales campaign can be developed creatively yet fall flat on its face if salespeople haven't been sold on the use and significance of the materials.

Seek and ye shall find!

Promotion and sales managers have heavy responsibilities in relation to promotional programs. They are not only responsible for developing promotional materials for customers but must also promote the programs to their sales forces. Managers must take the necessary time to explain promotional materials thoroughly and to motivate salespeople to use them. Salespeople share this responsibility. They must seek out on their own as much information as possible in order to be adequately informed.

"Although sales promotion departments or managers are responsible for the development of sound sales promotion programs, you, the salesperson, are a key figure in determining their success or failure."

Basically, the means used by many firms to stimulate their own salespeople are related to motivational concepts, sort of the carrot-and-stick approach. For example, some firms periodically run *contests* that competitively pit one salesperson against the others for sales results. Other companies, as a means of stimulating selling efforts, offer salespeople the opportunity to win *vacations* at exotic holiday spas. Merchandise awards or *prizes* based on sales are also used. Opportunities for *profit sharing* or bonus plans are other enticements sometimes offered to salespeople. And perhaps less tasty than the proverbial carrot but nevertheless potentially effective are meetings and quotas. *Meetings* where new product lines can be "sold" to the sales force, or where tired and run down sales batteries can be recharged through educational and inspirational sessions, are fairly commonplace among larger firms. *Quotas,* too, are often established to motivate sales personnel to push a particular item or line of merchandise.

Sales promotion aimed at salespeople, as you have observed from our discussion, is really a two-pronged activity. First, it is designed to *motivate* the sales force; second, it is intended to *provide information* to salespeople that can be passed on to dealers and distributors. This information can help the latter in their own sales promotion activities. Now let's briefly explore some of the more customary types of sales promotion devices you may be expected to use with dealers and distributors.

SALES PROMOTION AIMED AT DEALERS AND DISTRIBUTORS

What are the promotional devices used by manufacturers?

Manufacturers usually have a strong desire to influence in a positive manner the sales activities of their merchant intermediaries, that is, their dealers and distributors. They use a number of methods to make this influence felt, and sales promotion is one of the most important. Among the sales promotion devices used by manufacturers are the following:

1. Point-of-purchase displays
2. Cooperative promotional activities
3. Specialty advertising
4. Store demonstrations
5. Dealer incentive travel
6. Trade fairs and exhibitions

Point-of-Purchase Displays

Have you ever wondered what attracted you to a particular counter in a retail store? Could it have been a creative and well-planned counter display? A good display can be highly effective in attracting the attention and interest of potential customers. Therefore many firms train their sales representatives to use aids that can help their dealers and outlets stimulate sales. Such aids, called **point-of-purchase (P.O.P.) displays**, are normally placed near the spot where sales transactions take place. There's a wide variety of displays available, including display racks, dummy packages, product facsimiles, photographs, plain and animated signs, window displays, and decals.

"The creative and persuasive techniques you've learned to sell products to dealers can also be used to sell P.O.P. displays."

Although you might imagine that your retail customers would welcome with open arms all the assistance you might offer in promoting sales, such is not always the case. Keep in mind that you are merely one of many salespeople selling products and competing for the limited sales promotion space in your dealer's outlet. Your dealers or distributors typically make their own decisions regarding the use of P.O.P. materials. As a result, customers must be sold on their use, just as they had to be sold to get your products on their shelves in the first place. The creative and persuasive techniques you've learned to sell products to dealers can also be used to sell P.O.P. displays. Once again, unless they see the benefits involved, customers are unlikely to want to use your promotional materials.

Remember the name of the game—selling!

Cooperative Promotional Activities

There are a number of sales promotion activities in which the producer and dealers share the costs of the program. For example, one type—**cooperative advertising**—can be quite useful for enlisting dealer involvement in a producer's advertising and promotional programs. We'll discuss cooperative advertising again in a later section of this chapter.

The salesperson often has the major responsibility for promoting the wide variety of co-op programs. Assume, for example, that you have taken a job as a field representative for a large insurance company. You know why you were hired: to persuade independent insurance agents to sell more of *your* company's policies rather than those of your competitors. You might be surprised, however, to discover that you are expected to sell not only your firm's insurance services. You are also expected to sell a wide variety of noninsurance items—ranging from outdoor signs to appointment books and letterheads—to the agents you deal with. The cost of a number of such promotional aids is shared mutually by the company and its dealers. Both parties likewise enjoy the benefits of cooperative promotional efforts.

Mr. Customer, I can put your name up in lights.

Specialty Advertising

Assume, for the sake of illustration, the unthinkable (and the unlikely?)—that all advertising media, in addition to the postal and telephone systems, have been unavailable for two years because of a prolonged nationwide strike. Negotiations have broken down between the representatives of management and their employees, and it appears that the strike might enter its third excruciating year starting next Thursday.

"A paperweight with your firm's name on it situated on the desk of an account is practically like a sales call between personal visits."

Your company's sales curve, however, has held its own fairly well during the long crisis. You analyze the factors that have helped to maintain your sales position and realize that all was not left solely to chance. Your firm has not only a highly organized and well-trained sales force but also an active sales promotion program,

Something **special's** *been working for you!*

especially in an area known as **specialty advertising.** In spite of the dearth of media and communications facilities available, the name of your firm and reminders of its products have continually been in your customers' minds and on their desks thanks to the many goodwill items your sales force has provided to customers and prospective customers in the past.

A prolonged strike like that described above may be an exaggeration. But it's no exaggeration to say that many firms are extensively involved with specialty advertising as a means of reminding prospective buyers of available products and services. A paperweight with your firm's name on it situated on the desk of an account is practically like a sales call between personal visits.

The list of specialty advertising devices is practically without end. Some of the more common giveaways or small-fee items include ballpoint pens, calendars, key rings, rulers, metric conversion slide charts, matchbooks, balloons, flying discs, and T-shirts emblazoned with advertising messages.

Store Demonstrations

"Hurry, hurry, hurry! Step right up, ladies and gentlemen, and see demonstrated—right before your very own eyes—the nifty, the thrifty, the all new and hefty, the fantabulous and the glamorous, the unique and the discrete, the hundred percent improved version of the Wizard Company's handsome structurally fortified hand-fed ferndock spreader."

¡Tranquilo, por favor!

Wow! Can you imagine hearing something like that coming from your neighborhood drugstore? Fortunately, the days of the shouting huckster are generally behind us. Today, in most instances, we prefer a more sophisticated and lower-decibel approach. We must admit, however, that the vociferous huckster of yesteryear was a master at attracting attention.

Today's salespeople may also be masters at attracting attention, but they usually use far more subtle approaches. One of these is the **store demonstration,** a technique in which those involved with sales promotion arrange with the owner or manager of a particular store to demonstrate the manufacturer's product. Counter space or display areas are usually arranged for the demonstrations. You—the salesperson—may make the product demonstration yourself, or you may train others to do it. Personal demonstrations of this nature help attract customers into a store and are often used to introduce a new product or rejuvenate the sales of an established one.

Dealer Incentive Travel

Let's take a trip to Bermuda!

Everybody loves to travel, don't they? Well, maybe not everybody, but enough people seem to like to "get away from it all" once in a while to make the reward of an expense-paid trip an effective incentive to produce more business. Something called **dealer incentive travel** has become an increasingly common sales promotion tool of many companies. Its major purpose is to reward dealers or agents with travel to resorts and conventions for meeting or exceeding sales quotas. Many sales promotion managers feel that being able to go to a domestic or foreign resort motivates dealers even more than comparable cash rewards.

Trade Fairs and Exhibitions

Lead on!

The use of **trade fairs and exhibitions** is another common sales promotion device. Retailers and wholesalers often participate with manufacturers in these exhibitions, which are designed to show and demonstrate a wide variety of products under one roof. Typical trade shows feature boats, electronic equipment, automobiles, and mobile homes. On-the-spot sales as well as leads for future sales often result from contacts made at trade shows and fairs.

Miscellaneous Promotional Devices

And much, much more!

The range and variety of sales promotion techniques is limited only by the imagination and ingenuity of the sales promotion staff. A number of miscellaneous devices are also used by companies to motivate dealers and distributors. *House organs* (company publications), *sales manuals,* and *sales training programs* are provided by some companies to give dealer outlets ideas on how to stimulate sales. *Gifts* and *contests* are other means sometimes used to motivate the retailer's sales force. The offering of something called "PM" (push money) is an additional promotion device. This technique provides financial incentives to salesclerks who make greater efforts to sell a manufacturer's products. Anyone planning to employ such practices, however, should first make certain that price discrimination laws are not being violated.

SALES PROMOTION AIMED AT CONSUMERS

Why aim sales promotion at consumers?

Sales promotion aimed at consumers is a highly critical activity, since its results are closely linked to other promotional areas. For example, if sales promotion is successful in motivating ultimate consumers to purchase certain brands, then merchant intermediaries, such as wholesalers and retailers, are more likely to stock and promote those items. Naturally, the major purpose of sales promotion aimed at ultimate consumers is to provide them with a greater incentive to buy—in a sense to provide them with offers they find difficult to refuse. Although sales promotion programs are often a blend of more than one technique, Table 16.1 treats them separately for purposes of classification. The more common types of sales promotion activities and devices directed toward consumers include:

1. Coupons
2. Samples
3. Premiums
4. Special offers
5. Special services
6. Contests, games, and sweepstakes
7. Sponsoring special events (event marketing)

TABLE 16.1 Summary of Major Types of Sales Promotion Aimed at Consumers.

Type	Description	Purpose
Coupons	A form or certificate with redeemable value; usually printed on the outside of or included inside containers of certain products; sometimes printed in magazines or newspapers, distributed at retail counters, or mailed in quantity to householders.	To encourage consumers to try a product and to continue to buy it in the future.
Samples	Small quantities of the product that are provided free of charge or at nominal cost; especially used to promote cereals, soaps, toothpastes, and cigarettes; frequently mailed to consumers or given away in commercial districts and on college campuses.	To enable consumers to become familiar with particular brands and make them more likely to pay the full price in the future.
Premiums and special offers	Items of value to consumers given away free or provided at nominal cost (e.g., small toys packed inside cereal boxes); also used regularly by financial institutions, house-to-house salespeople, and retail outlets; sometimes uses the "cash refund" approach, in which purchasers apply for a partial refund.	To induce consumers to purchase a manufacturer's product and become regular customers.
Special services	Services provided at no cost to consumers (e.g., classes on tax-sheltered retirement programs, ornamental horticulture, or wallpapering; home appraisals, travelers' checks, safety deposit boxes, and money orders).	To develop more appreciative and loyal customers.
Contests, games, and sweepstakes	Competitions that offer prizes awarded on the basis of skill (e.g., completing a poem or limerick, developing a name for a new product, developing a company slogan or logo); may merely involve returning "lucky numbers" that were mailed to householders.	To develop greater brand awareness among consumers, build store traffic, and stimulate new uses for old products.

Type	Description	Purpose
Sponsoring special events (event marketing)	Events of national interest sponsored by companies, usually popular spectator activities with sampling opportunities for the marketer. Signs with product's name on them generally are displayed. Heavily used by cigarette and beer companies.	To develop and maintain brand familiarity. Opportunities to enable potential consumers to sample products.
Public relations blitz	To develop brand familiarity, especially for new products, among consumers.	"Free" publicity acquired by marketers who employ PR (public relations) firms that contact various media with human-interest stories about the products.
Electronic sales promotion	The use of computer technology, such as videotex, videodisc kiosks, and electronic mail in contacting prospective customers, frequently interactive between consumer and the electronic device.	To promote consumer interest in the purchase of goods and services.
Direct mail	Promotional materials (e.g., sales letters, postcards, brochures, and catalogs) that are mailed to potential customers.	To accomplish a wide variety of promotional goals, ranging from developing prospects to selling products and services.

8. Public relations blitz
9. Direct mail (including catalogs)
10. Electronic sales promotion

Carefully study Table 16.1 to help you gain an understanding of the major types and purposes of sales promotion aimed at consumers. Because direct mail is so widely used as a sales promotion tool, and because electronic sales promotion is so novel, each will receive special treatment in the sections that follow.

DIRECT MAIL AND THE SELLING PROCESS

"Neither snow nor rain, nor gloom of night, neither German shepherds nor well-groomed poodles, stays these couriers from the swift completion of their appointed rounds. The mail must go through!" These are words that our postal system would have us believe. Although some question the validity of such optimism, most of the mail *does* get through, a thought that leads us to our next topic: the use of direct mail in selling. **Direct mail** is designed to supplement but not replace personal selling. Direct mail includes sales letters, envelope stuffers or inserts, postcards, circulars, and catalogs.

The Uses of Direct Mail

Why use direct mail? Is it really worthwhile in these times of high postage rates and continual public outcries against voluminous quantities of "junk mail" delivered to householders and businesses? Also, there are constant protests from some consumer advocates demanding the end of unsolicited promotional mailings to householders. Those who squawk the loudest generally receive the most attention, but in spite of such attitudes, most people, when given the choice, have elected to continue receiving advertising materials in the mail.

Where might you direct your mail?

Mail to householders, however, is only one facet of this type of sales promotion activity. Professional salespeople have discovered a host of uses for direct mail that can enhance their sales effectiveness. (See Table 16.2 for a summary of the more typical uses to which direct mail can be put.)

It should be clear by now that the sales job is varied and time-consuming. It also is quite costly. Typical sales calls cost hundreds of dollars. Any means that can increase your sales effectiveness, that is, increase the number of opportunities to obtain favorable buying decisions from a prospect, should be utilized. Direct mail is one of those means.

When used as a prospecting tool, direct mail can provide salespeople with a continual supply of leads. As one sales manager put it, "Direct mail serves as our envoy in envelopes. It helps to establish leads, sorting out the suspects from the prospects, in a far shorter time than can cold calls. And it helps to reduce our selling costs by increasing the number of actual sales presentations we can make in a day."

How to Make Effective Use of Direct Mail

The typical business or household receives tremendous amounts of advertising in the mail each week. Individuals discard a lot of this mail after giving it little or no

TABLE 16.2 Common Sales Applications of Direct Mail.

1. Selling products and services
2. Prospecting for new customers
3. Obtaining appointments
4. Arousing interest in products and services
5. Reminding customers of the need for service or maintenance of prior purchases
6. Notifying preferred customers about special sales
7. Following up sales calls
8. Maintaining contact with customers between sales calls
9. Establishing and maintaining goodwill

attention. When using direct mail as a promotional medium, you should realize that your competition for the recipient's attention is stiff. Adequate planning, organizing, and evaluation of your results are essential if mailing activities are to accomplish your intended goals. Mailing costs are far too high today for you to ignore methods that will maximize your efforts at reasonable cost. Let's now look at some of the specific ways you might maximize the effectiveness of your own direct mail activities.

Select Mailing Lists Carefully An up-to-date and relevant prospect list is essential to the success of any direct mail activity. Sources of mailing lists were discussed in Chapter 8. You might find it helpful to review them at this time.

Here today and gone tomorrow!

People are continually on the move in our society, changing occupations and jobs, changing houses and spouses, and even changing countries. Their tastes and interests also change with surprising rapidity. As a result, you should periodically evaluate your mailing lists to make certain they are current and relevant.

"An up-to-date and relevant prospect list is essential to the success of any direct mail activity."

A mailing list should not only be up to date but also somewhat selective. If you were a consultant, for example, attempting to market training programs for supervisors with less than one year of management experience, wouldn't you be wasting a considerable amount of your direct mail budget if you sent circulars or letters to everyone listed between pages 20 and 40 of the telephone directory? A more effective approach would be to obtain names of personnel managers or lists of members of management associations. To assist organizations in their sales promotion activities, there exist **list brokers,** which are organizations that compile lists of names and addresses that can assist you in targeting your own specific market.

Use Appealing Materials Your concept of direct mail should be more than a No. 10 envelope stuffed with a hastily word-processed letter; much more is involved. An important consideration should be the appearance and layout of your mailing pieces. Before designing mailing materials, plan soundly. Have you determined what your main objectives are? Too frequently, the tastes of those who develop materials dominate designs, with little consideration for how the public might react.

Guard against "ego mailings."

Most direct mail specialists feel that sales letters should be relatively short. A letter that looks like a legal document is likely to be ineffective and quickly discarded. Letters should be written in an understandable and friendly style, worded so that the prospect will want to read the entire message—*and then act!*

With circulars and catalogs, you can include more information in your mailings, but their design and format should also be carefully planned and developed. Color, photographs, and simplicity are believed to be effective eyecatchers. Black-and-white illustrations are less costly, but they are generally less appealing to the prospect.

Well, if it isn't my dear old friend, Mr. Occupant!

Personalize Materials Whenever possible, mailings should be personalized. Every day, householders or business managers are likely to find at least two or three invitations to buy in their mailboxes. Canned, impersonal letters, as you might imagine, don't exactly strike a warm, responsive chord in the breasts of prospective customers. How do you react when you receive an envelope addressed to "Occupant" or "Resident" stuffed with a letter saluting "Dear Reader" or "Dear Friend"? The more effective materials used today include the recipient's name not only on the envelope but also in the salutation and, if possible, in the sales message. Avoid using bulk postage stamps on the envelopes. Many prospects throw such envelopes away without even opening them.

Because large quantities of personalized mailings can be prohibitively expensive, many firms have turned to the computer, which can be programmed to insert names from mailing lists. As a result, thousands of "personalized" letters can be turned out with incredible speed. The experience of many firms indicates that letters with a personalized appearance pull far greater returns. Computers are also used to analyze individual customer records in order to select the most promising prospects.

How do I benefit?

Stress Benefits Don't overlook the opportunity to apply sound selling concepts to all of your direct mail activities. Try to appeal to the buying motives of consumers. Response to your messages will be negligible unless you show how the person receiving the direct mail can personally benefit by responding to your request.

What do you expect from me?

Request Specific Action An important but sometimes overlooked requirement for an effective direct mail program is that it should request specific action on the part of the recipient. Self-addressed, postage-paid postcards are often included with letters to facilitate customer response. When return cards are used, be certain to include all relevant information on the cards themselves. Without such information, the prospect may be unable to take the action you desire if the letter is misplaced. (See Figures 16.1 and 16.2 for examples of a sales letter requesting direct action and a return postcard.)

A specific, direct request can often be the motivating factor that stimulates the prospect into action. For example, one company soliciting credit card membership asks for a response this way:

> Why not apply for Cardmembership today? All you have to do is fill out and mail the enclosed application. When it is approved, we'll send along the Card, without delay.

Follow up on Inquiries Try to put yourself into the shoes of a person who has responded to a media or direct mail advertisement. Wouldn't you want and expect your request to be acted upon promptly? When you use direct mail materials, be certain to apply the cardinal rule of following up within a reasonable period of time.

Try the "HIFO" method: hot-in first-out.

Planning, once again, is essential for optimum results. If you have received a sizable number of inquiries, which do you contact first? Some salespeople rate the respondents, putting them into specific priority categories. In this way you can make certain that you're contacting the most interested—that is, the hottest—prospects

Commercial • Industrial Photography

PHOTOGRAPHY FOR THE PROS...

As a media professional, you place special demands on your photographers. You not only need creative images, you need them on time. We understand that. We also buy and sell services, and we know what deadlines are for. They're to be met.

We'll meet your deadlines with images that will make it easy to sell your services. Photographs that make people stop and take notice of the product or company involved. Photographs for many uses. Catalogs -- display prints -- new product releases -- executive portraits -- copy work -- slide shows -- the list goes on and on.

When you work with Pacific Photo Services, you get more than commercial/industrial photography. You get custom lab services second to none. You get Kodaliths that are clean and ready to be used as overlays. You get custom framing for display prints. And, of course, you get satisfied clients.

We would like to meet with you so that you can see some samples of our work, and to talk about how our photographic services can benefit your agency. Please fill out the post card today and one of us will call to make an appointment.

Sincerely yours,

Bob Nehrbass

Bob Nehrbass

P.S. If you are in our neighborhood, stop by and see our collection of display prints.

4900 BARRETT AVENUE • RICHMOND, CA 94805 • 415/232-4358

Figure 16.1 Example of Sales Letter Requesting Direct Action.

first. Some individuals, of course, respond almost automatically to practically any offer for free literature or information, whether they are really interested or not. Such persons can be placed low on your priority list. But be careful that you don't weed out someone because of false assumptions.

Serving the North Bay with commercial/industrial photography for manufacturers, retailers and contractors.

MAIL THIS CARD TODAY and we will set up an appointment to show our portfolio and to discuss any photographic projects you may have in mind. Naturally, there is no obligation.

NAME ______

COMPANY NAME ______

POSITION ______

PHONE ______

ADDRESS ______

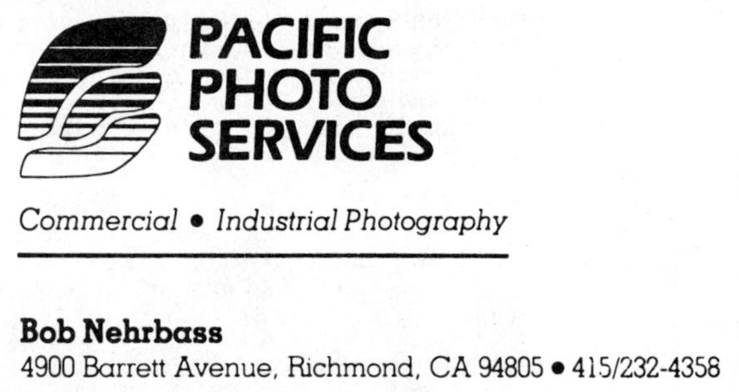

Figure 16.2 Example of Return Postcard and Business Card Included with Action Sales Letter.

You should also analyze which responses appear to require a personal sales call, which can be handled by a simple telephone call, and which can be handled by a return letter. Be certain that any customers placing orders with you in response to your mailing receive immediate acknowledgment of their requests.

Mail in Volume Did you realize that many businesses consider their direct mail campaigns to be successful when there is response from as little as 2 to 5 percent of the total mailing? Of course, you need a response as high as possible if your direct mail campaigns are to be economically feasible. Higher returns on your mailings lower the hourly cost of each sale. So, it's important for you to develop mailing lists and materials that increase as much as possible the probability of return. Because response rates typically are fairly low, direct mail tends to be more effective when used in volume.

Follow up to avoid foul-ups!

Evaluate Your Results Regular evaluation of direct mail effectiveness should be an integral part of your program. Have you analyzed costs in relation to revenues? Have you experimented with changes in format, color, photographs, and working in order to compare the effectiveness of various approaches? Sometimes a test market of different mail approaches to two similar groups of prospects can help determine which approach is more effective.

ELECTRONIC SALES PROMOTION

A relatively new area that has begun to alter the face of marketing is **electronic sales promotion.** Few householders in the early 1970s ever thought of owning personal computers. By the late 1980s, however, there were far more than a few "hackers" messing around with "bytes and bits" in their kitchens. In 1988, almost 20 percent of all homes in the United States had computers, with nearly 30 percent of all new personal computers purchased in that year installed in households.[2]

For our purposes we will define *electronic sales promotion* as the use of computer technology for the purpose of promoting consumer interest in the purchase of goods and services. New applications of electronic sales promotion are being put to use regularly. Its use in the past has been primarily for selling brand-name goods with strong customer identification. The three major areas of electronic sales promotion that we shall focus on in this section are:

1. Videotex
2. Videodisc kiosks
3. Electronic mail

Let's now take a brief look at each of these.

Videotex

Marketers are now able to sell their wares to consumers while the latter are sitting relaxed on the living room floor viewing TV through the medium of **videotex.** *Videotex* is a system that enables customers to order goods directly from manufacturers by combining their telephones with home computers by tapping into a central video catalog. A pioneer in this field, Compucard International, in a recent year offered more than 60,000 consumer durable goods at prices discounted as much as 50 percent below manufacturers' suggested retail prices to more than 2 million members nationwide.[3]

"Dear, would you please pass me the modem?"

The videotex system is an interactive system that has resulted in the computerization of traditional catalogs. Householders are able to sit in front of their televisions and select only those products or information they want to look at as they punch simple codes into their computer keyboards, rather than be forced to sit through a number of commercials that they do not want to see, as on conventional television. With videotex, householders can make immediate purchases or requests for information.

Videodisc Kiosks

A shortcoming of videotex is its inability to display anything other than text. A novel sales promotion medium that overcomes this handicap, one that can show products both in color and in motion as in movies and videotapes, is another electonic medium—the videodisc. There now exist firms that provide **videodisc kiosks** for their customers. A videodisc kiosk is a small booth located in a public place where customers use computer terminals to select products that they want to see demonstrated on a video screen. Viewers can also obtain information about products and even order items directly from the kiosks with their credit cards. Videodisc kiosks have primarily been installed in shopping malls, office buildings, and department stores.

You've gotta give those kiosks credit!

An interesting aspect of videodisc kiosks is that some are programmed to qualify prospective customers. For example, the Avon Corporation had its units equipped with special keyboards that women could use to enter data about their skin tone, PH factor, and other information related to the purchase of cosmetics. The videodisc displays only products compatible with the skin of the woman who enters the data.[4]

Electronic Mail

Another recent development is **electronic mail,** which is used by some firms to supplement ordinary third-class bulk mail. MCI Digital Service Information Corporation (MCI Mail) offers electronic mail service. For example, MCI Mail transfers data from a client's personal computer to any one of its 19 remote laser printers located throughout the United States and then transfers it to paper. If MCI Mail's clients supply letterheads, MCI Mail will print letters that are indistinguishable from originals.

"Original" copies!

Another form of electronic mail that is even faster than the use of electronic mail firms is owning and using a **facsimile machine,** also called a **fax machine.** Such devices are being used with increasing frequency for transmitting all sorts of documents, including pictures in various shades of gray from one fax machine to another. With a fax machine, for example, a standard letter can be transmitted virtually anywhere in the industrialized world in a mere 10 to 50 seconds. Some fax machines can even dial the recipient's phone number automatically.

Faster than a speeding mail truck!

Electronic mail has been used to obtain written confirmation of customers' telephone orders. It also has been used by direct marketers that sell mutual funds and by specialized catalog firms. Electronic mail enables the marketing firm to send to their customers prompt information about changes in prices and new product availability. With MCI Mail, for example, a company located in the Midwest can send a letter to either coast within four hours.[5]

THE NATURE OF ADVERTISING

> Two business people are talking. One says: "Is your new advertising getting results?" "It sure is," says the second. "Last week we advertised for a night security guard and the next night we got robbed."

This corny story about the business people and the night security guard helps to illustrate that "advertising truly gets results!"

Throughout the text we've emphasized the need to attract the attention of prospective customers. And just as the businessperson's advertising attracted the thief, creative advertising can help to attract the attention and interest of prospective buyers.

We've already concluded that salespeople have a number of responsibilities besides their personal, face-to-face selling activities. Still another responsibility that may be yours as a salesperson: understanding how company advertising programs can be used to further selling objectives. We've already explored a related topic: the use of sales promotion devices. What is the nature of advertising? What are the various types of media that you as a salesperson should understand? How might you be directly involved with advertising activities? These are some of the questions to be answered in this section.

Advertising—A Salesperson's Friend or Foe?

Does advertising compete with the salesperson?

Have you ever considered what you have in common with advertising? Both of you have been employed to help your firm sell its goods and services. Advertising, therefore, should not be considered in direct competition with you. Instead, it should be considered as one of your "silent" selling partners. Aren't you both really members of the same team?

Let's illustrate what this means. If you were the coach of an athletic team, would you be likely to look upon the members of your team as competitors? If you were a player, would you consider your teammates your principal competition? What is the major function of your fellow team members? Aren't they there for support as you try to win over your real competitors—other teams? The same is true of the supportive members of your sales team—advertising, sales promotion, and direct mail. They are there to help you and your firm accomplish the important goal of selling a product as often and as profitably as possible.

What is **advertising?**

We've been using the word **advertising,** but just what does it mean? *Advertising* can be defined as *a nonpersonal message or series of messages paid for by an identifiable sponsor for the purpose of persuading others to accept products, services, or ideas.*

Why Advertising Is Important to Salespeople

The major purpose of advertising is not to compete with sales activities but to make selling easier. One of the prime purposes of advertising, therefore, is to influence product and brand selection, that is, to create and cultivate markets for goods and

How can products be **presold***?*

services. Effective advertising can also help to keep a product known in the marketplace. In effect, products can be *presold* as a result of a well-planned, timely, and creative advertising program. By *presold* we mean that prospective customers have been motivated to act—to make a purchase—as a result of exposure to advertising media.

"An advertising campaign that helps to build or maintain favorable company and product images can remove many of the obstacles faced by the salesperson whose company or products are not familiar to prospective customers."

Unless your potential customers know of the existence and availability of your products, they can't very well have a desire for them. So advertising helps create this desire, and the salesperson, in most instances, closes the sale. An advertising campaign that helps to build or maintain favorable company and product images can remove many of the obstacles faced by the salesperson whose company or products are not familiar to prospective customers.

What's in it for you?

Advertising, therefore, can work with you to accomplish a common goal—the stimulation of prospective buyers. It can open numerous doors for you as a result of the presold familiarity customers may develop with your company and products. Because advertising is so widespread, it serves to penetrate markets and thus reach customers that might be inconvenient or difficult for you to contact. As a consequence, it helps to develop new leads for you and your firm. Furthermore, since you can't visit all of your accounts personally each day, your teammate—advertising—can be actively saturating your territory, both cultivating and selling your customers between sales calls.

How Advertising Helps Your Customers

And for your customers?

Customers, whether they are ultimate consumers, industrial or governmental buyers, or merchant intermediaries, also stand to gain from your firm's advertising programs. Advertising not only enables them to become more aware of new or improved products on the market, but also provides information regarding a product's use, quality, and performance.

Customers such as wholesalers and retailers who purchase your products for resale can significantly benefit from advertising that helps them move the goods they bought from you. With the increased demand can come increased turnover of merchandise, which can result in increased profits for your customers. And aren't increased profits one of their major goals?

Promotional Versus Institutional Advertising

Advertising generally falls into one of two broad categories: promotional or institutional. Either may be concerned with the selling of goods or services. The basic difference between them is the span of time leading to the ultimate goal of each.

For example, **promotional advertising** is usually used to gain short-run results. Sometimes termed *product advertising,* promotional advertising is customarily concerned with the *immediate* stimulation of demand. A large proportion of advertising is of this nature. It seeks to create immediate buyer interest and desire for specific products and services.

Institutional advertising, on the other hand, is concerned with broader and longer-term goals. It usually stresses such factors as goodwill, a company name, a theme or cause, or simply a class of products, such as prunes or milk, sold by a group of firms.

Can Advertising Ever Completely Eliminate the Personal Selling Function?

Although advertising is used principally to stimulate demand and arouse the desire for goods and services, in some cases the advertisement itself actually does most of the selling to consumers. For example, Procter & Gamble has expended literally millions of dollars on advertising that extols the virtues of Crest toothpaste. The typical consumer who enters a retail store in search of toothpaste has generally been presold on the brand. Seldom is there a need or desire to have a salesperson deliver a sales presentation to a customer on the merits of "floristat," the active decay-preventing ingredient added to the dentifrice.

Is it "bye, bye" to the selling function?

So we could say that, in some cases, the selling function has been eliminated through advertising. Yes, we could *say* that, but would we necessarily be completely right? How did the toothpaste originally get on the retailer's shelves? A salesperson undoubtedly had some influence over a buyer or buying committee. What influenced the store manager's decision regarding where to locate the toothpaste in the retail outlet? A salesperson probably expended considerable persuasive effort to get a desirable location and adequate shelf space in the store for the product. You can see, therefore, that advertising can sell, but it seldom eliminates the need for the personal selling process.

Major Types of Advertising Media

Why isn't the **desire** *to advertise enough?*

Advertising alone doesn't necessarily expand a firm's market. Some firms have painfully learned the lesson that certain types of advertisements are clever attention-getters but don't sell the product. Before a company enjoys positive results from its advertising efforts, it needs much more than a mere willingness to advertise. It needs to consider such factors as *timing,* the *markets* in which advertising takes place, and the *type of medium* that best suits the firm's goals. For example, in Minnesota, December would probably be a bad time to run newspaper ads for bikini bathing suits. And you wouldn't be likely to put your advertising for business jets into comic books.

"Some firms have painfully learned the lesson that certain types of advertisements are clever attention-getters but don't sell the product."

What is the best medium?

As to which medium is the most effective for a company's advertising budget, the answer is not always easy or clear-cut. The choice is relatively wide, since each medium has both advantages and disadvantages.

It is beyond the scope of this text to explore advertising in depth. We'll leave that task to textbooks in advertising and marketing. However, as a salesperson, you should be aware of the major types of advertising media. Carefully study Table 16.3, which briefly lists and summarizes the principal strong and weak points of the following types of advertising media:

1. Newspaper
2. Radio
3. Television
4. Outdoor advertising
5. Direct mail
6. Throwaway flyers
7. Magazines
8. Videocassettes

ADVERTISING AND THE ROLE OF THE SALESPERSON

I like it—but where can I buy it?

A significant problem faced by many manufacturers is how to let consumers know where products can be purchased. For example, your firm might spend huge sums on outstanding advertising campaigns getting millions of customers interested in your products. But much of your firm's advertising budget will have gone down that proverbial drain if prospective buyers don't know how or where to buy your merchandise.

A salesperson's role in relation to advertising may, at first glance, seem like a nonselling activity, but think for a moment: is this actually the case? Many manufacturers have discovered that advertising campaigns, to be truly successful, require the cooperative support and involvement of their dealers and outlets. Can you see now where you—the salesperson—can play a significant role? You are one of the few individuals in your company in direct contact with dealers, thus you're in the position to sell (motivate) them on becoming more involved with your firm's advertising programs. Read on for a brief examination of some of the ways in which you can develop this involvement.

". . . much of your firm's advertising budget will have gone down that proverbial drain if prospective buyers don't know how or where to buy your merchandise."

TABLE 16.3 Summary of Strong and Weak Points of Principal Types of Media.

Kind of medium	Strong points	Weak points
Newspaper	Permits product illustration Frequent publication Some flexibility in responding to sudden change Regularly used as a shopping guide Some geographical selectivity	Short life of individual issues Poor qualitative selectivity—everyone reads the paper
Radio	Personal—human voice can often be more persuasive than print Flexible—permits sudden change in message Particular stations may appeal to selective audience because of program content	Audio only—may make less impact than visual media Cannot use illustrations Short life of message
Television	Combines sound, sight, and motion to convey message Some flexibility in responding to sudden change Gives a sense of immediacy	Too expensive for small- or middle-sized firm Message is short-lived Time and production costs are high
Outdoor advertising	Time costs are low per person reached Low cost per impression delivered Frequent repetition of the message Good reinforcement medium Good geographical selectivity	Poor qualitative selectivity Copy limitations
Direct mail	Reaches a select market with precision Can be used on a limited budget Flexible in timing and message Can add a personal touch	High cost per person per message
Throwaway flyers	Allow specific geographic market coverage Easily prepared Low cost, easy distribution Allows immediate response	Are often not read
Magazines	Relatively long life Excellent reproduction Targeted audiences	Require long lead times
Videocassettes	Relatively long life Utilizes both sight and sound senses	Little flexibility Requires long lead times Relatively high cost per person viewing message

Relate Advertising Benefits to the Dealer

What's in it for the cooperating dealer?

We have mentioned that an advertising campaign gains effectiveness when the dealer feels involved with the program. But what motivates dealers into greater involvement? Here's where you—the salesperson—come into the picture. You should do all you can to relate your advertising programs and materials to the needs and goals of the dealers. One of their primary concerns is increasing profits. Dealers are not likely to become involved with advertising programs unless they've been convinced that they personally stand to gain. Dealers who have been sold on the benefits of advertising programs are often stimulated into making additional purchases to prepare for anticipated increases in sales.

Provide Advertising Materials and Assistance

There's much you can do to help!

There is much you can do to motivate your accounts toward greater involvement with advertising programs. Your company, for example, can provide you with a variety of advertising and promotional materials that can either be given to your dealers or offered at low cost. You may be able to help your accounts set up attractive display ads. You might provide them with creative ideas on ways to improve existing sales promotion activities.

Perhaps you can help them develop a direct mail advertising campaign. In addition, your firm might offer newspaper advertising copy or mats that are copy-ready for newspaper publication. Sometimes free or low-cost radio and television scripts are provided to dealers.

Use Advertising Facsimiles

You should carry copies of current advertisements, sometimes called **advertising facsimiles,** with you during sales calls. These not only lend prestige to your own firm but can also stimulate dealers' interest in your present and future advertising programs. Facsimile ads can also be used by dealers for promotional tie-ins and as mailers to their own customers.

The ways in which you can help your dealers with advertising are practically endless. By keeping up with changing trends, you can help your dealers with their advertising needs and improve your own sales record as a result.

Sell Mutually Paid Advertising

Dealers who can see the personal benefits in advertising programs tend to become more involved. Dealer involvement is even greater, however, when something is at stake, like an investment of money and time. As discussed earlier, many manufacturers have developed *cooperative advertising* programs in which the manufacturer shares advertising costs with its dealers. Any of the media already discussed can be utilized. Some manufacturers even share the cost of storefront signs and direct mail campaigns.

Typically, the manufacturer provides a **co-op allowance,** which is, in effect, a refund of a portion of the price paid for goods purchased from the manufacturer.

Most co-op advertising agreements stipulate that any payment made by the manufacturer is to be matched by the dealer, that is, the dealer contributes about 50 percent of all advertising costs.

Customarily, the dealer places the advertising locally (rates to local advertisers are usually lower than to national advertisers) and then submits proof (a bill or invoice) to the manufacturer that the advertising took place. Dealers are then reimbursed for their share or are given credit toward future purchases.

Since dealers contribute toward the cost of the advertising, co-op programs tend to be successful in getting them actively involved with promoting and merchandising the manufacturer's products.[6]

SUMMARY

Sales promotion is a broad concept, one that encompasses virtually any activity that "promotes" the selling of goods and services. Some marketers, however, prefer a narrower definition of *sales promotion* and exclude personal selling, advertising, and publicity from the meaning of the term.

Sales promotion activities are aimed principally at three groups: the company sales force, dealers and distributors, and ultimate consumers. The list of sales promotion activities is extensive. Since salespeople are often involved with carrying out sales promotion activities, they should become familiar with the more typical types of materials employed.

Direct mail is one of the most commonly used methods for the promotion of goods and services. It can be effective not only in developing leads for future sales but can also result in the more effective use of a salesperson's time by converting suspects into prospects.

Electronic sales promotion has become increasingly popular in recent years as a result of the proliferation of personal computers. The types of electronic sales promotion discussed in the chapter were videotex, videodisc kiosks, and electronic mail, including fax machines.

A key objective of direct mail activities is to stimulate some sort of action on the part of the recipient, such as a request for information, the arrangement of an appointment, or the purchase of a product. Direct mail results are enhanced when the following suggestions are followed: (1) select mailing lists carefully, (2) use appealing materials, (3) use personalized materials when possible, (4) stress benefits to the prospect, (5) request specific action, (6) follow up promptly, and (7) evaluate results regularly.

Advertising and the salesperson have something in common. Both serve to facilitate the sale of goods and services. Neither should be considered as being in competition with the other.

Advertising can be defined as a nonpersonal message or series of messages paid for by an identifiable sponsor for the purpose of persuading others to accept products, services, or ideas. Advertising performs a variety of useful functions for salespeople. It helps create demand for products, and thus, by preselling potential buyers, can reduce some of the obstacles commonly faced by salespeople. Advertising also serves to remind customers of a company and its products between sales visits.

Advertising helps customers become more aware of the availability of products and provides them with information regarding a product's use, quality, and performance. Advertising can also help dealers move merchandise more rapidly and thus increase profit potentials. Advertising is typically either promotional or institutional in nature.

Advertising can alter but seldom completely eliminate the personal selling function. Even consumer products that have been extensively presold to the public require some degree of personal selling. Salespeople, for example, must persuade merchants to provide ample shelf space and use suitable store locations for their products.

The medium is not the complete message. Other factors such as optimum timing, the specific markets, and the most relevant types of media must be considered when attempting to develop advertising that sells.

The principal media used for advertising are:

1. Newspaper
2. Radio
3. Television
4. Outdoor advertising
5. Direct mail
6. Throwaway flyers
7. Magazines
8. Videocassettes

Each medium, of course, has its own advantages and limitations.

Salespeople frequently play an active role in advertising programs. A principal responsibility of salespeople is to have their customers become more involved with present and future advertising programs. Dealer cooperation tends to increase substantially when the dealers have been convinced of the merits of participating in advertising campaigns. Such cooperation and involvement tends to improve the effectiveness of any advertising activities.

KEY TERMS

sales promotion
point-of-purchase (P.O.P.) displays
cooperative advertising
specialty advertising
store demonstration
dealer incentive travel
trade fairs and exhibitions
direct mail
electronic sales promotion
list brokers
videotex
videodisc kiosks

electronic mail
facsimile (fax) machines
advertising
promotional advertising
institutional advertising
advertising facsimilies
co-op allowance

QUESTIONS

1. In what way is sales promotion different from and in what way similar to personal selling?
2. Some sales managers feel that travel incentives are more effective motivators of salespeople and dealers than merchandise. Do you agree? Explain.
3. Assume that in two weeks you plan to open a sandwich shop near a local college campus. What types of sales promotion activities would you develop for your firm?
4. What are the two major purposes of sales promotion aimed at the sales force.
5. Why is it important for sales representatives to be sold on the application of sales promotion materials? How would you, as a sales manager, motivate your sales personnel into greater use of such materials?
6. What types of P.O.P. displays might be effective for the promotion of laptop computers? House paint? Roofing materials?
7. What are some ways in which you, as a salesperson, might become involved with specialty advertising?
8. What benefits might you, as a manufacturer's representative, derive from arranging to present a store demonstration in one of your customer's outlets?
9. Describe the ways in which direct mail can be made more effective as a sales promotion device.
10. Define the term advertising. How does it differ from the activity of selling? What does it have in common with selling?
11. Evaluate the following statement: "The intent of advertising is to wipe out the selling function. Basically, advertising people are interested in just one thing—eliminating the salesperson."
12. Examine four current publications and differentiate between the institutional and the promotional types of advertising in them.
13. Does anyone really benefit from product and service advertising, other than the advertising agency? Explain.
14. In recent years, advertising messages have been included with rental movies on videocassettes. For example, Pepsi had its jet plane TV commercial inserted at the start of the videocassette version of *Top Gun.* How do you feel about this form of advertising?
15. Describe some of the ways in which salespeople can get their customers more involved in advertising campaigns.

APPLICATIONS

16.1 THE UNSTUCK DECAL

Assume that you are a sales representative for the Lettam Toy Company. Among the sales promotion materials you are expected to use are decals intended to be placed on the windows or doors of your dealer outlets. The decals enable potential customers to know that your products are available within a particular store. You have never been especially active in promoting their use because of the negative reactions you usually receive from store managers.

Typical of the objections to using the decals was the one Werner Wearhardt, an account, gave to you this morning: "Why should I want your decals messing up my window? Besides, I handle the toys of Quickhammer, Oxtied, and about fifteen other manufacturers. If I put up your decal, then every peddler I deal with will want me to do the same thing. Before I know it, no one will be able to see through my store windows!"

Problems

1. Develop an effective response to Wearhardt's objections to the use of your decals.
2. Role play your response with someone else.

16.2 SEARCHING FOR PROMOS

Table 16.1 summarizes nine categories of sales promotion aids aimed at consumers. During the next week, locate examples of each category and then answer the questions below.

Questions

1. What do you feel was the primary objective of each of the promotion devices you observed?
2. How successful do you feel each promotion device will be? Why?
3. How might each sales promotion device that you examined be improved?

16.3 SELLING A CO-OP ADVERTISING PROGRAM

Assume that you are a sales representative for the Pentashi Camera Company. One of your responsibilities is to encourage camera dealers to tie in with your company advertising campaigns. Assume that your firm has a policy of reimbursing participating retailers up to 50 percent of their local advertising costs when they feature your company's products in their advertising.

Problem

Develop a sales presentation designed to motivate your retail accounts into committing themselves to a cooperative advertising program with your firm, Pentashi Camera Company.

16.4 "IS THIS WHAT THEY MEAN BY 'PRODUCT DIFFERENTIATION'?"

Fortune magazine reported in the latter 1980s that marketers were having a hard time coming up with products that were different from those of their competitors. As a result, they leaned more heavily on sales promotion than in the past as a means of attracting the public's interest. Three types of promotions that received substantial attention were coupons, PR blitzes, and event sponsorship.[7]

Coupons have become one of the most popular types of sales promotion for consumer nondurable goods. For example, in a recent year, consumers redeemed more than 6.5 billion coupons, thus saving more than $2 billion on their shopping bills.[8]

However, not everyone has been sold on the desirability of coupons as a marketing device. Critics of coupons say that price promotion turns people into selective shoppers who only buy when there's a "deal" and then buy from the competition when it too has "deals." As a result, brand loyalty is believed to have been significantly weakened through the use of cents-off coupons and rebates.[9]

PR (public relations) *blitzes* are also used quite extensively by marketers in recent years. There are PR agencies that marketers hire as they would an advertising agency to ensure that particular products get their share of "free" publicity.

For example, Cabbage Patch Kids were introduced with a PR blitz. Kraft also joined the blitz brigade by attempting to PR blitz its bagels at a Kraft-funded party given for members of the press in the hope that the well-wined and -dined journalists would help promote Kraft's new line of bagels nationwide. Efforts were also made by Sandeen, Inc., to popularize *SpinJAMMER,* a novel type of flying disc, through the use of PR blitzes. PR agencies contacted evening "TV magazine" programs, school paper editors, *People* magazine, and other media and gave them press releases about the new *SpinJAMMER.*

So much of what appears in the media as human-interest stories did not get there by chance but, instead, as a result of a glib-tongued PR representative who wined and dined media people who were hungry for human-interest items to present to the curious public. PR representatives, therefore, serve as a bountiful source of "new and different" topics for the media. Critics of PR blitzes, however, say that blitzes merely represent a manipulation of the media and don't truly present useful information or news. They contend that PR blitzes are merely a form of advertising adorned in different garb.

Finally, we come to *event marketing,* or *sponsorship,* which is another controversial sales promotion area. The tobacco and beer industries—big users of event marketing—have been attacked in recent years as a result of the increasingly more restrictive attitudes of the general U.S. public toward smoking and drinking.

For example, laws have been passed banning advertising on TV and radio and preventing beer from being sold in such places as minimarkets situated in gas stations. As a result, the tobacco and beer industries have switched their promotional emphases and are estimated to be involved in 50 percent of the events sponsored by corporations. These events include Philip Morris's sponsorship of Virginia Slims women's tennis tournaments, R. J. Reynolds' sponsorship of the 30-event Winston NASCAR stock car races, and various beer companies' sponsorship of ski races, truck pulls, and rock concerts. In the past, beer companies have even provided free beer in unlimited quantities for college student parties.

Over $1 billion was poured into event marketing in a recent year. However, legislation has been suggested to impose a ban on tobacco company event sponsorship. Organizations such as Mothers Against Drunk Driving (MADD) and Students Against Drunk Driving (SADD) have mobilized to provide pressure against alcoholic products being publicized at public events.

However, supporters of event marketing contend that because of the lack of adequate funding many events that the public enjoys and takes for granted would completely disappear from the face of the earth. And they flaunt the social contribution made by Philip Morris's sponsorship of tennis, which helped to bring women to the forefront of the sport. Women previously received a mere one-tenth of the prize money given to men for similar efforts.

Question

The purpose of sales promotion is to help create a positive public image and desire for products and services. However, as discussed, certain types of sales promotion activities are looked upon with disfavor by some segments of the public. Reexamine Table 16.1. What are your attitudes—both pro and con—toward each of the types of sales promotion summarized in the table?

NOTES

1. Joanne Lipman, "As Network TV Fades, Many Advertisers Try Age-Old Promotions," *The Wall Street Journal,* August 26, 1986, pp. 1, 15.

2. " 'Two-Computer Yuppies' Fuel a New Boom," *Business Week, International Edition,* November 9, 1987, p. 53.

3. Larry Riggs, "Direct Marketing Goes Electronic," *Sales & Marketing Management,* January 14, 1985, pp. 59–60.

4. Ibid.

5. Ibid.

6. For an extensive analysis and report on co-op advertising, see "Pulling Together," *S&MM Special Section/Cooperative Advertising, Sales & Marketing Management,* May 13, 1985, pp. 81–107; and "Cooperative Advertising," *Sales & Marketing Management,* May 1986, pp. 89–113.

7. Joanne Lipman, "As Network TV Fades, Many Advertisers Try Age-Old Promotions," *The Wall Street Journal,* August 26, 1986, pp. 1, 15.

8. Felix Kessler, "The Costly Coupon Craze," *Fortune,* June 9, 1986, pp. 83–84.

9. Kessler, "Coupon Craze."

Planning and Organizing Sales Activities

Next Week I've *Got* to Get Organized!

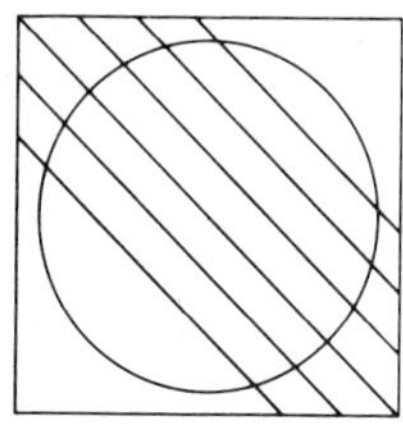

It is not enough to be busy. . . . The question is: what are we busy about?
HENRY DAVID THOREAU

In little more than a decade from now, virtually every marketing decision or plan will pass through your PC. You'll make use of the technology as casually as you now use the telephone.
RESEARCH INSTITUTE OF AMERICA (RIA)

Here's what you should be able to do after studying this chapter:

1. Explain how a salesperson is, in effect, a manager.
2. Understand how computers can assist salespeople in the accomplishment of their goals.
3. Recognize the importance of planning and establishing realistic goals and objectives.
4. Describe a method for systematically analyzing and managing the accounts in your territory.
5. Explain several ways in which salespeople can manage their time more effectively.

Someone once prophesied, "What I am to be, I am now becoming." Think about these words for a moment. How do they relate to you and your life? As you well know, your past experiences have significantly influenced what you are doing today, perhaps even what you are doing at this very moment. But have you given sufficient thought to the fact that everything you do *now* will exert a strong influence over what you do *tomorrow?*

This premise holds true whether we're talking about the end-of-the-month sales results in your territory or long-run aspirations, such as becoming a sales manager or retiring to an exotic South Sea island. Neither a high volume of sales nor an opportunity to become a sales manager nor even a South Sea retirement are likely to come about automatically. Your present activities coupled with realistic goals will determine what you will have achieved at the end of the month, the end of the year, and at some time far in the future.

In this chapter, we explore some of the ways in which you can manage your selling activities more efficiently. Regardless of your occupation, each of your days contains only 24 hours—converting to the metric system won't help to stretch your day one millisecond. So, how you organize your activities within those 24 hours will strongly influence the feelings of accomplishment and satisfaction you derive from your sales position.

THE SALESPERSON AS A MANAGER

In this chapter we shall see how you as a salesperson have a responsibility to manage your time and territory so that you operate with a fair degree of efficiency. We could say that, in a sense, a salesperson is a manager. If you have ever taken a course in the principles of management, you've probably learned that management involves planning, organizing, staffing, directing (motivating), and controlling. Managing, it has been said, is the art of doing.

How is a salesperson a manager?

Think back, if you will, on the many sales activities that we have covered in this text. How can you as a salesperson carry them out effectively? Only by behaving as a manager. Each function taught in a managment course is also performed by salespeople. In effect, salespeople are managers of time, activities, territories, and people.

You can also compare your sales activities with those of a business owner. Both of you have to plan most of your own activities. Usually, no one tells the businessperson when to start in the morning. You, too, are usually on your own, making decisions with little or no guidance from others. No one tells you what time to be on the job, on whom to make your sales calls each day, or precisely what to say to customers. Although your progress is continually measured and evaluated by your sales results, usually no one is watching your daily activities. Salespeople, therefore, must be self-starters, individuals who can work effectively with and through other people. They must be managers of people and activities. And to customers, remember, the salesperson is the company.

A tool that can aid you significantly in managing your time and territory is the computer. Let's look now at some of the principal ways in which computers assist salespeople today in their efforts to become more productive.

COUNTING ON COMPUTERS FOR SALES ASSISTANCE

A revolution of sorts has taken place in the selling field in recent years, a nonviolent one that involves the use of **personal computers (PCs)**—both desktops and portable laptops. Computers are not really new to the organizational world. Their use by salespeople, however *is* relatively new. Yet, it is estimated that by the end of this decade, one of every three laptop personal computers purchased will be for a salesperson versus only one in six that was destined for the sales force in 1986.[1]

". . . it is estimated that by the end of this decade, one of every three laptop personal computers purchased will be for a salesperson. . . ."

The Use of Data Base Management Systems

"You've come a long way from the shoe-shine-and-a-smile days!"

A "hot" buzzword of the 1980s was **data base management systems (DBMS),** a concept that has changed substantially the way modern salespeople function both in the field and in the office. A *DBMS* is a system that allows easy access to large amounts of data stored in a well-organized format.

A DBMS typically consists of both a **centralized data base** (i.e., data stored in a **host computer** at corporate headquarters or regional offices) and a **personal data base** (records and information that salespeople maintain with their own PCs in the field).

"Where did I put that customer order form?"

Until relatively recently, most marketing and sales information was stored in filing cabinets, in binders, in people's minds, on pieces of paper, and even on match book covers! Although to the uninitiated, the concept of DBMS may sound abstruse and complicated, it has actually simplified the lives of many salespeople. DBMS enables salespeople to maintain, combine, and analyze with relative ease large amounts of data related to their sales activities. The data are stored conveniently on **floppy** or **hard disks,** which are small revolving magnetic plates on which information and data are stored.

Today a myriad of computer **software systems** specifically aimed at selling and marketing activities is available. Table 17.1 lists the principal current-day uses of computers in the selling field. Limited space precludes our discussing each in detail. However, the following section explains six of the most important uses of computers, followed by a brief discussion of the principal benefits that computers provide to salespeople.

"2B or not 2B . . . That is the query!"

Prospecting Instead of having to wear out their Reeboks pounding the pavement in hot pursuit of prospects, salespeople can now take advantage of **market analysis software systems (MASS)** that help them locate key customer groups and develop strategies to reach them. Software is available that can be programmed to analyze specific areas or sales territories in terms of prospect characteristics, counties, ZIP Codes, and other relevant data.[2] The system can be programmed to allow **querying,** which is accessing the computer for the purpose of retrieving specific types of information, such as the names of all customers whose purchases have exceeded $100,000 during the previous year. The program may also allow **sorting**—arranging data in a specific order—such as alphabetically or by ZIP Code.

"Good Tandy. Lie down, Tandy. That's a good boy!"

Filing Information The modern salesperson can have the equivalent of a room full of filing cabinets stored in an 8- to 12-pound portable high-tech marvel that can be toted virtually anywhere. In effect, the salesperson can have an "electronic filing cabinet" at his or her knees. Computerized "folders" can be created for each customer or prospect and easily accessed for obtaining historical, or for inputting new, data. An account folder can be brought up to date after a sales call in only minutes when the salesperson returns to his or her car.

Some types of computer-stored information may be available only at the salesperson's regional or corporate office. If so, he or she has **field access** to the host computer, which means that communication can take place between the salesperson's computer in the field and one in the office through the use of a telephone and

TABLE 17.1 Major Uses of Computers in Sales.

General applications
Word processing
Spreadsheet
Data base management
Telemarketing
Specific applications
Prospecting
Filing information
Order entry
Electronic data interchange (EDI)
Checking order status
Recording and reporting financial data
Checking inventory
Preparing forecasts
Planning and scheduling
Territory management
Account management
Reporting sales calls
Analyzing customer requirements
Preparing bids or proposals
Managing sales leads
Electronic mail
Sales force management
Computer-based training

Adapted from John B. Kennedy, "Start With a Data Base," *Sales & Marketing Management,* December 3, 1984; and Thayer C. Taylor, "Marketers and the PC: Steady as She Goes," *Sales & Marketing Management,* August 1986.

a **modem.** A modem, built into many computers, is what enables the transmission of data from one computer to another by telephone.

"This . . . is . . . your . . . com . . . put . . . er . . . speak . . . ing."

Order Entry Another increasingly common use of the computer in sales is for entering customer orders. A standard order entry form can be created and formatted for the computer. It can then be readily accessed when needed merely by hitting a few keys. The program can also be made interactive so that prompts appear on the computer video screen thus guiding the salesperson in making the order entries. The order can then be easily **uploaded** to the host computer of the salesperson's company and quickly processed. Product availability, delivery dates, or other relevant information can then be **downloaded** from the host computer to the salesperson's PC.

Electronic Data Interchange Another buzzword reverberating off the office walls of marketers these days is **electronic data interchange (EDI),** which is a system for transferring purchase orders, invoices, and related transactions between manufacturers and their wholesalers and dealers.[3] EDI is simply computer-to-computer ordering between manufacturers and their distributors. The salesperson is thereby bypassed. Oops! What did we just say? The salesperson . . . *bypassed?* Does this mean the end of salespeople? There are a few prophets of doom who believe so.[4] Many others, however, disagree. They contend that the salesperson's job is making the first sale, whether it is a new account, a new product, or a new service. Computers, the more optimistic soothsayers believe, will merely place follow-up orders.[5]

Nunca!

Checking Order Status A fairly common question that customers ask their vendors is, "What happened to my order?" In the past, trying to trace an order could take hours or even days. Today, however, the salesperson has access to a fast medium. By dialing into a host computer through the modem in his or her personal computer, the salesperson can check on order status and shipment schedules and reassure the customer of the delivery date or, if necessary, provide alternative information. The salesperson can also reserve inventory and place additional orders for the customer at the same time.

Push-pull, click-click!

If in his or her office, the salesperson's computer software can dial a customer automatically and even view the customer's dossier on the screen while talking to the customer.

Financial Recording and Reporting Software is also available that enables salespeople to track auto mileage, auto and selling expenses, and commissions. The programs can also compare commissions to selling expenses by individual account for the purpose of determining how profitable a particular account is.

Imagine being stuck in a traffic jam with nothing productive you could be doing. *Ce n'est pas une problème, monsieur!* If you have a cellular telephone in your car, you can merely plug your portable PC into the telephone, upload your order reports and expenses to your company's host computer, and even receive a downloaded update on the next customer that you are scheduled to see.[6]

"Hey, Mac! Get movin'!"

How Computers Assist Salespeople

The use of computers by sales personnel provides many benefits. Some of the principal ones include providing a ready link with corporate or regional offices, reducing paperwork, increasing sales productivity, and enhancing customer goodwill. Each benefit will be described briefly.

A Link with Corporate or Regional Offices Field access to host computers is a boon to salespeople on the run. Salespeople frequently require information immediately, but sometimes no one at the regional or corporate office is either available or has enough time to obtain the information. In addition, some salespeople are situated in different time zones, and their corporate offices are closed when they need information. For example, when the time is only 2:00 P.M. in San Francisco, it is 5:00

"I'm sorry, but Ms. Info is in a meeting."

P.M. in New York. *¡No problema, señora!* Not anymore, at least, since—as a computer manufacturer's advertising director might say—"You can now access your headquarters for up-to-date information with fingertip ease!" Having such access can save salespeople a considerable amount of time.

Fingertip access!

Reducing Paperwork Paperwork can be readily reduced with the use of computers, For example, standard reporting forms and sales letters can be stored for later retrieval without their having to be retyped. Many **word processing systems,** that is, text-editing programs that allow electronic writing and correcting of material that formerly had to be typewritten, are highly flexible. Mistakes can be corrected with ease, blocks of textual material can be moved or deleted in an instant, special types of printing—for example,

expanded,

boldface

italics,

and

condensed

—can be utilized, and material can be readily exchanged with other software packages, such as data base managers and spreadsheets. Many individuals who have switched to word processing systems argue that they would never again use a typewriter if given the choice. Your author, for example, has not used a typewriter for more than a decade.

Computerphobia is on the wane.

Increasing Sales Productivity Because salespeople with PCs tend to have less paperwork and thus save time through the use of their electronic devices, they are able to spend more time in face-to-face contact with their customers and prospects. Consequently, many firms have found that salespeople with computers tend to have increases in sales productivity up to 25 percent—sometimes even more.[7]

And much, much more!

Enhancing Customer Goodwill Salespeople with computers typically can respond faster to customer or prospect inquiries. Customers generally appreciate a quick turnaround to their questions. Consequently, this faster response time tends to enhance customer goodwill.

"That was good, Will!"

"Many individuals who have switched to word processing systems argue that they would never again use a typewriter if given the choice."

THE NEED FOR PLANNING AND ESTABLISHING GOALS

Goals have considerable psychological value, especially to those in the selling field. They tend not only to be a motivating force, but also to provide us with a certain degree of faith in our futures. In addition, they help give us a sense of direction. And especially important, reaching our goals tends to provide us with feelings of achievement and satisfaction. However, to accomplish our goals and aspirations requires careful planning. Laurence J. Peter, author of *The Peter Principle,* once said, "If you don't know where you are going, you will end up somewhere else." The salesperson who fails to plan may also end up somewhere else, possibly somewhere outside of the selling field!

The Long and the Short of It

Salespeople generally are not closely supervised and, as a result, require a high degree of self-discipline. When things are not going too well or you feel somewhat tired, it's easy to escape into an activity far less demanding than calling on customers. However, your income and career path are directly tied to how effectively you can work without close direction.

Could there be a football game without goals?

Goals tend to have the psychological effect of spurring people on. Effective salespeople don't just go out and get orders; they generally set targets and work toward them. Goals for salespeople typically range in time frames from a "to-do list" for tomorrow to a one-year territorial analysis and forecast. Let's now examine some of the typical types of annual goals.

Annual Sales Goals in Dollars or Units Many salespeople establish their own sales quotas or are assigned them by their managers. Sales quotas are a type of goal typically expressed in *dollar volume* or *number of units* of a product that salespeople are supposed to have sold within a specific period—typically one year. Both dollar and unit goals have their shortcomings, however.

For example, when goals are set solely on the basis of *dollar volume,* there is the tendency for salespeople to promote more expensive items as a means of achieving a higher dollar volume. Furthermore, when sales objectives are expressed in terms of dollar volume, goals are much more easily achieved during periods of rising product prices, which is not particularly a desirable outcome for companies attempting to maximize profits. Goals established on the basis of *units sold,* however, do tend to overcome problems associated with dollar sales volume and price changes.

Unfortunately, goals set solely on a *unit volume basis* have their shortcomings also. There is a tendency for some salespeople to "push" products that are easy to sell at the expense of other equally important items in their product line.

Product Mix Goals As a means of overcoming both dollar volume and unit goal shortcomings, many salespeople are encouraged to establish *product mix goals.*

A product mix goal involves developing unit goals, but, in addition, making a list of all items in a product line and determining individual sales objectives for each product. This method tends to ensure a more balanced distribution of the company's entire product line. An unbalanced distribution may result in losing the opportunity to sell certain items because low sales volume resulted in their being discontinued. Yet, these products may have been potentially important to customers and profitable for the manufacturer.

A balancing act!

Mix it up!

In reality, a salesperson would be wise to establish goals for all three categories, sales by dollar volume, by unit volume, and by product mix. These larger goals should then be broken down into smaller ones that can be achieved on *weekly* and *monthly* bases. Furthermore, it's not satisfactory to evaluate your territory solely at the end of each year to see if your goals have been achieved. Goals should be monitored on a continual basis and activities modified when they are off target. Goals themselves should be modified in cases where they turn out to be unrealistic or unattainable.

Let's now turn to an examination of some of the specific methods for managing your accounts, territory, and time for the purpose of achieving your goals.

"Goals should be monitored on a continual basis and activities modified when they are off target."

MANAGING ACCOUNTS AND TERRITORIES

Every territory is unique. Some territories consist of a large number of high-volume accounts; others have mostly medium or small accounts. Some may cover several states (or even countries); others may consist of only several blocks in the downtown section of a large city. Some have many accounts; others have few. But regardless of the nature, location, and size of your territory, it must be analyzed and managed carefully if you're to extract maximum benefit from it.

Account Analysis

Let's assume that you're a sales representative for a firm called the More Business Records Company and that you've been assigned to a territory consisting of 85 accounts scattered throughout the fictitious state of New Delafornia. Your manager informs you that you should be able to average about five calls a day in your territory. Your main question now is how often you should call on each customer.

What influences the frequency of sales calls?

Since you've been hired to sell, a principal factor influencing how often you call on your established customers would be their *present* and *potential* sales volume. Of course, you should allow for exceptions. Some customers may be large purchasers yet require little attention, while others may be small but demand an inordinate amount of your time. In general, however, the more profitable the account, the more time you are likely to spend with it. But what is your plan for calling on accounts? How should you go about analyzing your accounts? How would you do an **account analysis?**

Let's assume that you classify your 85 accounts by potential annual sales and label them classes AA, A, B, C, and D. These letters, as you can see in Table 17.2, symbolize the potential dollar volume of each category.

After you determine your account classifications based on sales, you then should decide how often each category should be seen per year. As you can see in Table 17.3, you decide that class AA accounts should be seen at least twice a month (24 times per year). Since you have ten class AA accounts, you should plan to make about 240 calls annually on your best accounts (10 accounts × 24 visits each = 240 calls). Remember, though, that this is not a hard and fast rule. Planning flexibility is essential unless you intend to manage your territory like an automaton. Look again at Table 17.3. You can see that you've planned to make 800 sales calls per year. Assuming 240 working days in a year and the ability to make 5 calls per day, you could make 1200 sales calls per year. However, you have wisely allowed for 400 calls for prospecting new accounts.

TABLE 17.2 Account Categories.

Account classification	Potential annual sales	Number of customers
AA	Over $150,000	10
A	$75,000–$150,000	30
B	$25,000–$75,000	25
C	$5,000–$25,000	10
D	Under $5,000	10

TABLE 17.3 Number of Calls by Account Classification.

Account classification	Number of customers	Number of calls on each customer	Total calls by classification (per year)
AA	10	Twice a month	240
A	30	Once a month	360
B	25	Every two months	150
C	10	Every four months	30
D	10	Every six months	20
	85		800

Making Travel More Efficient

What can influence the size of a sales territory?

"Join the Navy and See the World," is an old U.S. Navy slogan. One can also say, "Join Consolidated Technologies' sales force and see the world." Sales representatives employed today by large multinational organizations can have territories ranging in size from a four-square-block downtown area to several countries.

The time spent by salespeople on travel depends to a great extent, of course, on the size of their sales territories. Salespeople in rural areas, for example, typically spend nearly 40 percent of their time in travel, those operating in urban areas between 20 and 25 percent, and those with suburban territories roughly 30 percent. Some sales representatives spend considerable time traveling by airplane or automobile, while others use shoe leather and high-speed elevators in high-rise buildings. Retail selling may require no more traveling than 3 to 5 meters back and forth behind a product display counter.

"The unorganized sales representative will find that time spent on travel is far more costly than necessary."

In addition to territory size, another important influence on the amount of time spent on travel is how well the salesperson organizes and plans travel. You should be aware that most travel is costly and unproductive. You're not generating revenues for your company when you're driving 30 miles to your next appointment. Such costs, however, can be reduced through adequate planning and organizing. Continual reevaluation of your travel activities can help you improve the management of your territory.

How can travel costs be reduced?

You should plan your **itinerary,** or schedule of appointments, in a logical fashion—don't scatter your activities over too wide an area during any given day. You should also attempt to reduce, as much as possible, the distance between calls on customers. Many salespeople firm up each day's plan the night before through the activity called **routing,** which is determining the most effective *pattern* of territory coverage. They carefully route their calls so that they're not backtracking or zig-zagging, and thus wasting valuable time.

Not *here, there, and everywhere!*

As a salesperson, you must coordinate two important, and sometimes conflicting, goals: (1) minimizing travel time between customers and (2) visiting customers at proper intervals. The characteristics of a particular sales territory will significantly influence what sort of pattern is most effective.

A helpful tool for planning is called a **daily call schedule** (see Figures 17.1a and b). This is customarily a pocket-sized card on which you can write the names of customers and prospects whom you plan to visit.

Wherever possible, make appointments in advance, which can save you both travel and waiting time. Instead of taking a chance that buyers will be in their offices, call or send a postcard notifying them of your intended visit. You can reduce wasted travel time this way. Familiarity with the usual flow of traffic can also help. Try to arrange your automobile trips so they don't coincide with rush-hour traffic. The

PLAN YOUR WORK — WORK YOUR PLAN

LIST BELOW CALLS YOU PROPOSE TO MAKE TODAY

DATE

CUSTOMER CALLS

	√	FIRM	PARTY TO SEE	SAMPLES	REMARKS
1					
2					
3					
4					
5					
6					
7					
8					
9					
10					
11					
12					
13					
14					
15					
16					
17					
18					
19					
20					

NEW ACCOUNT CALLS

1				
2				
3				
4				
5				
6				

Figure 17.1a Example of a Daily Call Schedule.

unorganized sales representative will find that time spent in travel is far more costly than necessary.

"Wherever possible, make appointments in advance, which can save you both travel and waiting time."

Planning Sales Calls to Save Time

We discussed the need to evaluate how often you should call on your customers. The next step is to develop a realistic plan related to *when* and *how* you are going to make your sales calls. Well-organized salespeople generally plan their itineraries at least

MEMORANDA	DAILY CALL SCHEDULE

Figure 17.1b Reverse Side of Daily Call Schedule.

two weeks to one month in advance. Tentative plans can be made six months to a year in advance. As you may recall, an itinerary is the salesperson's guide, or traveling plan, for future sales calls.

Daily, Weekly, and Monthly Planning

Of mice and **what?**

Even though you may have given considerable thought to your tentative itinerary, it's essential to have handy, easy-to-use records of your plans. The best made plans of mice and women sometimes go awry due to emergencies that arise, unexpected meetings, or service calls that have to be made. Flexibility is essential to allow for exceptional situations. The documents can be prepared on a computer for ease of editing or can be made into standardized, preprinted forms.

Plans often change out of necessity. It is essential, therefore, that you know in advance what you are going to do tomorrow. A useful tool for planning on a daily basis is a simple **daily organizer** (see Figures 17.2a and b). It is typically made from index paper, printed on both sides, and can be folded in the middle. It can provide you with a handy device for maintaining a daily "to-do" record. It can include phone calls and appointments you have to make, and expenses that you've incurred.

Another tool that you should carry with you is a **pocket-sized appointment book.** This aid provides you with a ready reference to, and record of, appointments and planned activities regardless of where you might be at the moment. Sales expenses that are reimbursable or tax deductible and business mileage can be recorded as they are incurred rather than kept for a short time in your mind and possibly forgotten.

"Eh . . . gosh, Ms. Gomez . . . Eh . . . I . . . really don't know."

Both the daily organizer and the appointment book should be carried with you. If one of your customers, for example, asks you if you are free to meet with her next Wednesday at 9:00 A.M., you can simply take out your pocket daily organizer, turn to next Wednesday's date, and see at a glance if you're available.

Figure 17.2a Example of Front Side of a Pocket-Sized Daily Organizer.

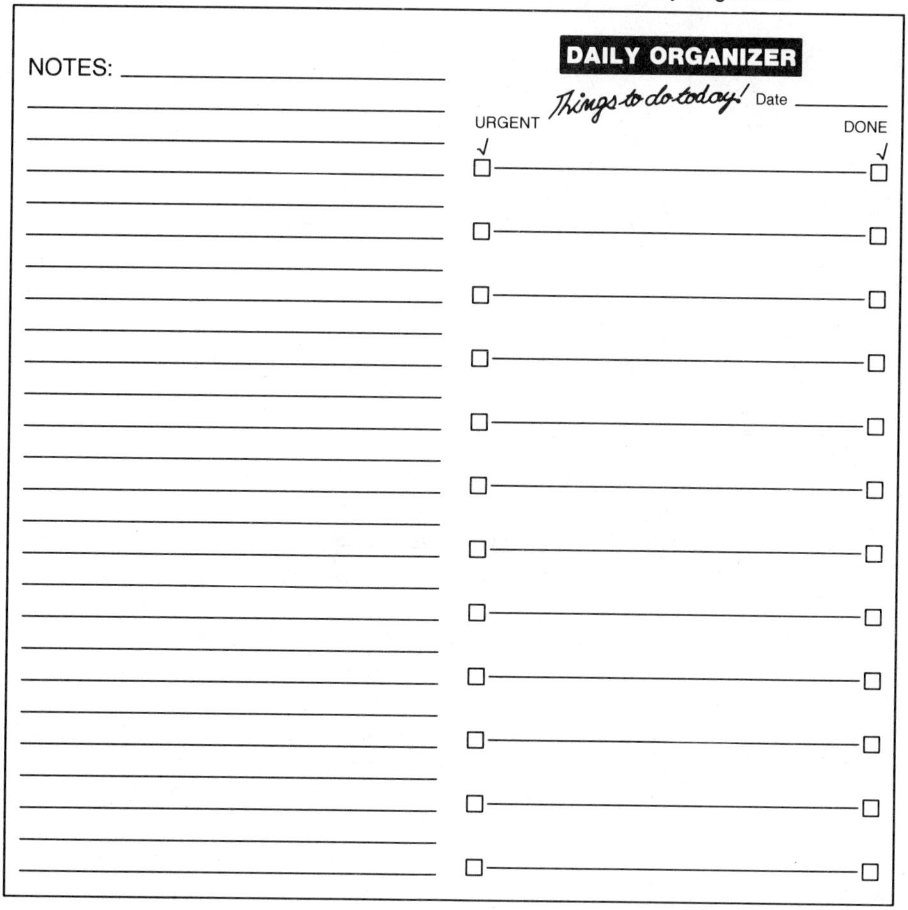

NOTES: ____________

DAILY ORGANIZER

Things to do today! Date ______

URGENT √ ☐ ____________ ☐ √ DONE

APPOINTMENTS

Morning:

Lunch:

Afternoon:

Evening:

PHONE CALLS

URGENT ✓	Name	Phone No.	DONE ✓
☐			☐
☐			☐
☐			☐
☐			☐
☐			☐
☐			☐
☐			☐
☐			☐
☐			☐
☐			☐
☐			☐
☐			☐
☐			☐
☐			☐
☐			☐
☐			☐
☐			☐

DAILY EXPENSES

Figure 17.2b Example of Reverse Side of a Pocket-Sized Daily Organizer.

Most salespeople have to plan many of their activities at least a month in advance—often longer. A useful form that provides you with an overview of your schedule for an entire month is a **monthly planner** (see Figure 17.3). This tool is also helpful in giving you a better sense of direction and organization.

Each Sales Call Should Be Planned

Do you know who decides?

Another method to avoid wasting time is to plan each sales call carefully. Have you determined in advance *who makes the buying decision?* Calling on the wrong person can be a real time waster. You might assume, for example, that the purchasing manager makes all of the purchasing decisions. But often this isn't the case. A production manager, administrative manager, or even an assistant to a manager may be the key individual in determining a purchase. Knowing in advance who has buying authority as well as when they can be seen can be a substantial time saver.

Plan for the Month ______________________

Name ______________________

Sunday	Monday	Tuesday	Wednesday	Thursday	Friday	Saturday
	Town	Town	Town	Town	Town	
Sunday	Monday	Tuesday	Wednesday	Thursday	Friday	Saturday
	Town	Town	Town	Town	Town	
Sunday	Monday	Tuesday	Wednesday	Thursday	Friday	Saturday
	Town	Town	Town	Town	Town	
Sunday	Monday	Tuesday	Wednesday	Thursday	Friday	Saturday
	Town	Town	Town	Town	Town	
Sunday	Monday	Tuesday	Wednesday	Thursday	Friday	Saturday
	Town	Town	Town	Town	Town	
Sunday	Monday					
	Town					

1. Number the days.
2. Complete for each day.
3. If you intend to stay overnight indicate the town.

Figure 17.3 Example of a Monthly Planner.

Analyzing a customer's needs in advance of a call can save you time. The more you know about the customer's operations and activities before your interview, the less time you have to spend probing for information.

"The best made plans of mice and women sometimes go awry due to emergencies that arise, unexpected meetings, or service calls that have to be made."

Develop a Sales-Call Planner

Don't consider the effort spent on planning and organizing a waste of your time. Such activities actually enable you to utilize your available sales time more effectively. Many salespeople have discovered that planning a specific sales-call strategy can be an excellent way to maximize selling efforts. You might develop a **sales-call planner** or worksheet similar to the one illustrated in Figure 17.4 to help you develop your sales-call strategy.

Sales-Call Planner

Name of firm ____________________
Person with purchasing authority __________ Title __________

1. What do I want to accomplish from this call?
2. How can the prospect influence my sales objectives?
3. What are the prospect's needs, wants, or problems that I should be concerned with?
4. How can my product satisfy the prospect's needs or resolve his or her problems?
5. What evidence can I present to substantiate my claims?
6. What objections do I foresee?
7. Have I carefully answered item 1? Do I know specifically what I expect from this call?

Figure 17.4 An Aid for Planning Sales Calls.

Make a Time-Waste Inventory

Often we get so bogged down with the routine of our jobs that we don't even take time to think about how we might be wasting time. The education and training department of the 3M Company suggests that its sales representatives periodically examine some of the areas that might limit their effective utilization of time. 3M has developed a checklist that can help reveal a salesperson's weaknesses and thus, it is hoped, put the salesperson in a much better position to build on the strengths. Sharpen your pencil and turn to Figure 17.5 to make your own **time-waste inventory.** Answer the questions honestly. If you answer any of the questions yes, then there is undoubtedly room for improvement in how you manage your time.

Postcall Analysis

Each sales call should be evaluated as soon as possible after it has been made, especially before relevant details have faded from your memory. A **postcall analysis** isn't like closing the barndoor after the horse has escaped. Instead, it's more like finding the horse and planning how to prevent it from escaping a second time.

A sales-call analysis can serve as a record of what was discussed during your interview, what customer needs were uncovered, what objections were raised, and what your plans are for following up. This activity can save time during your next call. You saw one type of postcall analysis form illustrated in Figure 13.2. Another sample form with a different type of format is given in Figure 17.6.

MANAGING TIME AND ACTIVITIES

Is it time, or its careful utilization, that is scarce?

It is often said that we don't have enough time, that there just aren't enough hours in the day. Time does seem scarce, especially for those in responsible selling jobs. But is it really true that we don't have enough time, or could it be that we don't make effective use of the time we do have? Arthur Brisbane seemed to be on the right track when he said: "Time is the one thing we possess. Our success depends upon the use of our time and its by-product, the odd moment." A major problem for many sales personnel is their inefficient use of that valuable commodity, time. They operate more by instinct than by design. What they really need to do is plan their activities. But before salespeople develop sound plans for the future, they should first try to analyze where they've been in the past.

Where Do the Days Go?

Let's continue with our assumption that you are a fairly typical sales representative for the More Business Records Company. You recently completed an evening course in selling at a nearby college and have decided to apply some of your recently acquired knowledge. One of the topics covered was salespeople's need to account for

Place a check mark in the space that best answers the following questions:

		Yes	No
1.	Do I spend an excessive amount of time at my office or home in the morning?	_____	_____
2.	Could I reduce the time spent waiting for interviews by making appointments in advance?	_____	_____
3.	Am I making too many calls that do not result in interviews simply because I do not have an appointment or have not learned in advance through a phone call that my prospect will be out or busy?	_____	_____
4.	When forced to wait for interviews, do I usually overlook the opportunity to make the time productive by reading, writing, planning, making out reports, or at least thinking about something related to my work?	_____	_____
5.	Am I guilty of staying too long on interviews or engaging in too much general conversation?	_____	_____
6.	Do I take too many breaks in my work, such as stopping for coffee and shopping?	_____	_____
7.	Do I take too much time for lunch?	_____	_____
8.	Do I sometimes overlook the chance to talk to prospects at all possible times they are accessible, including before 8 A.M. and after 5 P.M., Saturdays, and the days preceding and following holidays?	_____	_____
9.	Do I make too many calls on friends or other individuals who are not likely to help me in accomplishing my sales objectives?	_____	_____
10.	Do I make personal visits for canvassing purposes when it could be handled just as effectively by phone?	_____	_____
11.	Do I make personal visits on customers when my objectives could be accomplished just as effectively by phone?	_____	_____
12.	Do I waste time trying to decide what to do next?	_____	_____
13.	Do I waste time trying to decide whom to see or call?	_____	_____
14.	Am I traveling more miles than I would if I planned my sales calls?	_____	_____
15.	Are my reports and letters longer than necessary?	_____	_____
16.	Have I overlooked developing well-defined objectives that have been jointly agreed upon with my manager?	_____	_____

Figure 17.5 Checklist for Making a Time-Waste Inventory.

Customer information:	Sales call method:
	☐ Telephone
Company ________________	☐ Sales meeting
Division ________________	☐ ________________
Name ________________	If new contact:
Title ________________	Source, if new prospect:
Address ________________	☐ Cold call
City/state ________________	☐ Advertising lead
Telephone ________________	☐ Customer request
Date time ________________	☐ Referral
Product/service ________________	Details ________________
________________	________________
Objective of sales call:	________________
________________	Benefits accepted:
________________	________________
Present at meeting:	________________
________________	________________
________________	Outcome/action planned:
Needs expressed:	________________
________________	________________
________________	________________
________________	
Objections/answers:	
________________	
________________	
________________	

Next activity:	Letter	Telephone	Sales call
When:			
Estimated dollar sales:			
Estimated closing date:			

Figure 17.6 Sample Postcall Analysis Form.

their time. The idea seems reasonable, so you decide to start keeping an accurate record of the time spent on your daily activities.

Each of your workdays varies somewhat from the next. Some days require substantial travel. Others require numerous service calls. Some require entertaining customers. At the end of most days you generally have reports to prepare. At times you feel that you should be called a busywork rep, not a sales rep, since you hardly have any time left for selling after you take care of all the nonselling activities expected of you.

You decide, though, that you can't lose sight of your major responsibility—selling your products to customers. One of your prime concerns, therefore, is finding

How can you increase selling time?

ways to increase the time available for face-to-face selling. If only you could manage your time in a more efficient manner. An analysis of your daily activities over a period of time, you conclude, will help you see at a glance specifically what you've done with your time. You then will be able to see if you're spending a disproportionate amount of time on activities other than selling.

Here is what you do. You purchase a small notebook to carry with you and start keeping a log of your activities. You break down your activities into five major categories:

1. Traveling and waiting
2. Service calls
3. Paperwork and meetings
4. Telephone selling
5. Face-to-face selling

Activities Summary Log

At the end of the working day you enter the total hours spent on each of the five categories in an **activities summary log** (see Figure 17.7). At the end of your first week, you add the totals of each activity and can now readily see where your time has been spent.

You note from the activities summary log that you are spending 38 percent of your time traveling and waiting, 7 percent servicing accounts, 22 percent on paper-

	Traveling and Waiting	Service Calls	Paperwork and Meetings	Telephone Selling	Face-to-Face Selling
Monday	3 hrs 40 min	35 min	2 hrs	40 min	1 hr 5 min
Tuesday	3 hrs 25 min	20 min	1 hr 45 min	1 hr	1 hr 30 min
Wednesday	3 hrs 30 min	—	1 hr 30 min	1 hr 20 min	1 hr 40 min
Thursday	2 hrs 5 min	20 min	1 hr 30 min	1 hr 20 min	2 hrs 40 min
Friday	2 hrs 30 min	1 hr 15 min	2 hrs 15 min	40 min	1 hr 20 min
Totals	**15 hrs 15 min**	**2 hrs 30 min**	**9 hrs**	**5 hrs**	**8 hrs 15 min**
Av./day	3 hrs 3 min	30 min	1 hr 48 min	1 hr	1 hr 39 min
Percentage	**38**	**7**	**22**	**12**	**21**

Figure 17.7 Activities Summary Log.

work and attending meetings, 16 percent in selling customers and prospects by telephone, and 27 percent in face-to-face selling activities. Your eyes open wide with amazement and you exclaim: "This can't be true! I'm spending 22 percent of my time on paperwork and attending meetings and 38 percent of it on travel and waiting. Why, that's 60 percent of my time spent solely on those *nonselling* activities!"

Now is the time for careful analysis and for you to answer some important questions. Are you necessarily working at optimum efficiency? This doesn't mean "busting your back" running helter-skelter from one account to another until you drop from physical and mental exhaustion. But couldn't it mean that with slightly better planning you might be able to reduce the amount of time spent on travel, waiting, and even paperwork?

How can careful planning save you time?

How about your paperwork? It can be a big stealer of time. Try to avoid handling paper more than once. For example, if you've just opened and read an incoming letter that requires a response, rather than putting it aside for an additional handling later, you could prepare your answer immediately, thus saving you some valuable time. You can save even more time by using the incoming letter for your response, rather than writing a new one. Merely jot down your response on the incoming letter and send it back. If you need a copy for your files, you could make a photocopy of the original letter.

Sometimes it's not even necessary for you to write a letter of response to an incoming letter or memo. A short telephone call could accomplish the same as a letter in less time.

Keeping your letters and memos short and simple can also save you time. Try to restrict your letters or memos to no more than one page, which is usually ample for most messages. Furthermore, the use of computer systems that are able to retrieve already prepared formats and documents can also save you paperwork time, as we've already seen in an earlier section of this chapter.

You can see from the log that you're spending more time on traveling and waiting than on face-to-face selling with your customers. Is there any way you might organize your appointments so that you spend *less* time traveling and waiting and *more* time selling? Do many of your customers keep you waiting longer than ten minutes? If so, how might you avoid long waits?

Small savings of time each day can add up to large amounts over long periods. For example, assume that through more effective time and territory management you reduce your travel and waiting time. You lop off 2 percent from travel and waiting time and 4 percent from paperwork activities. This 6 percent may not seem like much, but let's analyze how significant it really is: *You have increased the time available for selling by nearly one-half an hour in each eight-hour day.* Adding a half hour to your daily selling time could result in an *additional 120 hours of extra personal selling time per year,* assuming about 240 working days per year (after deducting Sundays, holidays, vacations, and sick leave). Can you see the importance of this? You have added roughly *fifteen workdays*—three five-day work weeks—to your sales activity. Can you imagine how this extra selling time could affect your sales record? And isn't it your sales record that influences your future income and promotional opportunities?

A minute saved is hours earned.

How to Save a Dollar and Lose a Sale

Rep: Boss, I saved us a buck!
Mgr.: Great, how much did it cost?
Rep: Oops! $1000.

Salespeople should manage their expenses carefully. Sometimes, however, the frugal salesperson, in order to save a few dollars, may actually lose a few thousand. Here's an example: Parking fees, like most everything else, have risen over the years. Some salespeople hate to part with the relatively small amount of money typically charged by parking lots and garages. Instead, they may drive around town for 20 minutes looking for a free spot or an available parking meter space. Sometimes they find that they then have to walk an additional 10 minutes or so to get to the customer's office. If delayed in an account's office, the salesperson then becomes fidgety worrying about the parking meter time expiring. So, after being frustrated by not finding a parking space immediately and then worrying about an expired meter, the salesperson is not likely to be in top form when meeting the prospect.

Fifteen minutes may not seem like a lot of time, but consider how 15 minutes wasted here and another 15 minutes wasted there can add up over a period of a year. Consider too the number of sales that may be lost by trying to save a few dollars.

Why Wait When You Have to Wait?

A waiters' conspiracy?

Customers make you wait; dentists and doctors make you wait; post office personnel make you wait; automobile repair firms make you wait; even gas stations make you wait. Everybody seems to make you wait—it's almost like a conspiracy!

Waiting seems to be a basic part of living and working, but it also can be a substantial waste of our time. If you, on the average, spend 45 minutes of each day idly waiting for something, you have allowed 270 of your hours in a year to melt away into oblivion.

You have to weigh the merits versus the disadvantages of waiting for a specific customer. If it is an important and valuable account, you may be willing to wait somewhat longer than for one with little potential. On the other hand, some salespeople refuse to wait for anyone longer than 10 or 15 minutes. Instead, they check with the receptionist to find out when the customer will be available. If the wait seems like it will continue, they then politely inform the receptionist that they must leave and try to arrange for a more convenient appointment later.

How might you utilize waiting time?

Waiting can sometimes be a blessing in disguise though. Most salespeople have a lot of routine paperwork to prepare. Instead of complaining about how many forms you have to fill out each evening on your own time, why not do what you can while you're waiting. Review the quote by Arthur Brisbane at the beginning of this section and see how his words can relate to the problem of waiting.

Why Just Drive When You Have to Drive?

Driving a car for many people used to be a lot of fun. Today, with so many excessively clogged highways and byways, driving is more of an unpleasant chore than a pleasure, even when driving an expensive car. And for some salespeople, driving can cut drastically into their productive face-to-face selling time.

Well, then, why just drive when you have to drive? We've already suggested what you can do with your cellular phone and laptop computer if caught in traffic jams. However, what about those times when you're "fortunate" enough to be able to cruise right along on the turnpike, expressway, or freeway at a "brisk" 15 miles an hour—or even faster? How can you utilize that time? Why not have a cassette player in your car and become better educated while driving between sales calls? There are many training cassettes now available that can provide much useful information. Or have you always wanted to *habla Español* or *parle Français?* You might be amazed at how much of a foreign language you can learn in six months listening for only one-half hour per day to a language tape.

***"I don't care what the book said. Keep your eyes* on the road!"**

Another way to utilize travel time is to plan future activities. There are many quality pocket-sized microcassette recorders available into which you can conveniently dictate your thoughts.

Maintaining Records and Preparing Reports

"Paperwork, paperwork, how in heck do they expect me to get any selling done with all these confounded reports I have to prepare! Gads, they call me a sales rep, but I hardly have any time for selling after I take care of all the other busywork they expect me to do."

What is your reaction to these words? Salespeople with attitudes like the one expressed often create miserable situations for themselves. Their problems are usually caused by their lack of awareness that a salesperson's duties and responsibilities include far more than personal, face-to-face selling. One of these key responsibilities is preparing reports. Many ambitious salespersons feel that time spent on preparing reports and maintaining records is time lost to personal selling—and they're right! But, one of the favorable offshoots of report preparation is that it may result in more effective selling activities. To the person who likes interacting with other individuals but dreads paperwork, report preparation may seem like drudgery. An understanding of the purpose of reports, however, tends to make their preparation more endurable.

So now I'm a bookkeeper?

Why is report preparation essential?

In a nutshell, the major purpose of report preparation and record keeping is to enable both you and your company to operate more efficiently. Reports are frequently the main form of contact that managers have with their sales forces. The records and reports that sales personnel keep often influence production schedules, hiring policies, and plans for expansion of plant capacity. Records can be analyzed to see if certain customers should be discontinued because the costs of servicing exceed profitability. Records also help determine the profitability of specific lines of products.

Some salespeople are flooded with forms and reports they're expected to maintain. Of course, no record should be kept solely for the sake of keeping a record; *it should serve a useful purpose.* If you are in doubt as to the usefulness of a form, ask why it is used. One salesperson for a large toy manufacturing company complained bitterly to his friends for months about the many reports he had to mail to the division office daily. He felt that some of the forms were asking for the same information. Finally, instead of complaining, he asked his manager why the reports were required. His manager said, "No particular reason other than we've always used those forms. Come to think of it, you've asked a good question. Let me work on it for a while." The manager did, and the number of reports was reduced by 50 percent.

SUMMARY

Salespeople, in a sense, are managers. They must manage their sales activities and time in a professional and creative way to achieve their goals. A tool that an increasing number of salespeople use today to assist them in the management of their activities is the computer. Much of the burdensome paperwork of the past can be performed with relative ease by those familiar with computers and related software.

Salespeople should plan and establish goals, activities that help to motivate and give them a sense of direction.

Estimates indicate that most salespeople spend only about one-third of their time selling. The rest is spent on such activities as traveling, waiting, service calls, paperwork, and attending sales meetings. As a salesperson, you are likely to find that many of your potential frustrations are eased if you are aware of this. Did you notice the phrase "potential frustrations are eased"? Your potential frustrations won't be significantly reduced or eliminated, nor will you be a productive and successful salesperson over the long run, unless you utilize effective planning and organizing tools similar to those discussed in the text.

Costs per sales call have skyrocketed over the past two decades. In today's organizations, there is little room for the salesperson who lacks self-motivation. And a salesperson who does not plan and organize is likely to have mediocre results. As one anonymous sales philosopher has warned:

Failing to prepare,
you are preparing to fail.

KEY TERMS

personal computers (PCs)
data base management systems (DBMS)
centralized data base
host computer
personal data base
floppy disks
hard disks
software systems
market analysis software systems (MASS)
querying
sorting
field access
modem
uploaded
downloaded
electronic data interchange (EDI)
word processing systems
account analysis
itinerary
routing
daily call schedule
daily organizer
pocket-sized appointment book
monthly planner
sales-call planner
time-waste inventory
postcall analysis
activities summary log

QUESTIONS

1. In what ways is a sales job similar to a managerial position? In what ways do you feel it is different?
2. What is a *data base management system* (DBMS)? How can it aid sales people?
3. What is meant by the expression "electronic filing cabinet"?
4. Do you feel that *electronic data interchange* (EDI) will ultimately result in the decline in the need for salespeople? Why or why not?
5. What are the four ways discussed in the text in which computers can assist salespeople?
6. What are some shortcomings of annual goals established solely in terms of either dollar volume *or* in terms of units sold? How can these shortcomings be overcome?
7. What is your opinion of goals established on the basis of *product mix?*
8. What influences the amount of time a salesperson spends on travel? How might a salesperson reduce the high costs of travel and transportation?
9. What is the significance of the activity of *routing* to the salesperson?
10. What is the purpose of a *daily call schedule?*
11. What is a major purpose of an *activities summary log.*
12. If you've made a thorough weekly plan of sales activities, is it also necessary to plan on a daily basis? Explain.
13. In what ways can a *postcall analysis* assist you in subsequent sales activities? When should it be prepared? Explain.
14. Explain the following statement: "Waiting to see customers can sometimes be a blessing in disguise."
15. Would you agree with the attitude that time spent on travel by salespeople is a complete waste of time? Explain.
16. Salespeople, it is said, typically dread paperwork, such as preparing reports. Why should you attempt to convince yourself that adequate record keeping, along with prompt preparation and submission of reports, is essential for efficient territorial management? If you were a sales manager, how could you convince your sales staff of the same thing?

APPLICATIONS

17.1 MAKING PLANS FOR MY FUTURE

The activity of planning can help to give you a sense of direction and purpose. Accomplishing your plans can give you a sense of accomplishment and fulfillment.

The lack of planning creates uncertainty, and uncertainty tends to create stress. Consequently, one way to reduce stress caused by uncertainty is to reduce, as much as possible, the causes of uncertainty. A better understanding of yourself—your weaknesses and your strengths—as well as your future aspirations can give you improved feelings of direction and self-worth. Here's an opportunity for you to think about your present self and make some specific plans for the future.

Instructions

Indicate in the spaces provided the adjectives that best describe your *weaknesses* and *strengths.*

Self-description

Weaknesses	Strengths
1. ______________	1. ______________
2. ______________	2. ______________
3. ______________	3. ______________
4. ______________	4. ______________
5. ______________	5. ______________
6. ______________	6. ______________
7. ______________	7. ______________
8. ______________	8. ______________
9. ______________	9. ______________
10. ______________	10. ______________
11. ______________	11. ______________
12. ______________	12. ______________
13. ______________	13. ______________
14. ______________	14. ______________
15. ______________	15. ______________

In the spaces provided next, indicate in the *first column* where you would like to be five years from now. Indicate in the *second column* the specific reasons why your five-year objectives have not yet been achieved; that is, what are the obstacles currently blocking the achievement of your objectives? In the *third column,* make *general statements* regarding how you intend to overcome your obstacles. In the *last column,* make *specific statements* regarding how you

My Five-Year Plan

Where I want to be five years from now	Obstacles to achieving my objectives	General plans for overcoming my obstacles	Specific plans for overcoming my obstacles
1. Type of job I want to hold: ______	1. ______	1. ______	1. ______
2. Type of industry I want to work in: ______	2. ______	2. ______	2. ______
3. Geographical location where I prefer to work: ______	3. ______	3. ______	3. ______
4. Types of job-related responsibilities I want: ______	4. ______	4. ______	4. ______
5. Types of personal and family responsibilities I want: ______	5. ______	5. ______	5. ______
6. Material possessions I desire: ______	6. ______	6. ______	6. ______

Adapted from Stan Kossen, *Supervision: A Practical Guide to First-Line Management* (New York: Harper & Row, 1981), pp. 161–162.

will overcome your obstacles. Be certain to recognize both your strengths and weaknesses in establishing your goals and determining your plans.

17.2 YOUR WEEK'S ACTIVITIES

Prepare and maintain for one week an activities summary log related to your sales territory; then analyze how you might increase your face-to-face selling time in the future.

17.3 PLANNING SALES CALLS

Assume that you are a sales representative for a computer manufacturer and are planning to make a sales call on a purchaser for a large insurance company. Complete the sales-call planner in Figure 17.4 and explain why you answered the questions as you did.

17.4 TIME IS TOO SCARCE TO WASTE

If you currently are a salesperson, fill out the time-waste inventory in Figure 17.5 and critically evaluate your responses.

17.5 I'M SORRY I ASKED!

Informal small talk about a customer's interests is often a good way to "warm up" a sales interview. Assume that you once showed an interest in the coin collection of Nat Numismati, one of your customers. Since then, everytime you make a sales call, Nat seems to want to talk endlessly about his hobby. You want to be courteous, but you have other things to do besides fondle old coins during your visit with Nat.

Question

How would you handle this situation?

NOTES

1. "Have Laptop, Will Sell," *Sales & Marketing Management,* October 1986, p. 26; and "Don't Leave Home Without One," *Time, International Edition,* April 18, 1988, p. 33.
2. Thayer C. Taylor, "Marketers and the PC: Steady as She Goes," *Sales & Marketing Management,* August 1986, pp. 53–55.

3. "An Electronic Pipeline That's Changing the Way America Does Business," *Business Week,* August 3, 1987, pp. 80, 82.

4. "Death of the Sales Force?" *Sales & Marketing Management,* July 2, 1984, p. 124.

5. "John Diebold on PCs in Marketing: The Best Is Yet to Come," *Sales & Marketing Management,* July 1987, p. 40–45.

6. "Hewlett-Packard Creates Computerized Sales Force," *Sales & Marketing Management,* July 2, 1984, p. 124.

7. "Laptops and the Sales Force: New Star in the Sky," *Sales & Marketing Management,* April 1987, pp. 50–55.

APPENDIXES SPECIALIZED AREAS OF SELLING

14 The Essentials of Retail Selling

THE CHANGING FACE OF RETAILING

The Evolution of Department Stores ■ Challenges to Traditional Department Stores ■ So . . . Are Retail Salespeople Necessary or Not?

RESPONSIBILITIES AND OPPORTUNITIES FOR RETAIL SALESPEOPLE

Typical Responsibilities and Duties of Retail Salespeople ■ A Route to Other Opportunities?

PROSPECTING AND THE APPROACH

Avoid an Overagressive Manner ■ Avoid Overused Phrases

MAKING THE RETAIL SALES PRESENTATION

Demonstrations ■ Out-of-Stock Items ■ Trading Up or Down ■ Look for Add-on Opportunities ■ Handling Objections ■ Closing the Sale ■ Give a Choice

POSTSALE SERVICE

Remain Courteous After the Sale ■ And If You Don't Make the Sale?

"Retail selling is a misnomer. Retail selling doesn't even exist; it's dead. In fact, customers are presold by advertising and serve themselves in today's retail stores. Person-to-person selling isn't really necessary anymore."

Comments like these—believed by some but doubted by many—sound as though the obituary for retail selling has already been written. But is retail selling actually dead, or—more realistically—is it merely different? We can hardly deny that there have been substantial changes in the area of retailing in recent decades. In this special section, we'll briefly examine some of the key changes that have taken place in retail selling during recent decades. We'll also focus on some of the main techniques that many retail salespeople currently use to sell their goods.

THE CHANGING FACE OF RETAILING

We've just implied that retail selling hasn't irrevocably been laid to rest; it's merely changed in many respects. An indication that the field is still alive and kicking can be found in recent statistics. According to the U.S. Department of Commerce, retail sales more than doubled in a recent ten-year period. A large proportion of all sales positions—about 50 percent—fall into the retail selling category.

The Evolution of Department Stores

Having first evolved in the 1800s, the department store developed as a retail outlet where consumers could purchase a wide variety of products under one roof. It wasn't until the early 1950s that retailing began its move to the suburbs, a trend that accelerated during the 1960s and continues unabated today. Prior to the early 1950s, one rarely saw a giant suburban shopping mall of the kind that is so common today, with retail establishments of all varieties and sizes. Once situated only at downtown locations, many department stores have evolved into regional chains.

Challenges to Traditional Department Stores

Traditional department stores today are challenged from all sides. For example discount stores, mail order retailing, and buying clubs have made significant inroads in retailing. Videotex and videodisc kiosks, discussed in Chapter 16, are also trying their best to nibble away at the more traditional methods of retailing. A variety of products other than cigarettes and bubble gum are now being dispensed through vending machines.

Department stores haven't accepted all this competition passively; they've responded in kind with extensive promotions and by dispersing their advertising among newspapers, radio, and television. Department stores, too, now utilize direct mail catalogs and make use of telemarketing. In order to reduce costs, they have also responded to their competition by moving more in the direction of self-service. Montgomery Ward and Sears, for example, in an effort to cut millions of dollars from their payrolls, have switched to "area cashiering," in which cash registers are placed in a few locations rather than in each department. This change reduces the number of salespeople needed on each floor.

So . . . Are Retail Salespeople Necessary or Not?

Two schools of thought have emerged as to whether or not the consumer really wants the assistance that salespeople can offer. Some observers argue that *service* is defined by the customer as "the ability to get what I want and get it quickly, not having a salesperson wait on me." They contend that advertising presells most consumer products, thereby eliminating the need for skilled salespeople. Order-taking clerks, it is argued, can do the job amply.

Although many products *are* presold, other retailers are bucking the trend toward little or no service. For example, Nordstrom's, a Seattle-based retail chain, has been extremely successful by targeting the more affluent, "upscale," market, appealing to certain consumers' desires for higher quality and more, somewhat pampered, forms of service. Nordstrom's employees are trained that service to the store's customers is one of their most important responsibilities. Many consumers apparently are willing to pay nondiscounted prices for this added service, since the formula seems to be working fairly well for Nordstrom's.

RESPONSIBILITIES AND OPPORTUNITIES FOR RETAIL SALESPEOPLE

Regardless of the many changes that have taken place, there still remains a dire need for highly qualified retail sales personnel. Merely think back for a moment to the many times that you've shopped in plant nurseries, stereo equipment stores, computer stores, hardware stores, shoe stores, and many other types of retail outlets. Didn't you find that you frequently needed the assistance of a qualified salesperson to answer certain types of questions? The opportunities for qualified retail salespeople are still numerous.

Retail sales workers have continual contact with the public and must learn to respond promptly and courteously to the needs of prospective customers. Retail salespeople also have a wide variety of responsibilities and duties.

Typical Responsibilities and Duties of Retail Salespeople

In addition to writing up orders, suggesting additional purchases, and handling customer complaints, retail sales workers are usually expected to ensure that display counters are in proper order and that stocks are replenished as needed. They may also be concerned with the security of the store and attempt to devise means to prevent pilferage and theft of goods. Some retail salespeople also have the responsibility for ordering and buying, promoting new and seasonal merchandise, and even doing office work. Retail selling jobs vary significantly, depending on the marketing philosophy of the store managers. And, as we've already noted, some outlets are virtually self-service and may have few or even no clerks who actually perform selling activities.

A Route to Other Opportunities?

Many retail sales workers have found that their work experience has helped them to move up to more responsible jobs, such as assistant manager or manager. Retail selling experience also helps to provide the background necessary to start one's own retail establishment. Sometimes retail selling experience opens up other opportunities in selling. For example, GWG Limited, a large Canadian apparel manufacturer, has followed the practice of recruiting only individuals with prior retail sales experience for its field marketing sales positions.

Although many of the concepts already covered in this text apply also to retailing, there are some aspects of selling that relate especially to retail selling. Let's now examine some of these significant factors.

PROSPECTING AND THE APPROACH

Some retail sales workers creatively prospect for prospects by maintaining files on their regular customers and contacting them with information on special events or about new lines of articles that have recently arrived at the store. Automobile salespeople, too, often use specialized prospecting techniques. In general, however, most retail salespeople, unlike field sales representatives, are not involved with prospecting to a great extent. The approach, therefore, is usually the first step in the selling process for retail salespeople.

Avoid an Overaggressive Manner

Your approach is especially important in retail selling. Some retail sales workers tend to "scare off" prospects by approaching them too aggressively. It's critical for you to develop an approach that shows a supporting interest in the customer's needs but doesn't come across as being "pushy." Try to display genuine concern for your customers. Attempt to understand their possible anxieties about making certain types of purchases. Build up their egos whenever possible.

Avoid Overused Phrases

Try to avoid tired and worn phrases like "May I help you?" Doing so makes it too easy for the customer to say, "No thanks, I'm just looking." If you remain with the customer after such a negative response, you could make the customer feel somewhat uncomfortable.

A better approach is to say something more suggestive like, "Good morning. What size are you looking for?" Be certain to remain on the lookout for buying signals, either expressed in body language or in positive statements or questions about the product. Ask probing questions in a courteous manner in order to uncover the customer's needs. For example, a person selling electronic sound systems might ask something like, "Would you be likely to need a remote-control device when operating the equipment?"

Learn to distinguish the mere "lookers" from the hot prospects. Lookers tend to wander aimlessly around the store, usually trying to avoid contact with sales workers. The looker is more likely to be a real prospect after he or she starts to concentrate on a particular item in stock. Of course, be courteous to anyone who comes into your store.

MAKING THE RETAIL SALES PRESENTATION

Sales presentations on a retail level are actually not substantially different from many of the illustrations already cited in this text. As with any selling, you should avoid talking *only* about product features. Instead, you should relate the product's features, advantages, and benefits to the needs, desires, or problems of the potential customer. Remember to focus on what is important to the customer rather than on what you personally prefer.

Demonstrations

Demonstrate the product whenever possible, since this will tend to add impact to your presentation. Also, utilize the customer's senses if the product lends itself to such an activity. For example, you can ask the customer to touch a fabric to stress its quality or softness; to smell a perfume or after-shave lotion to emphasize scent; or to listen to a prerecorded audiotape through different sound systems to demonstrate and compare fidelity.

Out-of-Stock Items

In some instances, a person comes in for an item that is temporarily out of stock. Look for opportunities to provide substitute items. Sometimes an effective goodwill builder may be to recommend a competing source of the out-of-stock item. Even better, if possible, is to have the item transferred from one of your branch locations or delivered directly to your customer.

Trading Up or Down

"Trade ups" or "trade downs" may also be advisable in certain instances. For example, you may discover, after probing for needs, that the customer could benefit from acquiring a more elaborate model or more expensive style. Be careful when trading up a customer. At a later time the customer may feel that he or she was pressured into spending too much money.

Trading down can occur when you discover that the customer can't afford or doesn't need the more expensive or elaborate item. Some salespeople prefer to start at the top of the product line. Their assumption is that customers will settle on something better and more expensive than if a sales presentation begins with a more moderately priced product.

Look for Add-on Opportunities

Also, be continually alert to add-on or suggestion selling opportunities. For example, a person to whom you've just sold a pair of skis may be a potential customer for ski gloves, a hat, or some other accessory associated with skiing.

Handling Objections

Anticipate objections at any time during your presentation. Review the techniques for handling objections discussed in Chapter 12, since many of them also apply to retail selling. Keep in mind that a customer objection is not necessarily a definite and final rejection of your product but instead may merely indicate a desire for more information. Objections are often a sign that the prospect is really interested; people who don't object tend to leave the store because of lack of interest.

Closing the Sale

As we've already learned from Chapter 13, closing attempts can occur at any time during a sales presentation. In some cases, the less said by the salesperson to the customer the better. In other cases, the customer needs guidance, information, or even a "nudge" to make the buying decision. Once again, many of the techniques discussed in Chapter 13 apply to retail selling. Closing techniques that especially apply to retail selling are the forced-choice, agree-on-minor-points, and positive-assumption closes.

Give a Choice

Try to avoid the use of closed questions when attempting to close. It is generally more effective to give your customer a choice between something and something rather than between something and nothing. For example, you might ask, "Will this be cash or charge?" or "Would you like us to deliver or will you take it with you?" or "Which color do you prefer?" (Figure I.1 offers a number of reasons why some retail sales are lost.)[1]

Very often sales are lost through carelessness or indifference on the salesperson's part. Here are some reasons why:

1. **Disinterest**—Don't conduct a conversation with a fellow employee or another customer while waiting on someone. Give the customer your complete attention. Deadpan expressions, daydreaming, or "take it or leave it" attitudes leave unsold merchandise.
2. **Mistakes**—If you show the wrong item or make a mistake in change, acknowledge it and make the customer feel you are genuinely sorry.
3. **Appearing too anxious**—Show customers you want to serve their interests. Overinsistence and high-pressure tactics are objectionable to customers.
4. **Talking down other brands**—Talk up the brand you want to sell. Do not make unfair remarks about a competitive brand.
5. **Arguing**—Never argue with a customer. If it appears that an argument might develop, shift the conversation to another topic. There's little profit in winning an argument and losing the customer. If a customer makes an absurd statement, don't laugh or argue. You may anger the customer, and an angry customer is a lost customer.
6. **Being too long-winded**—A flood of words doesn't make many sales. Some people take time to make up their minds, and silence at the right time allows the customer to think and decide. Being a good listener often makes more sales than being a fast talker.
7. **Lack of courtesy**—Discourteous salespeople rarely last long on a job; they lose too many customers.
8. **Showing favoritism**—Never wait on your friends or favorite customers before taking care of customers who were there first.
9. **Being too hurried**—Take time to find out what a customer wants and then take time to show the merchandise properly.
10. **Embarrassing the customer**—Never laugh at a person who speaks with a foreign accent or correct a person who mispronounces words or product names.
11. **Misrepresenting merchandise**—Never guarantee any cures or make any claims for products that cannot be backed up by facts.
12. **Lack of product information**—Salespeople who are not well informed cannot expect to build a steady clientele for their store.
13. **Wasting customers' time**—When a customer is in a hurry, finish the sale as quickly as possible.
14. **Getting too personal**—Assume a professional attitude. Be sincere and friendly, but keep a touch of dignity and formality in all customer contacts. Never let familiarity creep into the conversation, for it is usually resented.

Figure I.1 Why Sales Are Lost.

POSTSALE SERVICE

As in any kind of selling, postselling activities are also important in retail sales. Before a customer leaves the premises, for example, you should be certain that he or she knows how to operate purchased equipment. The owner of a small retail appliance outlet in a California community even offers to make evening house calls to his customers' homes if any operating difficulties arise. Although few customers actually take advantage of the offer, they do appreciate his goodwill-building activities.

Remain Courteous After the Sale

Sometimes customers will have difficulties with or questions about the products and later telephone you for advice. Always treat such customers with dignity and courtesy. Don't imply that they are imposing on you. If the customer apologizes for bothering you, you might say, "No problem whatsoever, Ms. Jones; that's why I'm here." Be certain to *listen* to customer complaints. Try to avoid making the customer feel wrong or at fault regarding the problems they may be having with the product.

And If You Don't Make the Sale?

How about if you don't make the sale? It should go without saying—but can't—that you must avoid acting childish when the prospect turns you down. Continue to be courteous; don't lose your composure under any circumstances. The unsold customer may be impressed with your attitude and behavior and either change his or her mind later or recommend you to friends and acquaintances.

NOTE

1. R. Ted Will and Ronald W. Hasty, *Retailing* (New York: Harper & Row, 1977), p. 305.

Selling Real Estate

Real estate selling is a field that deserves special treatment because of the uniqueness of the real estate selling process and the influence real estate has on virtually everyone. The quality of our lives, for example, is often gauged by the structures we live and work in and by the types of structures nearby. Real estate provides us with shelter, a place to work, a place to farm, an investment opportunity, and much more. It significantly relates to our needs and wants. As someone once said, "We shape our buildings and they shape us."

In this special section, we examine some of the unique aspects of real estate sales. In the hope of providing an introductory guide for those interested in or new to the field, we will focus primarily on the essentials of selling real estate.

HOW REAL ESTATE SELLING IS DIFFERENT

Every field has its unique aspects, and real estate is certainly no exception. For example, the selling of real estate typically involves more parties than sales transactions in many other fields. Furthermore, the decision to buy or sell real estate is often an experience that is highly charged emotionally, especially for the buyer. Also, the nature of competition among real estate salespeople is, in general, much different from that in other fields. Let's now briefly examine each of these elements.

A Triple-Header Type of Activity

Unlike most fields in which a transaction takes place solely between two parties—the salesperson and the customer—real estate usually requires a three-pronged approach to selling. As a real estate salesperson, you have three elements to sell. You must:

1. *Sell potential disposers of property* on listing their properties with your agency, thus giving you the right to attempt to secure buyers
2. *Sell prospects* on making offers to buy listed properties
3. *Sell listed property owners* on accepting the prospective buyers' original offers or to make acceptable counteroffers

The Nature of Competition

Your principal selling activities of acquiring listings, obtaining offers to buy, and securing acceptances of offers are not without their obstacles. You will find that, as a real estate salesperson, competition strikes you from various directions. For example, you compete not only with *salespeople from other firms* for listings and sales but also with *salespeople in your own office.* You seldom have an exclusive territory. Anyone in your office can attempt to sell the listing you've brought in, although you do receive a percentage of the selling price on each of the listings you've personally acquired even when others sell the properties.

Another source of competition is with *property owners themselves.* Some property owners, for example, look at a commission rate of, say, 6 percent on a $250,000 piece of property and calculate that it amounts to $15,000. Consequently, some individuals are tempted to try to sell their properties themselves in order to save the realtor's commission, in spite of real estate statistics indicating that only 10 percent of owners manage to sell their own homes.

An Emotional Experience

Another somewhat unique aspect of real estate selling is that the activities surrounding a real estate transaction can create a tremendous amount of stress and anxiety for your clients. Most people find real estate transactions to be complex and frightening, something that they don't engage in often. Many of your clients may be having their first experience in effecting a transaction involving such a large amount of money. People tend naturally to fear the unknown. The jargon of the real estate field may sound like an unknown language to some of your clients.

The transaction tends to seem even more complex to the neophyte because of the numerous individuals and agencies involved, such as buyers, sellers, real estate brokers, title insurance companies, escrow companies, termite inspection companies, warranty companies, insurance agents, and attorneys.

The act of purchasing a home can change a family's entire life-style—a potentially traumatic experience for some. As a real estate salesperson, you should attempt to recognize and be supportive of your clients' feelings, continually reassuring them that they are making sound decisions.

WHAT SKILLS AND TRAITS DO YOU NEED?

If you are to be effective in the real estate field over the long run, you must have certain essential skills and traits. These characteristics include:

1. *Patience,* because of clients' lack of real estate knowledge, their anxieties, their reactions to having to uproot families, the size of the monetary transaction, and possible unforeseen complications.

2. *Credibility,* because few clients will want to make sizable purchases from someone they don't trust. Third-party references and a sincere desire to help your clients can help you to develop credibility.

3. *Communication skills,* because of the need to describe property in an interest-creating manner; to mediate differences of opinions between buyers and sellers, husbands and wives; and to be able to coordinate the various parties involved in real estate transactions.

4. *Motivation,* because of the need, in many instances, to work hard and at odd or long hours.

5. *Persistence,* because of the need to spend large blocks of time providing information and service to clients without being assured of any personal financial gain.

6. *Knowledge,* because of the complexity and rapidly changing nature of real estate markets, varying availability and types of financing, and specialized nature of real estate law.

7. *Diplomacy,* because of the frequent need to get buyers and sellers to compromise in order to consummate sales transactions.

8. *Creativity,* because of the need to see specific properties as one part of a larger total environment (e.g., a house situated within a community with its parks, schools, and so on) and the need to develop creative financing arrangements, especially during periods when loan funds are scarce.

THE REAL ESTATE SELLING PROCESS

In this section, we examine the all-important selling process as it applies to real estate. Much of what we've already covered in earlier sections of the text is also relevant to real estate. However, we now relate selling concepts specifically to the area of real estate selling.

Prospecting for Clients

Prospecting for both listings and potential buyers of property is a highly important activity in the selling of real estate. A factor that assists in prospecting is that many Americans tend to be highly mobile. Millions of Americans change addresses each year, which provides real estate salespeople with a potentially fertile source of prospects. A major problem, however, is to locate those prospects so that they can become your personal clients.

Typical sources of prospects for listings and sales include:

1. Phone- or walk-ins

2. Friends, acquaintances, and club associates

3. Centers of influence, such as bankers, personnel directors, mail carriers, or previous clients who might supply leads
4. Referrals from branch offices of franchised realtors
5. Newspaper articles that might supply leads, or advertisements inserted by property owners who are attempting to sell their properties themselves
6. Door-to-door canvassing
7. Direct mailings

Approaching Real Estate Prospects

As with the selling of virtually any product or service, your methods for approaching customers in the real estate field will significantly influence your selling success. For example, assume that you are holding an "open house" on a Sunday in one of your listed properties, a house on Elm Street. An approach that will help you to qualify your prospects can save you substantial amounts of selling time. Try to separate "hot prospects" from those who are merely "killing a Sunday" browsing through houses for sale.

Common sense dictates that you should be courteous to all comers. Some apparent browsers may actually be hot prospects who aren't yet ready to admit their true feelings.

Previewing the Property Site

Of course, you want to appear knowledgeable when you deliver your sales presentation to a client. The knowledge of real estate laws and financing arrangements is important but not enough. It's extremely important for you to do your homework in advance and carefully *study the property itself.* Each property is unique and has strengths and hidden values that may not be readily apparent to the client. Knowing your properties in advance aids you substantially in relating their features to the needs and desires of your clients.

The Sales Presentation

An effective sales presentation virtually requires that you show the property, since buyers typically want to see their prospective purchases before making a final decision. When arranging appointments, try to select convenient times for prospects to see the properties, times when they will not be preoccupied with other pressures or interests. In addition, try to arrange to have all individuals who might influence buying decisions present during the showings. Doing so will usually save you time later, since it often eliminates the need for repeat showings.

Two schools of thought exist regarding whether you should take prospects to property sites in their car or in your own. Realtors who favor the use of their own cars feel that they maintain greater control over the sales interview and presentation. For example, when you take your own car, you may be able to select a route to the property that tends to enhance, rather than to detract from, the property itself. In addition, even while driving, it is argued, you can use the time to find out more about the needs and interests of prospects.

On the other hand, those who favor traveling in their prospect's car feel that more control is maintained because the salesperson's hands and mind are free to handle documents and to plan sales strategies. If you, the salesperson, drive, it is also argued, you could run into legal difficulties with childrens' car seat legislation that requires infants under a certain age to sit in special safety car seats. So you can see, there are tradeoffs with either point of view.

Be certain to uncover the needs of your prospects before spending a lot of time showing properties. To illustrate, one of the most significant needs I had when in the market for a house several years ago was a room suitable to be used as an office where I could work on my writing commitments. Any real estate salesperson who failed to look for a house with a room for my writing activities was wasting time and energy. Therefore, keep in mind that seemingly inconsequential factors can be highly significant to prospects. Probe to uncover needs. Here are a few examples of qualifying questions that you might ask:

1. To what extent do you entertain guests? (Extensive entertaining could require a more elaborate and spacious dining room.)
2. What special space requirements do you have for your furniture? (The client may have oversized furniture with special space requirements.)
3. Do you have a piano? (Pianos require special space.)
4. Is it likely that you will need additional space in a few years? (For example, do they plan to have children?)
5. What are your expectations and attitudes toward local school districts?
6. Do you have plans to build a swimming pool on the property?
7. Do you have special side-yard access requirements for such items as a boats or recreation vehicles (RVs)?

Also, be alert to buying signals, such as those mentioned in an earlier chapter. For example, a statement such as "The people in this neighborhood certainly take good care of their yards" could indicate a favorable client attitude toward the property. Or something like "My pool table would fit perfectly in this family room" could also imply an interest in the property.

Handling Listing Objections

Since we've already offered, in an earlier chapter, a detailed treatment of techniques for handling objections, we take a somewhat different slant on the topic in this section. Both prospective listers and buyers of property are potential sources of objections that real estate salespeople must learn to handle skillfully. We first cite some of the more typical lister objections with some suggested responses and then give some of the more common examples of objections that potential buyers might offer.

As a reminder, remember that an objection doesn't necessarily indicate a lack of prospect interest but instead suggests that additional information is wanted before a buying decision can be made. Objections should really be viewed as feedback statements that enable you to find out how you must tailor your presentation to the prospect's interests and feelings. Be certain to look for meanings that are hidden behind the prospect's objections.

Listing Objection 1 An objection to providing you with a listing.

Prospect Nothing against you personally, but there's really no reason for me to list with you right now since I already have someone who expressed an interest in buying my property.

Salesperson As I understand your situation, Mr. Prospect, you already have someone whom you feel is a likely buyer of your property. If you didn't have that party in mind would you then consider listing with our agency?

Prospect Probably.

Salesperson If that's the case, then I have a suggestion. Why don't we try something like this: You continue to work on your prospect, and we'll work up a standard listing contract giving my agency the exclusive right to sell your property to anyone except your prospect. If your prospect buys during the next month, you pay nothing to us. On the other hand, if your prospect cools off and doesn't buy your property, we may have already lined up a number of potential buyers. After the month is up, we'll put your property on a multiple-listing service, which will give your property wide exposure. We'll do all of the necessary promotion and detail work while you haven't lost the freedom to work on your prospect. This arrangement doesn't cost you a cent until we sell your property. How does this proposal sound to you, Mr. Prospect?

Prospect I have to admit that it sounds pretty good.

Listing Objection 2 Prospect wants to eliminate broker's commission.

Prospect If I sell it myself instead of through a broker, I can save the commission.

Salesperson You're right, you would save the commission *if* you sell it yourself and *if* there are no complications. It's been my experience, however, that "by owner" signs tend to attract more of the "just-looking" types and unqualified people, or those merely looking for a bargain, rather than "hot prospects." That factor, plus all of the potential problems with escrow and financing, can end up costing you far more in time and headaches than the value of the commission you'd save. Wouldn't you really prefer to pay a reasonable but definite fee, receive the professional services of a real estate counselor, end up with far fewer complications, and receive a higher net?

The balance of the listing types of objections will merely be stated without a salesperson's response. Study the objections and then, on the basis of your own knowledge of selling and the real estate field, try to develop effective methods for handling the objections. If possible, compare your responses with those of an experienced realtor.

Listing Objection 3 The perennial "friend in the business."

Prospect I have a friend in the real estate business.

Salesperson ______________________________

____

____

Listing Objection 4 Seller feels listing price is too low.

Prospect The price you've suggested for listing my house is too low.

Salesperson ______________________________

____

____

Listing Objection 5 Seller wants to list at an unrealistically high figure.

Prospect Let's list it at a higher figure; we can always lower it later.

Salesperson ______________________________

____

____

Listing Objection 6 Seller knows another realtor who will list property at an unrealistically high price.

Prospect I know another realtor who will list it at my price.

Salesperson ______________________________

____

____

Listing Objection 7 Seller wonders why neighbors allegedly received higher price.

Prospect My neighbors got more than that when they sold.

Salesperson ______________________________

____

____

Listing Objection 8 Client wants to rent rather than accept too low a price for his or her property.

Prospect As far as I'm concerned, if I can't get the price I want, then I'll rent the house to others.

Salesperson ______________________________

____

____

Listing Objection 9 Seller wants to wait until the economy improves.

Prospect I'd like to sell, but I don't think economic conditions are quite right currently.

Salesperson ______________________________

____

____

Listing Objection 10 Seller wants to stall for various reasons.

Prospect I'd like to think it over.

Salesperson ______________________________

____

____

Handling Buyer Objections

As with listing objections, we now examine two typical types of objections that prospective buyers give, along with suggested salesperson responses. These are followed by additional examples for you to respond to.

Buyer Objection 1 Prospect indicates that it's too soon to think about buying.

Buyer We've just begun looking.

Salesperson That's fine, Mr. and Mrs. Prospect. One way that I can assist is to help you look and save you a lot of time in the process. My job is to study all new listings. After I find out what you want in a house, I will show you only those properties that suit your needs at a price you can afford.

Buyer Objection 2 Buyer feels house should be closer to schools.

Buyer This house seems too far from schools for our children.

Salesperson Have you ever lived near a school or known anyone who has? In spite of how much we may love children, hearing them trek by noisily twice a day can really grate on one's nerves, not to mention potential problems of littering and damage to lawns and gardens.

Now develop your own responses to the following buyer objections:

Buyer Objection 3 Client feels that current economic conditions are unsuitable for making a house purchase.

Buyer I really don't think that now is a good time for me to make a house purchase.

Salesperson ______________________________

____

____

Buyer Objection 4 Client doesn't like the neighborhood but does not qualify for a house in a more expensive neighborhood.

Buyer We really don't think too much of this neighborhood.

Salesperson ____

____

____

Buyer Objection 5 Client wants to wait until old house is sold.

Buyer We want to sell the house we have now before we actually buy.

Salesperson ____

____

____

Buyer Objection 6 Client feels that houses will drop in price soon.

Buyer It seems to me that prices are about to fall and that I should wait.

Salesperson ____

____

____

Buyer Objection 7 Client wants more ready access to public transportation.

Buyer This house is too far from public transportation.

Salesperson ____

____

____

Buyer Objection 8 Client feels that price is excessively high.

Buyer The price is too high.

Salesperson ____

____

____

Buyer Objection 9 Client believes that interest payments and taxes will place too much of a strain on his or her budget.

Buyer The taxes and interest are much too high for my income.

Salesperson ______________________________

____

____

Buyer Objection 10 Client believes that renting is a more favorable alternative than buying.

Buyer I think we'd be better off continuing to rent.

Salesperson ______________________________

____

____

The Close

Last but, as we well know by now, not least, comes that all-important activity—the close. Remember, however, that *last* applies only to the order of presentation in this special section, not to the sales presentation itself. In reality, you should be ready to try to close at any time during your sales presentation. In fact, you should close immediately in those rare instances when a buyer offers no objections. Ask for earnest money—a deposit—as a token of the buyer's good faith in the transaction.

Virtually any of the closing techniques already discussed in detail in an earlier chapter can be applied to real estate. Review the techniques already presented and attempt to develop specific closing responses related to the selling of real estate. Also keep in mind the following guidelines:

1. Focus on the positive features, advantages, and benefits of the property as they relate to the buyer's needs.
2. Be certain to get approval of all parties concerned with the transaction. For example, don't try to close with only one spouse present.
3. Explain that "buyer's remorse" (cognitive dissonance) is quite normal among buyers of high-dollar-valued items like houses.
4. Congratulate clients on their buying decisions.
5. Start working on getting the buyer's offer accepted as soon as possible to prevent others from getting their offer accepted first.

Closing activities in real estate selling are somewhat unique, since often *double closing* efforts are necessary. For example, if the potential buyer doesn't accept the seller's initial asking price, the buyer typically makes a counteroffer, that is, offers a lower price. You then must either attempt to sell the buyer's counteroffer to the seller or attempt to negotiate a compromise between the parties. Such activities, as you might imagine, require you to communicate effectively to both parties in order to help them arrive at some sort of compromise.

POSTSALE ACTIVITIES

Satisfied customers can often create additional prospects for you in any field, and—once again—real estate is no exception. The period after the sale can be a critical one from the standpoint of developing satisfied buyers who will refer you to their friends, acquaintances, and associates.

Sometimes postsale problems or questions that you can assist with arise in the mind of either the buyer or seller. Your image and reputation in the real estate field is significantly influenced by what you do to provide assistance when your clients need it.

Many realtors follow up after each sale to see how things are going for the buyer. One salesperson even provides his clients with a congratulatory bottle of champagne to celebrate their purchase and to express his appreciation for their use of his services. Regardless of what sort of postsale activities you personally engage in, your primary purpose should be to maintain a positive image in the minds of your clients.

Selling in Foreign Markets

In spite of protectionism pressures throughout the world in recent years, foreign markets continue to be extremely important. Merely watch national television in Spain, for example, and you can view commercials for 7-Up, Pepsi, Camels, Lucky Strike, Ford Motor Company, *y mucho mas.* Many U.S. firms have consistently earned greater profits in foreign markets than in domestic ones. Let's assume that the company you work for has also decided to jump into the global ring for the first time. How might you organize to operate in foreign markets? Let's now take a brief look.

TYPES OF FOREIGN VENTURES

In the Beginning—Intermediaries

A fairly simple way to begin operating in foreign markets is for you to export products through distributors termed **foreign trade intermediaries.** These are generally either *wholesale export merchants* who actually take title to and buy the merchandise for resale in foreign markets or *export agents* who do not take title to the goods but who may represent a variety of noncompeting American manufacturers in foreign markets. For the novice company venturing into foreign markets, this route tends to be one of the least risky. Little in the way of capital investment, time, or effort is necessary for the firm that desires to export a portion or even all of its output this way. Unfortunately, however, you typically have little control over intermediaries. They may be serving a large number of firms and therefore might not market your products as aggressively as you might desire.

Eliminating the Middlepeople—Sales Branches

If your potential volume of sales warrants it, a logical progression when marketing in other countries is to sell your products through **foreign-operated sales branches.** You continue to manufacture in your home country but employ either foreign nationals or an American marketing force to perform the functions of the foreign trade intermediary mentioned above. This approach gives you far greater control over your marketing efforts. An important requirement is that your sales force understand the differences in the laws and customs of other nations.

A License to Operate—Licensing Foreign Manufacturers

As you find your foreign markets expanding, you might take an additional step often taken by growing firms: **licensing.** This procedure allows a manufacturer located in a foreign country to produce your product, which then could be marketed through either your own salespeople or foreign nationals, or a combination of both. Licensing agreements enable a producer to enter markets that for various reasons might otherwise be impossible to penetrate. For example, Levi Strauss & Company in 1978 entered into a licensing agreement with Hungary to produce "genuine" Levi Strauss blue jeans. The PepsiCo, already with a foothold in the Soviet Union, negotiated in 1986 a joint venture deal to put Pizza Huts across the USSR.

We'll Walk Alone Together—Joint Ventures and Wholly Owned Subsidiaries

Another approach to marketing across borders is to set up production facilities in foreign countries, either with *joint ventures* or by establishing *wholly owned foreign subsidiaries.* If you took the **joint venture** route, you would be entering a partnership arrangement in which you share ownership of the foreign operation with foreign nationals—either individuals, a company, or sometimes even the foreign government itself. In some instances, you may have little choice if you want to enter certain foreign markets. Joint ventures or licensing may be the only alternatives because of strong nationalistic attitudes on the part of government officials in the foreign country. A typical foreign joint venture agreement allows the U.S. (or any non-domestic) company to own 49 percent of the venture.

As they expand, some firms prefer to go it completely alone. For example, you might decide to operate abroad through a **wholly owned foreign subsidiary.** Although costly, owning your own manufacturing and distribution facilities in another country gives you maximum control over operations. We'll discuss other aspects of global business in the following portion of this special section.

International Back Scratching—Production Sharing

"Necessity," it has been said, "is the mother of invention." One of those "necessities" that many manufacturing firms have long recognized and required is a readily available supply of people for traditional production work. In recent years, however, the more technologically advanced nations have experienced a shortage of semi-skilled manual workers. Capital-intensive nations have even developed surpluses of well-educated people.

The "invention" that has emerged in recent years to deal with this "necessity" is a world economic trend called **production sharing.** This innovative approach to production and marketing doesn't follow the traditional lines of exporting and importing. Instead, it integrates production along transnational lines.

An example of production sharing should make the concept clearer. Traditional statistics may show such products as hand-held calculators as "imports," but such figures don't tell the complete story. The silicon chip—the heart of a calculator system—may be made in America, shipped to a developing nation such as Singapore or South Korea, assembled into a fully functioning calculator, and then marketed principally in developed countries, such as the United States, Canada, and Europe.

European companies follow similar production-sharing approaches. For example, there is a large European textile group that spins, weaves, and dyes its unfinished products in superefficient European plants and then ships the cloth by air carrier to Indonesia, Malaya, or Morocco. The cloth is then converted into finished products, such as curtains, rugs, towels, bedding, and clothing. It is then air-freighted back for marketing in European markets. So you can see that marketing among nations exists in many forms.

GOOFS, RISKS, AND HAZARDS IN OVERSEAS MARKETING

Marketing concepts, if they work for managers of North American companies, should be applicable in the same manner all over the world, right? Not so right! Although communication networks and international travel have made people throughout the world similar in many of their tastes and behavior (the young people of almost every nation wear Levi's blue jeans, drink Pepsi or Coke, and dance to American music), there are still many cultural differences from one part of the world to another.

Ignorance of a host country's laws and culture can make both a marketer's face and a corporation's bottom line red! There's an old adage that advises, "What's good for the goose is good for the gander." Not necessarily so for the transplanted *norteamericano.* In fact, it has forced a number of well-intentioned Americans to eat crow, so to speak.

We can learn from the failures and successes of others. Failures can result from a variety of factors, ranging from risks associated with political events over which firms have little or no control to plain ignorance of the host countries' laws and culture. Let's briefly look first at some of the goofs made, risks taken, and hazards experienced by some North American companies in their efforts to do business abroad.

Some Experiences in Overseas Marketing

The Tandy Corporation The late Charles Tandy, who built Radio Shack into one of the leading merchandisers of amateur electronic gear in the United States, has been quoted as follows: "I see nothing different about the people in Europe from the people in the United States." Apparently Tandy turned out to be mistaken. His corporation lost $21 million from its European operations during a three-year period.[1]

Ignoring host country laws and customs didn't help Tandy a bit. In Belgium, Tandy belatedly discovered that he was supposed to have a government tax stamp on window signs. In Germany, Tandy discovered that he was breaking sales laws by giving away flashlights, a common sales promo device in the "good old U.S. of A." In Holland, Tandy missed the Christmas shopping crowds, learning the hard way that sales promotions geared to December 25 were too late. The Dutch, it turned out, are early birds. They give presents on December 6, St. Nicholas Day. Well, Happy New Year anyway!

The Xerox Corporation Xerox was doing business in Nicaragua, where it had contracts to service 800 copiers—more than half of all such machines in the country—which it lost after the Reagan administration slapped a trade embargo on Nicaragua. Xerox's local unit couldn't get the parts it needed for servicing the Nicaraguan copiers, so Japan's Canon, Inc., got all the business.[2]

Semitek Systems Corporation A small Silicon Valley electronics company, Semitek Systems, won a $9.5 million contract to install a solid-state relay factory in China. Semitek had an irrevocable letter of credit from the Bank of China, but over a dozen banks in California refused Semitek the $3.2 million in working capital it needed. Once again, a Japanese company ended up with the order. Obtaining adequate credit in the United States was the bugaboo this time.

Warner-Lambert The Warner-Lambert Company, a large multinational conglomerate, has had phenomenal success marketing its Schick products in Japan through independent wholesalers. In a recent year, for example, Shick controlled over 70 percent of the Japanese market for stainless-steel blades.[3]

Warner-Lambert tried the same approach—distributing through local independent wholesalers—to peddle its chewing gum line of Trident, Chiclets, Bubblicious, and others. This approach bombed because the wholesalers were apparently not working the retail outlets hard enough. So Warner-Lambert decided to bypass the wholesalers with its own sales force. Wholesalers, naturally, became quite upset. But retailers, too, became suspicious of a company that changed its marketing tactics. Warner-Lambert finally got together a formula that worked: it used its own sales force to get orders from the retailers and then passed the orders on to wholesalers. Everybody apparently became more contented, since Warner-Lambert went on to develop a 17 percent share of the Japanese market for chewing gum.[4]

Avon Company The Avon Company did poorly when it first attempted to market its personal-care products the way it did everywhere else—using a large number of women selling door-to-door to strangers. Avon found that most Japanese women were too reserved to call on strangers. Avon then allowed the timid ones to sell to acquaintances instead. Avon also started an advertising campaign that was low-key and poetic. In the 10 years that followed, Avon's sales grew annually at a rate exceeding 25 percent.[5]

Boeing Corporation The Boeing Corporation was flying high, so to speak, in the Middle East until politics, once again, got in the way of marketing. When the U.S. Department of Commerce refused to grant an export license for the sale of several 747s to Libya, other Arab nations became incensed at the action and started buying their airplanes elsewhere. Another "challenge" faced by Boeing was the three years it took to get U.S. government approval to sell two 767s to Ethiopia because of that country's Marxist leanings.[6]

All has not been a series of heartbreaks, however, for North American Marco Polos. There have been an amazing number of outstanding successes, a few of which we shall briefly examine below.

McDonald's McDonald's has been doing well overseas. Its foreign sales have been increasing four times more rapidly than its sales in the United States in recent years. Hamburgers? Not *that* unique in Bavaria and Frankfurt. But *Big Macs*—in Japan, the land of sushi? Something unheard of in the past. Asian traditions didn't discourage McDonald's. In fact, it helped create new tastes for Big Macs in Japan. McDonald's has since become the No. 1 fast-food business in Japan. Over a 15-year period, its sales went from zero to more than $800 million a year.

Part of McDonald's *secret* was obtaining a Japanese entreprenurial type of person—Den Fujita—to operate its Japanese unit. However, Fujita and McDonald's corporate people in the United States clashed heads at first. Corporate wanted outlets to follow the American pattern and be opened in the suburbs, since that was where McDonald's enjoyed so much success in the United States. Fujita won out and was able to convince corporate that outlets should be opened in large cities instead. His sense of the Japanese habits was correct. After only one year, his first unit in Tokyo set a McDonald's world record for one-day sales. The urban approach to marketing hamburgers was also tried in the United States, where it also was a hit.

As mentioned, hamburgers had not been typical Japanese fare. Fujita, however, didn't focus on Big Mac's American roots. Instead, he concentrated on promoting the product as a unique sort of food. He was so successful that the Japanese ministry of education complained that school children have lost their skills in the use of chopsticks![7]

Gillette Gillette's sales overseas are now greater than their U.S. sales. However, until the 1980s, it wasn't doing so well in developing countries. Tastes were different and income was low in these locations. Currently, however, Gillette is highly successful in developing countries through a practice of tailoring their products and packaging toward local tastes and budgets. For example, where personal incomes are relatively low, Gillette packages razor blades so that they can be sold one blade at a time. In some areas, it promotes shaving cream in lower-priced tubes and deodorants in plastic bottles, rather than in more costly aerosol cans.

In order to gain footholds in many developing countries, Gillette had to give up its policy of investing only where it could have 100 percent-owned subsidiaries. It now has joint ventures in such countries as Malaysia, China, Egypt, Thailand, and India.

Gillette's formula has been to begin with factories that only make double-edged blades—which are still popular in developing nations. After it achieves success in that area, Gillette then expands into the production of shampoo, toothbrushes, deodorants, and pens. Gillette's successes, thus far, have been phenomenal.[8]

And More A number of U.S. companies earn over 20 percent of their revenues overseas. Table III.1[9] summarizes some of the most successful overseas marketers. Others not on the list include IBM, Hewlett-Packard, General Electric, Commodore, and many more. U.S. industries that have the greatest export potential, according to the Small Business Administration, can be viewed in Table III.2.[10]

GUIDELINES FOR INNOCENTS ABROAD

The companies that have been successful in overseas marketing have chiefly been those that have done their homework. We shall now discuss briefly some guidelines that have generally been followed by companies that have succeeded abroad.[11]

Learn the Host Country's Laws, Business Practices, and Customs

We observed earlier the plight of Tandy in Europe. Mere conversational styles differ in various cultures. Latins, for example, tend to speak mere millimeters away from their listeners. They also touch each other more than do many North Americans, who generally prefer a bit more space except when kissing someone.

At a business club in Brazil, where frequent receptions are held for newly arrived North American businesspeople, terrace railings had to be strengthened to prevent so many "gringos" from tumbling into the flower garden below as they backed away from their effervescent hosts!

TABLE III.1 Some of the Most Successful U.S. Overseas Marketers.

Company	Exports as a percent of total sales (%)
Boeing	45
MGM/UA Communications	38
Advanced Micro Devices	37
Pittson	36
Teradyne	34
Kellog	30
Computervision	30
Caterpillar	28
Universal Leaf Tobacco	26
Cray Research	24
McDonnell Douglas	22

TABLE III.2 The 15 U.S. Industries with the Greatest Export Potential (Including Products and Services), Ranked in Descending Order.

Rank	Industry
1	Computers and peripherals (hardware)
2	Telecommunications equipment and systems
3	Computer software and services
4	Medical instruments equipment and supplies
5	Electronic parts
6	Analytical and scientific laboratory instruments
7	Industrial process control instruments
8	Aircraft and parts and avionics and ground support equipment
9	Automotive parts and service equipment and accessories
10	Electronic production and test equipment
11	Electronic power generation and distribution systems and transmission equipment
12	Food processing and packaging equipment and machinery
13	Safety and security equipment
14	Printing and graphic arts equipment
15	Water resources equipment

Words also mean different things in different cultures. For example, the faces of the Parker Pen Company's executives turned rosy red after the company blitzed Latin America with an advertising campaign that—much to their surprise—implied that its new ink would help to prevent unwanted pregnancies. Otis Engineering Company once startled potential customers at a Moscow trade show. There, its posters promised that Otis oil well completion equipment would work wonders for improving a person's sex life!

Be Patient

Marketers who rush into foreign markets tend to make a rash of mistakes due to their haste. Instead, it's wise to engage in both informal and formal feasiblity studies in the target countries. Visit the markets where you desire to do business. Find out if the resources that you require for operating will be available. McDonald's, for example, found that it couldn't easily obtain locally the potatoes that were necessary for its operations. McDonald's now grows its own Russet Burbank potatoes in 18 countries.

The U.S. Department of Commerce can also be a source of foreign market surveys at little cost. In addition, export management companies and export trading companies can also assist. Their fees, however, may be high, and they typically take complete control over the marketing process.

Hire Foreign Nationals for Management Positions

Natives of a particular country, of course, tend to have a much greater sense of their own lands than do North Americans. Many North American firms, therefore, hire a substantial amount of local talent. However, the nationals should also be immersed in the corporate culture of the North American concern as well. For example, many American companies operating abroad bring their foreign managers to the United States to gain a greater sensitivity toward their firms.

Learn the Host Country's Language

Americans, for some reason, are renowned for their lack of knowledge of foreign languages. A language is a major part of a culture. Kai Lindholst, a director with Egon Zehnder, a management recruiting firm, believes that "languages are important, especially a working knowledge of French and Spanish, and perhaps even Portuguese, for working overseas."[12]

Tailor Operations and Products to Suit the Host Country

We've seen how Gillette modifies its packaging in different countries. Boeing also had to make changes. It originally had little success with its 737 airliners in developing countries until it modified them to withstand damage on bumpy runways. Kellogg, too, had to change. It had to modify its commercials for Rice Krispies in Japan, where the words "snap, crackle, and pop" were hard to pronounce. The Japanese version goes "patchy, pitchy, and putchy"! Nor could Kellogg use the name "Bran Buds" for its cereal in Sweden, unless it wanted to promote "burned farmer" breakfast food!

Understand U.S. Laws

U.S. legislation can also influence your approach overseas. A significant act for Yanks abroad is the Foreign Corrupt Practices Act of 1977, which prohibits U.S. companies from paying fees (in effect, *bribes*) to foreign government officials and limits fees paid to consultants to "reasonable" amounts. Competitors from Europe and many other countries have no similar constraints. *Mordida,* or under-the-table bribes, are not uncommon in some cultures. Many American firms, in order to stay within the boundaries of U.S. laws but also access a market, have discovered the "need" for hiring the services of a substantial number of so-called consultants. However, *¡tenga cuidado!* Consultants could be considered by U.S. authorities as an innovative ploy for bribing foreign officials.

Opportunities Exist for Those Who Are Prepared

As we've already discussed, to avoid legal and cultural pitfalls, it's important for individuals who want to tap foreign markets to prepare for various differences. Basic areas where significant differences may exist include the availability of skilled and educated employees in the host country; the behavioral or cultural patterns (including language and attitudes toward time); the legal, political, and moral atmosphere; and the economic structure (including the local currency). Many firms doing business abroad, including Xerox, Dow, Levi Strauss, and Kaiser Aluminum & Chemical, provide guidelines to their transplanted employees. Those marketers who fail to do their homework in advance often find themselves making embarrassing and possibly costly mistakes.

Not all North American business people are willing to expose themselves to the hazards of overseas marketing. However, Anthony L. Anderson, president of H.B. Fuller Co., in spite of the many difficulties in the global market his company has experienced, believes that U.S. companies are losing a golden opportunity. Recognizing that international trade is a way of life for so many European and Asian companies, Anderson contends, "U.S. business people are unique in their seeming reluctance to venture out into the world."[13]

KEY TERMS

foreign trade intermediaries
foreign-operated sales branches
licensing
joint venture
wholly owned foreign subsidiary
production sharing

NOTES

1. "Radio Shack's Rough Trip," *Business Week,* May 30, 1977, p. 55.
2. Clifford Krauss, "Japan Gains from American Embargo Against Nicaragua," *The Wall Street Journal,* June 12, 1987, p. 7.
3. Michael Allen, "The Foreign Connection," *The Wall Street Journal,* May 15, 1987, p. 16D.
4. Kenneth Labich, "America's International Winners," *Fortune,* April 14, 1986, p. 36.
5. Ibid., p. 44.
6. Ibid., p. 46.
7. Frederick Hiroshi Katayama, "Japan's Big Mac," *Fortune,* September 16, 1986, pp. 114–116.
8. David Wessel, "Gillette Keys Sales to Third World Tastes," *The Wall Street Journal,* January 23, 1986, p. 26.
9. "Most U.S. Companies Are Innocents Abroad," *Business Week, International Edition,* November 16, 1987, p. 54.
10. Allen, "Foreign Connection."

11. Adapted from Labich, "America's International Winners," pp. 34–46; and Elizabeth M. Fowler, "Foreign Experience, Languages Boost Hopefuls up the Corporate Ladder," *Contra Costa Times, Business Times Section,* December 30, 1985, p. 12.

12. Fowler, "Foreign Experience."

13. "Fuller's Worldwide Strategy: Think Local," *Business Week International Edition,* November 16, 1987, p. 55.

Glossary

(The number following each definition indicates the chapter or appendix in which it is discussed.)

Account analysis: The activity of studying and evaluating customers in a sales territory for the purpose of categorizing them by potential sales volume; an aid in determining the frequency of future visits with each customer (17).

Acknowledging: An effort by the salesperson to show the prospect that the salesperson understands and sympathizes with the prospect's feelings of resistance (12).

Activities summary log: A territory management tool used to summarize daily activities over a week in order to analyze how effective past utilization of time has been (17).

Actual self: The way we *really* see ourselves in relation to our environment (5).

Advantages: Factors inherent in a product that may provide benefits to a prospective customer (10).

Advertising: A nonpersonal message or series of messages paid for by an identifiable sponsor for the purpose of persuading others to accept products, services, or ideas (16).

Advertising facsimiles: Copies of current advertisements used by salespeople in their presentations to lend prestige to their firms and to stimulate dealers' interest in present and future advertising programs (16).

Agreeing and neutralizing: The effort by the salesperson to "disarm" the prospect by appearing to recognize the merits of the prospect's objection before returning to the sales message with renewed vigor (12).

AIDA concept: AIDA is an acronym that symbolizes four steps or stages that a prospect's mind goes through, with assistance from a salesperson, on the way to a buying decision; the steps are Attention, Interest, Desire, and Action (10).

Alternate-choice question (forced-choice question): A question, such as "Which do you prefer?," that allows the receiver to make a choice between two or more alternatives (7).

Annual percentage rate: The actual rate of interest computed and quoted on an annual basis (3).

Approach: The step in the selling process intended to gain the prospective customer's attention for the purpose of arousing interest and desire in the product and salesperson's message (9).

Asch conformity studies: Research by Solomon E. Asch that showed the effect of group pressure on the perception and attitudes of individual members of a group (5).

Aspirational reference groups: Groups an individual is not a member of but would like to belong to (5).

Attitude: The belief and feelings individuals have that influence the ways they behave toward other people, objects, and ideas (5).

Audiovisual presentation: An automated type of sales presentation that makes use of various kinds of equipment to relate product features and advantages to customer benefits; usually requires a salesperson to answer additional questions and to close the sale (10).

BAD-C bad-news technique: An acronym that symbolizes the four major elements of bad-news messages, which are Buffer, Analysis, Decision, and Close (14).

Bad-news messages: As applied to customer relations, messages, often in letter form, to customers expressing unpleasant information in a manner that does not cause a deterioration of customer goodwill (14).

Bait-and-switch tactic: An illegal advertising ploy that exists when a retailer advertises a lower-priced item that is either unavailable or disparaged by the salesperson for the purpose of selling attracted customers higher-priced items (3).

Benefits: In selling, a product characteristic that can prove useful or profitable to a prospective customer (10).

Bird dogs: Individuals who don't work for the same firm as the salesperson but who are in the position to provide leads to the salesperson (8).

Blind referral: An approach technique that makes vague, rather than specific, reference to third parties as a means of arousing prospect interest in the salesperson's message and products (9).

Blitz technique: An approach to prospecting intended to saturate a particular region or group in a short period of time (8).

Body language: A form of nonverbal communication in which body movements convey meaning (7).

Brand loyalty: The tendency for consumers to prefer a particular product over others because of past satisfaction with it (4).

Breach of warranty: Occurs when a seller's statements related to a good or service prove to be false or misleading (3).

Bribes: An effort to stimulate sales to customers through the use of kickbacks or elaborate gifts (3).

Bulletin board systems: Electronic computer systems into which special interest groups upload and download data through their personal computers and telephone modems (8).

Buyer's remorse: The feelings of doubt or regret that some customers develop shortly after making an affirmative buying decision (13).

Buying center: A concept, rather than a formal group or place, that represents all of the people who either directly or indirectly influence purchases (5).

Buying committees: Ongoing, established groups whose function is to determine the best sources for their organizational purchases (5).

Buying motives: Factors that cause or drive people to purchase particular products (5).

Buying signals: Expressions, either physical or verbal, of a prospect's desire to make a buying decision (10, 13).

By-the-way close: A closing technique in which the salesperson appears to have given up and then attempts one more close; tends to relax the prospect's defenses (13).

Call-ahead approach: The practice of telephoning in advance of calling personally on customers; often results in reduced waiting time and less likelihood of "no shows" (15).

Catalogs: Booklets provided to salespeople that contain reference and sales information related to product specifications, prices, and terms (11).

Caveat emptor: An outdated and illegal business philosophy that meant "let the buyer beware"; a belief that when goods were sold without an express warranty, the buyer had to take the full risk of loss from potential defects in the goods (3).

Centers of influence: Individuals who are well known in a community and who may serve as sources of prospective customers (8).

Centralized data base: Data stored in a host computer at corporate headquarters or regional offices (17).

Channels of distribution: The route that goods follow from producer to consumer (4).

Civic and social groups: Organizations whose members can be excellent sources of prospective customers (8).

Close (closing): The attempt by the salesperson to motivate the prospective customer into making an affirmative decision regarding the purchase of a product or service (10, 13).

Closed question: A question that typically can be answered only with a yes or no (7).

Clubs: Social groups whose members can be excellent sources of prospects (8).

Cognitive dissonance: A form of stress caused by uncertainty as to whether a purchase should have been made at a particular time (5).

Cold calls: Calling on prospects who have not been contacted previously (8).

Cold canvass approach: An approach to prospecting that involves contacting as many individuals as possible in a particular group or area; frequently used by door-to-door salespeople (8).

Communication: A two-way process resulting in the transmission of information and understanding between individuals (7).

Company knowledge: The kinds of information that salespeople must have about their own companies, such as company history, performance, philosophy, policies, procedures, future plans, and socially responsible activities (6).

Company philosophy and values: The "personality" of a firm; may be progressive, aggressive, or conservative; tends to reflect the philosophy and values of its founders or senior management (6).

Competitor knowledge: An understanding of the strengths and weaknesses of goods or services offered by companies similar to your own (6).

Complimenting-customers approach: An approach technique that extends to customers sincere flattery related to achievements or events that have affected the customers or their firms (9).

Computer software programs: Computer systems that enable salespeople to utilize such elements as word processing, telemarketing, autodial, tickler systems, call reporting, form letters, mailing labels, and notation space for account profiles (8).

Computer user groups: Special interest organizations whose members are especially good prospects for computer hard- and software products and services (8).

Consumer goods: Goods intended for personal use and consumption rather than for resale or use in producing other goods (4).

Consumer market: The portion of the buying public that purchases goods intended for personal use and consumption rather than for resale or use in producing other goods (4).

Contingency close: A closing technique in which the salesperson agrees to do something provided the prospect agrees to make a purchase (13).

Convenience goods: Products, such as candy, pencils, and notebook paper, that consumers are willing to purchase with little expenditure of time, effort, and money (4).

Converting (boomerang): The sales activity of converting objections into reasons for buying a product or service (12).

Cooling-off period: As applied to purchases from house-to-house salespeople, the period of time that must be provided to enable the purchaser to reconsider and cancel the order (3).

Co-op allowance: A refund by the manufacturer to the dealer of a portion of the price paid for purchased goods or part of the costs of approved dealer advertising (16).

Cooperative advertising: A type of sales promotion in which the manufacturer and the dealer share in the cost of the advertising medium or device (16).

Counselor close: A closing technique in which the salesperson advises the customer how and what to buy (13).

Culture: The environmental influences handed down from one generation to another (5).

Curiosity-appeal approach: An approach technique that attempts to arouse a prospective customer's interest by appealing to his or her natural curiosity (9).

Customer-benefit approach: An approach technique that uses statements or questions for the purpose of enabling prospects to see how they can benefit from the purchase of a product or service (9).

Customer requirements: The features, advantages, and benefits that are necessary in a product to satisfy the needs of a particular customer (6).

Custom production: Products that are produced to satisfy the specific needs of a particular customer rather than customers in general (5).

Cyclical demand: Demand for a product that tends to fluctuate widely depending on economic conditions, inventory, policies, and buyer expectations (5).

Daily call schedule: A form or pocket-sized card used for keeping a convenient record of customers and prospects to be visited (17).

Daily organizer: A form, typically made from index paper, that provides a person with a handy daily "to-do" record (17).

Data base management system (DBMS): A computer system that allows easy access to large amounts of data stored in a well-organized format (17).

Dealer incentive travel: A method of sales promotion that offers dealers expense-paid trips as an incentive to meet or exceed sales quotas (16).

Decline stage: The final stage in a product's life cycle; characterized by disappearing demand for the product (4).

Demand creation: The activities involved with assisting or influencing others in recognizing their needs and desires for specific goods and services (1).

Denying: The act of refuting an untrue accusation made by a prospect toward the salesperson or company; must be used with caution (12).

Departure: The various activities associated with making a smooth exit from the customer's premises (13).

Derived demand: Demand for a product or resource, such as silicon chips, that results from demand for another product, such as computers (5).

Direct mail: Sales promotion devices, such as sales letters, postcards, brochures, and catalogs, mailed to potential customers (16).

Direct request close: A closing technique in which the salesperson simply asks the prospect for the order (13).

Downloaded: Data that have been electronically transferred from a host computer to peripheral equipment (17).

Dramatizing: Related to sales presentations, efforts by the salesperson to use product demonstration techniques that tend to stir a prospective customer's imagination or emotions (11).

Drawing account: A system that provides salespeople with advances charged (drawn) against future commissions; must ultimately be earned through actual sales (2).

Earmuff problem: A condition that exists when a person tunes out incoming communication; sometimes exists among certain individuals who perceive their roles as authoritative (7).

Economies of scale: A concept that shows how the costs of producing each unit of a product tend to decline as the scale of a firm's productive operations and activities increases (1).

Effective demand: The actual ability—rather than mere desire—to purchase a product or service; based on the purchasing power of potential customers (4).

80/20 rule: A concept based on the experience of many sales managers indicating that about 80 percent of their customers are responsible for only about 20 percent of total sales volume. Therefore about 80 percent of their sales volume comes from only about 20 percent of their customers (14).

Electronic data interchange (EDI): A system for transferring purchase orders, invoices, and related transactions between manufacturers and their wholesalers and dealers; computer ordering between manufacturers and their distributors (17).

Electronic mail: Correspondence that is transferred from one computer to other electronic equipment, such as laser printers, geographically dispersed (16).

Electronic sales promotion: The use of computer technology for the purpose of promoting consumer interest in the purchase of goods and services (16).

Empathy: The ability to feel as another person does; to attempt figuratively to place yourself into the other person's shoes (2).

Employee benefit programs: Indirect employee financial rewards that include paid leave, insurance, retirement plans, stock options, and educational assistance (2).

Endless-chain method: The activity of obtaining names of prospective customers from existing customers (8).

Entertaining customers: Providing various types of hospitality, such as dinner in a restaurant, for the purpose of building customer goodwill and making potential customers more receptive to sales messages (3).

Equal Credit Opportunity Act: A law that prevents creditors from discriminating in any aspect of a credit transaction on the basis of sex, marital status, ethnic background, or receipt of public assistance funds (3).

Ethics: The standards of conduct or morals established by the current and past attitudes, moods, and practices of a particular society (3).

Expense accounts: Financial allowances or reimbursements provided for salespeople to cover work-related expenses (2).

Expressed warranty: A direct statement or promise by a seller concerning the nature, quality, character, use, and purpose of a particular good. It helps to induce the prospect to buy and becomes a part of the sales contract (3).

Facsimile (fax) machines: Devices used for rapidly transmitting documents, including pictures in various shades of gray, from one fax machine to another virtually anywhere in the industrialized world (16).

Facsimiles: Replicas of original products that can be used to visually demonstrate an actual product; may be working models (11).

Fair Debt Collection Practices Act: A law that makes it illegal for collection agencies to use unfair or abusive collection practices (3).

Features: The prominent parts or characteristics that can help to sell a product when they are related to product benefits and customer needs (10).

Federal Trade Commission (FTC): A federal agency, created by the Federal Trade Commission Act of 1914, primarily responsible for preventing false and misleading advertising and the misrepresentation of products (3).

Feedback: The activity that makes communication a two-way process; an activity that enables the effectiveness of communication to be determined (7).

Fiduciary relationship: A position of trust, confidence, and responsibility that a salesperson should hold toward his or her customers (3).

Field access: A condition that exists when communication can take place between a salesperson's computer in the field and one in the office through the use of a telephone and a modem (17).

Field intelligence: A nonselling activity of salespeople that involves uncovering and reporting information of concern to company managers. It includes such information as competitor activities and the changing needs of customers (1).

Finance charge: The total interest paid in dollars plus any other charges related to purchasing something on credit (3).

First-person sensitivity: The ability to perceive what another person thinks about you (2).

Fixed costs: Costs associated with producing a product or service and that continue relatively unchanged regardless of the level of output (1).

Flip chart: A series of illustrations on individual sheets of paper or cards that is used to present an attention-getting, organized sales presentation (11).

Floppy disks: Small, relatively flexible revolving magnetic plates on which computer information and data are stored (17).

Follow-up: The types of sales and service activities that follow the sales call; activities that tend to assist customers and foster favorable customer attitudes toward you, your company, and its products (14).

Forced-choice close: A closing technique in which the salesperson provides the prospect with a choice between two positive alternatives (see also *alternative-choice question*) (13).

Foreign market: Potential customers of goods and services that are situated beyond the borders of domestic producers; may be further segmented on the same bases as domestic markets; that is, consumer, industrial, and governmental (4).

Foreign-operated sales branches: A marketing channel used by firms that want to sell in foreign countries through their own marketing organizations but that continue to manufacture products in their home countries (App. III).

Foreign trade intermediaries: *Wholesalers* or *agents* who perform the marketing functions for firms doing business in foreign countries (App. III).

Forestalling: An effort by a salesperson to anticipate specific objections and answer them before they arise (12).

Founders: Individuals who risk capital and energy for the purpose of establishing a new firm (6).

Fraud: The intentional misrepresentation of the truth in order to induce another to act in a particular manner, as to purchase a good or service (3).

Free-service approach: An approach technique that offers something free for the purpose of showing interest in the customer and arousing his or her interest (9).

FUN-FAB OPTIC concept: An acronym symbolizing the essential ingredients of most sales presentations; stresses the importance of First Uncovering Needs, relating the Features, Advantages, and Benefits of the product to the customer's needs, and the elements of handling Objections, Proving, Trial closing, Insuring, and Closing (10).

Future-event close: A closing technique in which the salesperson attempts to motivate the prospect to buy now in order to avoid the greater future losses that would result if the purchase were postponed (13).

Gatekeeper: An individual, or individuals, in a "buying center" who creates obstacles to the making of a sale by a salesperson (10).

Goodwill: An intangible factor related to the attitudes that customers hold toward a company and its products; an essential factor in maintaining customers over time (14).

Government markets: Usually considered to be a segment of industrial markets, including local, state, and federal levels; purchases generally made for the purpose of performing governmental functions rather than for resale (4).

Graphs: Diagrams that present statistical information in a more dramatic manner than do raw data; types include line graphs, bar graphs, and pictorial graphs (11).

Gratuities: The giving of gifts to customers as a means of developing goodwill. Gift-giving that might interfere with the objective judgment of customers is usually considered an unethical business practice (3).

Gross national product (GNP): The total sales price of all goods and services produced annually in a country, such as the United States (1).

Growth stage: The second stage of a product's life, characterized by increased marketing efforts tending to result in increased sales and profit margins (4).

Guarantees/warranties: Promises by a manufacturer that assure a particular condition with or outcome from a purchased product (11).

Guiding: The sales activity of supporting favorable comments made by the prospect toward the product in order to move the prospect away from focusing on negative feelings (12).

Hard disks: Rigid revolving magnetic plates on which large amounts of computer information and data are stored (17).

Hierarchy of needs: A theory developed by Abraham Maslow that refers to the arrangement of a person's needs in order of priority (5).

High involvement products: More expensive products that are infrequently purchased and require more consumer information prior to purchase (5).

Host computer: A computer situated in a centralized location, such as a corporate or regional office, from which individuals can download data and information or into which they can upload data and information (17).

Ideal self: The way we *want* to be seen or *would like* to view ourselves (5).

Ignoring: A technique for handling objections that simply sidesteps a prospect's objections when they appear flimsy and without merit; should be used with caution (12).

Implied warranty: A right that a purchaser has to believe that the goods will be of a quality comparable to those described or demonstrated and will be delivered free of anyone else's interest in them, that is, with a clear title (3).

Inbound telemarketing: A concept that relates to the various services available through telephone systems that assist salespeople in obtaining prospects and that aid in the marketing process (15).

Industrial distributors: Intermediaries who acquire the products of manufacturers for resale to industrial, institutional, and governmental purchasers; they are the counterparts of the wholesaler in the consumer goods channels (4).

Industrial goods: Products, such as raw materials, that are typically used to help manufacturers produce consumer goods or other types of industrial goods (4).

Industrial market: The portion of the buying public that purchases goods used either directly or indirectly to produce other goods for resale (4).

Institutional advertising: A type of advertising concerned with the longer-term goals and concerns of a firm, such as a company name or image, a theme or cause, or a general class of product, such as milk or prunes (16).

Institutional buyers: A category of industial buyers, such as hospitals, hotels, restaurants, and schools, that buys large quantities of relatively standard items, such as towels, soap, and furniture (4).

Insuring: An element in a sales presentation that offers information intended to reassure the prospect that minimal risk will result from his or her purchasing the product (10).

Integrated Services Digital Network (ISDN): A form of transmission technology that enables users to transmit voices, video images, and computer data along the same line simultaneously (15).

Introduction stage: The first stage of a product's life; characterized by low sales and profits and substantial promotional efforts (4).

Itinerary: A proposed route or schedule of future appointments with prospective customers or prospects (17).

Joint venture: A type of partnership agreement between a firm in one country and a firm or government officials in another country for the purpose of doing business in markets where "going it alone" might be difficult or impossible (App. III).

Junior salespeople (spotters): Employees of a company whose responsibility is to locate leads for more experienced salespeople (8).

K.I.S.S. concept: K.I.S.S. is an acronym that symbolizes the need to communicate in simple, understandable terms. It represents Keep It Short and Simple (7).

Last-chance (SRO) close: A closing technique in which the salesperson suggests the importance of buying now to avoid disappointment later (13).

Licensing: An agreement between one company (the licenser) and another (the licensee) whereby the licensee is permitted to manufacture and/or market a product patented by the licenser; licensee makes royalty payments to licenser (App. III).

List brokers: Organizations that compile lists of names and addresses that can assist those using direct mail to target their own specific markets (16).

Listening: An important activity that enables salespeople to uncover needs, discover reasons for buyer resistance, and calm down excessively emotional customers (12).

Listening responses: Verbal or physical interaction with speakers that helps to convey to them that you are interested and want them to continue (7).

Low involvement products: Lower-priced products that are routinely bought without a lot of analysis (5).

Marginal accounts: Customers that typically cannot be given much attention because they do not provide a lot of sales income and do not have much potential for increased purchases in the future (15).

Market: A group of potential customers who share some common needs or wants and have the financial authority and ability to purchase particular products or services (4).

Market analysis software systems (MASS): Computer systems that help marketers locate key customer groups and develop strategies to reach them (17).

Market concentration: A characteristic of the marketplace when large numbers of customers are situated within a relatively small geograpical area (5).

Marketing: The process of planning and executing the conception, pricing, promotion, and distribution of ideas, goods, and services to create exchanges that satisfy individual and organizational objectives (1).

Marketing concept: The belief that the needs and wants of customers should be determined before goods are produced and sold to meet those desires (4).

Market segmentation: The grouping or categorizing of customers whose needs and wants are similar enough to be satisfied by the purchase of a particular product (4).

Maturity stage: The third stage of a product's life, characterized by increased competition if the product has been successful and declining profit margins; a critical stage in the product life cycle (4).

Medical service representative: Formerly called a *detail man,* a person who calls on doctors and pharmacists to provide them with "details" on the products the representative is responsible to sell (1).

Merchant wholesalers: Traditionally referred to as *middlemen,* firms that serve as links in the distribution chain between manufacturers and ultimate consumers (4).

Minor-point close: A closing technique in which the salesperson attempts to obtain agreement on a minor point so as to check the receptiveness of a prospect (13).

Mirroring: The act of restating to the prospect what the salesperson thinks the prospect has just said; allows prospects to reconsider their own words (12).

Missionary salespeople: Individuals who are typically involved in promoting products new to the marketplace; they may also be responsible for assisting buyers in the resale of purchased products (1).

Modem: An electronic device attached to, or built into, a computer that enables the transmission of data from one computer to another by telephone (17).

Monthly planner: An organizing tool that provides a person with an overview of his or her schedule for an entire month (17).

Moonlighting: The holding of a second job by an employee; an activity usually discouraged by sales managers in relation to their sales force (3).

Motive: A feeling or condition that leads to specific activity intended to bring about satisfaction (5).

Multiple-acceptance close: A closing technique in which the salesperson obtains a series of agreements leading to a final close (13).

Multiple buying decisions: Decisions as to whether or not to purchase that are made by more than one person (5).

Multiple-sense appeals: Factors in a sales presentation that tend to appeal to more than one of the prospect's senses (11).

Need(s): The condition of deprivation; occurs when something, such as food, is missing from a person's environment (5, 10).

Negative reference groups: Groups that a person doesn't want to identify with, so that he or she adopts attitudes opposed to them (5).

Noncash sales compensation: Benefits, other than cash, such as company cars, expense accounts, and employee benefit plans (2).

Nonverbal communication: All forms of communication other than the spoken or written word, such as vocal tones, facial expressions, gestures, and body posture (7).

Nonverbal symbols: Objects or conditions that convey meaning without words, such as space, height, and status symbols (7).

Objections: Resistance by a prospective customer toward various aspects of a salesperson's sales message (10).

"OK-names" approach: An approach technique that attempts to gain attention by offering prospective customers the names of well-known users of the salesperson's products (9).

One-way communication: A message flowing in one direction with no feedback or signs of understanding involved (7).

On-route calls: Telephone calls made for the purpose of expanding territorial coverage; an activity that enables salespeople on sales trips to contact larger numbers of prospects, customers, and marginal accounts (15).

Open question: A question that typically cannot be answered with a simple yes or no; sometimes referred to as "the five W's and an H": Who, What, When, Where, Why, and How (7).

Open-question-and-pause close: A closing technique in which the salesperson asks a question that can't be answered with a simple yes or no and then waits for the prospect to answer (13).

Outbound telemarketing: The activity of contacting prospective customers by telephone for the purpose of closing sales (15).

Outlined presentation: An organized sales presentation that follows a predetermined checklist of major points to be covered (10).

Participational reference groups: A group that individuals are integral members of, such as their families, clusters of friends, and their neighbors; buying habits are often derived from such reference groups (5).

Party groups: Gathering of relatively large numbers of prospective customers, typically in the home of host persons who have invited them to sales demonstrations of certain products such as cosmetics and household wares (8).

Patronage motives: The reasons why people repeatedly and consistently buy from a particular firm (5).

Peer effect: The influence our associates have on what we see, think, and do (5).

Perception: An activity or skill related to seeing things as they really are rather than as we expect (2, 5).

Personal computers (PCs): Electronic equipment that performs high-speed mathematical calculations or that assembles, stores, correlates, or otherwise processes and prints information derived from various computer systems (17).

Personal data base: Records and information that salespeople maintain with their own personal computers in the field (17).

Pocket-sized appointment book: An item that provides a salesperson with a portable and handy reference to, and record of, appointments and planned activities (17).

Point-of purchase (P.O.P.) displays: Promotional materials, such as banners and counter cards, that the marketer gives or sells to dealers to help promote product sales (16).

Policies: Guides to decision making and action for a company's employees (6).

Portable audiovisual aids: Various types of equipment that appeal to the senses of sight and sound; used by many organizations in meetings, training programs, and sales presentations (11).

Portfolios: Visual aids often in the form of looseleaf binders that contain material, such as testimonial letters or photographs of products, designed to provide graphic assistance in the course of a sales presentation (11).

Positive-assumption close: A closing technique in which the salesperson assumes that the prospect wants to make a purchase and will act accordingly (13).

Postcall analysis: A form completed after a sales call by the salesperson for the purpose of recording and analyzing the nature of the discussion, what customer needs were uncovered, what objections were raised, and future plans for a follow-up sales call (13, 17).

Postponing: The intentional delaying by a salesperson of a response to an objection until ample sales information has been presented to the prospect (12).

Post-sales-call period: A critical period that follows the sales interview; sales and service activities during this period significantly influence future customer relationships and goodwill (14).

Preapproach: The sales activity that involves obtaining as much relevant information as necessary about prospects before contacting them personally (8).

Presentation skills: The ability to deliver well-organized, persuasive presentations to individuals and groups (2).

Preventive maintenance: As applied to the communication process, the practice of active listening which can help to prevent friction and misunderstanding between salespeople and their customers (7).

Primary needs: Factors that are vital to human survival, such as oxygen, food, clothing, shelter, sleep, and so on; also termed *physical needs* (5).

Probing: The activity during a sales presentation of asking questions and listening for clues that enable the salesperson to obtain information related to the customer's needs and buying motives (10).

Problem-solving approach: An approach technique that emphasises how the purchase of a particular good or service can create solutions to specific customer problems (9).

Procedures: Guidelines to decision making and action for a company's employees (6).

Product approach: An approach technique that uses the product itself or various visual aids as a means of arousing a potential customer's interest in the salesperson's message and products (9).

Product comparison: The comparing of the features of your products with those of competing firms (6).

Product data sheet: A document that provides the reader with technical information and specifications, dimensions, prices, cost savings, colors, efficiency, and performance data; can also serve as an effective advertising tool (11).

Production concept: A philosophy of production management that is concerned with producing the most goods at the least cost (4).

Production sharing: A manufacturing process whereby production is integrated along international lines; a company may manufacture an item in one nation, ship it to another for further processing, and then market it in other countries (App. III).

Product knowledge: The understanding of any aspect of a product that will help the salesperson relate it to the needs and problems of customers, thus making sales more easily and/or maintaining goodwill (6).

Product life cycle: The phases that a product goes through from its introduction to its demise; includes introduction, growth, maturity, and decline (4).

Programmable telemarketing: The use of computerized telephones that enable the phone numbers of prospective customers to be dialed automatically; may allow for interactive communication between prospects and the programmed telephone (15).

Programmed or survey presentation: A sales presentation that attempts during the first visit to examine and analyze a prospect's problems and needs. Typically, a follow-up sales call is then required to offer a combined written and oral presentation (10).

Projection: The tendency to attribute to others some of our own values and motives (5).

Promotional advertising (product advertising): A type of advertising concerned with the immediate stimulation of buyer interest in and demand for goods and services (see also *institutional advertising*) (16).

Prospecting: The step in the selling process that involves locating potential customers (8).

Prospects: Persons or organizations who qualify, have buying authority, and can benefit from the purchase of a particular good or service (8).

Proving: The sales activity of using available evidence to substantiate the benefit claims made by a salesperson (10).

Purchase decision process: The stages that most purchasers are believed to go through when trying to decide whether to make a purchase (5).

Qualifying prospects: The activity of obtaining the information necessary to determine whether a lead or suspect is likely to be a good prospect (8).

Querying: Accessing a computer for the purpose of retrieving specific types of information (17).

Questioning: When used as a technique to handle objections, the effort to move a prospect's objections from the general to the specific so that the salesperson can understand and deal more effectively with them (12).

Questioning approach: A technique of approaching customers that helps to maintain interest even when an answer is not expected; can be used to uncover needs of prospective customers (9).

Rational buying motives: Reasons for purchasing goods or services that are based on thought rather than emotion (5).

Reciprocity: A situation in which a firm buys products or services from its own customers (3).

Reference groups: Groups that we tend to identify with and derive many of our attitudes from (5).

Referral approach: An approach technique that makes use of the names of or letters of introduction from personal acquaintances of the prospective customer as a means of gaining his or her attention (8, 9).

Reprints: Samples of a firm's advertising programs that may be used in dramatizing a sales presentation (11).

Restaging: Utilizing a new ingredient, package design, or marketing technique to extract additional profits from the marketplace (4).

Routing: Determining the most effective pattern of territory coverage (17).

Salary plus commission: A system of remuneration that provides salespeople with a predetermined and guaranteed floor below which their income will not fall regardless of sales volume (2).

Salary plus commission plus bonus: A system of remuneration that provides salespeople with a salary that serves as a floor and commissions and bonuses that are provided in addition to the salary and related to actual performance (2).

Salary plus group bonus: A system of remuneration that provides salespeople with added rewards based upon an entire sales department, or sometimes the company as a whole, achieving or exceeding predetermined goals (2).

Salary plus individual bonus: A system of remuneration that provides salespeople with a fixed salary plus rewards for particular achievements (2).

Sales aids: Items used to help dramatize a sales presentation and appeal to the buying motives of prospects (11).

Sales associates: (see *bird dogs*) (8).

Sales-call planner: A worksheet designed to assist salespeople in planning specific sales-call strategies (17).

Sales concept: The belief that a marketer's principal responsibility is to sell the products that have been manufactured regardless of the needs or desires of customers (4).

Sales contests: Motivational campaigns that typically pit one salesperson against others in a region, or one division against other divisions; prizes are provided as noncash sales compensation (2).

Sales engineers: Often called *field engineers,* these are salespeople whose specialized backgrounds and training enable them to provide technical advice and assistance to their industrial accounts (1).

Sales kits: Kits, generally including materials or samples, that aid in demonstrating a product (11).

Sales presentation: A message given by a salesperson to a prospective customer for the purpose of arousing a feeling of need and showing how the product can satisfy this recognized need (10).

Sales promotion: Marketing activities designed to inform, persuade, or remind potential customers about a company's goods or services or to improve dealer effectiveness through the use of displays, shows, expositions, and demonstrations; a narrower definition preferred by some marketers excludes personal selling, advertising, and publicity (16).

Sales quotas: Types of goals assigned to salespeople, typically expressed in dollar volume or number of units of a product that salespeople are expected to attain within a specified period of time (2).

Sample/gift approach: An approach technique that offers free samples or gifts for the purpose of arousing the prospective customer's interest in the salesperson's message and products (9).

Secondary needs: Factors of a social or psychological nature that tend to motivate people, such as the needs to feel secure, to be with people, to be respected, and to have feelings of accomplishment (5).

Second-person sensitivity: The ability to perceive what others are feeling, thinking, or experiencing about a particular situation or problem (2).

Selective perception: The tendency for people to see or hear only what they want or are set to see and hear and to tune out much of the rest of a given situation (5).

Self-concept (self-image): The way we view ourselves and the way we feel others view us (5).

Self-discipline: A self-imposed form of control and influence over one's own behavior (2).

Seller's market: A condition in which the seller can determine purchase terms and price with little interference from the buyer; usually exists when there are shortages of particular goods (4).

Selling: The process of analyzing potential customers' needs and wants and assisting them in discovering how such needs and wants can be best satisfied by the purchase of a particular product, service, or idea (1).

Selling process: The essential elements involved in the activity of personal selling: includes prospecting, the approach, the presentation, handling objections, the close, and the follow-up (8).

Senior account managers: Typically, experienced salespeople entrusted with the responsibility of developing and maintaining large, more complex, and major customers of a particular company (1).

Service facilities: Units of an organization that are available in the event of product malfunction or difficulty; may provide replacement parts, repairs, or information (6).

Shopping goods: Products obtained usually only after considerable effort has been made to compare the characteristics and prices of competing goods; such goods include furniture, jewelry, household appliances, and used cars (4).

Showmanship: The act of vividly and dramatically demonstrating the features, advantages, and benefits of a product or service; should have multiple-sense appeals where possible (11).

Showmanship approach: An approach technique that presents product features in a dramatic fashion for the purpose of gaining a prospective customer's attention and interest in the product (9).

Situational dramatization: The recognition that each prospective customer is unique and that the type of dramatization used should be one that appeals to the particular prospect (11).

Situational ethics: The application of moral standards that relate to the attitudes and laws in a particular social and cultural environment (3).

Situational selling: The process of drawing on past sales experiences and knowledge when confronting a prospective buyer while also recognizing that each selling situation and customer are somewhat unique and may require a flexible and distinct presentation (2, 10).

Slide chart: A sales aid, often pocket size, with movable parts that are used to show such things as product features, capacities, dimensions, and characteristics; also used for various types of calculations (11).

Snap judgments: The tendency to form hastily conceived first impressions of people and things (5).

Social class: A group of people who have similar status in society, generally determined by attained educational levels, occupations, and location of residence (5).

Social responsibility: The attitude and behavior expressed and practiced toward the public by key representatives of an organization; expressed by such activities as aid to the socially disadvantaged, concern for the environment, and waste prevention programs (6).

Social sensitivity: A person's awareness of and responsiveness toward the needs and feeling of others (2).

Software systems: Programs that instruct computers what to do (17).

Sorting: Arranging data in a specific order, such as alphabetically or by ZIP Code (17).

Special-offer close: A closing technique in which the salesperson provides the prospect with an added inducement, such as a discount (13).

Specialty advertising: Goodwill-building sales promotion devices—such as inscribed ballpoint pens, calendars, and matchbooks—that are given or sold at nominal cost to customers for the purpose of reminding them of a marketer's products and name (16).

Specialty goods: Particular brands of products that consumers will make special efforts to obtain (4).

Standard memorized presentation: A highly structured or "canned" sales presentation in which the salesperson expresses a predetermined message (10).

Store demonstration: A technique in which those involved with sales promotion activities arrange with the owner or manager of a particular store to demonstrate or train store employees to demonstrate the manufacturer's products (16).

Straight commission: A system of remuneration that provides a salesperson with a specific percentage of an item's selling price as income (2).

Straight/guaranteed salary: A system of remuneration that provides a salesperson with a fixed sum of money each pay period regardless of his or her volume of sales (2).

Suggestion close: A closing technique in which the salesperson relates to a previous point that suggested a purchase should be made (13).

Summarize-the-benefits close: A closing technique in which the salesperson attempts, by blending a summary of the benefits with one of the other closing techniques, to guide the prospect into making a positive buying decision (13).

Surprise/shock approach: An approach technique that utilizes the element of nonexpectation as a means of gaining the prospective customer's attention (9).

Surveys: A prospecting technique that involves the use of questionnaires to uncover potential needs of potential customers (8).

Suspects (leads): People or organizations that could be buyers of a good or service but have not yet been qualified as definite prospects (8).

Sympathy: The state of feeling sorry for someone (see also *empathy*) (2).

Team selling: A sales situation in which two or more salespeople make a sales presentation to a potential customer (5).

Telemarketing: A set of activities that involves the use of the telephone to support and, at times, to serve as a substitute for personal face-to-face selling (15).

Telephone and mail inquiries: A source of prospects that develops when prospective customers telephone or write for additional product information (8).

Testimonial letter: A written document indicating that a customer has been pleased with a salesperson and his or her company's products and service; such a letter may be an aid in prospecting and in approaching prospective customers (8, 9).

Test marketing: Positioning a product in select markets to determine the likelihood of sales in additional markets (4).

Thank-you letter: A goodwill-building item that expresses to customers or prospects a salesperson's appreciation for having been granted a sales interview or having received an order (14).

Tickler files: A system designed to remind a salesperson when to make follow-up calls on and what to discuss with prospective customers (8).

Time-waste inventory: A questionnaire that enables salespeople to evaluate how effectively they have been utilizing their time and organizing their activities (17).

T.O. method: The activity of *turning over* a difficult customer to another salesperson (12).

Trade fairs and exhibitions: Displays of manufacturers' products at gatherings of prospective customers (8, 16).

Trial closing: An effort by a salesperson, made at any time during a sales presentation, to obtain an affirmative buying decision from the prospect (10).

Trial-order close: A closing technique in which the salesperson attempts to get the prospect to test the product on a limited scale (13).

Truth in Lending Act: A law that requires lenders to disclose the actual costs of credit (3).

Two-way communication: Communication that allows for feedback, recognizing that all parties to certain types of communication are simultaneously both producers and consumers of communication (7).

Ultimate consumers: The end users of goods produced for consumption by householders (4).

Unit costs: The cost per each item produced, calculated by dividing the total cost by the number of units produced (1).

Unit pricing: A marketing procedure that permits shoppers to compare the prices of like items packaged by different weights or quantities (1).

Unsought goods: Products or services that consumers don't necessarily want to buy but feel they must buy, such as prescription drugs, burial plots, and life insurance (4).

Uploaded: Data that has been transferred from a peripheral computer to a host computer (17).

Useful-idea approach: An approach that attempts to gain a prospective customer's attention by offering helpful ideas (9).

Variable costs: Costs associated with producing a product or service that change with changes in the level of output (1).

Varied commission: A method of remuneration that provides salespeople with commissions that are higher on items that generate greater gross profits and lower on items of lesser profitability (2).

Verbal communication: Forms of communication involving words, such as oral conversations or printed messages (7).

Videocassettes: As applied to sales promotion and prospecting, a VHS or Beta format tape that can display advertising on TV intended to spark consumer interest; videocassettes requested by mail can furnish prospecting leads to salespeople (8).

Videodisc kiosks: Small booths located in public places where customers use computer terminals to select products that they want to see demonstrated on a video screen; capable of showing products both in color and in motion (16).

Videotex: An interactive system that enables householders to order goods directly from manufacturers by combining their telephones with home computers and tapping into a central video catalog (16).

Visual aids: Items that can be used in sales presentations to appeal to a prospect's sense of sight, such as flip charts, graphs, and portfolios (11).

Weighing: A technique for handling objections that shows a prospect how advantages of a product outweigh disadvantages; often makes use of a "T-account" by listing advantages on one side and disadvantages on the other (12).

Wholly owned foreign subsidiary: Exists when a firm has separate manufacturing and distribution facilities located in a foreign country (App. III).

Word processing systems: A text editing program that allows electronic writing and correcting of words, letters, forms, etc. (17).

Workaholism (work addiction): A compulsive type of behavior inherent in persons who experience withdrawal symptoms or guilt feelings when they are not working (3).

Index